Great Britain, International Law, and the Evolution of Maritime Strategic Thought, 1856–1914

Great Britain, International Law, and the Evolution of Maritime Strategic Thought, 1856–1914

GABRIELA A. FREI

OXFORD
UNIVERSITY PRESS

OXFORD
UNIVERSITY PRESS

Great Clarendon Street, Oxford, OX2 6DP,
United Kingdom

Oxford University Press is a department of the University of Oxford.
It furthers the University's objective of excellence in research, scholarship,
and education by publishing worldwide. Oxford is a registered trade mark of
Oxford University Press in the UK and in certain other countries

First Edition published in 2020

Impression: 1

Published in the United States of America by Oxford University Press
198 Madison Avenue, New York, NY 10016, United States of America

British Library Cataloguing in Publication Data

Data available

Library of Congress Control Number: 2019951995

ISBN 978-0-19-885993-2

Printed and bound in Great Britain by
Clays Ltd, Elcograf S.p.A.

Acknowledgements

This book has taken many years to prepare, and many people and institutions have contributed to the result. I am grateful for the generous financial support I received from Merton College throughout my time in Oxford as a Greendale Scholar and as a recipient of a Simms Fund Bursary. The bursary from the Guy Hudson Memorial Trust, administered by the Oxford University Royal Navy Unit, was also a timely help.

This book would have been impossible without the guidance and advice of my supervisor Sir Hew Strachan, whom I would like to thank for his great insight and sharp analysis from which my research has greatly benefited. His challenging questions and his generosity in sharing his knowledge with me have shaped the research of this book. Particular thanks are also due to Stig Förster whose approach to history has always been an inspiration to me. His passion about the big picture, and his curiosity to explore history beyond disciplinary boundaries, profoundly formed my understanding of history at the outset of my career.

Oxford has always been a stimulating place, and I would like to thank the community of the Faculty of History for the opportunities to discuss my research. I am grateful for the conversations I have had with Jeremiah Dancy, Basil Germond, Steven Haines, Rob Johnson, and Nicholas Rodger. My research stays abroad have been inspiring breaks from my routine at Oxford. Particular thanks to Tom Long from George Washington University for our numerous conversations on American naval history and international law when we were Summer Fellows in Military History at the US Military Academy West Point, NY. Twice I enjoyed the hospitality of the US Naval War College, Newport, RI; the first time as a researcher and the second time as Edward S. Miller Research Fellow. Both times, I received generous support for my research from John B. Hattendorf, Evelyn Cherpack, and James Kraska, and I would like to thank them for sharing with me their views on American maritime strategic thought in relation to international law. During my time as a Brettschneider Scholar at Cornell University, Ithaca, NY, I was fortunate to meet Dan Baugh and Isabel V. Hull, who both gave me invaluable feedback on my research.

Many friends and colleagues have read early drafts of the manuscript, and I would like to thank Lawrence Hill-Cawthorne, Meighen McCrae, and Stephen C. Neff, for their comments and suggestions. I am particularly indebted to Marion Wullschleger, who spent many hours commenting on draft versions of the book. Special thanks to her for her time and commitment, and for always being in good spirits despite short-notice corrections.

My sincere thanks to my husband, Philipp, who has not only commented on drafts of the manuscript, but also for his encouragement, humour, and love while I spent long hours writing. Last but not least, I would like to thank my family and friends for their enduring support, their toleration of my absences, and their love. I especially thank my parents Erna and Josef Frei-Sonderegger who have made everything possible in my life, and have always encouraged me to pursue my dreams. This book is dedicated to them.

Contents

Contents

Introduction

This book is about the relationship between sea power and international law. From the mid-nineteenth century, an increasingly interconnected world saw the rise of international law as a discipline, as a tool in international politics, and as an expression of a society that was becoming more international.[1] Pioneers of the newly founded discipline envisioned the future codification of international law as a process which would transform the practice of international relations guided by international rules.[2]

This book illuminates key developments of international maritime law surrounding state practice, custom, and codification, and outlines the complex relationship between international law and maritime strategy, from the mid-nineteenth century to the outbreak of the First World War in 1914. In 1856 the European great powers signed the Treaty of Paris, which ended the Crimean War. The signatories also agreed to the Declaration of Paris, which marked not only the beginning of the codification of international maritime law but also the beginning of the age of multilateralism.[3] These developments found their culminating point in the Hague peace conferences of 1899 and 1907, as well as the London naval conference of 1909. The book

---

[1] Rainer Klump and Miloš Vec (eds), *Völkerrecht und Weltwirtschaft im 19. Jahrhundert* (Baden-Baden, 2012); Luigi Nuzzo and Miloš Vec, 'The Birth of International Law as a Legal Discipline in the 19th Century', in Luigi Nuzzo and Miloš Vec (eds), *Constructing International Law: The Birth of a Discipline* (Frankfurt/Main, 2012), ix–xvi; Miloš Vec, *Recht und Normierung in der Industriellen Revolution: Neue Strukturen der Normsetzung im Völkerrecht, staatlicher Gesetzgebung und gesellschaftliche Selbstnormierung* (Frankfurt/Main, 2006).

[2] Jean d'Aspremont, 'Professionalisation of International Law', in Jean d'Aspremont, Tarcisio Gazzini, André Nollkaemper and Wouter Werner (eds), *International Law as a Profession* (Cambridge, 2017), 19–37; Martti Koskenniemi, *The Gentle Civilizer of Nations: The Rise and Fall of International Law 1870–1960 (Hersch Lauterpacht Memorial Lectures)* (Cambridge, 2001), 46–51; Mark Mazower, *Governing the World: The History of an Idea* (London, 2012), 66–70; Barry Nichols, 'Jurisprudence 1', in Michael G. Brock and Mark C. Carthoys (eds), *The History of the University of Oxford: Volume VII: Nineteenth-Century Oxford, Part 2* (Oxford, 2011), 385–96.

[3] Matthias Schulz, ' "Defenders of the Right"? Diplomatic Practice and International Law in the 19th Century: An Historian's Perspective', in Luigi Nuzzo and Miloš Vec (eds) *Constructing International Law: The Birth of a Discipline* (Frankfurt/Main, 2012), 251–75; Matthias Schulz, *Normen und Praxis: Das Europäische Konzert der Grossmächte als Sicherheitsrat, 1815–1860* (München, 2009); Paul W. Schroeder, *Austria, Britain, and the Crimean War: The Destruction of the European Concert* (Ithaca, NY, 1972).

Great Britain, International Law, and the Evolution of Maritime Strategic Thought, 1856–1914. Gabriela A. Frei, Oxford University Press (2020). © Gabriela A. Frei.
DOI: 10.1093/oso/9780198859932.001.0001

concludes at the outbreak of the First World War in 1914, which ended the long period of relative peace between the great European powers.[4]

This book focuses on Britain, which shaped state practice as well as the codification of international maritime law like no other sea power at the time. Britain was the global maritime power in the nineteenth century and its empire spanned the globe, holding semi-formal and informal ties to most parts of the world.[5] Britain was not only the predominant sea power but also the world's largest carrier of goods. To a lesser extent, the book also examines the views on international maritime law of other European powers, such as France, Germany, Russia, and Austria-Hungary, in order to understand the broader international context of Britain's actions. Last but not least, this book analyses the role of the United States in advancing international maritime law.

Focusing on the practice and codification of international maritime law, I argue that state practice was important for the codification of international maritime law, and that both international law and maritime strategy are based on long-term state interests, and are closely interwoven. Hence, state practice and codification shaped maritime strategic thought as much as maritime strategy shaped state practice and codification. Examining these interrelations more closely shows three key results. First, state practice provided an important reference point for the codification of international maritime law. Second, state practice needed to be consistent to gain wide recognition, and as a result, state practice constrained political decisions which meant that ambitious codification projects without reference to state practice were less likely to be adopted. Third, strategic concerns limited a state's ambition to change its own practices or to propose new domestic and international legislation. These results also illustrate that Britain used international law to balance its conflicting interests, and that it effectively used international law as an instrument of foreign policy to defend its strategic and economic interests.

Analysing state practice requires examination of how government administrations and administrators work, what procedures they develop

---

[4] Gabriela A. Frei, 'International Law and the First World War: Introduction', *European Journal of International Law (EJIL)*, 29, 1 (2018), 229–32; see also the contributions in *EJIL* 2018 from Jochen v. Bernstorff, Andrew Norris, Stephen C. Neff, Marcus M. Payk, Randall Lesaffer, Thomas Graditzky, Neville Wylie, and Lindsey Cameron. See also Isabel V. Hull, *A Scrap of Paper: Breaking and Making International Law during the Great War* (Ithaca, NY, 2014).

[5] Peter J. Cain and Anthony G. Hopkins, *British Imperialism, 1688–2000*, 2nd edn (Harlow, 2002); John Darwin, *The Empire Project: The Rise and Fall of the British World-System, 1830–1970* (Cambridge, 2009).

and follow, and how they interpret treaties or customs underlying their work. Hence, this book focuses less on politicians than on government administrators, such as legal advisers, civil servants, strategic advisers, and port officials, to name but a few. I argue in this book that their views shaped state practice far more than recent literature has acknowledged. Apart from government administrators, international lawyers, both then and now, occupy an important place between the theory and practice of law. As academics, international lawyers contributed to the development of their discipline, but many of them also acted as external experts advising the government on specific legal questions, or served as judges in national or international courts, where they interpreted and applied the respective laws. In their different functions, international lawyers criticised governments as much as they advised them. Hence, their writings are valuable sources for this book, giving a broader insight into the subject matter.[6] Significantly, international lawyers were also organized in professional organizations such as the Institut de droit international or the International Law Association. These non-governmental bodies provided essential preparatory work for the codification of international maritime law. Moreover, I argue that in their multiple functions within and outside the administration, international lawyers were knowledgeable in the theory of war, which enabled them to assess the broader military and naval strategic context of state practice and of the codification of international maritime law.

This book focuses on the development of international maritime law in the nineteenth century. It is important to understand how contemporaries defined international law, of which international maritime law was an integral part, and, importantly, which sources international law used. The 1882 law textbook by the British international lawyer, William E. Hall, was widely used as a reference by the British government and serves as an example. Hall described international law as 'certain rules of conduct which modern civilised states regard as being binding on them in their relations with one another'. Those claims for 'rules' and 'principles' needed to be substantiated, but at the time 'no formal [international] code has been adopted by the body of civilised states'. As a result, 'national acts' provided evidence and Hall argued that their 'international usage...can be looked upon as authoritative' and binding in nature.[7] For Hall it was the task of the international

---

[6] d'Aspremont, 'Professionalisation', 19–37; Koskenniemi, *Gentle Civilizer*; Nuzzo and Vec, 'The Birth of International Law', ix–xvi.

[7] William E. Hall, *A Treatise on International Law*, 2nd edn (Oxford, 1884), 5.

lawyer to test 'the validity of practices claiming to be legal' and to assess 'appropriate modes of regulating new facts or relations...within the scope of the principles in question, in going beyond the rules which can be drawn from the bare facts of past practice'. Changes to usage could not easily be made as 'the principle governs until an exceptional usage is shown to have been established, or at least until it can be shown that the authority of the principle has been broken by practice at variance with it, but not treated as an infringement of the law'.[8]

Hall's emphasis on 'practice' and 'international usage' shows that they were important sources of international law in the nineteenth century, in addition to international treaties and custom.[9] Even today there is no easy answer about the sources of international law, a fact which recent literature on the subject has highlighted.[10] In order to understand how international law originates, it is essential to know the sources of international law. One is the concept of custom. As defined in the Statute of the Permanent Court of International Justice from 1920, international custom is defined as 'evidence of a general practice accepted as law', a definition which the International Court of Justice has since adopted in the same wording.[11] For Hall, custom had to be 'authoritative', a term which Hugh Thirlway also used in his 2014 publication on the sources of international law.[12] For custom to reach an authoritative meaning, state practice and *opinio juris* were essential. Another source of international law is the concept of practice. 'Practice' is a term which Hall had already used in his early textbook to describe the action of states. According to a Committee Report by the International Law Association in 2000, practice is the verbal and physical acts of states. Even more important is the prerequisite that those acts have to be public.[13]

---

[8] Hall, *Treatise*, 2nd edn, 6.

[9] Caspar Sylvest, 'International Law in Nineteenth-Century Britain', *The British Yearbook of International Law*, 75, 1 (2005), 9–70.

[10] Anthony D'Amato, *The Concept of Custom in International Law* (Ithaca, NY, 1971); Jean d'Aspremont, *Formalism and the Sources of International Law: A Theory of Ascertainment of Legal Rules* (Oxford, 2011); Clive Parry, *Sources and Evidence in International Law* (Manchester, 1965); Hugh Thirlway, *The Sources of International Law* (Oxford, 2014).

[11] James Crawford, *Brownlie's Principles of Public International Law*, 8th edn (Oxford, 2012), 20–47; Anthony Carty, 'Doctrine versus State Practice', in Bardo Fassbender and Anne Peters (eds), *The Oxford Handbook of the History of International Law* (Oxford, 2012), 972–96; Hilary Charlesworth, 'Law-Making and Sources', in James Crawford and Martti Koskenniemi (eds), *The Cambridge Companion to International Law* (Cambridge, 2012), 188–202.

[12] Thirlway, *Sources*, 55–7.

[13] Thirlway, *Sources*, 63–8; For more detail, see International Law Association, *Final Report of the Committee. Statement of Principles Applicable to the Formation of General Customary International Law* (London, 2000).

In the nineteenth century, history was an important source for the construction of a legal argument.[14] The American international lawyer Theodore D. Woolsey explained in the third edition of his textbook in 1872 the value of the study of history for international law because 'from the changes and improvements in the law of nations, it is evident that the history of this science—both the history of opinion and of practice—is deserving of especial attention'. Historical examples were important for the illustration of 'the progressive character of the science, and of conferring a benefit on the student of history'. At the same time, Woolsey warned that 'historical precedents must be used with caution. History tells of crimes against the law of nations, as well as of its construction and its observance, of old usages or principles given up and new ones adopted. There is no value in the mere historical facts apart from the response or pretexts for them, and from their bearings on the spread of justice and the sense of human brotherhood in the world.'[15] Woolsey's warnings show his understanding of the use of history in his discipline. The study of history, of people, and of states was essential to the understanding of international law and its development as a discipline in the nineteenth century. International lawyers used the historical approach to describe the organic development of states, the origins and development of customs, practices and traditions, and, beyond that, the study of treaties in the wider context of international law.

In the last few decades, a historical perspective has returned to the study of international law. International lawyers, historians, and legal historians have produced innovative new research, demonstrating the many facets of the theory and practice of international law. As the legal historian Randall Lesaffer has recently pointed out, history and law have been close disciplines.[16] Martti Koskenniemi, a former Finnish diplomat and international lawyer, has contributed immensely to this new interest in the history of international law, and his publications are testimony to his ambition to bring history and law together.

Koskenniemi's examination of the construction of a legal argument provides a critical analysis of the function of international law in politics.

[14] Theodore D. Woolsey, *Introduction to the Study of International Law, Designed as an Aid in Teaching and in Historical Studies*, 3rd edn (New York, 1872), 4–5, 14–16, 26–8; Hall, *Treatise*, 2nd edn, 1–16. See also Kunal M. Parker, *Common Law, History, and Democracy in America, 1790–1900: Legal Thought before Modernism* (New York, 2011).

[15] Woolsey, *Study of International Law*, 31–2.

[16] Randall Lesaffer, 'International Law and Its History: The Story of an Unrequited Love', in Matthew Craven and Malgosia Fitzmaurice (eds), *Developments in International Law: Time, History, and International Law* (Leiden, 2006), 27–41.

His work is a direct response to those who criticize the close relationship between law and state, to those who argue that international law is a mere expression of a state's policy and therefore apologetic, and to those who see international law as being too moralistic and therefore utopian. Koskenniemi calls this contradiction the apology/utopia dilemma, and argues that the dilemma is an inherent inconsistency of international law. The understanding of the underlying mechanisms of a legal argument will be invaluable for this book.[17]

There is a diverse literature on the history of international law and the approaches and scopes of these studies are similarly diverse.[18] Koskenniemi's second book offers a history of ideas underpinning the discipline of international law, and many scholars focus on the philosophical basis of the discipline, and of international lawyers.[19] Legal theorists use a much more systematic approach to examine the structure of international law, as the works of Gerry Simpson or Mary Ellen O'Connell illustrate.[20] Historians have approached the subject from a different angle, illuminating the context

[17] I would like to thank my former flatmate at Merton College, Dr Lawrence Hill-Cawthorne, now Associate Professor in Law at the University of Reading, for introducing me to Koskenniemi's work. This book has profoundly changed my understanding of international law for which I am very grateful. Martti Koskenniemi, *From Apology to Utopia: The Structure of International Legal Argument. Reissue with New Epilogue* (Cambridge, 1989, reprint: Cambridge, 2005). See in particular his epilogue as it offers a summary and reflection of Koskenniemi's argument, 562–617. For critical reviews, see Alexandra Kemmerer and Morag Goodwin (eds), 'From Apology to Utopia: A Symposium', *German Law Journal*, 7, 12 (2006), 977–1176; Vaughan Lowe, 'Book Review of *From Apology to Utopia*', *Journal of Law and Society*, 17 (1990), 384–9.

[18] Frederik Dhondt, 'Recent Research in the History of International Law', *Tijdschrift voor Rechtsgeschiedenis/Revue d'Histoire du Droit/The Legal History Review*, 84 (2016), 313–34; Marcus Payk, 'Institutionalisierung und Verrechtlichung: Die Geschichte des Völkerrechts im späten 19. und frühen 20. Jahrhundert', *Archiv für Sozialgeschichte*, 52 (2012), 861–83.

[19] Koskenniemi, *Gentle Civilizer*. See also Arnulf Becker Lorca, *Mestizo International Law: A Global Intellectual History, 1842–1933* (Cambridge, 2014); Bardo Fassbender and Anne Peters (eds), *The Oxford Handbook of the History of International Law* (Oxford, 2012); Mónica García-Salmones, *The Project of Positivism in International Law* (Oxford, 2013); Emmanuelle Jouannet, *The Liberal-Welfarist Law of Nations. A History of International Law* (Cambridge, 2012); Randall Lesaffer, *European Legal History: A Cultural and Political Perspective* (Cambridge, 2009); Stephen C. Neff, *Justice Among Nations: A History of International Law* (Cambridge, MA, 2014); Caspar Sylvest, 'The Foundations of Victorian International Law', in Duncan Bell (ed.), *Victorian Visions of Global Order. Empire and International Relations in Nineteenth-Century Political Thought* (Cambridge, 2007), 47–66.

[20] Gerry Simpson, *Great Powers and Outlaw States. Unequal Sovereigns in the International Legal Order* (Cambridge, 2004); Gerry Simpson, 'International Law in Diplomatic History', in James Crawford and Martti Koskenniemi (eds), *The Cambridge Companion to International Law* (Cambridge, 2012), 25–46; Mary Ellen O'Connell, *The Power and Purpose of International Law: Insights from the Theory and Practice of Enforcement* (Oxford, 2008).

in which international law developed, and so broadening the scope beyond the focus on individual lawyers or networks.[21]

This book embraces a historical approach. The centenary of the First World War resulted in the publication of numerous new historical studies on the origins of the war, including particularly economic warfare. Together with the previous literature, they provide an excellent historical analysis of British politics, and yet they often neglect the legal dimension of economic warfare. Blockade and the right of search and capture, which are so essential to economic warfare, are based on legal concepts and shaped through state practice.[22] There are some notable exceptions, such as John Coogan's book *The End of Neutrality*, which provides a brilliant analysis of Anglo-American relations and the United States' position of neutrality.[23]

---

[21] Benjamin Allen Coates, *Legalist Empire. International Law and American Foreign Relations in the Early Twentieth Century* (Oxford, 2016); Marcus M. Payk, *Frieden durch Recht? Der Aufstieg des modernen Völkerrechts und der Friedensschluss nach dem Ersten Weltkrieg* (Berlin, 2018); Juan Pablo Scarfi, *The Hidden History of International Law in the Americas: Empire and Legal Networks* (Oxford, 2017); Daniel M. Segesser, *Recht statt Rache oder Rache durch Recht? Die Ahndung von Kriegsverbrechen in der internationalen wissenschaftlichen Debatte 1872–1945* (Paderborn, 2010).

[22] Stephen Cobb, *Preparing for Blockade, 1885–1914: Naval Contingency for Economic Warfare* (London, 2013); Shawn T. Grimes, *Strategy and War Planning in the British Navy, 1887–1918* (Woodbridge, 2012); Nicholas A. Lambert, *Sir John Fisher's Naval Revolution* (Columbia, SC, 1999); Nicholas A. Lambert, *Planning Armageddon: British Economic Warfare and the First World War* (Cambridge, MA, 2012); Lambert's latter work deals with international law from the Admiralty's point of view, which offers a rather distorted picture on the role of international law in naval planning prior to 1914 (for a critical reflection on Lambert's book, see John W. Coogan, 'The Short-War Illusion Resurrected: The Myth of Economic Warfare as the British Schlieffen Plan', *The Journal of Strategic Studies*, 38 (2015), 1045–64); William Mulligan, *The Origins of the First World War* (Cambridge, 2010); Eric W. Osborne, *Britain's Economic Blockade of Germany 1914–1919* (London, 2004); Andreas Rose, *Between Empire and Continent: British Foreign Policy before the First World War* (New York, 2017).

[23] John W. Coogan, *The End of Neutrality: The United States, Britain, and Maritime Rights, 1899–1915* (Ithaca, NY, 1981). See also John R. Ferris, 'To the Hunger Blockade: The Evolution of British Economic Warfare, 1914–1915', in Michael Epkenhans and Stephan Huck (eds), *Der Erste Weltkrieg zur See* (Berlin, 2017), 83–97; Douglas Howland, 'Contraband and Private Property in the Age of Imperialism', *Journal of the History of International Law*, 13 (2011), 117–53; Douglas Howland, 'The Sinking of the S.S. Kowshing: International Law, Diplomacy, and the Sino-Japanese War', *Modern Asian Studies*, 42 (2008), 673–703; Scott A. Keefer, *The Law of Nations and Britain's Quest for Naval Security: International Law and Arms Control, 1898–1914* (Cham, 2016); Christopher Martin, 'The 1907 Naval War Plans and the Second Hague Peace Conference: A Case of Propaganda', *Journal of Strategic Studies*, 28, 5 (2005), 833–56; Christopher Martin, 'The Declaration of London: A Matter of Operational Capability', *Historical Research*, 82, 218 (2009), 731–55; Avner Offer, *The First World War: An Agrarian Interpretation* (Oxford, 1989); Avner Offer, 'Morality and Admiralty: "Jacky" Fisher, Economic Warfare and the Laws of War', *Journal of Contemporary History*, 23 (1988), 99–118; Matthew S. Seligmann, 'Failing to Prepare for the Great War? The Absence of Grand Strategy in British War Planning before 1914', *War in History*, 24, 4 (2017), 414–37; Matthew S. Seligmann, *The Royal Navy and the German Threat 1901–1914. Admiralty Plans to Protect British Trade in a War Against Germany* (Oxford, 2012); Bernard Semmel, *Liberalism and Naval Strategy: Ideology, Interest, and Sea Power during*

This book also draws on recent works on sea power, international law, and maritime strategy. Daniel O'Connell's book, *The Influence of Law on Sea Power*, is a classic in its own right. Each historical example he discusses underscores the importance of law for naval planning and the conduct of maritime operations.[24] James Kraska provides a much more recent study, arguing that international law offers a more flexible tool than maritime strategy for adapting to new maritime operations. Hence, he argues, international law influences policy-making far more than maritime strategy.[25] Steven Haines' study offers a more sceptical view on the influence of law on maritime strategy. Haines argues that legal influence is limited to the tactical and operational levels, and does not pertain to the strategic level, as Kraska has suggested.[26] Their conclusions differ because of a different understanding of strategy—Kraska uses a broad understanding of strategy while Haines emphasizes the different levels of war. Both offer valuable tools to examine the relationship between international law and maritime strategy.

Today, international law is omnipresent in the analysis of contemporary conflicts. In fact, as David Kennedy argues, 'warfare has become a legal institution', and the term 'lawfare' is a clear expression of that.[27] However, Kennedy argues that international lawyers today have mostly forgotten about the development of international law in the nineteenth century, although it provides many concepts still used today. In the narrative of the discipline of international law, the period before the First World War was a classical or traditional legal system with clear concepts of neutrality, belligerency, and sovereignty. Yet, Kennedy doubts the narratives of a

---

the Pax Britannica (Boston, MA, 1986); Nicholas Tracy (ed.), *Sea Power and the Control of Trade: Belligerent Rights from the Russian War to the Beira Patrol, 1854–1970* (Aldershot, 2005); Nicholas Tracy, *Attack on Maritime Trade* (London, 1991).

[24] Daniel P. O'Connell, *The Influence of Law on Sea Power* (Manchester, 1975).

[25] James Kraska, 'Grasping "The Influence of Law on Sea Power"', *Naval War College Review*, 62, 3 (2009), 113–35; James Kraska, *Maritime Power and the Law of the Sea. Expeditionary Operations in World Politics* (Oxford, 2011).

[26] Steven Haines, 'The Influence of Law on Maritime Strategy', in Daniel Moran and James A. Russell (eds), *Maritime Strategy and Global Order: Markets, Resources, Security* (Washington, DC, 2016).

[27] David Kennedy, *Of War and Law* (Princeton, NJ, 2006), here: 111; David Kennedy, 'Lawfare and Warfare', in James Crawford and Martti Koskenniemi (eds), *The Cambridge Companion to International Law* (Cambridge, 2012), 158–83. See also Charles J. Dunlap Jr, 'Lawfare Today: A Perspective', *Yale Journal of International Affairs*, (2008), 146–54; Charles J. Dunlap Jr, 'Lawfare Today...and Tomorrow', in Raul A. 'Pete' Pedroso and Daria P. Wollschlaeger (eds), *International Law and the Changing Character of War* (Newport, RI, 2011), 315–25.

formalized international law, and argues instead that sovereignty was not absolute in the nineteenth century. According to Kennedy, international law was understood for most of the nineteenth century to be part of domestic law and therefore based on practice and custom rather than on formalism. Only at the beginning of the twentieth century did states attempt to create an international legal order with themselves as its subjects and with a system of international law designed to regulate an increasingly interdependent world. Since the making of international law put the state at its heart, sovereignty received a stronger connotation than it had before, and, yet, only after the First World War did this development come to be associated with an absolute sovereignty.[28]

Historical studies on the development of the laws of war in the nineteenth and twentieth centuries, such as those by Geoffrey Best or Michael Howard, and, more recently, Stephen C. Neff, provide some answers to Kennedy's questions.[29] The recent publications about the Hague peace conferences equally contribute to a better understanding of the 'Hague' law and provide an assessment of the long-term impact of those developments.[30] Rarely, however, do historians engage with the development of state practice.

Examining Britain's sea power in relation to the development of international maritime law is inherently tied to British imperial politics. Lauren Benton and Lisa Ford's recent book *Rage for Order* focuses on the British Empire in the first half of the nineteenth century and examines how Britain created an imperial legal order.[31] In Benton's earlier work on sovereignty,

[28] David Kennedy, 'International Law and the Nineteenth Century: History of an Illusion', *Nordic Journal of International Law*, 65 (1996), 385–402. See also Wilhelm G. Grewe, *The Epochs of International Law*. Translated and revised by Michael Byers (Berlin, 2000).

[29] Geoffrey Best, *Humanity in Warfare: The Modern History of the International Law of Armed Conflicts* (London, 1980); Geoffrey Best, *War and Law since 1945* (Oxford, 1994); Michael Howard, George J. Andreopoulos, and Mark R. Shulman (eds), *The Laws of War: Constrains on Warfare in the Western World* (New Haven, CT, 1994); Stephen C. Neff, *War and the Law of Nations: A General History* (Cambridge, 2005). See also Stephen C. Neff, *Friends but no Allies: Economic Liberalism and the Law of Nations* (New York, 1990); Stephen C. Neff, *Justice in Blue and Gray: A Legal History of the Civil War* (Cambridge, MA, 2010); Stephen C. Neff, *The Rights and Duties of Neutrals: A General History* (Manchester, 2000).

[30] Maartje Abbenhuis, *The Hague Conferences and International Politics, 1898–1915* (London, 2018); Maartje Abbenhuis, Christopher Ernest Barber, and Annelise Higgins (eds), *War, Peace and International Order? The Legacies of the Hague Conferences of 1899 and 1907* (London, 2017).

[31] Lauren Benton and Lisa Ford, *Rage for Order: The British Empire and the Origins of International Law, 1800–1850* (Cambridge, MA, 2016), 147. See also Lauren Benton and Adam Clulow, 'Legal Encounter and the Origins of Global Law', in Jerry Bentley, Sanjay Subrahmanyam, and Merry Wiesner-Hanks (eds), *The Cambridge World History, Vol 6, Pt 2* (Cambridge, 2015), 80–100.

she argues that 'sovereign claims to ocean space brought the ocean, or parts of it, within an inter-imperial regulatory order'.[32] This book builds on the works of Benton and Ford, and develops their analysis further by investigating how Britain as a sea power shaped international maritime law in the latter half of the nineteenth and early twentieth centuries.

The transdisciplinary field of the history of international law has inspired this research, and it is hoped that this book may be of interest not only to historians but also to international lawyers, legal historians, international relations theorists, and strategists.

The chapters are arranged chronologically, but the complexity of the topic means that figures and legal concepts appear in several chapters. To avoid repeating introductions, they will only be explained the first time, and referred to in subsequent chapters. Chapter 1 serves as an introductory chapter, exploring the idea of the sea as a legal and strategic space. When steamships conquered the sea, early naval thinkers reflected on how to use the sea in time of war. They asked what the future of a maritime conflict would look like. Simultaneously, the scholarly discipline of international law was established, and the codification of custom and practices changed the role of international law in international politics. The adoption of the Declaration of Paris in 1856 was the first multilateral treaty to define principles for the laws of naval warfare. This chapter explores how the process of the codification of international law shaped international relations in the second half of the nineteenth century and vice versa.

Chapter 2 examines how the concept of neutrality developed in the mid-nineteenth century and shows how Britain profoundly changed its foreign policy in the period after 1856. After the American Civil War, Britain adopted new domestic legislation which formed the basis of its neutrality policy until 1914. The implementation of Britain's neutrality policy through state practice is the focus of Chapter 3. It examines the challenges Britain faced in the application of the domestic legislation, and how Britain shaped the law of neutrality more generally as part of international law during this period.

Chapter 4 analyses the early attempts at codification. For most of the second half of the nineteenth century, the process was not state-driven but put forward by non-governmental organizations such as the Institut de droit international. The chapter illustrates the challenges of codification in the context of the practice of international maritime law. Since the codification

---

[32] Lauren Benton, *A Search for Sovereignty: Law and Geography in European Empires, 1400–1900* (Cambridge, 2010), 111.

was a significant change to the customary tradition of international law, Chapter 5 evaluates the importance of state practice for the process of codification and the role of non-governmental organizations in advancing international maritime law. The Hague and London conferences signified a departure from the cabinet diplomacy of great powers, and the embrace of an interconnected world with many more players coming to the negotiating table. Yet, there were only a limited number of sea powers which shaped the codification of international maritime law to the extent that Britain did. This chapter illuminates Britain's position on the process of codification, and how it shaped an international legal order, providing a legal framework for a future maritime conflict.

Chapter 6 turns to the development of maritime strategic thought in Britain in the period from 1872 to 1914 when naval strategic thinkers, such as John and Philip Colomb, Alfred T. Mahan, and Julian S. Corbett, produced influential works on the understanding of sea power and maritime strategy. This chapter examines not only how maritime strategic thought developed but also how the practice and codification of international maritime law shaped ideas about a future maritime conflict, and how law and strategy interacted with each other.

Chapter 7 explores the question of the immunity of private property from capture at sea, which posed a serious challenge to sea powers fearing a further curtailment of belligerent rights, and which the naval thinkers Mahan and Corbett saw as an existential danger to waging maritime warfare. The chapter also examines the views of opponents and supporters of the immunity of private property, illustrating the limitation of the adoption of such a far-reaching proposal.

Finally, the Conclusion outlines how a sea power such as Britain used international maritime law as an instrument in foreign policy to protect its economic and strategic interests, and how international maritime law in turn affected visions of future warfare. Custom, state practice, and codification provided important reference points for the legal framework governing international relations in the nineteenth and early twentieth centuries. The Conclusion explores the shifts from custom to codification in international maritime law.

1

The Sea as a Legal and Strategic Space

The sea spans more than 70 per cent of the globe's surface. Throughout history, the sea has divided and connected different regions and continents. The sea can be relentless, swallowing ships and men, and limiting human ambition to conquer and govern its space. With the onset of the age of steam, with steamships replacing sailing ships, ever more naval transport connected people while goods could be transported more easily and further afield.[1] Excited about new opportunities, people dreamed of oceans becoming like the land—an assimilation which reflected a fundamental change in the perception of the ocean. It was no longer a hostile space. Understanding the sea as a social space is important for this book. This chapter explores how international lawyers and early strategists envisioned the sea as a space to be governed and, at times, conquered.[2] There were important differences in how lawyers and strategists looked at the sea as a space, and yet there were also significant overlaps in their thinking. This chapter illuminates the interaction between international law and maritime strategy, serving as a basis for the following chapters of this book.

The Sea as a Legal Space

The claims to freedom of the sea versus sovereignty of the sea, or in other words ownership of the sea, is one of the oldest disputes in international law. The concept of freedom of the seas (*mare liberum*) had been developed

---

[1] Akira Iriye, *Global Community: The Role of International Organizations in the Making of the Contemporary World* (Berkeley, CA, 2002), 1–24; Robert Kubicek, 'British Expansion, Empire, and Technological Change', in Andrew Porter and Alaine Low (eds), *Oxford History of the British Empire. Vol. 3: The Nineteenth Century* (Oxford, 1999), 247–69.

[2] Philipp E. Steinberg, *The Social Construction of the Ocean* (Cambridge, 2001). For a more detailed analysis of the idea of space, see Akira Iriye and Jürgen Osterhammel (eds), *A World Connecting: 1870–1945* (Cambridge, MA, 2012); Valeska Huber 'Multiple Mobilities, Multiple Sovereignties, Multiple Speeds: Exploring Maritime Connections in the Age of Empire', *International Journal of Middle Eastern Studies*, 48 (2016), 763–6; John Pickles, *A History of Spaces: Cartographic Reason, Mapping and the Geo-Coded World* (London, 2004).

Great Britain, International Law, and the Evolution of Maritime Strategic Thought, 1856–1914. Gabriela A. Frei, Oxford University Press (2020). © Gabriela A. Frei.
DOI: 10.1093/oso/9780198859932.001.0001

in Asian and African cultures long before the Romans and Greeks implemented these ideas in their codes of maritime law. However, it was the anonymous publication in 1609 of *Mare Liberum*, which had a lasting impact on the concept of the freedom of the seas. The author, who was later identified as Hugo Grotius, was then an advocate of the Dutch East India Company. Originally, he prepared the work as a brief to counter Portuguese and Spanish claims to the sovereignty of the sea, and thus deny them the exclusive rights to navigate and trade with the East Indies. Grotius argued that 'the sea is common to all, because it is so limitless that it cannot become a possession of any one, and because it is adapted for the use of all, whether we consider it from the point of view of navigation or of fisheries'.[3] Since the sea could not be possessed, he argued, the sea should be free for every ship, which would mean that the Dutch were free to navigate in the Indian Ocean and to trade in the East Indies.[4]

Grotius' book on freedom of the seas did not go unanswered. Rather, it marked the beginning of the 'battle of the books'—a dispute between the idea of freedom of the seas versus that of the sovereignty of the sea. Portuguese and Spanish authors both defended their claims separately, and the concept of the sovereignty of the sea more generally. In the early seventeenth century, a dispute broke out between the Dutch and the British over the same issue when King James I proclaimed sovereignty over parts of the sea in 1609. The Dutch objected to the British practice of seizing Dutch ships in waters upon which the British claimed territorial rights. As a result, the English lawyer, John Selden, wrote a defence of the claim to ownership of the sea in 1618 in a work entitled *Mare Clausum Seu de Dominio Maris Libri Duo*, which was published in 1635 by the order of King Charles I. Selden argued that claims to the sovereignty of the sea (*mare clausum*) were legitimate as long as a power was able to defend those claims by force. He rejected the Portuguese and Spanish claims over vast areas of ocean on the

---

[3] Hugo Grotius, *The Freedom of the Seas or, The Right which Belongs to the Dutch to Take Part in the East Indian Trade*, ed. James Brown Scott, trans. Ralph Van Deman Magoffin (New York, 1916), 28.

[4] Ram P. Anand, 'Freedom of the Seas: Past, Present and Future', in Rafael Gutiérrez Girardot et al. (eds), *New Directions in International Law: Essays in Honour of Wolfgang Abendroth-Festschrift zu seinem 75. Geburtstag* (Frankfurt/Main, 1982), 215–33; Ram P. Anand, *Origin and Development of the Law of the Sea: History of International Law Revisited*, Publications on Ocean Development (The Hague, 1983), 10–39; Grotius, *The Freedom of the Seas*; Stephen C. Neff, 'Introduction', in Stephen C. Neff (ed.), *Hugo Grotius and the Law of War and Peace* (Cambridge, 2012), i–xxxv; Mónica Brito Vieira, 'Mare Liberum vs. Mare Clausum: Grotius, Freitas, and Selden's Debate on Dominion over the Seas', *Journal of the History of Ideas*, 64, 3 (2003), 361–77.

grounds that they lacked the power to effectively defend those claims. Selden's understanding of the sovereignty of the sea was much more relative than that of the Portuguese and Spanish. Thus, the ability to control the sea was at the heart of Selden's definition of sovereignty of the sea.[5] For him, the sea was a space of power projection, and sea powers used the control of the sea to make territorial claims. Rather than seeing *mare clausum* and *mare liberum* as opposites, these claims complemented each other. Selden's concept of sovereignty of the sea would later be known as territorial waters, whereas freedom of the seas would later define the legal status of the high seas because the high seas could not be controlled effectively enough to claim ownership. Overall, the 'battle of the books' illustrated that there was a limitation to the ownership of the sea. For Grotius and Selden, the sea was a space which was generally free to use, particularly the part of it that is today known as the high seas.[6]

Blockade and the Right of Search and Capture

The concepts of sovereignty and freedom of the sea clashed in wartime, with belligerents claiming the former and neutrals demanding the latter. This caused conflicts between belligerents and neutrals as the exercise of belligerent rights raised fundamental questions about the control of the sea. Belligerents exercised the control of the sea through the law of blockade and the right of search and capture. A sea blockade enabled a belligerent power to deny an enemy's war fleet and its merchant marine the use of the sea, resulting in the control of the enemy's trade and lines of communication.

---

[5] Anand, *Origin and Development*, 94–109; William E. Butler, 'Grotius and the Law of the Sea', in Hedley Bull, Benedict Kingsbury, and Adam Roberts (eds), *Hugo Grotius and International Relations* (Oxford, 1990), 209–20; Thomas W. Fulton, *The Sovereignty of the Sea; an Historical Account of the Claims of England to the Dominion of the British Seas, and of the Evolution of the Territorial Waters, with Special Reference to the Rights of Fishing and the Naval Salute* (Edinburgh, 1911); John B. Hattendorf, 'Maritime Conflict', in Michael Howard, George J. Andreopoulos, and Mark R. Shulman (eds), *The Laws of War: Constraints on Warfare in the Western World* (New Haven, CT, 1994), 98–102; A. Pearce Higgins, 'The Growth of International Law: Maritime Rights and Colonial Titles, 1648–1763', in *Cambridge History of the British Empire, Vol. 1: The Old Empire from the Beginnings to 1783* (Cambridge, 1929), 538–60; Lassa Oppenheim, *International Law: A Treatise*, 2 vols (London, 1912), vol. 1, 315–22; Efthymios Papastavridis, 'The Right of Visit on the High Seas in a Theoretical Perspective: Mare Liberum versus Mare Clausum Revisited', *Leiden Journal of International Law*, 24, 1 (2011), 45–69.

[6] Gabriela A. Frei, 'Freedom and Control of the Seas, 1856–1919', in N. A. M. Rodger (ed.), *The Sea in History: The Modern World/La mer dans l'histoire: La période contemporaine* (Woodbridge, 2017), 59–69; Steinberg, *Social Construction*, 68–109.

A blockade was also directed against neutral trade. Generally, there were two forms of blockade. The military blockade was part of a military operation to intercept communication and supplies for the enemy by denying its war fleet use of the sea. The economic blockade aimed at blockading the enemy's coastline or individual ports in order to put economic pressure on the enemy. Both forms of blockade were often used in combination and aimed at limiting the enemy's capacity to wage war. Blockade laws can be traced back to the sixteenth century when the Dutch proclaimed that enemy ships meant enemy goods, and free ships meant free goods. In other words, the Dutch made no distinction between enemy ships transporting neutral goods and neutral ships carrying enemy goods. As a result, a blockade affected neutrals as much as the enemy. When a ship breached the blockade, it constituted a punishable act and the blockading power was allowed to capture the ship. In any case, belligerents determined the conditions of a blockade.[7]

The exercise of the right of search and capture was another means to control the sea. Belligerents were generally allowed to stop and search any ship on the high seas or in enemy waters in order to verify the identity of the ship, its destination, and its cargo. When a ship carried contraband of war, it was subject to capture and brought to a port where a prize court decided on the lawfulness of capture. Contraband goods were usually goods which directly assisted the enemy's war efforts such as arms and ammunition. A belligerent usually published a list of contraband of war and was free to put any good on that list.[8]

The Rule of 1756

Belligerents could not forbid a neutral to trade with the enemy per se, but they could try to restrict neutral trade with the enemy. In wartime, neutrals often tried to take advantage of the situation by establishing a risky but lucrative trade with both sides. The Seven Years War is a good example of

---

[7] Lance E. Davis and Stanley L. Engerman, *Naval Blockades in Peace and War: An Economic History since 1750* (Cambridge, 2006), 2, 6–7; Phillip Drew, *The Law of Maritime Blockade: Past, Present, and Future* (Oxford, 2017); Eric J. Grove, 'Blockade', in John B. Hattendorf (ed.), *The Oxford Encyclopedia of Maritime History, Vol. 1* (Oxford, 2007), 298–303; William E. Hall, *A Treatise on International Law*, ed. J. B. Atlay, 6th edn (Oxford, 1909), 695–714; Higgins, 'Growth of International Law', 555–7; Lassa Oppenheim, *International Law*, vol. 2, 450–565.

[8] William E. Hall, *A Treatise on International Law*, ed. J. B. Atlay, 5th edn (Oxford, 1904), 719–35; Hattendorf, 'Maritime Conflict', 106; Higgins, 'Growth of International Law', 554–5.

how the British endeavoured to restrict neutral trade with adversaries. During that conflict, France opened its trade to the neutral Dutch, because it was unable to maintain its trade with the colonies. The British reacted by capturing Dutch ships on the grounds that they supported the French enemy. The Rule of 1756, which the British introduced in that war, restricted neutral trade to that in peacetime. The aim of the Rule of 1756 was twofold: first, to regulate neutrals and, second, to cut off the French colonies from France. In reaction, the Dutch circumvented the British policy by transshipping goods which originated from French colonies and which were destined for French ports. This meant that goods were not directly shipped from the French colonies to France but rather that those goods were first transported to neutral ports of the Dutch colonies like St Eustatius and Curaçao. From there, the goods were shipped further to France. For the British, the Dutch practice was unacceptable, and the British condemned such goods as enemy property arguing that they were on a 'continuous voyage' from the French colonies to France. The transshipment via a neutral port had no effect on the status of the property, they argued. This British policy would later be known as the doctrine of continuous voyage and would develop further during the American Civil War.[9]

Claims of Neutrality

The right of neutrals to trade in wartime could not be completely ignored on the international stage and neutrals gained ground by the end of the eighteenth century. The League of Armed Neutrality, founded in 1780 under the auspices of Russia, which united several neutral states, aimed at regulating neutral rights. For the protection of neutral trade it proclaimed four principles: first, a free ship meant free goods except contraband of war; second, agreement on a list of contraband of war; third, blockades had to be effective in order to be legal; fourth, free passage for neutral ships. A second League of Armed Neutrality (1800–1801) supplemented those claims and added the

---

[9] Daniel Baugh, *The Global Seven Years War, 1754–1763: Britain and France in a Great Power Contest* (Harlow, 2011), 323–6; John W. Coogan, *The End of Neutrality: The United States, Britain, and Maritime Rights, 1899–1915* (Ithaca, NY, 1981), 17–24; Davis and Engerman, *Naval Blockades*, 3–4, 7; Hattendorf, 'Maritime Conflict', 104–8; Higgins, 'Growth of International Law', 551–2; Stephen C. Neff, *The Rights and Duties of Neutrals: A General History* (Manchester, 2000), 65–9; Oppenheim, *International Law*, vol. 2, 352–3; Richard Pares, *Colonial Blockade and Neutral Rights, 1739–1763* (Oxford, 1938), 180–204.

neutral right of convoy to the list of principles. The formation of an alliance of neutrals and their putting forward a proposal for an international regulation can be seen as an attempt to define principles of international maritime law with regard to neutral rights. The claims were also formulated in response to Britain's dominance of the sea at the time, and whose prize court rulings had strengthened belligerent rights through the right of blockade and the right of search and capture.[10]

The War of 1812 was in part a direct consequence of Britain antagonizing a neutral power, namely the United States. The Napoleonic Wars had imposed strains on neutrals and the United States went to war against Britain over the rights of neutrals, among other reasons. The Americans challenged the Rule of 1756 and the doctrine of continuous voyage in particular. Yet, the United States only had limited naval resources to fight the British, and the war ended in 1815 without resolving any of the issues at stake. In 1818, when the US Supreme Court decided on the last prize case from the War of 1812, Justice William Johnson highlighted the need to resolve the diverging practices at sea to avoid another war.[11]

Neither the Napoleonic Wars nor the War of 1812 had resolved diverging practices at sea. Only when Britain and France, the two major sea powers, fought as allies in the Crimean War, did Britain give up the practice of the Rule of 1756 and acknowledge the principle of 'free ship, free good', while France abstained from the principle of 'enemy ship, enemy good'. After the war in 1856, Britain and France agreed to define principles to govern future maritime conflicts, signing the Declaration of Paris. The aim was to regulate the relationship between belligerents and neutrals at sea. Celebrated as a

---

[10] James Brown Scott (ed.), *The Armed Neutralities of 1780–1800: A Collection of Official Documents Preceded by the View of Representative Publicists* (New York, 1918). See also Davis and Engerman, *Naval Blockades*, 7.

[11] Gabriela A. Frei, 'Prize Laws in the War of 1812', in Tim Voelcker (ed.), *Broke of the Shannon and the War of 1812* (Barnsley, 2013), 51–6; John B. Hattendorf, 'The War of 1812: A Perspective from the United States', in Tim Voelcker (ed.), *Broke of the Shannon and the War of 1812* (Barnsley, 2013), 1–15. See also Wade G. Dudley, 'The Flawed British Blockade, 1812–15', in Bruce A. Elleman and S. C. M. Paine (eds), *Naval Blockades and Seapower: Strategies and Counter-Strategies, 1805–2005* (London, 2006), 35–45; Paul A. Gilje, *Free Trade and Sailors' Rights in the War of 1812* (New York, 2013); A. Pearce Higgins, 'International Law and the Growth of the Empire', in *Cambridge History of the British Empire, Vol. 2: The Growth of the New Empire 1783–1870* (Cambridge, 1940), 851–2; J. Richard Hill, *The Prizes of War: The Naval Prize System in the Napoleonic Wars, 1793–1815* (Stroud, 1998), 45–59; Andrew D. Lambert, *The Challenge: America, Britain and the War of 1812* (London, 2012); Alfred T. Mahan, *Sea Power in its Relations to the War of 1812*, 2 vols (London, 1905); Neff, *Rights and Duties of Neutrals*, 69–85; Carlton Savage, *Policy of the United States Toward Maritime Commerce in War*, 2 vols (Washington, DC, 1934), vol. 1, 36–41, 277–98; J. C. A. Stagg, *War of 1812: Conflict for a Continent* (Cambridge, 2012), 18–47.

milestone in the codification of international maritime law, the Declaration of Paris marked the beginning of a broader process in the codification of international law. The Declaration of Paris consisted of four principles: first, the abolition of privateering; second, protection of enemy goods under a neutral flag except contraband of war; third, neutral goods except for contraband of war were not subject to seizure when under enemy flag; and fourth, blockade had to be effective in order to be binding. In essence, the Declaration of Paris was a compromise between the conflicting interests of belligerents and neutrals over the use of the sea in wartime. It limited the right of search and capture to enemy ships and defined what represented a lawful blockade. With these two concessions, neutral rights gained in significance.

By adopting the Declaration of Paris, Britain accepted stricter rules regarding the law of blockade and the right of search and capture. With the adoption of the principle of 'free ship, free good', Britain also agreed to the practice that neutrals could freely transport enemy goods, with the exception of contraband. In return, for an increase in neutral rights, all parties agreed to abolish privateering, a condition very dear to the British. In sum, the Declaration of Paris marked an important step towards the regulation of war at sea. It also had a lasting impact on Britain's position regarding international maritime law and British thinking on maritime conflict as well as on Britain's maritime strategy.[12]

Central to the understanding of the sea as a legal space, in the sense of Grotius and Selden, was the ability of men to control the sea. Disputes arose in wartime when neutrals insisted on the right of an uninterrupted voyage and used the principle of freedom of the seas to underline their claim, while belligerents exercised the right of controlling the sea in the name of the sovereignty of the sea. While the British had claimed sovereignty of the sea in the early seventeenth century, Britain's expanding empire and growing economy demanded the adoption of the principle of freedom of the seas. By

---

[12] C. I. Hamilton, 'Anglo-French Seapower and the Declaration of Paris', *The International History Review*, 4, 2 (1982), 167–84; Higgins, 'International Law and the Growth of the Empire', 842–81; Jan M. Lemnitzer, *Power, Law and the End of Privateering* (Basingstoke, 2014), 872; Jan M. Lemnitzer, ' "That Moral League of Nations against the United States": The Origins of the 1856 Declaration of Paris', *The International History Review*, 35 (2013), 1068–88; Stephen C. Neff, *Rights and Duties of Neutrals*, 94–100; Francis T. Piggott, *The Declaration of Paris, 1856: A Study, Documented* (London, 1919); Bryan Ranft, 'Restraints on War at Sea Before 1945', in Michael Howard (ed.), *Restraints on War: Studies in the Limitation of Armed Conflict* (Oxford, 1979), 44–5; Bernard Semmel, *Liberalism and Naval Strategy: Ideology, Interest, and Sea Power during the Pax Britannica* (Boston, MA, 1986), 56–9; Charles H. Stockton, 'The Declaration of Paris', *The American Journal of International Law*, 14, 3 (1920), 356–68.

the mid-nineteenth century, the principle of the freedom of the seas was an integral part of Britain's free trade policy.[13] In 1865, John K. Laughton, a pioneer of naval history, who worked as a Mathematical and Naval Instructor at the Royal Naval College, Greenwich, described the change as Britain opening 'the grand highway of European commerce and civilisation'.[14] In a later publication, Laughton reminded his readers that, although Britain had adopted a free trade policy, the concept of the sovereignty of the sea should not be neglected. Laughton rejected the absolute claims of the Spanish and Portuguese in the sixteenth century as sovereignty of the sea could not be applied 'to the open, the blue sea, the ocean', but he argued that control of the sea was an important concept, describing a relative sovereignty of the sea.[15] The control of the sea was therefore also a question of great interest to strategic thinkers in Britain in the mid-nineteenth century.

The Sea as a Strategic Space

In the 1860s and 1870s, a series of war scares and invasion threats prompted reflection on Britain's defences and its maritime strategy. In 1867, Captain John C. R. Colomb from the Royal Marine Artillery published anonymously a pamphlet in which he highlighted how vital the protection of Britain's overseas trade was for Britain's very existence and for its empire, writing that 'it is beyond dispute that the general welfare of the empire depends chiefly upon its commercial prosperity, and therefore we conceive that our regular forces abroad should be distributed in time of peace in such a manner as would best secure protection to our commerce in the event of sudden war'.[16] Colomb was one of Britain's early strategic thinkers. His innovative approach to dealing with Britain's defence gives a unique insight into the making of British maritime strategy in the second half of the nineteenth century, and conveys a sense of the complexity of the issue, which he took into account in his works.

[13] Anand, *Origin and Development*, 124–58; David H. Anderson, 'Early Modern through Nineteenth-Century Law', in John B. Hattendorf (ed.), *The Oxford Encyclopedia of Maritime History*, Vol. 2 (Oxford, 2007), 330–2; Daniel P. O'Connell, *The International Law of the Sea*, 2 vols (Oxford, 1982), vol 1, 1–20.

[14] John K. Laughton, 'Sovereignty of the Seas', *Fortnightly Review*, 5 (1866), 718–33, here: 733.

[15] John K. Laughton, 'The Scientific Study of Naval History', *Journal of Royal United Service Institution*, 18 (1874), 510–11.

[16] John C. R. Colomb, *The Protection of our Commerce, and Distribution of our Naval Forces Considered* (London, 1867), vi–vii.

Colomb's writings directly attacked Britain's dominant fortress strategy, which had been defined in the Report of the Royal Commission on the Defence of the United Kingdom of 1860. The report focused on the threat to Britain's security from invasion, but Colomb did not see invasion as Britain's greatest danger. Rather, he wrote, 'the defence of the United Kingdom is only a part of the question of "national defence".... The vital question is not how to defend Great Britain and Ireland; but how can we best secure the British Empire against attack.'[17] Colomb published these lines in 1871 in *The Times* where he openly pleaded for the formulation of a British defence strategy in response to Prussia's victories over Austria at Königgrätz (1866) and over France at Sedan (1870). Colomb understood 'national defence' as imperial defence, which he described as an overall strategy for the defence of the empire, including naval and military operations and administration.[18]

Colomb's concept of imperial defence consisted of three aspects: first, the defence of Britain and Ireland; second, the protection of trade; and third, the occupation of India. These aspects were based on Colomb's belief that the empire and international commerce were the sources of Britain's wealth, and, thus, vital to defend.[19] In Colomb's thinking, the empire was 'an immense commercial speculation' based on 'English money,...laid out in investments in all parts of the world'. The sea connected the island nation with its far-flung empire and Colomb highlighted that 'upon the freedom of communication the commercial existence of the empire depends'. He feared that these communication channels could be 'cut off' in time of war, and, thus, according to Colomb, securing the lines of communications should be central to Britain's defence strategy.[20]

Colomb saw the sea as a commercial highway connecting Britain with the empire. It was also a means of 'communication', and in this context,

---

[17] John C. R. Colomb, *Imperial Strategy with Introductory Letters Addressed to 'The Times'* *Forming Part 1 of 'Imperial Defence'* (London, 1871), 8.

[18] Colomb, *Imperial Strategy*, 5–6; Colomb, *Protection of our Commerce*, 3–7. For a conceptual analysis of imperial defence, see Greg Kennedy, 'Introduction: The Concept of Imperial Defence, 1856–1956', in Greg Kennedy (ed.), *Imperial Defence: The Old World Order, 1856–1956* (Abingdon, 2008), 1–8, as well as the chapters by David French, Andrew Lambert, and T. G. Otte in the same volume. See also Richard A. Preston, *Canada and 'Imperial Defense': A Study of the Origins of the British Commonwealth's Defense Organisation, 1867–1919* (Durham, NC, 1967), xiv; Bryan Ranft, 'The Naval Defence of British Sea-Borne Trade 1860–1905' (University of Oxford, DPhil thesis [unpublished], 1968), 1–2; Donald M. Schurman, *The Education of a Navy: The Development of British Naval Strategic Thought, 1867–1914* (London, 1984), 16–35; W. C. B. Tunstall, 'Imperial Defence 1815–1870', in *The Cambridge History of the British Empire, Vol. 2: The Growth of the New Empire 1783–1870* (Cambridge, 1940), 807.

[19] Colomb, *Imperial Strategy*, 5–6; Colomb, *Protection of our Commerce*, 3–7.

[20] Colomb, *Protection of our Commerce*, 3.

'freedom of communication' meant that the sea was free for everyone to use. In time of war, the protection of lines of communication became paramount. Colomb's imperial strategy called for a joint approach in which the army and the navy played significant roles. The protection of lines of communication was foremost the task of the navy. Yet, Colomb argued that wars were not decided at sea, and that the role of the navy was 'to carry war into that [the territory] of an enemy', as wars were primarily fought and won on land.[21] Again, the sea was a highway rather than a battlefield. The navy's role was therefore confined to transporting troops to the enemy's territory, and to keeping open lines of communication so as to give the army the maximum leverage it needed to operate globally. The army's defensive role was to garrison naval and military bases at home and abroad, and its offensive role was to fight the enemy on their territory.[22]

Colomb's writings commented on the ongoing army and navy reforms of the 1860s, which had caused a general debate about British home and colonial defence. Edward Cardwell as Secretary of State for War (1868–74) reorganized the army for colonial defence in order to meet the demands of the Liberal government for reductions in army estimates. The core of the reforms consisted of a shorter period of active service, the abolition of the purchase system, the reorganization of the regimental districts, and an overall reorganization of battalions in overseas and local units. In this way Cardwell sought to transform the British army to meet the demands of both home and colonial defence.[23]

Colomb wrongly criticized the Cardwell reforms for focusing too much on home defence, instead of the army's role in colonial defence. While Colomb supported the idea of the colonies making financial and manpower

---

[21] Colomb, *Imperial Strategy*, 8.

[22] John C. R. Colomb, 'On Colonial Defence: A Paper read before the Royal Colonial Institute, 28 June 1873', in John C. R. Colomb, *The Defence of Great and Greater Britain. Sketches of its Naval, Military, and Political Aspects* (London, 1880), 35–92; Colomb, *Protection of our Commerce*; John C. R. Colomb, *The Reorganization of our Military Forces: Forming Part 2 of 'Imperial Defence'* (London, 1871).

[23] Brian Bond, 'The Effect of the Cardwell Reforms in Army Organization, 1874–1904', *Journal of the Royal United Service Institution*, 105 (1960), 515–24; Brian Bond, 'Prelude to the Cardwell Reforms, 1856–68', *Journal of the Royal United Service Institution*, 106 (1961), 229–36; Anthony Bruce, 'Edward Cardwell and the Abolition of Purchase', in Ian Beckett and John Gooch (eds), *Politicians and Defence: Studies in the Formulation of British Defence Policy 1845–1970* (Manchester, 1981), 24–46; Thomas F. Gallagher, 'British Military Thinking and the Coming of the Franco-Prussian War', *Military Affairs*, 39, 1 (1975), 19–22; Thomas F. Gallagher, '"Cardwellian Mysteries": The Fate of the British Army Regulation Bill, 1871', *The Historical Journal*, 18, 2 (1975), 327–48; Edward M. Spiers, *The Army and Society 1815–1914* (London, 1980), 177–200.

contributions to defence expenses, he objected to the withdrawal of troops from overseas possessions for two reasons. First, Colomb doubted the ability of any foreign navy or merchant marine to land large contingents of foreign troops on British shores. Consequently, he saw no need to station more British troops at home to man the fortifications. Second, he argued that the security of the colonies was crucial for the existence of Britain and the empire, and therefore the capacity to deploy British troops to the colonies had to be maintained at all times in order to continuously guarantee their defence. The navy had to ensure rapid intervention by transporting troops in case of emergency and by keeping lines of communication open.[24]

The navy was similarly affected by the anxiety of the Liberals to reduce its estimates. H. C. E. Childers, then First Lord of the Admiralty, introduced navy reforms between 1868 and 1870, which transformed the administration of the Admiralty so that it could cope better with developments in technology. While Colomb generally supported the Childers reforms, he envisioned the transformation of the navy based on the Prussian army model, as 'the naval service [was] gradually assimilating itself to that of the army'.[25] Colomb imagined the future navy as an army afloat. By adopting the organization and discipline intrinsic to armies, Colomb developed the idea of a 'standing navy', as only a well-administered and organized navy would enhance Britain's efficiency and readiness for war.[26] Colomb's vision of a 'standing navy' suggests that he envisioned the sea as an expansion of the land—a place which could be governed as the land was.

The Protection of Trade

The concept of sea power and its relation to the protection of trade were widely discussed by army and navy officers in the 1860s and 1870s. War scares and invasion fears were the main reasons for reflecting on the capabilities of the Royal Navy in a future maritime conflict, despite the fact that

---

[24] Colomb, *Imperial Strategy*; Colomb, 'Colonial Defence', 35–92; Colomb, *Reorganization of our Military Forces*, 30.

[25] Colomb, *Protection of our Commerce*, 86–7.

[26] John Beeler, *British Naval Policy in the Gladstone–Disraeli Era, 1866–1880* (Stanford, CA, 1997); C. I. Hamilton, 'The Childers Admiralty Reforms and the Nineteenth-Century "Revolution" in British Government', *War in History*, 5 (1998), 37–61; C. I. Hamilton, *The Making of the Modern Admiralty: British Naval Policy-Making, 1805–1927* (Cambridge, 2011), 149–55; N. A. M. Rodger, 'The Dark Ages of the Admiralty, 1869–85. Part 1: "Business Methods", 1869–1874', *Mariner's Mirror*, 61, 4 (1975), 331–44.

Britain's rival naval powers, notably France and Russia, were not of comparable strength. Colomb and others were not primarily concerned that another naval power would challenge Britain's command of the sea. Rather, they were worried about partially losing control of the sea and the ability to protect Britain's trade. It is important to note that they and their contemporaries did not use the term 'control of the sea', but rather 'protection of trade'.[27]

The *guerre de course* strategy, which French naval thinkers, such as Louis-Antoine-Richild Grivel, Jurien de Gravière, and Théophile Aube, made popular in the 1860s, fuelled the British debate on the necessity of trade protection. Rather than seeking decisive battles, the French thinkers suggested that inferior navies should attack the enemy's trade with small but fast ships, such as torpedo boats or cruisers. The aim was to undermine a superior naval power's control of the sea. Britain feared a *guerre de course* strategy because it pursued a strategy of economic warfare, targeting merchant ships rather than the battle fleet.[28]

Economic Warfare and International Law

Sea power and economic warfare were closely intertwined. Economic warfare primarily aimed at destroying the enemy's economic resources and the interception of trade was an important means for undermining the enemy's war efforts. However, waging economic warfare was also a question of a navy's ability to control the sea and to exercise belligerent rights, such as the right to form a blockade and the right of search and capture. These means enabled a sea power to seize neutral and enemy ships, to enforce contraband lists,

---

[27] T. B. Collinson, 'The Strategic Importance of the Military Harbours in the British Channel as Connected with Defensive and Offensive Operations', *Journal of Royal United Service Institution*, 18 (1874), 227–64; Philip H. Colomb, 'Great Britain's Maritime Power: How Best Developed etc.', *Journal of Royal United Service Institution*, 22 (1878), 1–55; Sydney M. Eardley-Wilmot, 'Great Britain's Maritime Power, How Best Developed etc.', *Journal of Royal United Service Institution*, 22 (1878), 435–60; Gerard H. U. Noel, 'Great Britain's Maritime Power, How Best Developed etc.', *Journal of Royal United Service Institution*, 22 (1878), 461–97. See also John F. Beeler, 'A One Power Standard? Great Britain and the Balance of Naval Power, 1860–1880', *Journal of Strategic Studies*, 15, 4 (1992), 548–75.

[28] Collinson, 'Strategic Importance of the Military Harbours', 232, 238, 262. See also Arthur J. Marder, *The Anatomy of British Sea Power. A History of British Naval Policy in the Pre-Dreadnought Era, 1880–1905*, 3rd edn (London, 1972), 68–95; Martin Motte, *Une éducation géostratégique: La pensée navale française de la jeune école à 1914* (Paris, 2004), 94–210; Arne Røksund, *The Jeune Ecole: The Strategy of the Weak* (Leiden, 2007), x–xi, 1–23; Theodore Ropp, *The Development of a Modern Navy: French Naval Policy, 1871–1904*, ed. Stephen S. Roberts (Annapolis, MD, 1987), 19–210.

and to prevent unneutral service.[29] In other words, economic warfare brought together the sea as a legal and strategic space. Both international law and maritime strategy were primarily concerned about control of the sea. While strategic considerations were mostly based on theoretical reflections of the use of the sea, legal considerations embraced a more practical stance.

Naval circles in Britain were hesitant in their support of the development of international maritime law and its consequences for a future war at sea. In the 1870s, naval threats led to demands for a withdrawal from the Declaration of Paris of 1856 in order to restore essential belligerent rights. The reason for the outcry was uncertainty as to the importance of economic warfare in a future maritime conflict. The capture of enemy and neutral ships was regarded as essential for a successful British maritime strategy. Economic warfare would have the decisive effect of not only ending a war but also of doing so quickly. The expansion of Britain's overseas trade raised concerns as to the ability to protect trade in a future maritime conflict. At the same time, the principles laid out in the Declaration of Paris were too vague to ensure the protection of British trade. The law of blockade as well as the right of search and capture were only vaguely defined, and the lack of a definition of contraband of war left both neutrals and belligerents exposed to uncertainty, as the following chapters illustrate.[30]

In the debate on economic warfare, legal aspects, such as the definition of contraband or blockade, were treated as parts of strategic, tactical, and technological considerations. For instance, the strategic importance of coal, which Sir Alexander Milne, Fourth Naval Lord, had pointed out as early as 1859, was a recurrent topic. Coal considerably restricted the radius of naval operations due to the ships' dependence on coaling stations and the limited capacity to store coal on board. Since Britain had more coaling stations in the world than any other power, their protection became important. At the same time, Britain produced the highest quality steam coal and possessed a near monopoly on exporting coal.[31] These circumstances were advantageous

---

[29] Neill H. Alford Jr, *Modern Economic Warfare (Law and the Naval Participant)* (Washington, DC, 1967), 4–5.

[30] W. Vernon Harcourt, 'The Rights and Duties of Neutrals in Time of War. Part 1', *Journal of Royal United Service Institution*, 9 (1865), 313–28; W. Vernon Harcourt, 'The Rights and Duties of Neutrals in Time of War. Part 2', *Journal of Royal United Service Institution*, 9 (1865), 329–45; William S. Lindsay, 'On Belligerent Rights: The Declaration of Paris, 1856', *Journal of Royal United Service Institution*, 21 (1878), 179–227; John Ross-of-Bladensberg, 'Maritime Rights', *Journal of Royal United Service Institution*, 20 (1876), 423–46.

[31] John Beeler, 'Steam, Strategy and Schurman: Imperial Defence in the Post-Crimean Era, 1856–1905', in Greg Kennedy and Keith Neilson (eds), *Far-Flung Lines: Essays on Imperial Defence in Honour of Donald Mackenzie Schurman* (London, 1996), 27–54; Bob Wilson,

for Britain as a sea power in time of war. In conflicts in which Britain remained neutral, however, the situation looked different as the American Civil War illustrated. Britain remained neutral and provided belligerents with coal. The main question was whether coal should be treated as contraband or not. In 1862, the British government had declared that coal was not contraband—a decision which reflected Britain's neutral and economic interests.[32] Colomb and other officers did not agree with this decision and demanded that coal be declared contraband, so as to halt maritime operations and terminate war quickly. In their view, the question of coal was treated only from the perspective of a belligerent, which explains their disagreement with the government.[33]

Blockade

Steamships' dependence on coal also raised concerns as to their capacity to maintain a blockade. Blockade was an important means of economic warfare and yet technological advances questioned its feasibility in modern naval warfare. Most discussants were also sceptical about the effectiveness of blockade in the future—because Britain was 'by far the largest carriers by sea, any measures which stop or diminish our [Britain's] intercourse with other countries, must inflict more injury on us [Britain] than on any other neutral nation'.[34] Despite the potentially negative effect of blockade on Britain's vast overseas trade, those who believed that blockade would remain effective in a future maritime conflict stressed its military purpose.[35]

'Fuelling the Steam Navy: Naval Coal Supplies in the Early Steam Period, 1820–1870' (University of Exeter, MA degree [unpublished], 2006); Bob Wilson, 'Fuelling the Victorian Steam Navy', *Warship* (2009).

[32] Memorandum by E. Hertslet on the Question whether or not Coals are Considered Contraband of War (Confidential), 20 Jan. 1862, TNA, FO 881/1017.

[33] Collinson, 'Strategic Importance of the Military Harbours', 233, 244; John C. R. Colomb, 'The Naval and Military Resources of the Colonies', *Journal of Royal United Service Institution*, 23 (1879), 421–5.

[34] Lindsay, 'On Belligerent Rights', 183.

[35] Collinson, 'Strategic Importance of the Military Harbours', 227–64; John. C. R. Colomb, 'Naval Intelligence and Protection of Commerce in War', *Journal of Royal United Service Institution*, 25 (1881), 553–90; Philip H. Colomb, 'Blockades: Under Existing Conditions of Warfare', *Journal of Royal United Service Institution*, 31 (1887), 733–58; Philip H. Colomb, 'The Naval Defences of the United Kingdom', *Journal of Royal United Service Institution*, 32 (1888), 565–601; Donald Currie, 'On Maritime Warfare; the Importance to the British Empire of a Complete System of Telegraphs, Coaling Stations, and Graving Docks', *Journal of Royal United Service Institution*, 21 (1877), 228–47; Lindsay, 'On Belligerent Rights', 179–227; Samuel Long,

Strategic Importance of Foodstuffs

Britain's strategic vulnerability was intertwined with the composition of the economy. By the mid-1870s, Britain had a highly interdependent economy. On the one hand, it was dependent on the import of foodstuffs and raw materials, and, on the other, on the export of manufactured goods. The rapid expansion of the formal and informal empire in this period added to its vulnerability. The causes for these structural changes in the British economy lay in the period prior to the depression of 1873.[36] First, the introduction of steam facilitated production, reduced the costs of production and transport, and boosted the expansion of trade.[37] Second, rising economic powers like the United States and Germany challenged Britain's leading position in international trade. The introduction of steam not only increased the number of steamships but also boosted the construction of railways. While Britain had the largest merchant marine, Germany had heavily invested in its railway network, which facilitated transport on land. The United States, with its huge domestic market potential, could easily

'Study of the Tactics of Naval Blockade as Affected by Modern Weapons', *Journal of Royal United Service Institution*, 25 (1882), 316–49.

[36] Nicholas Crafts, 'Long-Run Growth', in Roderick Floud and Paul Johnson (eds), *The Cambridge Economic History of Modern Britain Vol. 2: Economic Maturity, 1860–1939* (Cambridge, 2004), 2; François Crouzet, *The Victorian Economy*, trans. Anthony Forster (London, 1982), 101–4; Albert H. Imlah, *Economic Elements in the Pax Britannica: Studies in British Foreign Trade in the Nineteenth Century* (Cambridge, MA, 1958); C. Knick Harley, 'Trade, 1870–1939: From Globalisation to Fragmentation', in Roderick Floud and Paul Johnson (eds), *The Cambridge Economic History of Modern Britain. Vol. 2: Economic Maturity, 1860–1939* (Cambridge, 2004), 161; Martin Lynn, 'British Policy, Trade, and Informal Empire in the Mid-Nineteenth Century', in Andrew Porter and Alaine Low (eds), *Oxford History of the British Empire. Vol. 3: The Nineteenth Century* (Oxford, 1999), 101–21; Gary B. Magee, 'Manufacturing and Technological Change', in Roderick Floud and Paul Johnson (eds), *The Cambridge Economic History of Modern Britain. Vol. 2: Economic Maturity, 1860–1939* (Cambridge, 2004), 74–98; Peter Mathias, *The First Industrial Nation: An Economic History of Britain, 1700–1914*, 2nd edn (London, 1983); R. C. O. Matthews, C. H. Feinstein, and J. C. Odling-Smee, *British Economic Growth, 1856–1973* (Oxford, 1982), 527; David Reynolds, *Britannia Overruled: British Policy and World Power in the Twentieth Century*, 2nd edn (Harlow, 2000), 1–82; Keith Robbins, *The Eclipse of a Great Power: Modern Britain, 1870–1975* (London, 1983); Samuel Berrick Saul, *Studies in British Overseas Trade, 1870–1914* (Liverpool, 1960), 11; Werner Schlote, *British Overseas Trade from 1700 to the 1930s*, trans. W. O. Henderson and W. H. Chaloner (Oxford, 1952), 41–50; Alan Sked, *Britain's Decline: Problems and Perspectives* (Oxford, 1987).

[37] Crouzet, *Victorian Economy*, 102; Harley, 'Trade, 1870–1939', 163–8; Daniel R. Headrick, *The Tentacles of Progress: Technology Transfer in the Age of Imperialism, 1850–1940* (New York, 1988), 18–48; Magee, 'Manufacturing', 88–96; Mathias, *First Industrial Nation*, 286–9; Brian R. Mitchell, *British Historical Statistics* (Cambridge, 1988), 536; Saul, *British Overseas Trade*, 13.

compete with Britain in terms of productivity.[38] The rise of land powers in the second half of the nineteenth century put Britain under economic and political pressure. Britain was dependent on exports and imports via sea, and thus was vulnerable if a political or economic crisis occurred elsewhere in the world. Germany and the United States, on the other hand, were much less affected by external factors as they primarily used local raw materials and produced for domestic markets, meaning that their economies were less influenced from outside.[39] Third, Britain's free trade policy, which it had adopted in the mid-1840s with the repeal of the Corn Laws in 1846 and of the Navigation Laws in 1849, opened not only new markets abroad but also its own economy. The consequences of free trade were only felt in the mid-1870s, when foreign competition became noticeable, and prices for foodstuffs fell due to a dramatic increase in imports. Undoubtedly, free trade reduced trade barriers whilst also making Britain's economy more vulnerable. As a result, the protection of overseas trade became a matter of strategic importance.[40]

In the 1870s, statistical societies examined Britain's increasing dependence on imported foodstuffs and raw materials, and warned of the consequences of its free trade policy. For instance, the Manchester Statistical Society, founded in 1833, systematically studied the socio-political effects of Britain's dependence on imported foodstuffs and raw materials. Stephen Bourne, a civil servant, presented an impressive set of data illustrating that the import of foodstuffs had tripled between 1854 and 1877. What worried him most was the fact that Britain's imports mainly derived from foreign countries, such as the United States. He suggested, therefore, investing in British colonies rather than in the informal empire, and so favoured a form of protectionism over free trade.[41]

---

[38] Paul Kennedy, *The Rise and Fall of British Naval Mastery* (London, 1976; reprint with new introduction London, 2004), 177–202; Magee, 'Manufacturing', 84–8.

[39] Harley, 'Trade, 1870–1939,' 172; Mathias, *First Industrial Nation*, 289–93.

[40] Mathias, *First Industrial Nation*, 268–314; Avner Offer, *The First World War: An Agrarian Interpretation* (Oxford, 1989), 81–103, 218–21; Sarah Palmer, *Politics, Shipping and the Repeal of the Navigation Laws* (Manchester, 1990); Barry Turner, *Free Trade and Protection* (Harlow, 1971).

[41] Thomas S. Ashton, *Economic and Social Investigations in Manchester, 1833–1933. A Centenary History of the Manchester Statistical Society* (Hassocks, 1977); Stephen Bourne, 'Increasing Dependence of this Country upon Foreign Supplies for Food: Read at Manchester Statistical Society, 11 Apr. 1877', in Stephen Bourne (ed.), *Trade, Population and Food: A Series of Papers on Economic Statistics* (London, 1880), 76–102.

Protection of Trade as Strategic Importance

John C. R. Colomb, who had pointed out the importance of trade protection in the past, re-emphasized his argument in 1881 in an often-cited paper entitled 'Naval Intelligence and Protection of Commerce in War', in which he provided a comprehensive set of data to underline his argument. Statistical data, tables, and maps were used to identify vital sea-lanes and to illustrate Britain's extensive economic network and even more so the country's vulnerability. In all, Britain's dependence on the import of foodstuffs and raw materials put domestic security at risk, and thus Colomb proposed the protection of vital sea-lanes in wartime. Using maps to visualize the sea as a space helped Colomb to illustrate his case. In these maps, the sea appeared as a space with carefully drawn lines, symbolizing sea-lanes, and red circles, which marked strategically important areas within that space, giving a sense of closely described areas comparable to territories on maps drawn by military staff. However, the picture of Britain's overseas economic interests and activities was incomplete, as Colomb highlighted, and he urged the British government to collect more data to gain a comprehensive picture to serve as a basis for strategic planning.[42]

The Admiralty recognized the importance of the protection of trade. War scares in 1878, 1884, and 1885 illustrated Britain's vulnerability and the Admiralty's response to the French and Russian threats showed that the protection of trade was Britain's foremost strategic concern.[43] In fact, the British government had only started to analyse the defences of Britain and the empire in 1879 when it was threatened by Russia and France. The government appointed a Royal Commission, also known as the Carnarvon Commission, to enquire into the defence of ports and coaling stations. Colomb commented ironically that 'for the first time in the history of our Empire we are about to enquire how to defend it'. Although Colomb was

---

[42]   Colomb, 'Naval Intelligence', 553–90. See also John C. R. Colomb, 'The Distribution of our War Forces. Part I', *Journal of the Royal United Service Institution*, 13 (1869), 37–56; John C. R. Colomb, 'The Distribution of our War Forces. Part II', *Journal of the Royal United Service Institution*, 13 (1869), 57–71.

[43]   Remarks by Captain W. H. Hall on a Naval Campaign (Most Confidential), 24 Sept. 1884, TNA, ADM 231/5; General Outline by Captain W. H. Hall of Possible Naval Operations against Russia (Most Confidential), 14 Mar. 1885, TNA, ADM 231/6; The Protection of Commerce by Patrolling the Ocean Highways and by Convoy by the Foreign Intelligence Committee (Most Confidential), May 1885, TNA, ADM 231/6. See also Tunstall, 'Imperial Defence, 1870–1897', in *The Cambridge History of the British Empire, Vol. 3: The Empire-Commonwealth 1870–1919* (Cambridge, 1959), 231–2.

influential in the creation of the commission, he was not a member, which may explain the tone of his writing and his attacks against it. He accused the commission of excluding colonial representatives and of not considering the wider dimension of Britain's defence strategy. The final report of the commission, which was submitted in 1882, acknowledged the necessity for Britain to protect its trade and specifically dealt with the maintenance of the war fleet in order to exercise trade protection. Despite the importance of the results of the Carnarvon Commission, the reports were withheld and only partially published in 1887 in Parliamentary Papers, due to the sensitivity of the matter at the time.[44]

In summary, the mid-nineteenth century marked a watershed in the understanding of the sea as a legal and strategic space. Britain was the world's leading economy in the 1870s, and its wealth and prosperity were founded upon command of the sea. The adoption of a free trade policy led to a rapid expansion of Britain's overseas trade prior to 1870. Yet, this development undermined the Royal Navy's ability to defend British trade and its economic interests in a future maritime conflict. With domestic security at risk, protection of trade became Britain's foremost strategic concern, as John C. R. Colomb's analysis of the defences of Britain and the empire illustrated. Central to the discussion on Britain's defences was the question of control of the sea. Britain's vulnerability was a result not only of the expansion of trade, or of advances in technology, but also of changing perceptions of international maritime law and its role within international politics. The British government imagined a future maritime conflict as an economic war in which blockade, contraband, and the right of search and capture would play central roles. However, the British government needed to create a legal framework which reflected Britain's economic and strategic interests. The following chapters explore how the British government developed new practices at sea and shaped international politics as a means to protect British trade and economic interests.

---

[44] Third and Final Report of the Royal Commission Appointed to Inquire into the Defence of British Possessions and Commerce Abroad (Confidential), 22 July 1882, TNA, CAB 7/4; John C. R. Colomb, *The Defence of Great and Greater Britain: Sketches of its Naval, Military and Political Aspects* (London, 1880), 1, 5. See also Donald M. Schurman, *Imperial Defence*, ed. John Beeler (London, 2000), 107; Schurman, *Education of a Navy*, 20.

2
The Making of the Neutrality Policy

Neutrality became an important concept in international politics in the nineteenth century, and the Crimean War of 1853–6 showed the challenges and the benefits of neutrality. While Britain was a belligerent during the Crimean War, neutrality was politically appealing. This chapter addresses the development of the law of neutrality in the mid-nineteenth century, and examines the making of Britain's neutrality policy in the latter half of the nineteenth century. Crucially for Britain's change in policy was its experience as a neutral during the American Civil War. Hence, the chapter is concerned with the legal framework upon which Britain's neutrality policy was based until the outbreak of the First World War in 1914.

Early Concepts of Neutrality

The law of neutrality was the result of a gradual development in state practice. In the just war tradition of the early Middle Ages there was no space for neutrality or for the idea of the rights and duties of neutrals. Recognizing neutrality depended solely on the benevolence of belligerents. The first evidence of the concept of neutrality can be traced to the late Middle Ages. Although neutrality was associated with impartiality towards belligerent parties, neutrals' territory was used for the transit of troops or the recruitment of soldiers or sailors. With the development of sovereign states in the sixteenth century, the concept of neutrality gained ground. As a result, the law of neutrality was defined more closely in relation to sovereignty.[1]

Neutrality's golden age spanned from the end of the Napoleonic Wars to the outbreak of the First World War. As Maartje Abbenhuis convincingly argues, neutrality became an important political tool in international

---

[1] Maartje Abbenhuis, *An Age of Neutrals: Great Power Politics, 1815–1914* (Cambridge, 2014), 1–2, 22–38; Stephen C. Neff, *The Rights and Duties of Neutrals: A General History* (Manchester, 2000), 1–25, and particularly 63–108 for an overview of the development of neutral rights in the early nineteenth century until the Declaration of Paris of 1856.

Great Britain, International Law, and the Evolution of Maritime Strategic Thought, 1856–1914. Gabriela A. Frei, Oxford University Press (2020). © Gabriela A. Frei.
DOI: 10.1093/oso/9780198859932.001.0001

politics in the nineteenth century.[2] Nineteenth-century textbooks on international law discussed neutrality in great detail. For instance, the widely used textbook by American international jurist, Theodore D. Woolsey, distinguished different degrees of neutrality. First, strict neutrality demanded a state to abstain absolutely from any involvement with the belligerents. Second, imperfect neutrality meant that a neutral allowed both, or one, of the belligerents to use its territory for the transit of troops or to recruit soldiers or sailors. In this case, the recognition of its neutral status depended on other states. Third, perpetual neutrality, as declared by Switzerland and Belgium, meant that the sovereign state abstained from the right to declare war, and depended on the recognition of its neutrality by other states. In addition, the term 'armed neutrality' often appeared in this context, which meant that a neutral would defend its neutral status in the case of an attack.[3]

The relationship between the state and neutrality was crucial and the British international jurist, William E. Hall, wrote that 'a neutral state is not merely itself bound to refrain from helping either of two belligerents, but...it is also bound to take care to a reasonable extent that neither one nor the other shall be prejudiced by acts over which it is supposed to have control'.[4] Not only was abstention essential but so too was the state's control of neutral behaviour. Neutrality was not an expression of passivity. On the contrary, neutrality demanded a neutral state to actively engage in controlling its actions. Hall argued that 'the highest attribute of a state, that of sovereignty itself, has become the root of neutral duty'.[5] Thus, a state was responsible for enforcing neutrality within its jurisdiction. For instance, a state was obliged to ensure that no belligerent used neutral territory for military operations. It was also not allowed to lend money to, or support the troops of, a belligerent.[6]

However, there was also a limitation to a state's responsibility with regard to the enforcement of neutrality. Naturally, the borders of a state formed a judicial limitation, as 'no state can be asked to take cognizance of what occurs outside its own borders; in another country it cannot, and on the sea it need not act; there it washed its hands of responsibility'. Hall further

---

[2] Maartje M. Abbenhuis, 'A Most Useful Tool for Diplomacy and Statecraft: Neutrality and Europe in the "Long" Nineteenth-Century, 1815–1914', *The International History Review*, 35, 1 (2013), 1–22.

[3] Theodore D. Woolsey, *Introduction to the Study of International Law, Designed as an Aid in Teaching and in Historical Studies*, 3rd edn (New York, 1872), 261–3.

[4] William E. Hall, *A Treatise on International Law*, 2nd edn (Oxford, 1884), 73.

[5] William E. Hall, *The Rights and Duties of Neutrals* (London, 1874), 16.

[6] Hall, *Rights and Duties*, 16–18. See also Woolsey, *Study of International Law*, 265.

argued that the state's control over its citizens ceased outside its jurisdiction as a state 'is not expected to follow its subjects beyond its jurisdiction to protect a belligerent; of whatever hostile conduct its subjects may be guilty, his remedy is upon them personally, and not upon the nation to which they belong'.[7]

This latter point touches on a difficult issue as conflicts between neutrals and belligerents often occurred because individuals of a neutral state infringed the state's neutrality policy. Here Hall distinguished between a state's intent to breach neutrality, and that of a neutral individual, whose main interest was to make 'a business profit'. If an individual infringed neutrality, Hall argued that the individual was 'left face to face with the belligerent nation' and the belligerent power 'alone determines whether he [the individual] has infringed its privileges'.[8] It was then up to the prize court of the belligerent state to make a final decision, and a neutral state could only intervene on behalf of its citizen when the belligerent state 'overstepped the boundaries of his [the belligerent state's] rights'.[9] More generally, the law of neutrality did not recognize an individual's rights. Hall argued further that 'the only duty of the individual [was] to his own sovereign; and so distinctly is this the case, that acts done even with the intent to injure a foreign state are only wrong in so far as they compromise the nation of which the individual is a member'.[10] This clear hierarchy of the treatment of individuals in international law was characteristic for the nineteenth century. The emphasis on the state's sovereignty meant that the individual was subordinate to the state.[11]

Since states rather than individuals were the focus of the law of neutrality, international jurists were particularly interested in the complex relation-ships between neutrals and belligerents, as well as in the conflicts between them. A look at the rights and duties of neutrals helps to understand the concept of neutrality more thoroughly. Neutrality primarily meant impar-tiality. In practical terms, a neutral state was obliged to maintain friendly relations with the belligerent parties. This meant, for instance, that troops or ships, which fled to a neutral territory or waters, were protected as disarmed civilians. In case of bad weather or other emergencies which required the

---

[7] Hall, *Rights and Duties*, 18. See also Hall, *Treatise*, 2nd edn, 76–9.

[8] Hall, *Rights and Duties*, 19–20. See also Lassa Oppenheim, *International Law: A Treatise*, 2 vols (London, 1912), vol. 1, 362–9.

[9] Hall, *Rights and Duties*, 20.   [10] Hall, *Rights and Duties*, 21.

[11] Robert Kolb, 'The Protection of the Individual in Times of War and Peace', in Bardo Fassbender and Anne Peters (eds), *The Oxford Handbook of the History of International Law* (Oxford, 2012), 317–58.

immediate use of a port, a belligerent ship was allowed to enter a neutral port as an act of humanity. A misuse of the neutral's benevolence constituted a violation of neutrality and was an act of war on the part of the belligerent. The examples again illustrate that nineteenth-century neutrality was closely linked to the sovereignty of a state, which had to be respected at all times.[12]

By the mid-nineteenth century, a 'consolidation' of the law of neutrality can be noticed.[13] After the Crimean War, the two major sea powers, Britain and France, had agreed on the Declaration of Paris of 1856, which outlined a series of principles governing maritime warfare (see Chapter 1). Although intended to regulate some of the most contentious issues between neutrals and belligerents in a war at sea, the vagueness of the principles left room for interpretation. Yet, the Declaration of Paris was celebrated as a major achievement in the recognition of neutral rights. How enduring those principles would be, only future wars, and, in particular, state practice would show.[14]

The concept of neutrality gained in importance in international politics after 1856. The Second War of Italian Unification in 1859 provided the first opportunity to observe how neutrals positioned themselves in a conflict. Britain, Russia, and Prussia declared neutrality with the aim of containing the war, while simultaneously dealing with domestic issues. The British government's pragmatic decision proved not only to be successful but also popular. Moreover, the case illustrated that neutrality could be used as a diplomatic tool to localize wars and, at the same time, to protect national interests.[15] Yet, it was the American Civil War that had a lasting impact on Britain's neutrality policy.

The American Civil War: A Turning Point

The outbreak of the American Civil War in 1861 meant that European powers had to position themselves in the conflict. Britain decided to stay neutral despite calls for its intervention. The main reason was the protection

---

[12] Hall, *Rights and Duties*, 16–21; Hall, *Treatise*, 2nd edn, 75–7; Woolsey, *Study of International Law*, 262–5.

[13] Neff, *Rights and Duties of Neutrals*, 86–108. See also Abbenhuis, *Age of Neutrals*, 66–95.

[14] Jan M. Lemnitzer, *Power, Law and the End of Privateering* (Basingstoke, 2014). See also Jan M. Lemnitzer, '"That Moral League of Nations against the United States": The Origins of the 1856 Declaration of Paris', *The International History Review*, 35 (2013), 1068–88.

[15] Abbenhuis, *Age of Neutrals*, 96–108; Neff, *Rights and Duties of Neutrals*, 99–101.

of British economic interests on the American continent. Neutrality allowed the maintenance of good economic relations with both belligerent parties.[16] On 14 May 1861, Britain published a proclamation of neutrality in *The London Gazette*, the official publication of the Crown.[17] It not only informed other states of Britain's neutrality, but also addressed its own citizens and informed them of the laws applicable at the time. Apart from a reference to the Law of Nations, the proclamation drew particular attention to domestic law, especially the Foreign Enlistment Act of 1819. The act had been adopted in the aftermath of the Napoleonic Wars when British officers joined forces fighting for the independence of Spanish American states. Modelled on the American Foreign Enlistment Act of 1794, it explicitly forbade British subjects from enlisting in foreign services, or from equipping or arming vessels for foreign services. The aim was to control the activities of individual citizens, who could otherwise compromise the state's neutrality.[18] Citizens were warned that in the case of 'misconduct' they would 'in nowise obtain any Protection' from the British government 'against any liabilities or penal consequences'.[19]

Throughout the American Civil War, the Union accused Britain of unneutral behaviour.[20] The *Trent* affair in November 1861 almost caused an outbreak of hostilities between the Union and Britain. The Unionists seized the British mail ship *Trent* and captured two Confederate envoys who were on a mission to Britain and France to lobby for the recognition of the Confederacy as a sovereign state. The British government protested against the unlawful seizure and accused the Unionists of violating British neutrality. From the Union's point of view, though, carrying enemy subjects on board a British ship was an act of un-neutral behaviour.[21]

While the *Trent* affair illustrated the vagueness of the concept of neutrality, Britain's domestic legislation was another point of conflict. The Confederates lacked strong naval forces that could safeguard the imports of war material

---

[16] Nir Arielli, Gabriela A. Frei, and Inge Van Hulle, 'The Foreign Enlistment Act, International Law, and British Politics, 1819–2014', *The International History Review*, 38, 4 (2016), 642–3. More generally on the American Civil War, see Howard Jones, *Blue and Gray Diplomacy: A History of Union and Confederate Foreign Relations* (Chapel Hill, NC, 2010).

[17] 'A Proclamation of Neutrality by the Queen Victoria', *The London Gazette*, No. 22510, 14 May 1865, 2046–7.

[18] Arielli, Frei, and Van Hulle, 'Foreign Enlistment Act', 637–40.

[19] Arielli, Frei, and Van Hulle, 'Foreign Enlistment Act', 637–40.

[20] James P. Baxter III, 'The British Government and Neutral Rights, 1861–1865', *The American Historical Review*, 34, 1 (1928), 9–29.

[21] Charles F. Adams, 'The Trent Affair', *The American Historical Review*, 17 (1912), 540–62; Norman B. Ferris, *The Trent Affair: A Diplomatic Crisis* (Knoxville, TN, 1977); Gordon H. Warren, *Fountain of Discontent. The Trent Affair and Freedom of the Seas* (Boston, MA, 1981).

and other essential goods. The Unionists' strategy was to blockade the southern ports in order to stop all trade with the Confederates. Despite the Unionists' considerable success, the Confederates could count on British support. The city of Liverpool had strong business connections with the South dating back to the slave trade and later the cotton trade. Thus, many of the Confederates' commerce raiders that operated off the coast of the southern states and interfered with the Unionists' naval operations, were built in Liverpool shipyards.[22]

This situation led to further diplomatic tensions between the Union and Britain. The section of the Foreign Enlistment Act dealing with the 'fitting out, arming, or equipping' of vessels for foreign belligerent service started to receive particular attention. The CSS *Florida* was one of the first vessels completed in March 1862 in a Liverpool shipyard and operated successfully until her capture in 1864. The most prominent case, however, was that of the commerce raider CSS *Alabama* that was also built in Liverpool in 1862 and sunk in 1864. The Union accused Britain of breaching neutrality by supporting the enemy's war efforts, and pressured the British government to apply the Foreign Enlistment Act more vigorously within its jurisdiction. Following the evidence provided by the Union's consul in Liverpool, Thomas H. Dudley, the Foreign Office ordered the detention of the CSS *Alexandra* in April 1863 while she was still in the Liverpool shipyard. Intending to set a precedent, Sir Frederick Pollock, the Lord Chief Baron of the Exchequer, who had to judge on the matter, ruled that the *Alexandra* had to be released due to lack of evidence.[23] The ruling was a major defeat for the British government, and illustrated the major weakness of domestic legislation. Nevertheless, it sent a strong signal to the British shipbuilding industry, warning it against the lure of commercial opportunities that could potentially compromise Britain's neutrality.[24]

While the American Civil War ended in 1865, the legal disputes between Britain and the United States continued to occupy arbiters. The United

---

[22] Frank L. Owsley, *King Cotton Diplomacy: Foreign Relations of the Confederate States of America*, 2nd edn (Chicago, IL, 1959); David G. Surdam, 'The Union's Navy's Blockade Reconsidered', in Bruce A. Elleman and S. C. M. Paine (eds), *Naval Blockades and Seapower: Strategies and Counter-Strategies, 1805–2005* (London, 2004), 61–9.

[23] Court of the Exchequer at Westminster, *Attorney-General v. Sillem and Others, Claiming the Vessel 'Alexandra' Seized under the Foreign Enlistment Act (59 George III. Chapter 69). Report of the Trial before the Lord Chief Baron and a Special Jury* (London, 1863).

[24] Arielli, Frei, and Van Hulle, 'Foreign Enlistment Act', 643–4. For more details, see Coy F. Cross, *Lincoln's Man in Liverpool: Consul Dudley and the Legal Battle to Stop the Confederate Warships* (DeKalb, IL, 2007).

States held Britain liable for the damage that the commerce raiders had caused during the war and demanded compensation.[25] The claims were only settled in 1872 in the Geneva Arbitration, and the British had to pay US$ 15 million in compensation. Apart from the compensation, the 1871 Treaty of Washington addressed the status of neutrals more generally. Most famously, Britain and the United States agreed on the 'three rules' in Article 6 of the treaty that defined the rights and duties of neutrals more precisely:

> Article 6: A neutral Government is bound—
>
> First, to use due diligence to prevent the fitting out, arming, or equipping within its jurisdiction, of any vessel which it has reasonable ground to believe is intended to cruise or to carry on war against a Power with which it is at peace; and also to use like diligence to prevent the departure from its jurisdiction of any vessel intended to cruise or carry on war as above, such vessel having been specially adapted, in whole or in part, within such jurisdiction to war-like use.
>
> Secondly, not to permit or suffer either belligerent to make use of its ports or waters as the base of naval operations against the other, or for the purpose of the renewal or augmentation of Military supplies or arms, or the recruitment of men.
>
> Thirdly, to exercise due diligence in its own ports and waters, and, as to all persons within its jurisdiction, to prevent any violation of the foregoing obligations and duties.[26]

These 'three rules', as the regulations were commonly known, formed the legal basis for Britain's neutrality policy in the second half of the nineteenth century.[27]

British Neutrality Policy

The British government also considered changes to the Foreign Enlistment Act itself. The public had been outraged about the government's decision to

---

[25] Tom Bingham, 'The Alabama Claims Arbitration', *The International and Comparative Law Quarterly*, 54 (2005), 1–25; Adrian Cook, *The Alabama Claims: American Politics and Anglo-American Relations, 1865–1872* (Ithaca, NY, 1975).

[26] Annexed to Art. 6 of Treaty of Washington (Confidential), 8 May 1871, TNA, FO 881/7040.

[27] Stephen C. Neff, *Justice in Blue and Gray: A Legal History of the Civil War* (Cambridge, MA, 2010), 167–85.

detain the *Alexandra* in 1863, and sided with the Confederates. As a *Times* editorial of 27 April 1863 highlighted, the Confederates required ships but the British domestic legislation forbade their export, while the export of arms and ammunition, which the Unionists needed, was not restricted. The editors spoke 'of a practical inequality which the public will not be likely to overlook'.[28] Following Pollock's ruling on 23 June 1863, *The Times* triumph-antly wrote that 'we are so far from being surprised at the verdict that we are tempted at first to grudge the time expended by much eminent council on so simple a question'. In their opinion the Foreign Enlistment Act was phrased peculiarly regarding the meaning of 'equipping' as building.[29] Felix H. Hamel, a barrister and law clerk at the Board of Trade, argued similarly and warned that this law seriously harmed the British shipbuilding industry.[30] Some Liverpool shipbuilders, on the other hand, disagreed with this position and suggested to the Foreign Office a revision of the Foreign Enlistment Act so that the government could intervene more swiftly.[31]

In January 1867 the British government appointed the Neutrality Laws Commissioners to deal with the reform of the Foreign Enlistment Act, so that it could enforce neutrality more effectively within its jurisdiction while fulfilling 'international obligations'. The commissioners Sir Robert Joseph Phillimore, Travers Twiss, and William Vernon Harcourt, possessed exten-sive knowledge of international maritime law.[32] Phillimore and Twiss had both served as Advocate-General to the Admiralty and later as Queen's Advocate. Harcourt, the youngest of them, wrote legal commentaries for *The Times* during the American Civil War, in which he ardently supported strict British neutrality against the popular support for the Confederates.[33]

The commission sat from March 1867 to May 1868, and its report, pub-lished in 1868, contained several recommendations for the improvement of

---

[28] 'Editorial', *The Times*, 27 Apr. 1863.   [29] 'Editorial', *The Times*, 25 June 1863.

[30] Felix H. Hamel, *International Law in Connexion with Municipal Statuses Relating to the Commerce, Rights, and Liabilities of the Subjects of Neutral States Pending Foreign War Considered with Reference to the Trial of the Case of the 'Alexandra', Seized under the Provisions of the Foreign Enlistment Act* (London, 1863).

[31] North America. No. 13 (1863). Memorial from Certain Shipowners of Liverpool, Suggesting an Alteration in the Foreign Enlistment Act, 8 July 1863, 1863 (3200) LXXII.563.

[32] Stephen Lushington, Judge of the High Court of Admiralty, was also listed as commissioner but since he did not attend the meetings, he consequently did not sign the report in 1868. See Report of the Neutrality Laws Commissioners Together with an Appendix Containing Reports from Foreign States and Other Documents. 1867–68 (4027). Command Papers. Vol. XXXII.265.

[33] [W. Vernon Harcourt], *Letters by Historicus on Some Questions of International Law. Reprinted from the Times with Considerable Additions* (London, 1863); [W. Vernon Harcourt], *American Neutrality by Historicus. Reprinted from the London Times of December 22d, 1864* (New York, 1865).

the Foreign Enlistment Act. The foremost concern had been the 'equipping, fitting out, and arming' of vessels for foreign belligerent service and, thus, the commissioners suggested adding the clause 'dispatch, or cause to be dispatched, any ship with the intent or knowledge that the same shall or will be employed in the military or naval service of a foreign power'. Here the aim was to clarify the vague phrasing of the existing Foreign Enlistment Act, and thus avoid any future disputes as to the infringement of the act. Moreover, a new provision should be added which made it illegal to build a ship in Britain and then send it to a British dominion to 'fit out and arm' before employment in a foreign belligerent service. The next recommendation concerned the expansion of executive powers, so that the government could act more swiftly on suspicion rather than evidence. Here, the commissioners suggested granting the Secretary of State the 'power to issue a warrant' if there was 'reasonable and probable cause' that a ship had been so built or equipped. The warrant should also allow customs or port authorities to 'arrest and search . . . and to detain' ships. The Court of the Admiralty then had to decide upon the ship's condemnation or release. Most importantly, though, it was the owner of the ship who had to provide the evidence rather than the government. With these measures, the commissioners hoped to avoid cases such as the *Alexandra* in future, and to enable the government to apply the Foreign Enlistment Act more vigorously.[34]

The only commissioner who did not sign the report was Harcourt, who explained his dissenting opinion in a separate statement. He disagreed with his colleagues on the question of 'building' vessels. He feared that the proposed change in legislation would 'hamper, and probably ultimately destroy' British shipbuilding, one of the country's key industries. Even worse, foreign clients of British shipyards would choose to build their ships elsewhere, and thus give the yards of others the impetus to jump into the gap opened by British legislation. In many ways, Harcourt's concerns echoed Hamel's criticism of the Foreign Enlistment Act.[35]

---

[34] Report of the Neutrality Laws Commissioners Together with an Appendix Containing Reports from Foreign States and other Documents. 1867–68 (4027). Command Papers. Vol. XXXII.265, 1–7. For a detailed analysis on the report, see Memorandum by Lord Tenterden on the Analysis of the Report of the Neutrality Laws Commission (Confidential), 10 June 1868, TNA, FO 881/1629. See also John Macdonell, 'Recent Changes in the Rights and Duties of Belligerents and Neutrals According to International Law, Part 1', *Journal of Royal United Service Institution*, 42, 2 (1898), 801–3; Oppenheim, *International Law*, vol. 2, 375–7.

[35] Report of the Neutrality Laws Commissioners Together with an Appendix Containing Reports from Foreign States and other Documents. 1867–68 (4027). Command Papers. Vol. XXXII.265, 7–11.

However, Lord Tenterden from the Foreign Office, who had been present at the meetings of the commission and who later represented Britain at the Geneva Arbitration, disagreed with Harcourt. Tenterden argued that 'no legitimate and open transaction for the construction of ships of war for belligerent service can take place in England, nor is likely to be permitted on the continent'. He mentioned France, where police regulations rather than neutrality laws dealt with un-neutral behaviour. Tenterden therefore rejected Harcourt's fears of a disadvantage to the British ship-building industry. On the contrary, the commissioners had been careful to phrase the recommendations in such a way that the actual building of vessels was not prohibited. Rather, 'the fear of such a prosecution will, it may confidently be anticipated, prove a powerful deterrent' for the British shipbuilding industry. Holding the shipbuilders liable for their business transactions was a primary goal of the changes, and it 'would make most men think twice before they engage' in such business.[36]

The recommendations contained two tools which enabled the British government to intervene and detain suspected vessels much more easily than under the old provisions. The phrase, 'with intent or knowledge, or having reasonable cause to believe', allowed the government to act on suspicion alone, rather than requiring it to have evidence. The phrase, 'despatches, or causes or allows to be despatched, any ship with intent or knowledge', allowed the government to intervene at an early stage, when the ship was still in port, focusing on the supposed destination, rather than on the work of the ship itself. This was a fundamental change from the old rules.

Other recommendations declared it illegal to enlist persons in a foreign service, or to hire persons for businesses that directly supported war efforts. While the first clause referred to the mercenary business, which had ceased, the latter clause was added in response to cases reported from Ireland, of persons who were hired for the building of railway lines for the Union. As the railway lines were built for the transport of men and goods, the persons were accused of directly supporting the Union's war efforts. A final body of recommendations dealt with the prize law. They recommended that prizes were not be allowed to be brought into British ports and that no asylum be granted to belligerent ships. While most recommendations aimed at enforcing neutrality, the last few recommendations addressed belligerents and their duty to respect British neutrality. Finally, Tenterden hoped that the

---

[36] Memorandum by Lord Tenterden on the Analysis of the Report of the Neutrality Laws Commission (Confidential), 10 June 1868, TNA, FO 881/1629.

new legislation would 'eventually be adopted by other Powers, and so lead the way to a mutual understanding for the exclusion of vessels fitted out in violations of neutral rights'.[37]

The Foreign Enlistment Act of 1870

The report of the Neutrality Laws Commissioners did not immediately lead to the revision of the Foreign Enlistment Act. The actual revision of the act only happened shortly after the outbreak of the Franco-Prussian War on 19 July 1870. The British government hastily introduced a Foreign Enlistment Bill into parliament that had been based on the report. The Attorney-General, Sir Robert Collier, emphasized that the bill only considered neutrality from a domestic point of view and that the government wished to introduce a 'more stringent' law to prevent cases such as the *Alabama* and *Alexandra*. The British government went a step further than the report suggested on the point of executive powers. Not only the Secretary of State but also the 'local authorities' (meaning customs and port officials) should be given the power to detain ships on suspicion. In all, the bill enabled the government to enforce neutrality more strictly within its jurisdiction.[38]

The parliamentary debate about the Foreign Enlistment Bill addressed the question of neutrality broadly.[39] For some the bill exceeded the principles of international law regarding neutrality, while others thought that the bill should not only have dealt with the building and equipping of ships but also have included contraband goods. Similar discussions on neutrality took place in other European states, which had proclaimed neutrality during the Franco-Prussian War, but no other country went as far as Britain in its efforts to change its domestic laws to enforce neutrality more vigorously than before.[40]

The Foreign Enlistment Act, dated 9 August 1870, provided the domestic tool to enforce Britain's neutrality policy for decades to come. According to paragraph 8 of the Act, the following cases were liable to prosecution:

---

[37] Memorandum by Lord Tenterden on the Analysis of the Report of the Neutrality Laws Commission (Confidential), 10 June 1868, TNA, FO 881/1629.

[38] Hansard, 3rd series, HC Deb., 1 Aug. 1870, vol. 203, cc.1365–72.

[39] Foreign Enlistment. A Bill to Prevent the Enlisting or Engagement of Her Majesty's Subjects to Service in Foreign Service, and the Building, Fitting out, or Equipping, in Her Majesty's Dominions, Vessels for War-Like Purposes, without Her Majesty's License, 1870 (228), II.61.

[40] Arielli, Frei, and Van Hulle, 'Foreign Enlistment Act', 645. For a broad overview, see Abbenhuis, *Age of Neutrals*, 123–43.

(1) Builds or agrees to build, or causes to be built any ship with intent or knowledge, or having reasonable cause to believe that the same shall or will be employed in the military or naval service of any foreign state at war with any friendly state: or

(2) Issues or delivers any commission for any ship with intent or knowledge, or having reasonable cause to believe that the same shall or will be employed in the military or naval service of any foreign state at war with any friendly state: or

(3) Equips any ship with intent or knowledge, or having reasonable cause to believe that the same shall or will be employed in the military or naval service of any foreign state at war with any friendly state: or

(4) Despatches, or causes or allows to be despatched, any ship with intent or knowledge, or having reasonable cause to believe that the same shall or will be employed in the military or naval service of any foreign state at war with any friendly state.[41]

Paragraph 24 of the Act gave 'special powers' to port officials and customs officers, allowing them to detain ships deemed suspicious.[42]

Britain proclaimed neutrality in most international conflicts in the latter nineteenth and early twentieth centuries. The revised Foreign Enlistment Act of 1870 was first applied in the Franco-Prussian War of 1870–1. While the original proclamation was published in the *London Gazette* at the outbreak of war on 19 July 1870, the revised act was published on 9 August 1870, soon after the Foreign Enlistment Bill had passed through parliament.[43] In contrast to previous declarations, the 1870 proclamation addressed British citizens directly, acknowledging their rights but also urging them 'to maintain a strict and impartial neutrality'. Moreover, the Foreign Office published a letter addressed to the Lords Commissioners of the Admiralty and other government departments, in which it stated that Britain would 'observe the duties of neutrality'. Four points were listed: first, no warship of a belligerent was allowed in a British port. Second, if a warship of a belligerent

---

[41] Foreign Enlistment Act, 1870 (33 and 34 Vict., cap. 90), http://www.legislation.gov.uk/ukpga/1870/90/pdfs/ukpga_18700090_en.pdf (accessed 30 Oct. 2018).

[42] Foreign Enlistment Act, 1870 (33 and 34 Vict., cap. 90).

[43] 'A Proclamation of Neutrality by the Queen Victoria', *The London Gazette*, No. 23635, 19 July 1870, 3431–2; 'A Proclamation of Neutrality by the Queen Victoria', *The London Gazette*, No. 23642, 9 Aug. 1870, 3743–5. See also Memorandum by E. Hertslet as to the Time when British Proclamations of Neutrality were Issued in Cases of Wars between Foreign States (Confidential), 16 July 1870, TNA, FO 881/3362.

was in a British port at the time of the neutrality proclamation, the vessel was 'required to depart and to put to sea within twenty-four hours after her entrance into such port'. The only exception was in case of distress or need of repair. Third, warships in a British port would only be allowed to take in supplies for the crew, and coal would only be permitted once in a three-month time span. Fourth, belligerent ships were not allowed to bring prizes into British ports.[44] The instructions were intended as information not only for other government departments but also for the belligerents. With these public statements, the British government pursued a much clearer and more explicit neutrality policy than it had previously. Three principles guided the neutrality policy: first, a neutral was impartial towards the belligerent parties; second, belligerents had to respect a neutral; and third, a neutral was responsible for enforcing neutrality within its jurisdiction, and ensuring that its waters or territory were not used for belligerent purposes.[45] All three principles were addressed in the neutrality proclamation, defining the relationship between belligerents and neutral Britain.

In summary, the Foreign Enlistment Act of 1870 as well as the Treaty of Washington of 1871 were important pillars of Britain's neutrality policy and provided the legal framework for the British government domestic enforcement of neutrality. The wide-ranging powers the British government conferred on local authorities were remarkable. No other power at the time had so explicitly outlined the rights and duties of a neutral. The fact that the major sea power had committed itself to such a stringent neutrality policy gave force to the concept of neutrality domestically as well as internationally. Only time would show if and how the new legislation would work in practice.

---

[44] 'Copy of a Letter from Earl Granville (Foreign Office) to the Lords Commissioners of the Admiralty and other Government Departments, 19 July 1870', *The London Gazette*, No. 23635, 19 July 1870, 3432–3.
[45] Hall, *Rights and Duties*, 47.

3

The Law of Neutrality and State Practice

Britain's neutrality policy would be put to the test in many conflicts after 1870. Despite the new legal framework, belligerents often accused Britain of breaching neutrality, mostly because neutral individuals were alleged to have engaged in un-neutral behaviour. Not always, but often, the provisions of the Foreign Enlistment Act were concerned. This chapter examines the practice of Britain's neutrality policy and shows how the Foreign Office dealt with various cases. The cases illuminate not only the development of the legal framework as an effective machinery but also the challenges to its application. This chapter examines a range of disputes that arose between neutrals and belligerents: first, building, fitting out, selling, or dispatching vessels; second, coaling in neutral and international waters; third, the trade in contraband goods; and, fourth, the destruction of neutral ships. These cases show not only Britain's commitment to neutrality but also its strategic implications.

The Shipbuilding Industry and the Sale of Ships

The building, fitting out, arming or dispatching of ships became a primary concern for the British government. Since the revised Foreign Enlistment Act only came into power shortly after the outbreak of the Franco-Prussian War, the Foreign Office was careful to avoid drastic action. When British customs officials reported to the Foreign Office the imminent sale of steam-colliers to the French, they intervened too late. The British shipowner had sold the ships, and they were already on their way to Cherbourg. The Law Officers, Robert P. Collier and John D. Coleridge, as well as the Queen's Advocate General, Travers Twiss, were angry and demanded a full investigation by the Customs Solicitor and a prosecution if possible. For them, it

Great Britain, International Law, and the Evolution of Maritime Strategic Thought, 1856–1914. Gabriela A. Frei, Oxford University Press (2020). © Gabriela A. Frei.
DOI: 10.1093/oso/9780198859932.001.0001

was obvious that the sale and transfer of the ships had been hastily completed to avoid infringement of the Foreign Enlistment Act.[1]

Similar cases occurred on the eve of the Russo-Turkish War of 1877–8. British shipowners Messrs. Watson had a contract with the Turkish government to build the ironclad *Mendoukié*, which was ready for dispatch when Russia declared war on the Ottoman Empire on 24 April 1877. Since Britain had proclaimed neutrality on 30 April 1877, the customs officials warned the shipowner that the transfer of the ship to the Turkish government violated the Foreign Enlistment Act.[2] When Customs reported that the preparations for departure were continuing, the Law Officers decided to detain the ship. Since the shipowner had cooperated in the investigation so far, they suggested that 'the warrant should only be issued to the officer of the Customs to be used in case of need, and should not be actually executed till the necessity arises'.[3] Customs reported further that the ship had already changed owner prior to the declaration of war, and thus the ship belonged to the Turkish government. Yet, the Law Officers upheld their order to detain the ship, which was executed on 2 June 1877. The Turks protested and the Law Officers felt that only the Court of the Admiralty could make a final decision about the case.[4]

The two examples illustrate that shipowners and builders were well informed about the new legislation, which would explain why they hurriedly completed their business transactions in time of crisis or before the outbreak of war. The British government, on the other hand, could only formally implement the Foreign Enlistment Act after the belligerent parties had declared war and Britain had declared neutrality in the conflict. However, shipowners and builders used the opportunity during crises to complete business transactions in order to avoid infringements of the Foreign Enlistment Act. The cases also demonstrate that the enforcement of

---

[1] The Law Officers of the Crown (R. P. Collier, J. D. Coleridge, Travers Twiss) to Earl Granville, 5 Aug. 1870 (No. 98), TNA, FO 834/9; The Law Officers of the Crown (R. P. Collier, J. D. Coleridge, Travers Twiss) to Earl Granville, 10 Aug. 1870 (No. 101), TNA, FO 834/9.

[2] Law Officers of the Crown (John Holker, Hardinge S. Giffard) and Dr Deane to Earl Derby, 2 May 1888 (No. 69), TNA, FO 834/12; Law Officers of the Crown (John Holker, Hardinge S. Giffard) and Dr Deane to Earl Derby, 3 May 1877 (No. 71), TNA, FO 834/12; Law Officers of the Crown (John Holker, Hardinge S. Giffard) and Dr Deane to Earl Derby, 17 May 1877 (No. 83), TNA, FO 834/12.

[3] Law Officers of the Crown (John Holker, Hardinge S. Giffard) and Dr Deane to Earl Derby, 25 May 1877 (No. 87), TNA, FO 834/12.

[4] Law Officers of the Crown (John Holker, Hardinge S. Giffard) and Dr Deane to Earl Derby, 1 June 1877 (No. 88), TNA, FO 834/12; Law Officers of the Crown (John Holker, Hardinge S. Giffard) and Dr Deane to Earl Derby, 3 Nov. 1877 (No. 101), TNA, FO 834/12.

the Foreign Enlistment Act required swift reporting and decision-making from different sections within government. Customs and port officials, who were given special powers under the domestic legislation, had to report suspicious behaviour to the Foreign Office. In fact, the Permanent Under-Secretary to the Foreign Office, Lord Tenterden, highlighted in a letter to the Admiralty that it was 'the duty of all officers in public service to give the earliest information of any intended or actual infraction of neutrality which may come to their knowledge, and to lend assistance in the prevention of any such intended infraction'. The Admiralty had been wondering how it was involved in the enforcement of the Foreign Enlistment Act, and it became clear that the Foreign Office was primarily responsible but that the Admiralty and other departments were crucial in providing information and assisting in the execution.[5] The decision as to whether a case was further investigated remained with the Foreign Office, which could then forward the matter to the Law Officers of the Crown for consultation. Only if the Foreign Office received a legal opinion from the Law Officers would customs and port officials be informed about the further procedures of the case. Since acting on suspicion was a delicate matter, investigations were treated as highly confidential. Shipowners and builders were only asked at a later stage to give more detailed information about the business transaction, and so received a warning from the Foreign Office. Only in the event of an actual breach of domestic law did the Law Officers intervene by ordering the detention of a ship.[6] As the two cases illustrate, the Law Officers had either reacted too late or too hastily. Timing was essential, and the Foreign Office still needed to find a practical solution as to when and how the Foreign Enlistment Act was applied.

Its implementation proved to be a balancing act for the government, especially with regard to the building of ships. It was not in Britain's interest to hurt one of its key industries, and so it negotiated the terms and conditions under which shipowners and builders could fulfil their contracts without compromising neutrality. One of these cases occurred during the Sino-French War of 1884–5 when Messrs. White had a contract with the French government to build steam-cutters. Since these ships were able to carry

---

[5] Lord Tenterden to the Secretary of the Admiralty, 8 June 1877 (Annex to No. 91), TNA, FO 834/12; The Law Officers of the Crown and Dr Deane to the Earl of Derby, 6 June 1877 (No. 91), TNA, FO 834/12.

[6] Memorandum by T. G. Staveley on the Course to be Pursued by Foreign Office in Communicating Direct with Customs in Urgent Cases Involving Detention or Seizure of Vessels under Foreign Enlistment Act, 1872, TNA, FO 881/2125.

weapons, the Foreign Office requested a reassurance from the buyer, in this case the French government, confirming that the ships were not to be used for any military operations. After a satisfactory assurance had been presented to the Foreign Office, the ships could be transferred to France.[7] Similar sales were approved throughout the conflict.[8]

With the government's approval of sales, it became directly involved in private business affairs. This proved a challenging task for the Foreign Office, which had to approve the contracts. First, the Foreign Office had to investigate the situation thoroughly before taking a decision. Many cases were dubious, and it was difficult for the Foreign Office to judge the real intentions of the seller and buyer, particularly with regard to the true destination and usage of the vessel. Thus, Foreign Office involvement in approving those contracts had to negotiate between the private business interests of the British shipbuilding industry and the state's neutrality policy.

A case which was debated during the Sino-French War of 1884–5 serves as a good example. On 24 December 1884, Customs informed the Treasury that Sir Donald Currie, a British shipowner, wanted to sell seven ships to a French agent, whom Customs believed was acting on behalf of the French government. Initially, the Secretary of Lloyd's, an insurer and reinsurer, had informed Customs of the case in a confidential letter. The customs officials suspected that Currie wanted to proceed quickly with the sale to evade the restrictions of the Foreign Enlistment Act given the ongoing crisis between the French and the Chinese in the region of the South China Sea. Therefore, they brought the case to the attention of the Foreign Office.[9] After an initial evaluation of the situation, the Law Officers advised the Foreign Office to warn the shipowner 'that any such sale would be contrary to the provisions of the Foreign Enlistment Act, and would subject the vendors and persons concerned to heavy penalties'.[10] For the Law Officers, Henry James and Farrer Herschell, the evidence was not strong enough to detain the ships. Yet, the Admiralty Advocate, and legal adviser to the Foreign Office, James

---

[7] Law Officers of the Crown (Henry James and Farrer Herschell) and Dr Deane to Earl Granville, 3 Jan. 1885 (No. 55), TNA, FO 834/15; Law Officers of the Crown (Henry James and Farrer Herschell) and Dr Deane to Earl Granville, 15 Jan. 1885 (No. 57), TNA, FO 834/15.

[8] Law Officers of the Crown (Henry James and Farrer Herschell) and Dr Deane to Earl Granville, 16 Apr. 1885 (No. 90), TNA, FO 834/15.

[9] Customs to Treasury, 24 Dec. 1884, TNA, FO 27/2780; Mr H. Murray (Customs) to Sir R. Lingen (Treasury), 2 Jan. 1885 (No. 1, Inclosure), TNA, FO 881/5163; Sir R. Lingen (Treasury) to Sir J. Pauncefote (Foreign Office), 3 Jan. 1885 (No. 1), TNA, FO 881/5163; Sir R. Lingen (Treasury) to Sir J. Pauncefote (Foreign Office), 5 Jan. 1885 (No. 2), TNA, FO 881/5163.

[10] Law Officers of the Crown (Henry James and Farrer Herschell) to Earl Granville, 9 Jan. 1885 (No. 56), TNA, FO 834/15.

Parker Deane, argued that it was obvious that the French needed ships for troop transports, and he therefore urged the ships to be detained as 'the selling owners may so easily ignore the intended real destination and use of the ships'.[11] Subsequently, Customs warned Currie that any sale would infringe the Foreign Enlistment Act. Currie instantly protested against the Customs' decision. He could not see any wrongdoing as neither France nor China had issued a declaration of war and, thus, the British government could not enforce the provisions of the Foreign Enlistment Act.[12] However, the Foreign Office defended its position and argued that the Foreign Enlistment Act applied in this case as 'a state of war' existed between France and China.[13] In a letter dated 16 January 1885, the Board of the Company stated that it 'promised' not to violate the Foreign Enlistment Act.[14] It is not known, though, what happened after, or whether the sale was completed or not.

The government's frustration in this case illustrates the difficulty of enforcing the Foreign Enlistment Act. Britain depended on the belligerent parties to issue formal declarations of war but China was not a fully recognized member of the family of nations and so France never issued one. As a direct consequence of the Currie case, and to avoid any unlawful behaviour from British citizens in the conflict, Britain unilaterally decided to implement the Foreign Enlistment Act in its Eastern Colonies on 27 January 1885 without a formal proclamation of neutrality. The government justified its decision by referring to the fact that the French had installed a blockade and exercised the right of search and capture, which equalled a *quasi*-declaration of war in international law. The implementation of the Foreign Enlistment Act was the result of prolonged diplomatic correspondence between Britain and France as to whether a state of war existed or not. For a long time, the French denied there was, but the British felt the need to act in order to protect its citizens.[15] The case shows that the implementation of the act was not

---

[11] Dr Deane to Sir J. Pauncefote, 9 Jan. 1885 (No. 56 Annex), TNA, FO 834/15.

[12] T. V. Lister (Foreign Office) to Sir R. Lingen (Treasury), 9 Jan. 1885 (No. 5), TNA, FO 881/5163; Donald Currie to H. Murray (Customs), 12 Jan. 1885 (No. 8), TNA, FO 881/5163.

[13] Sir J. Pauncefote (Foreign Office) to Sir R. Lingen (Treasury), 15 Jan. 1885 (No. 10), TNA, FO 881/5163.

[14] R. Smith to H. Murray (Customs), 16 Jan. 1885 (No. 12, Inclosure 2), TNA, FO 881/5163.

[15] Law Officers of the Crown (Henry James, Farrer Herschell) and Dr Deane, 27 Sept. 1884 (No. 31), TNA, FO 834/14; Law Officers of the Crown (Henry James, Farrer Herschell) and Dr Deane, 25 Oct. 1884 (No. 32), TNA, FO 834/14; Law Officers of the Crown (Henry James, Farrer Herschell) and Dr Deane, 22 Dec. 1884 (No. 36), TNA, FO 834/14; Mr Wingfield (Colonial Office) to Sir J. Pauncefote (incl. draft telegram), 20 Jan. 1885 (No. 13, and Inclosure to No. 13), TNA, FO 881/5163; Sir J. Pauncefote to the Law Officers of the Crown and Dr Deane, 23 Jan. 1885 (No. 18), TNA, FO 881/5163; Colonial Office (John Bramston) to Foreign Office

always beyond doubt, particularly in those conflict situations which lacked recognition from the international community in the form of a declaration of war. In fact, a declaration of war was not necessary, and yet as the international lawyer, William E. Hall, pointed out, a declaration of war warned an enemy and was also 'a matter of duty towards neutrals'.[16]

On 7 August 1894, a few days after the First Sino-Japanese War broke out on 25 July 1894, the British government implemented the Foreign Enlistment Act.[17] By then, the Law Officers, John Rigby and Robert T. Reid, had already received information from the customs officials of the sale of a torpedo-catcher, a gunboat used for destroying torpedo boats, to the Japanese government. As the British shipbuilder did not want to reveal the ship's destination, the Law Officers immediately ordered the detention of the ship because the work was being 'pressed on rapidly day and night at the present' even though the government had not yet issued a neutrality proclamation.[18] The same day, Francis Bertie from the Foreign Office informed the Treasury of the government's intention to detain the ship, because 'there would be a certain risk of the Treasury being made liable to costs in case of a mistake being made as regards the issue of a warrant for detaining this vessel', so it would be up to the Treasury to decide whether or not to proceed with the warrant.[19] As soon as the Foreign Enlistment Act was in force, arrest warrants were issued.[20] The shipbuilder informed the Foreign Secretary, the Earl of Kimberley, that the torpedo-catcher had been sold to a British

---

(Sir J. Pauncefote), 27 Jan. 1885 (No. 24), TNA, FO 881/5163; Sir J. Pauncefote to the Law Officers of the Crown (Henry James, Farrer Herschell) and Dr Deane, 27 Jan. 1885 (No. 25), TNA, FO 881/5163; Earl Granville to Viscount Lyons, 28 Jan. 1885 (No. 26), TNA, FO 881/5163; The Law Officers of the Crown (Henry James, Farrer Herschell) and Dr Deane to Earl Granville, 28 Jan. 1885 (No. 60), TNA, FO 834/15; The Law Officers of the Crown (Henry James, Farrer Herschell) and Dr Deane to Earl Granville, 28 Jan. 1885 (No. 61), TNA, FO 834/15.

[16]   William E. Hall, *A Treatise on International Law*, 5th edn (ed. J. B. Atlay) (Oxford, 1904), 377–95, 574–5, here: 384. See also Memorandum by E. Hertslet as to the Time When British Proclamations of Neutrality Were Issued in Cases of Wars between Foreign States (Confidential), 16 July 1870, TNA, FO 881/3362; John F. Maurice, *Hostilities without Declaration of War. An Historical Abstract of the Cases in which Hostilities Have Occurred between Civilized Powers Prior to Declaration or Warning. From 1700 to 1870* (London, 1883).

[17]   'A Proclamation of Neutrality by the Queen Victoria', *The London Gazette*, No. 26540, 7 Aug. 1894, 4599–602.

[18]   The Law Officers of the Crown (John Rigby, R. T. Reid) to the Earl of Kimberley, 3 Aug. 1894 (No. 19), TNA, FO 881/6692; Foreign Office (Francis Bertie) to Customs, 4 Aug. 1894 (No. 23), TNA, FO 881/6692.

[19]   Foreign Office (Francis Bertie) to Treasury, 4 Aug. 1894 (No. 24), TNA, FO 881/6692.

[20]   Foreign Office to Law Officers, 8 Aug. 1894 (No. 45), TNA, FO 881/6692; Customs to Foreign Office, 9 Aug. 1894 (No. 48), TNA, FO 881/6692; Foreign Office to Customs, 9 Aug. 1894 (No. 52), TNA, FO 881/6692; Foreign Office to Customs, 9 Aug. 1894 (No. 55), TNA, FO 881/6692.

subject, and he hoped for its release.[21] When the Law Officers looked at the case, they were suspicious as 'no private person would be likely to purchase such a vessel except for re-sale to a foreign Government, and if he is acting for a neutral Government, he can have no difficulty in proving the fact'.[22] When news reached the Foreign Office that the ship was almost ready to sail, the Law Officers ordered that every measure should be taken to prevent it leaving port, and consequently Customs removed parts from the machinery. The shipowner was furious and demanded compensation from the government. Yet, the Law Officers were only willing to release the ship on condition that the new owner provided evidence as to its destination. Only on 17 April 1895 when the war between China and Japan ended, did the Foreign Office release the torpedo-catcher. Compensation claims were denied since the vessel had been lawfully detained under the Foreign Enlistment Act.[23]

This case showed that the British government was able to intervene swiftly and effectively. Customs, the Foreign Office, and the Law Officers worked hand in hand to enforce the provisions of the act. Interestingly, port officials had been monitoring the activities in the shipyard even before the outbreak of war, so allowing Customs to react quickly when the conflict escalated. This smooth administrative machinery also proved effective in the Russo-Japanese War of 1904–5. To leave no doubt about the provisions of the Foreign Enlistment Act, the Home Office suggested to the Foreign Office that leaflets be distributed to British shipowners and builders, informing them of the restrictions. It is not clear whether this measure had any positive effect on the number of cases reported during the conflict. Yet, shipowners and builders contacted the Foreign Office much more frequently to enquire about the political situation in different parts of the

---

[21] Messrs. Sir W. Armstrong, Mitchell and Co. to Mr Macklin (Confidential and Private), 13 Aug. 1894 (Inclosure of No. 75), TNA, FO 881/6692; Messrs. Sir W. Armstrong, Mitchell and Co. to the Earl of Kimberley, 13 Aug. 1894 (No. 82), TNA, FO 881/6692; Mr Rennison to the Earl of Kimberley (Telegraphic), 15 Aug. 1894 (No. 88), TNA, FO 881/6692.

[22] Law Officers Report (John Rigby, R. T. Reid), 16 Aug. 1894 (No. 92), TNA, FO 881/6692.

[23] Foreign Office (Francis Bertie) to Admiralty, 16 Aug. 1894 (No. 95), TNA, FO 881/6692; Foreign Office to Customs, 16 Aug. 1894 (No. 98), TNA, FO 881/6692; Customs to Foreign Office, 17 Aug. 1894 (No. 100), TNA, FO 881/6692; Admiralty to Foreign Office, 22 Aug. 1894 (No. 109), TNA, FO 881/6692; Customs to Foreign Office, 24 Aug. 1894 (No. 129), TNA, FO 881/6692; Foreign Office to Customs, 25 Aug. 1894 (No. 143), TNA, FO 881/6692; Mr Palmer to Mr Head, 31 Aug. 1894 (No. 178), TNA, FO 881/6692; Customs to Foreign Office, 3 Sept. 1894 (No. 178), TNA, FO 881/6692; Customs to Foreign Office, 28 Sept. 1894 (197), TNA, FO 881/6692; Customs to Foreign Office, 18 Apr. 1895 (No. 265), TNA, FO 881/6692; Foreign Office to Customs, 29 Apr. 1895 (No. 267), TNA, FO 881/6692; Customs to Foreign Office, 10 May 1895 (No. 271), TNA, FO 881/6692.

world and whether it affected their businesses and contracts, so seeking the approval of their businesses from the government department.[24]

Coaling in Neutral Ports and International Waters

In the age of steam, coaling was of strategic importance, and thus a frequent source of conflict between neutrals and belligerents in time of war. Steamships required regular re-coaling in order to continue their voyages, and so coaling stations around the world became strategically important to belligerents' vessels. Britain possessed more coaling stations than any other power in the world, and thus controlling access became a central task. The Foreign Enlistment Act explicitly prohibited coaling as part of 'fitting out a ship'. However, it was customary law that neutrals allowed belligerent ships into their ports in case of distress, for essential repair, or for other emergencies, as humanitarian acts. In the age of steam, this custom was expanded and also included the re-coaling of a ship. Since this opened up the possibility for misuse during the American Civil War, Britain defined more precisely those cases in which ships could enter a neutral port for re-coaling. The rule said that a belligerent ship was only granted as much coal as it required to reach 'the nearest port of her own country' and no further coaling was allowed in another British neutral port within a three-month period.[25] Since those rules concerned belligerents in particular, the Foreign Office attached a letter to the Crown's proclamation of neutrality with an additional public announcement of the rules applicable during the conflict.[26] The Foreign Office's proactive approach showed that the issue was an integral part of Britain's neutrality policy. Despite Britain's strict adherence to its practice throughout the latter half of the nineteenth and the beginning of the twentieth centuries, it could not avoid criticism from belligerents, as the following cases illustrate.

[24] Foreign Office to Home Office, 21 Mar. 1904 (No. 476), TNA, FO 881/8404; Home Office to Foreign Office, 28 Mar. 1904 (No. 509), TNA, FO 881/8404; Notice to Shipbuilders and Others, 15 Mar. 1904 (No. 434), TNA, FO 881/8404.

[25] Memorandum by E. Hertslet on Coaling of French and Chinese Vessels of War at British Colonial Ports during the Present Hostilities, Foreign Office, 27 Nov. 1884, TNA, FO 27/2780; Law Officers of the Crown (Henry James, Farrer Herschell) and Dr Deane to Earl Granville, 28 Jan. 1885 (No. 60), TNA, FO 834/15.

[26] For example: 'Earl Granville to the Lords Commissioners of the Admiralty', *The London Gazette*, No. 23635, 19 July 1870, 3432–3.

During the Franco-Prussian War of 1870–1, the belligerent parties accused Britain of un-neutral behaviour because it granted coal to both parties. However, Britain defended its position and stressed that it only granted the re-coaling of belligerent ships which were in distress. The action was declared an act of humanity and, therefore, did not violate domestic or international law. Both sides, the French and the Prussians, relied on British coal, which was the actual reason for their protests. The Foreign Office defended Britain's neutral position, and the Law Officers ruled that 'if colliers are chartered for the purpose of attending the French fleet and supplying them with coal to enable them to pursue their hostile operations, such colliers become "store-ships" employed in their service, and (if this fact be established) that they should be detained under the provisions of the Foreign Enlistment Act'.[27] With this decision, the Law Officers had created a precedent, and it would be referred to in later conflicts.[28]

The Sino-French War of 1884–5 constituted a special case, particularly with respect to the question of re-coaling, due to the large geographical distance between the belligerent parties. When Britain unilaterally applied the Foreign Enlistment Act in the colonies of Hong Kong, Ceylon, and the Straits Settlements at the end of January 1885, the Law Officers modified the wording of the act in terms of the supply of coal. The modified act allowed belligerent ships as much coal as necessary to reach 'the nearest national port, or nearer destination'. With these changes, the Law Officers tried to find a practicable solution to allow French warships to re-coal in Chinese ports where no hostilities were taking place. The relaxed restrictions on coaling meant that port authorities in British colonies, such as Hong Kong, needed to be extra vigilant and report any misuse of the provisions in place.[29] Yet, the situation became tense when the French government announced that it would exercise 'strict belligerent rights' also on the high seas, which meant it would seize neutral vessels carrying contraband goods. Enquiries reached the Foreign Office with regard to Australian coal on

---

[27] The Law Officers of the Crown (R. P. Collier, J. D. Colderidge and Travers Twiss) to Earl Granville, 25 July 1870 (No. 1), TNA, FO 881/8508.

[28] The Law Officers of the Crown (R. P. Collier, J. D. Colderidge and Travers Twiss) to Earl Granville, 29 July 1870 (No. 94), TNA, FO 834/9; The Law Officers of the Crown (R. P. Collier, J. D. Colderidge and Travers Twiss) to Earl Granville, 10 Aug. 1870 (No. 200), TNA, FO 834/9; The Queen's Advocate (Travers Twiss) to Earl Granville, 19 Nov. 1870 (No. 152), TNA, FO 834/9; The Queen's Advocate (Travers Twiss) to Earl Granville, 11 Jan. 1871 (No. 83), TNA, FO 834/9.

[29] Law Officers of the Crown (Henry James, Farrer Herschell) and Dr Deane to Earl Granville, 28 Jan. 1885 (No. 60), TNA, FO 834/15; Law Officers of the Crown (Henry James, Farrer Herschell) and Dr Deane to Earl Granville, 28 Jan. 1885 (No. 61), TNA, FO 834/15.

British ships on their way to Chinese ports, and the Law Officers warned that, although France did not treat coal as absolute contraband, ships could always be stopped on the grounds that coal could be used for military purposes.[30]

When hostilities ceased between France and China in late April 1885, the Foreign Office wanted to lift the restrictions of the Foreign Enlistment Act with regard to re-coaling following a letter received from Lloyd's. One of the Law Officers, Farrer Herschell, pointed out that the act should only be lifted if the French no longer exercised belligerent rights, and suggested discussing this matter with the French Ambassador.[31] However, before the French officially replied, the Foreign Office informed the belligerent parties on 8 May 1885 that British ports would again be open and free for coaling.[32] When the French Ambassador to Britain, William Waddington, finally informed the Foreign Office on 15 May 1885 that the French government had not 'renounced these belligerent rights', the Law Officers were under pressure since they had approved lifting the Foreign Enlistment Act. The Law Officers suggested protesting against the position of the French, arguing that a 'de facto state of war now no longer exists, and there never having been any declaration of war, the two Powers cannot, in the view of Her Majesty's Government, be any longer regarded as at war'. More strongly, they argued that the French government had no right to continue exercising belligerent rights. Currie and Bergne from the Foreign Office thought that the Law Officers had reacted too strongly, and in an attempt to avoid diplomatic frictions, they suggested using a less strongly worded reply to the French government.[33] Before the Foreign Office could finalize its position towards the French statement, it received news of the seizure by the French of the British steamer *Kowshing*, which was suspected of carrying contraband goods to

[30] Law Officers of the Crown (Henry James, Farrer Herschell) and Dr Deane to Earl Granville, 6 Feb. 1885 (No. 63), TNA, FO 834/15; Law Officers of the Crown (Henry James, Farrer Herschell) and Dr Deane to Earl Granville, 7 Feb. 1885 (No. 64), TNA, FO 834/15; Law Officers of the Crown (Henry James, Farrer Herschell) and Dr Deane to Earl Granville, 10 Feb. 1885 (No. 65), TNA, FO 834/15.

[31] Sir F. Herschell to Mr Currie, 6 May 1885 (No. 94), TNA, FO 834/15.

[32] Law Officers of the Crown (Henry James, Farrer Herschell) and Dr Deane to Earl Granville, 2 May 1885 (No. 346), TNA, FO 881/5163; Earl Granville to M. Waddington, 8 May 1885 (No. 356), TNA, FO 881/5163; Foreign Office to Colonial Office, 8 May 1885 (No. 354), TNA, FO 881/5163; M. Waddington to Earl Granvillle, 15 May 1885 (No. 363), TNA, FO 881/5163; Mr P. Currie to the Law Officers of the Crown (Henry James, Farrer Herschell) and Dr Deane, 18 May 1885 (No. 365), TNA, FO 881/5163.

[33] Law Officers of the Crown (Henry James, Farrer Herschell) and Dr Deane to Earl Granville, 22 May 1885 (No. 95), TNA, FO 834/15.

Hong Kong, on 20 May 1885.[34] Shortly after, another incident was reported with the detention of the British steamer *Waverley*. The incidents raised doubts as to whether hostilities had really been terminated, and called the decision of the Foreign Office and the Law Officers to lift the Foreign Enlistment Act into question.[35] Yet, the Law Officers adhered to their opinion and insisted, threatening the French with the reimposition of 'the restrictions existing under the powers of the Foreign Enlistment Act'.[36] Pressure grew on the Law Officers after the Lord Chancellor, Lord Selborne, criticised their decision to lift the Foreign Enlistment Act as premature. Since the British government had de facto recognized the state of war between China and France, it had to wait until the belligerent parties announced the end of the war. It was not enough that hostilities had ceased or that the parties had agreed on a preliminary peace.[37] The Law Officers defended their position, saying that their opinion 'was not so much founded upon general principles as upon the circumstances of this particular case, which are very peculiar'.[38] Despite the disagreement between the Law Officers and the Lord Chancellor, the Foreign Secretary, the Earl of Granville, demanded from Waddington, the French Ambassador to London, that France immediately discontinue its exercise of belligerent rights, warning that the British government would otherwise be forced to reinstate the Foreign Enlistment Act as a measure to protect neutral ships from capture by French warships. In reality, though, the measure was intended to deny French warships re-coaling in British ports, and thus deprive them of their operational basis for the exercise of belligerent rights.[39] Only a day later, on 9 June 1885, the French signed a peace treaty with the Chinese, marking the end of the conflict.[40]

Britain's pushiness illustrates how, as a neutral power, it used the Foreign Enlistment Act to put pressure on belligerents. Unsurprisingly, Britain's

[34] Foreign Office (P. Currie) to Law Officers of the Crown, 20 May 1885 (No. 366), TNA, FO 881/5163. The Law Officers had later confirmed that the seizure was legitimate, as the vessel carried contraband of war on board: see Law Officers of the Crown (Henry James, Farrer Herschell) and Dr Deane to Earl Granville, 13 June 1885 (No. 400), TNA, FO 881/5163.

[35] Law Officers of the Crown (Henry James, Farrer Herschell) to Earl Granville, 27 May 1885 (No. 98), TNA, FO 834/15.

[36] Law Officers of the Crown (Henry James, Farrer Herschell) to Earl Granville, 27 May 1885 (No. 98), TNA, FO 834/15.

[37] Memorandum by the Lord Chancellor (Lord Selborne), 1 June 1885 (No. 99), TNA, FO 834/15.

[38] Law Officers of the Crown (Henry James, Farrer Herschell) and Dr Deane to Earl Granville, 8 June 1885 (No. 101), TNA, FO 834/15.

[39] Earl Granville to M. Waddington, 8 June 1885 (No. 101, Annex 1), TNA, FO 834/15.

[40] Sir Nicholas R. O'Conor (Secretary of Legation in Peking) to Earl Granville (Telegraphic), 9 June 1885 (No. 395), TNA, FO 881/5163.

interference in the conflict was not well received in France and Waddington criticized Britain's course of action, pointing out to Granville that the Foreign Enlistment Act was a domestic matter rather than a foreign issue.[41] Waddington was entirely correct in his criticism, and yet the case is a good illustration of the reverse point, that neutrality was not only a domestic but also a foreign policy matter. In that sense using the Foreign Enlistment Act to threaten a belligerent party showed how influential domestic law could be in diplomatic encounters. Britain, as a neutral power, was a serious player on the world stage, even if it was not directly involved in a conflict, and so belligerent parties were watchful.

The question of re-coaling in neutral ports reached a new peak at the turn of the century. When the Spanish-American War broke out on 21 April 1898, Spanish warships left their home waters for the Philippine Islands, sailing through the Suez Canal. The long voyage was not possible without re-coaling, and Port Saïd and Suez were the two obvious coaling stations along the way. As both coaling stations were in the British-French influence zone, Lord Cromer, the British Consul-General in Egypt, urgently contacted the Foreign Secretary, the Marquess of Salisbury, after the Consul-General of the United States urged the Egyptian government to refuse re-coaling for Spanish warships. After some internal discussions, the Foreign Office suggested applying the Foreign Enlistment Act to both Port Saïd and Suez despite the fact that Egypt had not issued a formal proclamation of neutrality.[42] Since it was obvious that the Spanish warships were on their way to the theatre of war in the Philippines, the provisions of the act were interpreted strictly. In fact, on 28 April 1898, Salisbury himself had already ordered that 'no coal should be supplied to any belligerent vessels except for the specific purpose of enabling them to proceed direct [sic] to the port of their own country or other nearer neutral destination with reference to which the supply of coal is given'. Furthermore, Salisbury instructed that '[c]oal should not be supplied at all if there is reasonable ground for supposing that the coal is in fact to be used for another purpose'.[43] Such a strict interpretation of the Foreign

[41]   M. Waddington to Earl Granville, 20 June 1885 (No. 409), TNA, FO 881/5163.

[42]   The Earl of Cromer to the Marquess of Salisbury, 23 June 1898 (No. 667), TNA, FO 881/7267.

[43]   The Marquess of Salisbury to Sir A. Hardinge (Telegraphic) (also to Captain Gallwey), 28 Apr. 1898 (No. 264), TNA, FO 881/7267.

Enlistment Act surprised Cromer, who wanted reassurance from the Foreign Office about the desired action to take.[44]

When the Spanish fleet neared Port Saïd, the situation was more complicated than expected. The French, who also had a stake in the Suez Canal, were the coal contractors at Port Saïd, and thus Cromer had to inform them about the British position on re-coaling. The French only reluctantly agreed to the rules of the Foreign Enlistment Act as their opinion differed from the British on this point.[45] When re-coaling was denied to the Spanish fleet in Port Saïd, a solution was quickly found. At night, the Spanish fleet sailed beyond the three-mile-limit and coaled in international waters and returned to port at dawn. Cromer was angry but he could not do anything other than demand that the Spanish fleet leave the port within twenty-four hours.[46] While the American government was pleased with the British government's strict implementation of the neutrality proclamation, the case also illustrated the difficulty of implementing the Foreign Enlistment Act in legally complex situations such as the Suez Canal. The British and French had no agreement on how to proceed in such a situation. State practice had to be created as new situations presented themselves to the British government.

The advance of the Spanish fleet from their home waters to the Philippines also alerted the Straits Settlements, such as Singapore, Labuan, Sarawak, and other territories known as British North Borneo. In anticipation of the Spanish fleet's voyage through the Strait of Malacca, the Colonial Office asked the Foreign Office for guidance on the application of the neutrality proclamation for these regions. While the Foreign Office replied affirmatively, the territories of British North Borneo were legally speaking protectorates and thus enjoyed some legal independence. When the Acting Consul-General, Sir J. Alexander Swettenham, wrote to the Foreign Office that Rajah Brooke of Sarawak had issued his own neutrality declaration, the Foreign Office was not pleased: 'I think that we have all along treated British Protectorates as if they were British Colonies, so far as the Proclamation of Neutrality and

---

[44] The Earl of Cromer to the Marquess of Salisbury, 24 June 1898 (No. 671), TNA, FO 881/7267.
[45] The Earl of Cromer to the Marquess of Salisbury, 26 June 1898 (No. 678), TNA, FO 881/7267; The Earl of Cromer to the Marquess of Salisbury, 26 June 1898 (No. 679), TNA, FO 881/7267.
[46] The Earl of Cromer to the Marquess of Salisbury, 2 July 1898 (No. 702), TNA, FO 881/7267; The Earl of Cromer to the Marquess of Salisbury, 2 July 1898 (No. 711), TNA, FO 881/7267; The Earl of Cromer to the Marquess of Salisbury, 4 July 1898 (No. 717), TNA, FO 881/7267; The Earl of Cromer to the Marquess of Salisbury, 5 July 1898 (No. 722), TNA, FO 881/7267; Consul Donald A. Cameron to the Marquess of Salisbury, 5 July 1898 (No. 779), TNA, FO 881/7267.

Rules are concerned....I should doubt, moreover, whether as a matter of policy it is desirable that Rajah Brooke should magnify his sovereignty by issuing Proclamations of his own motion.'[47] The Foreign Office demonstrated that it wanted to be in full control, and would not accept independent neutrality proclamations issued within the British Empire.

Re-coaling again became an issue in late 1903 when tensions grew between Russia and Japan. Lord Cromer had anxiously turned to the Foreign Secretary, the Marquess of Lansdowne, to ask for advice on how to handle the situation with regard to re-coaling in Egyptian ports, such as Suez and Port Saïd. After consultation with the Attorney-General, the Foreign Office took the same position as it had during the Spanish-American War, which meant that the Russian Baltic Fleet would only be allowed to re-coal once at a British port and then not again for another three months, as laid out in the neutrality proclamation.[48]

At the same time, the Foreign Office discussed with the Admiralty whether the wording 'to some nearer destination' should be further specified as 'on the way to the nearest national port'. The Admiralty was against such a wording. The Assistant Secretary of the Admiralty, C. Inigo Thomas, replied that 'such limitation would invest the neutral with power to dictate to the belligerent the direction in which he should go, which, in itself, might constitute a breach of neutrality in unduly favouring the other belligerent'.[49] Not everyone in the Admiralty shared this view. The First Lord of the Admiralty, Lord Selborne,[50] feared that, if Britain did not prescribe a destination after re-coaling, Russian warships would take advantage of neutral British ports and take enough coal on board to proceed eastwards to the Sea of Japan, which could be interpreted as assisting a belligerent.[51] Selborne's fears were justified, and yet the Foreign Secretary could not so easily overturn the established practice of granting coal to belligerents. With the backing of the Attorney-General, R. B. Finlay, Lansdowne instructed Cromer that 'no coal should be supplied at all except on the undertaking of the

---

[47] Acting Consul-General Sir J. Swettenham to the Marquess of Salisbury, 16 May 1898 (No. 629), TNA, FO 881/7267; C. B. R., Minutes, Foreign Office, 15 June 1898 (No. 629), TNA, FO 881/7267.

[48] The Earl of Cromer to the Marquess of Lansdowne (Telegraphic), 21 Dec. 1903 (No. 1), TNA, FO 881/8404; The Earl of Cromer to the Marquess of Lansdowne, 26 Dec. 1903 (No. 5), TNA, FO 881/8404.

[49] Admiralty to Foreign Office (Confidential), 30 Dec. 1903 (No. 7), TNA, FO 881/8404.

[50] Not to be confused with his father Lord Selborne (1812–1895), who served as Lord Chancellor 1872–4 and again 1880–5.

[51] Lord Selborne to Marquess of Lansdowne, 29 Dec. 1903 (No. 12), TNA, FO 881/8404.

Russian ship to proceed to the nearest available Russian port (Baltic) or to some nearer neutral destination, irrespective of whether this be to the eastward or to the westward'. He also reminded him that, under the British legislation, belligerent ships were only allowed to coal once in a British neutral port and then not again for another three months.[52] Cromer was not entirely satisfied with his answer.[53] It seemed to him that the Foreign Office had not taken the Suez Canal Convention of 1888 into account, which stated not only in Article 1 that the Suez Canal should 'always be free and open, in time of war as in time of peace, to every vessel of commerce or of war, without distinction of flag', but also in Article 4 that 'vessels of war of belligerents shall not revictual or take in stores in the canal and its ports of access, except in so far as may be strictly necessary'.[54] The application of 'strictly necessary' was a matter of interpretation, but the Foreign Office did not want to deal with it. The Suez Canal Convention of 1888 had been ratified by all signatory powers, but Britain had reserved the right to withdraw from the convention if its provisions clashed with its national interests, which meant that the convention was not formally in force. When Britain and France agreed to the Entente Cordiale on 8 April 1904, the two powers also settled the Suez Canal question, and Britain dropped its objections to the convention. Thus, the convention became relevant in this context.[55]

Japan declared war on Russia on 8 February 1904, and the British government issued its neutrality proclamation on 11 February.[56] Shortly after the outbreak of the war, the situation escalated when Russia declared coal to be absolute contraband. The Admiralty and the Foreign Office considered the restriction of coal to Russian warships as a retaliatory measure. At this point, the Law Officers intervened and warned that 'we do not think that coal should be refused to Russian vessels, unless it is determined to *retaliate* against Russia for treating coal as absolutely contraband'. This, however, would 'be a very serious step', which would significantly change the duties of

---

[52] The Marquess of Lansdowne to the Earl of Cromer (Telegraphic), 2 Jan. 1904 (No. 13), TNA, FO 881/8404.

[53] The Earl of Cromer to the Marquess of Lansdowne, 6 Jan. 1904 (No. 15), TNA, FO 881/8404.

[54] 'Convention Respecting the Free Navigation of the Suez Maritime Canal, Signed at Constantinople on 29 Oct. 1888', in *American Society of International Law Proceedings of the Seventh Annual Meeting, 24–26 Apr. 1913*, 295–302.

[55] Declaration respecting Egypt and Morocco, 8 Apr. 1904, in *Parliamentary Papers, France, No. 1, 1904 [Cd. 1952]*, 10. See also Edward A. Whittuck, *International Canals* (London, 1920), 34–5.

[56] The Marquess of Lansdowne to Admiralty, 10 Feb. 1904 (No. 99), TNA, FO 881/8404. The letter was also reprinted in *The London Gazette*, No. 27644, 11 Feb. 1904, 933–4.

neutrals, and the Law Officers warned the British government that it would not seriously want to consider such drastic action.[57]

The progress of the Russian Baltic fleet to the Sea of Japan through the English Channel and the Suez Canal again posed questions about how to deal with its re-coaling, particularly since Russia had not changed its view on treating coal as absolute contraband.[58] F. A. Campbell from the Foreign Office approached the Law Officers, R. B. Finlay and Edward Carson, on this point, and they clarified upfront that there was 'no obligation on the part of a neutral to receive into his ports vessels of war of a belligerent not in actual distress. He may forbid their entrance, or impose such conditions as he thinks fit. The same treatment must, of course..., be extended to the vessels of both belligerents.'[59] Generally, the neutrality proclamation out-lined the rules and regulations regarding coaling in British ports. Yet, the Law Officers were also aware that 'indirectly, of course, every supply of pro-visions or coal to a belligerent vessel may facilitate its taking part in the war'. Rather than prohibiting coal as it was 'not supplied directly for the purpose of any hostile operations', the Law Officers suggested not allowing the Russian war fleet 'to use any British ports for the purpose of coaling'. As the overall tone of the diplomatic correspondence between Britain and Russia reflected the strained relations between the two countries, the Law Officers highlighted that all measures had to apply strictly to both belligerents. They warned that treating one side differently from the other would constitute a breach of neutrality and cause a diplomatic incident.[60]

With these special regulations in place, the Russian Baltic fleet was forced to coal in international waters or in the territorial waters of other states. The situation also provided an opportunity for British and foreign colliers to take coal on board in British ports and follow the Russian Baltic fleet to coal them outside British waters. Since the colliers left British ports for other neutral destinations, particularly the Canary Islands and North Africa, the Foreign Enlistment Act did not apply directly. Customs officials and port

[57] Law Officers Report (R. B. Finlay, Edward Carson), 11 Mar. 1904 (No. 29), TNA, FO 834/21; Foreign Office to Admiralty, 14 Mar. 1904 (No. 431), TNA, FO 881/8404.

[58] Foreign Office (F. A. Campbell) to the Law Officers of the Crown (R. B. Finlay, Edward Carson), 3 June 1904 (No. 708), TNA, FO 881/8404. See also Ian Nish, 'Introduction', in Kenneth Bourne, D. Cameron Watt, and Ian Nish (eds), *British Documents on Foreign Affairs. Reports and Papers from the Foreign Office Confidential Print, Series E Asia, 1860–1914, Vol. 11: China and the Russo-Japanese War 1903–1904* (Frederick, MD, 1993), xvii–xviii.

[59] Law Officers Report (R. B. Finlay, Edward Carson), 6 June 1904 (No. 720), TNA, FO 881/8404.

[60] Law Officers Report (R. B. Finlay, Edward Carson), 6 June 1904 (No. 720), TNA, FO 881/8404.

authorities closely monitored the situation, and when an increasing number of reports of coaling in international waters reached the Foreign Office in late September 1904, they turned to the Attorney-General, R. B. Finlay. He had experienced a similar situation in 1870 when French and Prussian warships had also coaled in international waters. Finlay suggested that Customs should issue a letter about the government's position on coaling and the infringement of the Foreign Enlistment Act.[61] Cecil J. B. Hurst, the legal adviser to the Foreign Office, remarked that they should be 'prudent to press the enforcement of the Act in these cases', as traders would not like restrictions to their business. The Foreign Secretary, Lansdowne, agreed and wanted to 'let the matter alone'. He did not think that the Japanese would react in any way.[62] Nevertheless, the Foreign Office informed Customs that they should issue some instructions to the masters of ships, requiring them to give reassurance as to the destination of their cargoes. The Solicitor of Customs, N. J. Highmore, did not find this a practicable solution as port authorities and customs officials could hardly verify the 'real intention' of a ship's master.[63] Despite the uncertainty as to a ship's real destination, port authorities produced detailed lists, which they sent to the Foreign Office, reporting on their activities. The Foreign Office was slow in responding to the rising number of British and foreign ships that had taken British coal on board and sailed to neutral ports elsewhere.[64] The situation escalated when Japan accused Britain of allowing British ships to operate from British neutral ports, supplying the Russian Baltic fleet with British coal. In the eyes of the Japanese, this constituted a breach of neutrality. Although the Foreign Office protested against those allegations, they agreed to monitor the situation more closely.[65]

Two cases can serve here as an illustration of the difficulties verifying a ship's destination. The first case concerned the British steamer *Roddam*, which was suspected of following the Russian fleet and operating from Vigo

[61] Memorandum by the Attorney-General (R. B. Finlay), 30 Sept. 1904 (No. 6), TNA, FO 881/8508.

[62] Minute by C. J. B. Hurst, 1 Oct. 1904 (No. 6), TNA, FO 881/8508; Minute by Lansdowne, 2 Oct. 1904 (No. 6), TNA, FO 881/8508.

[63] Foreign Office (F. A. Campbell) to Customs (Confidential), 18 Oct. 1904 (No. 8), TNA, FO 881/8508; Customs (R. Henderson) to Foreign Office (Confidential), 24 Oct. 1904 (No. 9), TNA, FO 881/8508; Report by the Solicitor of the Customs (N. H. Highmore), 24 Oct. 1904 (No. 9, Inclosure), TNA, FO 881/8508.

[64] Customs (R. Henderson) to Foreign Office, 25 Oct. 1904 (No. 10), TNA, FO 881/8508.

[65] The Marquess of Lansdowne to Sir C. MacDonald (British Ambassador to Japan), 16 Nov. 1904 (No. 23), TNA, FO 881/8508; The Marquess of Lansdowne to Viscount Hayashi, 26 Nov. 1904 (No. 39), TNA, FO 881/8508.

in Spain with Welsh coal, which it had taken on board in a British port.[66] The case of the *Roddam* was first brought to the attention of the Foreign Office when customs officials filed suspicious port activities. After the *Westminster Gazette* reported the activity of the *Roddam*, Customs contacted the Foreign Office about the case. Although there was sufficient evidence, W. Edward Davidson as the legal adviser to the Foreign Office thought that a prosecution under the Foreign Enlistment Act would not 'be at all wise at the present juncture of affairs *qua* Russia, and in the present state of feeling amongst our shipping community'.[67] Lansdowne consulted the Law Officers, Finlay and Carson, who acknowledged the evidence, but thought that the case was 'far from clear'. They were most concerned that an 'abortive prosecution would be very unfortunate' and that would send the wrong signal to the shipping industry and other countries.[68] This principal decision guided future dealings in the case. For Davidson it was clear that 'the question has really passed beyond the realm of law, and has become one of high policy to be decided by the Government'.[69] The Japanese were unhappy, and Sir C. MacDonald, the British Ambassador to Japan, tried to appease them.[70] While the Foreign Office circulated a memorandum to the Chambers of Commerce reminding them about the Foreign Enlistment Act, the Secretary of State for War, H. O. Arnold-Forster, suggested the prohibition of the export of coal under the Customs and Inland Revenue Act of 1879 and the Act to Amend the Law relating to the Exportation of Arms, Ammunition, and Military and Naval Stores of 1900. In his opinion, this would solve the problem of coaling once and for all. Yet, the Foreign Office and the Law Officers rejected such a measure because it might hurt the British economy.[71]

The *Roddam* case took a new turn when crew members of the ship contacted Cromer in Cairo, informing him of their intention to leave the ship when they docked in Port Saïd because they did not want to proceed any

[66] Customs (R. Henderson) to Foreign Office (Confidential), 8 Nov. 1904 (No. 20), TNA, FO 881/8508; Board of Trade (Walter J. Howell) to Foreign Office, 16 Nov. 1904 (No. 26), TNA, FO 881/8508.

[67] Minute by W. E. Davidson, 10 Nov. 1904 (No. 20), TNA, FO 881/8508.

[68] The Law Officers of the Crown to the Marquess of Lansdowne, 25 Nov. 1904 (No. 37), TNA, FO 881/8508.

[69] Minute by W. E. Davidson, 26 Nov. 1904 (No. 38), TNA, FO 881/8508.

[70] The Marquess of Lansdowne to Sir C. MacDonald, 16 Nov. 1904 (No. 23), TNA, FO 881/8508.

[71] Customs and Inland Revenue Act, 1879 (42 and 43 Vict., cap. 21), http://www.legislation.gov.uk/ukpga/1879/21/pdfs/ukpga_18790021_en.pdf (accessed 7 Oct. 2018); Memorandum by H. O. Arnold-Forster respecting the Stoppage of the Export of Coal in Time of Peace, 25 Nov. 1904 (No. 33), TNA, FO 881/8508.

further with the Russian war fleet.[72] Although this provided an opportunity to strengthen the evidence base in the case of the *Roddam*, the Foreign Office did not have any intention of pursuing the case further.[73] However, the Treasury Solicitor, Lord Desart urged the Foreign Office to instruct Cromer to take statements from the crew as 'it is quite possible this may turn into a case on which we may act'.[74] Desart forwarded communications from the Admiralty and the Board of Trade to the Foreign Office containing information about the voyage of the *Roddam* and her intention to follow the Russian war fleet.[75] It turned out that the Hamburg America Line, a German company, had chartered the British colliers, and their crew had followed their orders. When the *Roddam* berthed in Port Saïd, the customs officials questioned her master.[76] Desart was content that they were 'doing all they can for us locally'. And yet, he was also aware of the challenges in 'get[ting] evidence of intention when it cannot be inferred from action on a previous voyage'.[77] The statement from the master and the crew proved that the ship had indeed followed the Russian war fleet but she had only coaled a Russian auxiliary in Spanish territorial waters.[78] From Port Saïd the *Roddam* returned to Glasgow, where Customs made further inquiries. By that point, the Foreign Office were no longer interested in pursuing the case, and Desart, who had been keen to prosecute, also concluded that there was 'little prospect of there being material for any prosecution of English owners or charterers'.[79] The Law Officers agreed with that view.[80]

---

[72] The Marquess of Lansdowne to Viscount Hayashi, 26 Nov. 1904 (No. 39), TNA, FO 881/8508; London Chamber of Commerce to Foreign Office, 28 Nov. 1904 (No. 41), TNA, FO 881/8508; The Earl of Cromer to the Marquess of Lansdowne (Telegraphic), 29 Nov. 1904 (No. 44), TNA, FO 881/8508.

[73] Foreign Office (F. A. Campbell) to Customs, 29 Nov. 1904 (No. 49), TNA, FO 881/8508.

[74] Treasury Solicitor (Lord Desart) to Foreign Office, 30 Nov. 1904 (No. 52), TNA, FO 881/8508.

[75] Treasury Solicitor (Lord Desart) to Foreign Office (Campbell) (Confidential), 1 Dec. 1904 (No. 58), TNA, FO 881/8508; Admiralty (C. Inigo Thomas) to Treasury Solicitor (Lord Desart), 30 Nov. 1904 (No. 58, Inclosure 1), TNA, FO 881/8508; Consul Keyser to Board of Trade, 7 Nov. 1904 (No. 58, Inclosure 2), TNA, FO 881/8508.

[76] Consul Cameron to the Marquess of Lansdowne (Telegraphic), 2 Dec. 1904 (No. 69), TNA, FO 881/8508.

[77] Treasury Solicitor (Lord Desart) to Foreign Office (Campbell), 5 Dec. 1904 (No. 83), TNA, FO 881/8508.

[78] Consul Donald A. Cameron to the Marquess of Lansdowne, 3 Dec. 1904 (No. 110), TNA, FO 881/8508. See also Inclosures of No. 110 (Affidavit of Captain Stevenson and List of Crew of the Steam-ship 'Roddam').

[79] Lord Desart to Foreign Office (Campbell), 29 Jan. 1905 (No. 179), TNA, FO 881/8508.

[80] Mr E. Bates (Collector) to the Solicitor, Customs, 23 Jan. 1905 (No. 174), TNA, FO 881/8508; Minute by Mr Davidson respecting the 'Roddam' Case, 9 Feb. 1905 (No. 202), TNA, FO 881/8508.

The second case deals with the German steamer *Captain W. Menzell*. The ship had taken coal on board at Cardiff, sailed to Vigo and Tangier, and returned to Cardiff where it waited for further instructions. In port it underwent repair work to the hull.[81] Due to suspicious behaviour by the master of the ship and the crew, the local superintendent became interested, and started an investigation and obtained witness reports. The evidence strongly suggested that the ship had coaled Russian warships in international waters, and that the damage to the hull had been the result of a collision with one of them during the transshipment of coal in heavy seas.[82] When the reports reached the Foreign Office, it immediately ordered the detention of the ship under the provisions of the Foreign Enlistment Act.[83] However, Lansdowne was careful in handling this case as the detention of a foreign ship could easily lead to a diplomatic crisis. But since the ship had operated from a British port and transported British coal, Lansdowne had to act.[84] The pressure to find a diplomatic solution was considerable and, in the end, the ship was released on condition that it returned to Hamburg.[85]

The two cases illustrate the difficulties of enforcing the Foreign Enlistment Act with regard to coaling in international waters, not least because the act was domestic legislation, and therefore not applicable in international waters. Although customs officers gathered sufficient evidence to seek prosecution under the act, the Foreign Office was cautious. It abstained from any prosecutions because they could hurt the British economy, and because they might lead to diplomatic disputes with other powers if they concerned foreign ships and individuals.

Trade in Contraband Goods

Contraband trade was another area of conflict between neutrals and belligerents. It was customary law for a belligerent state to issue a list of

---

[81] Memorandum by W. E. Davidson on Case of Steam-ship 'Captain W. Menzell', 1 Dec. 1904 (No. 65), TNA, FO 881/8508.

[82] Customs Solicitor (N. J. Highmore) to Foreign Office, 2 Dec. 1904 (No. 67), TNA, FO 881/8508; Treasury Solicitor (Lord Desart) to Foreign Office, 2 Dec. 1904 (No. 66), TNA, FO 881/8508.

[83] Foreign Office to Collector of Customs, Cardiff (Telegraphic), 3 Dec. 1904 (No. 78), TNA, FO 881/8508.

[84] Memorandum by W. E. Davidson, 3 Dec. 1904 (No. 79), TNA, FO 881/8508.

[85] Memorandum by F. A. Campbell respecting Case of 'Captain W. Menzell', 8 Dec. 1904 (No. 98), TNA, FO 881/8508.

conditional and absolute contraband goods at the outbreak of a conflict. Attempts to agree on a common list of contraband goods were often made but Edward Hertslet, the Foreign Office librarian and archivist, dismissed this thought as a hopeless endeavour. Particularly at a time of rapid techno-logical development, such a list would have required continuous updating. By deciding not to define a definite list of contraband goods, the signatories of the Declaration of Paris of 1856 left room for interpretation.[86]

In Britain, prize laws distinguished between absolute and conditional contraband of war. Absolute contraband of war were goods intended for direct and 'exclusive' military use, such as arms, ammunition, or uniforms. Conditional contraband of war were goods not exclusively used for military but also for civilian purposes, such as timber or coal. Here the destination of the goods determined whether they could be classified as conditional contraband or not.[87] Only a prize court could verify in such cases whether the goods could be declared conditional contraband, and thus be claimed as a lawful prize.[88]

What and when goods could be declared as conditional contraband was the root of numerous disputes between belligerents and neutrals. Here the doctrine of continuous voyage needs to be examined more closely. The doctrine of continuous voyage was first developed during the Seven Years War, and it received a much broader interpretation during the American Civil War with the decision on the *Springbok* case. On 3 February 1863, an American cruiser seized the British ship *Springbok* while she was on her way to Nassau, a neutral port in the Bahamas. The *Springbok* was alleged to have carried contraband goods on board destined for a blockaded port of the Confederates. The US Supreme Court, which considered prize cases in the highest instance in the United States, had judged that, while the *Springbok* was sailing for a neutral port, it had carried contraband goods on board whose ultimate destination was a blockaded port of the Confederates rather than neutral Nassau. For this reason, the judges had dismissed the fact that the *Springbok* sailed for a neutral port. Decisive for the judges was the fact that the goods were transshipped and consigned to a blockaded port. Consequently, the US Supreme Court condemned the entire cargo,

---

[86] Memorandum by E. Hertslet on the Definition of the Term 'Contraband of War' (Confidential), 3 May 1877; TNA, FO 881/3880.

[87] Thomas E. Holland, *A Manual of Naval Prize Law. Founded upon the Manual prepared in 1866 by Godfrey Lushington* (London, 1888), 18–21.

[88] Memorandum by E. Hertslet respecting Contraband of War (Confidential), 28 Mar. 1887, TNA, FO 881/5429.

not just the contraband goods, in order to send a strong signal to the per-petrators.[89] The Foreign Office and the Law Officers protested against the US Supreme Court's ruling, but the decision was final and thus set a new interpretation of the doctrine of continuous voyage. The doctrine had become increasingly important with the development of infrastructure on land, which allowed goods to be transported more easily from ports to the hinterland. This made the identification of the ultimate destination of cargo more difficult.[90]

Trade in contraband goods was not directly treated under the Foreign Enlistment Act. However, it was an integral part of Britain's neutrality policy, and thus the British government saw itself obliged to warn its citizens in its neutrality proclamation that 'articles considered and deemed to be contraband of war, according to the law or modern usages of nations, for the use or service of either of the said Sovereigns, that all person so offend-ing, together with their ships and goods, will rightfully incur, and be justly liable to, hostile capture, and to the penalties denounced by the law of nations in that behalf'.[91]

The British government had the powers to regulate the import, export, and prohibition of goods under the Customs Laws Consolidation Act of 1853.[92] Yet, the debates about the Foreign Enlistment Bill in parliament in 1870 showed that enforcing the Customs Laws Consolidation Act to pro-hibit contraband trade was not in Britain's economic interest. In fact, no neutral government ever prohibited the export of goods to its citizens,

---

[89] The Springbok, 72 U.S. 5. Wall. 1 1 (1866).

[90] Memorandum by E. Hertslet respecting Contraband of War (Confidential), 28 Mar. 1887, TNA, FO 881/5429; Memorandum by A. Pearce Higgins for H.M. Procurator General on Contraband Trade and Continuous Voyage, 1914, TNA, FO 881/10593X;Charles Noble Gregory, 'The Doctrine of Continuous Voyage', *Harvard Law Review*, 24, 3 (1911), 167–81; A. G. Leech, 'The Doctrine of Continuous Voyage: Its Origin and Development from the Seven Years' War (1756) to the Boer War', *Journal of the Royal United Service Institution*, 46 (1902), 1524–32. See also Stuart L. Bernath, *Squall Across the Atlantic: American Civil War Prize Cases and Diplomacy* (Berkeley, CA, 1970), 85–98; Stephen C. Neff, *Justice in Blue and Gray: A Legal History of the Civil War* (Cambridge, MA, 2010) , 187–202.

[91] 'A Proclamation of Neutrality by the Queen Victoria', *The London Gazette*, No. 23635, 19 July 1870, 3432.

[92] Customs Laws Consolidation Act, 1853 (16 and 17 Vict., cap. 107) was later replaced: see Customs Laws Consolidation Act, 1876 (39 and 49 Vict., cap. 36), http://www.legislation.gov. uk/ukpga/1876/36/pdfs/ukpga_18760036_en.pdf (accessed 15 Oct. 2018); Synopsis of the Customs Law Consolidation Bill, 1876, and the Unrepealed Sections of Existing Acts, 18 May 1876, in *Nineteenth Century House of Commons Sessional Papers, 1876, Vol. II*, 133; Joseph Nathaniel Highmore, *The Customs Laws including the Customs Consolidation Act, 1876, with the Enactments Amending and Extending that Act and the Present Customs Tariff for Great Britain and Ireland; also the Customs Laws and Tariff for the Isle of Man*, 2nd edn (London, 1907).

unless it served its purposes.[93] Lord Tenterden, who had been the Secretary of the Neutrality Laws Commission as well as Secretary of the Joint Arbitration Commission looking into the *Alabama* claims (see Chapter 2), explained the political decision in a memorandum, writing that the Customs Laws Consolidation Act had 'always been put in force as a precaution against the export of arms to an enemy of this country, never as a measure of neutrality'. Tenterden further argued that the British government had 'always contended, during the American controversy, that neutrals are not bound or called upon to prohibit the sale of arms, &c., to a belligerent. It is an offence against the belligerent which carries with it its appropriate penalty by exposing the vessel carrying the contraband of war to capture and confiscation.'[94] In other words, a neutral government could not be forced to prohibit the export of contraband goods; rather a belligerent government had to prosecute those involved in contraband trade—a position which Britain regularly defended against allegations from belligerents.

Coal

In the age of steam, both coaling and the supply of coal to the enemy had become a significant issue. Britain had been the biggest supplier of coal, and Welsh steam coal was the best in the world. Unsurprisingly, belligerents repeatedly accused neutral Britain of supplying coal to the enemy. During the Franco-Prussian War, Prussia treated coal as absolute contraband while France did not. Prussia accused Britain of supplying coal to the French navy, and the Prussian Ambassador, Count Bernstorff, demanded the British government prohibited the export of coal. The Law Officers replied that British legislation did not prohibit the export of coal and 'had no power by the law' to do so.[95] In fact, Britain had not considered coal as contraband since its principal ruling in 1859 during the Second Italian War of Independence. The rise of steam meant that coal had gained strategic importance and Britain needed to weigh up carefully the advantages and

[93] John Macdonell, 'Recent Changes in the Rights and Duties of Belligerents and Neutrals According to International Law (Part 1)', *Journal of Royal United Service Institution*, 42, 2 (1898), 801–3.

[94] Memorandum by Lord Tenterden on the Export of Arms during War (Confidential), 18 July 1870 (No. 51), TNA, FO 881/5163.

[95] Law Officers of the Crown (R. P. Collier, J. D. Coleridge, Travers Twiss) to Earl Granville (No. 200), 10 Aug. 1870, TNA, FO 834/9.

disadvantages of this development. If coal were declared contraband, neutral trade would be greatly affected and the British government concluded that it would 'probably lose more than we can gain by contending for the prohibition'. Undoubtedly, economic interests played a decisive role in the discussions, particularly since Britain possessed more coal resources and coaling stations around the world than any other power.[96] Yet, Bernstorff pushed further and generally criticized the Foreign Enlistment Act. The Law Officers advised the Foreign Office to remind Bernstorff of the fact that no other country had adopted stricter rules regarding the law of neutrality than Britain. In fact, 'in proposing this provision [of the Foreign Enlistment Act] they were going beyond any duty cast upon neutrals by international law'.[97]

When the Russo-Turkish war broke out in April 1877, the British government wanted to avoid another confrontation with the belligerent parties over coal. It successfully persuaded Russia, which had declared coal to be contraband, to exempt neutral colliers from capture at sea under certain circumstances. In practice this meant that neutral colliers could bring coal into belligerent ports, provided that the cargo was certified for civilian usage. The Law Officers had been sceptical about the introduction of certificates as belligerents could still argue that they were not 'genuine', but the Russians as well as the Turks were willing to accept them. This was a major negotiating success for the British, demonstrating how diplomacy shaped state practice. Most importantly, Britain was able to safeguard its economic interests.[98]

In the Sino-French War of 1884–5, British merchants enquired about the status of coal. Since France had not declared coal to be contraband in previous wars, the Law Officers assumed that France would adhere to its old practice. As a result, the Law Officers reaffirmed British practice that coal would not be declared absolute contraband because coal was 'so largely used for innocent purposes that no sufficient presumption that it is intended

---

[96] Memorandum by E. Hertslet on the Question whether or not Coals are Considered Contraband of War (Confidential), 20 Jan. 1862, TNA, FO 881/1017.

[97] Law Officers of the Crown (R. P. Collier, J. D. Coleridge, Travers Twiss) to Earl Granville, 14 Oct. 1870 (No. 211), TNA, FO 834/9.

[98] The Law Officers of the Crown (John Holker, Hardinge S. Gifford) and Dr Deane to the Earl of Derby, 3 May 1877 (No. 70), TNA, FO 834/12; The Law Officers of the Crown (John Holker, Hardinge S. Gifford) and Dr Deane to the Earl of Derby, 25 May 1877 (No. 86), TNA, FO 834/12; The Law Officers of the Crown (John Holker, Hardinge S. Gifford) and Dr Deane to the Earl of Derby, 6 July 1877 (No. 93), TNA, FO 834/12; The Law Officers of the Crown (John Holker, Hardinge S. Gifford) and Dr Deane to the Earl of Derby, 30 July 1877 (No. 96), TNA, FO 834/12.

for warlike use is afforded by the simple fact of its destination to a belligerent port'. Consequently, the Law Officers argued that if coal was 'conveyed in the ordinary course of business, consigned to a merchant at a belligerent port, it ought not to be regarded as contraband of war'. However, if coal was destined 'to a naval arsenal or station, [then] it might be regarded as contraband.'[99] Accordingly, the Foreign Office did not even warn British merchants against transporting coal to belligerent ports provided that the ultimate destination was of civilian nature.

During the Russo-Japanese War the issue of coal again received attention from the British government. Russia had declared coal to be absolute contraband on 28 February 1904, while coal was on Japan's conditional list.[100] The Foreign Office, following the advice of the Attorney-General, R. B. Finlay, condemned the Russian measure and protested formally against it.[101] Charles Hardinge, the British Ambassador to Russia, stressed to Count Lamsdorff, the Russian Foreign Secretary, the 'generally pacific use' of coal. Moreover, he pointed out that no 'belligerent had the right to extinguish British trade with a country at war when that trade was of a peaceful character'.[102] At the peak of the crisis, Britain even considered the refusal of coal to Russian warships as a retaliatory measure, which demonstrated how far the British government was prepared to go to press Russia into changing its practice.[103] Finally, Russia caved in. Yet, the dispute had raised broader questions, namely whether in the age of steam the old practice had reached its limits, and whether new political solutions were needed to resolve the issue of conditional contraband.

Foodstuffs

Foodstuffs were generally considered conditional contraband of war, and yet, the control of the flow of foodstuffs to the enemy forces was of strategic importance for belligerent parties. Furthermore, it was also a delicate matter as the civilian population was equally dependent on foodstuffs. The

---

[99] Law Officers of the Crown (Henry James, Farrer Herschell) and Dr Deane to Earl Granville, 7 Feb. 1885 (No. 64), TNA, FO 834/15.
[100] Foreign Office (F. A. Campbell) to the Law Officers of the Crown, 3 June 1904 (No. 33), TNA, FO 834/21.
[101] Memorandum by the Attorney-General (R. B. Finlay), 22 Sept. 1904 (No. 43), TNA, FO 834/21.
[102] Sir Charles Hardinge to the Marquess of Lansdowne, 21 Sept. 1904, TNA, FO 881/8433.
[103] Minute by W. Maycock (Foreign Office), 24 Sept. 1904, TNA, FO 881/8433.

Sino-French War gives an insight into the controversy surrounding food-stuffs as contraband.[104] In February 1885, France declared rice a 'general' contraband of war in an attempt to control its import into China. Although the measure was restricted to cargo destined for ports north of Canton, the British government vehemently protested against the measure, which it argued was not in accordance with 'the law and practice of nations'. Only foodstuffs intended for direct military usage could be treated as contraband, but this was a matter for prize courts to judge on a case-by-case basis.[105] Despite Britain's protest, the French upheld their position, and Britain publicly announced the new measure in the *London Gazette* in order to warn its citizens. Since the Law Officers feared that a public announcement equalled an acceptance of the new practice, they suggested a question in parliament should reaffirm the government's general disagreement with the French decision.[106]

The French Ambassador, Waddington, continued defending the position of his country, arguing that France had only adopted a practice that Britain had pursued in the past. He referenced the Crimean War, in which the destination rather than the good itself had been decisive in declaring a good as contraband. Furthermore, Waddington cited the case of the Franco-Prussian War in which coal had also been treated as conditional contraband, and Britain had accepted the judgements of the prize courts. Therefore, he could not accept Britain's objection.[107] Neither the Lord Chancellor nor the Law Officers objected to the right of a foreign prize court to decide upon the lawfulness of a prize given sufficient evidence. The actual dispute concerned the question of whether a foreign prize court had the right to make a principle decision on what constituted contraband or not. The Lord Chancellor argued that 'we ought not hold ourselves bound by any decisions of any belligerent Prize Courts'.[108] A few days later, Selborne wrote more strongly

---

[104] M. Waddington to Earl Granville, 20 Feb. 1885 (No.1), TNA, FO 881/8167.

[105] The Law Officers of the Crown (Henry James and Farrer Herschell) to Earl Granville, 24 Feb. 1885 (No. 4), TNA, FO 881/8167; Law Officers Report, 26 Feb. 1885 (No. 72), TNA, FO 834/15; M. Waddington to Earl Granville, 24 Feb. 1885 (No. 3), TNA, FO 881/8167; Earl Granville to M. Waddington, 27 Feb. 1885 (No. 5), TNA, FO 881/8167.

[106] Law Officers of the Crown (Henry James and Farrer Herschell) and Dr Deane to Earl Granville, 5 Mar. 1885 (No. 73), TNA, FO 834/15; Law Officers of the Crown (Henry James and Farrer Herschell) and Dr Deane to Earl Granville, 11 Mar. 1885 (No. 77), TNA, FO 834/15; 'Note from the Foreign Office, March 20, 1885', *The London Gazette*, No. 25453, 20 Mar. 1885, 1251.

[107] M. Waddington to Earl Granville, 10 Mar. 1885 (No. 6); TNA, FO 881/8167.

[108] Lord Chancellor (Lord Selborne) to Earl Granville, 30 Mar. 1885 (No. 8), TNA, FO 881/8167.

to Granville explaining that 'I do not think diplomatic courtesy can possibly require, after the French Government have expressively stated, and reiterated, their claim to act on a principle contrary to international law.'[109] Accordingly, Granville informed the French that belligerents were in no position to dictate what constituted contraband or not. Moreover, he argued that such a decision would also violate the Declaration of Paris of 1856, in particular the provision of 'free ship, free good'.[110]

The British protest aimed at preventing at all costs the French practice becoming accepted in international law. While Britain had declared food-stuffs to be contraband during the French Wars, it had changed its policy since then. The repeal of the Corn Laws and the Navigation Act in the 1840s marked the beginning of Britain's free trade policy. The Law Officers stated that Britain had previously 'endeavoured to act upon a different principle, and sought to prevent provisions entering any French port, but [since then] such action has been condemned by other nations, and by many writers of authority, and such a view certainly cannot now be maintained'.[111] The Lord Chancellor, Lord Selborne, was quite outspoken about the consequences of Britain's free trade policy, which undoubtedly affected its legal position in a future maritime war. He argued that it was 'of *most vital* importance to all nations who, like ourselves, depend for the food of our population on imports from abroad, to maintain the right of neutrals to trade with us (or with any other country) in time of war, in provisions and other commodities, which are neither in their own proper nature contraband of war, nor intended for naval or military use, without being liable to capture'.[112] Selborne feared that expanding the contraband list would empower minor sea powers, giving them a weapon similar to that of block-ade in the hands of the major sea powers. Ultimately, this would undermine the role of major sea powers and their capability to uphold a blockade, as this would no longer be necessary to keep the upper hand in a war at sea. Moreover, the French practice would also undermine the provisions of the

---

[109] Lord Chancellor (Lord Selborne) to Earl Granville, 3 Apr. 1885 (No. 85), TNA, FO 834/15.

[110] Law Officers of the Crown (Henry James, Farrer Herschell) and Dr Deane to Earl Granville, 31 Mar. 1885 (No. 81), TNA, FO 834/15; Earl Granville to M. Waddington, 4 Apr. 1885 (No. 11), TNA, FO 881/8167.

[111] The Law Officers of the Crown (Henry James and Farrer Herschell) to Earl Granville, 24 Feb. 1885 (No. 70), TNA, FO 834/15.

[112] Lord Chancellor (Lord Selborne) to Earl Granville, 30 Mar. 1885 (No. 80), TNA, FO 834/15.

Declaration of Paris, which protected neutral shipping, and more generally, 'such a doctrine would make a clean sweep of all international law'.[113]

A few days later, in April 1885, the German Chancellor, Otto von Bismarck, remarked in the *Norddeutsche Zeitung* that he explicitly supported the French decision to put rice on the contraband list.[114] These remarks sent shockwaves through Britain, and Selborne felt betrayed by the continental powers. Angrily he wrote that '[a]ll the concessions made, to the disadvantage of a Maritime Power, by the Treaty of Paris, will be expected to be observed by us; and they [continental powers] will, at the same time, submit, as neutrals, to whatever law of contraband the other belligerent may choose to lay down'.[115] Indeed continental powers held a different position compared to that of Britain as a major sea power. Bismarck had justified the French measure as an act of military necessity with the aim of terminating the war more quickly.[116] However, for the British, the contraband question revealed the fundamental dispute between major and minor sea powers.

Contemplating the far-reaching strategic consequences of such a development, Selborne concluded that, 'I do not hesitate to say, that, if this should ever happen, we should have to denounce, and shake ourselves free from, the Declaration of Paris; to resume the old rights, of taking enemy's goods in neutral bottoms, and of employing privateers against the enemy'.[117] The Declaration of Paris had become an important instrument enabling Britain to protect its economic interests and its trade. And yet, Britain's dependence on foodstuffs made it vulnerable to a future maritime war not least because international law generally, and the Declaration of Paris in particular, left too many questions open. Although no British ship with rice on board was stopped during the Sino-French War, the conflict illustrated how emotionally laden the contraband issue was.

Some decades later, during the Boer War of 1899–1902, the British government under Lord Salisbury again had to deal with the question of foodstuffs. This time, though, Britain was a belligerent party in the conflict. With

---

[113] Lord Chancellor (Lord Selborne) to Earl Granville, 30 Mar. 1885 (No. 80), TNA, FO 834/15.

[114] Extract from the 'Norddeutsche Allgemeine Zeitung', 8 Apr. 1885 (No. 91, Annex), TNA, FO 834/15.

[115] Memorandum by the Lord Chancellor (Lord Selborne), 24 Apr. 1885 (No. 91), TNA, FO 834/15.

[116] Extract from the 'Norddeutsche Allgemeine Zeitung', 8 Apr. 1885 (No. 91, Annex), TNA, FO 834/15.

[117] Memorandum by the Lord Chancellor (Lord Selborne), 24 Apr. 1885 (No. 91), TNA, FO 834/15.

war in South Africa looming, news reached the Colonial Office that British and foreign ships with arms, ammunition, and foodstuffs were headed to the Portuguese port of Lourenço Marques (today known as Maputo) from where goods were transshipped to destinations in the Orange Free State and the South African Republic (also known as Transvaal). Since the Boers had no direct access to the sea, Delagoa Bay and Lourenço Marques were of vital interest for the British to control, and thus Delagoa Bay became the centre of naval operations for the Royal Navy. In fact, Delagoa Bay and Lourenço Marques had been the key interests of Britain and Germany in the region for a long time.[118] Yet, as long as no official declaration of war had been issued, the seizure of neutral ships was delicate, and the Foreign Office suggested interfering 'as little as possible with neutral vessels, but to seize the goods if landed in a British port and to trust the Portuguese authorities at Delagoa Bay'.[119] In an initial telegram, the Foreign Office told Sir Alfred Milner, High Commissioner for South Africa, to abstain from seizing ships carrying foodstuffs unless there was 'reasonable ground for believing that they are directly destined for the supply of the enemy's forces'. The Foreign Office feared that this could otherwise open a discussion they wished to 'avoid'.[120] Two days later, Lord Salisbury instructed the Colonial Secretary, Joseph Chamberlain, and the Admiralty that British and foreign merchant ships should be searched and, if suspected of contraband trade, brought into a British port for a prize court procedure. He furthermore instructed that 'contraband of war should be regarded as including food suitable for feeding troops'.[121] After Milner's formal proclamation of a 'state of war' on 26 October 1899, prize courts were installed in the Colony of Natal (Durban) and the Cape Colony (Cape Town).[122] Swiftly, Lord Salisbury and the Foreign Office decided on provisional instructions for the colonial and naval administrators in South Africa, in which foodstuffs were declared

---

[118] Peter Henshaw, 'The "Key to South Africa" in the 1890s: Delagoa Bay and the Origins of the South African War', *Journal of Southern African Studies*, 24, 3 (1998), 527–43; F. H. Hinsley, 'British Foreign Policy and Colonial Questions, 1895–1904', in *The Cambridge History of the British Empire. Volume III: The Empire-Commonwealth* (Cambridge, 1959), 515–16.

[119] Foreign Office (Francis Bertie) to Admiralty, 13 Oct. 1899 (No. 15, Enclosure), TNA, CO 879/60/5.

[120] Mr Chamberlain to High Commissioner Sir Alfred Milner (Telegram), 21 Oct. 1899 (No. 27), TNA, CO 879/60/5.

[121] Foreign Office (Francis Bertie) to Colonial Office (Secret), 23 Oct. 1899 (No. 31), TNA, CO 879/60/5. See also Admiralty to Commander-in-Chief, Cape of Good Hope (Telegram), 23 Oct. 1899 (No. 32, Enclosure), TNA, CO 879/60/5.

[122] Admiralty (Evan MacGregor) to Colonial Office, 26 Oct. 1899 (No. 42), TNA, CO 879/60/5.

conditional contraband. This caused quite a stir since the Law Officers had not approved this decision.[123] Consequently, the Law Officers' report criticized the provisional instructions. For Richard E. Webster and Finlay, the government's decision was not tenable in the context of previous state practice as 'food-stuffs with a hostile destination can be considered contraband of war only if they are supplies for the enemy's forces. It is not sufficient that they are capable of being so used, it must be shown that this was, in fact, their destination at the time of seizure.' The adoption of a new practice would potentially have an unpredictable outcome in a future maritime conflict, and thus the Law Officers concluded 'that any extension of the doctrine of contraband as applied to food-stuffs would not be for the interest of this country'.[124] Moreover, the Law Officers warned of conflicts with neutrals if Britain exercised the right of search and capture. Rather, they urged the British government to negotiate with the Portuguese, so that they would then suppress contraband trade via Lourenço Marques.[125] Consequently, the British government reversed the provisional instructions sent to the colonial administrators and naval commanders. Chamberlain wrote in a telegram to Milner that foodstuffs should not be treated as contraband because 'it might form a dangerous precedent and the game is not worth the candle, as we intend not to starve the Boers but to beat them'.[126]

Milner did not agree with the decision, instead deeming it necessary to treat foodstuffs as contraband because he thought 'the question of supplies may prove a decisive factor if the war is prolonged'.[127] Although Milner's repeated attempts could not change the position of the British government with regard to foodstuffs as contraband, the control of trade with the enemy via Delagoa Bay and Lourenço Marques was absolutely essential.[128] Since treating foodstuffs as contraband was not an option for political reasons, the British government pursued a different course. The Foreign Office suggested declaring it 'a punishable offence' to trade with the enemy, which meant that British subjects and vessels could not continue trading with the Boers while

---

[123] Foreign Office (Francis Bertie) to Colonial Office (Secret), 23 Oct. 1899 (No. 31), TNA, CO 879/60/5.

[124] Law Officers Report (R. E. Webster, R. B. Finlay), 26 Oct. 1899 (No. 4), TNA, FO 834/19.

[125] Law Officers Report (R. E. Webster, R. B. Finlay), 26 Oct. 1899 (No. 4), TNA, FO 834/19.

[126] Mr Chamberlain to High Commissioner Sir Alfred Milner (Telegram), 2 Nov. 1899 (No. 67), TNA, CO 879/60/5.

[127] High Commissioner Sir Alfred Milner to Mr Chamberlain (Telegram), 2 Nov. 1899 (No. 68), TNA, CO 879/60/5.

[128] High Commissioner Sir Alfred Milner to Mr Chamberlain (Telegram), 7 Nov. 1899 (No. 80), TNA, CO 879/60/5.

the conflict was ongoing. This would allow naval officers and customs officials to search and detain British vessels carrying goods including foodstuffs.[129] The Colonial Office reacted hesitantly to Lord Salisbury's suggestion as Chamberlain thought the measure might disadvantage British traders and they would subsequently switch to other neutrals whose trade was not restricted.[130] Yet, a few days later, Chamberlain instructed Milner on this new policy and the Cape Colony issued a proclamation warning British subjects against trading with the enemy.[131] In mid-December 1899, the British army faced a series of defeats, known as the 'black week'.[132] The Admiralty sent the Commander-in-Chief a telegram, declaring that 'ordinary food-stuffs are still to be free, but such provisions as may fairly be regarded as intended for the supply of troops in the field are to be considered as contraband of war'.[133] For Milner, this posed another opportunity to high-light the necessity for the British to control Delagoa Bay as 'the Boers will require large supplies, certainly of food, and probably of ammunition, and these can only be obtained through the Portuguese possessions'. He thought that, although the Portuguese were neutral, they were not effective in stop-ping trade with the enemy and, thus, 'Delagoa Bay is a danger' to Britain.[134] When reports about smuggling through Delagoa Bay and also British colo-nial ports in the region reached London, the Colonial Office instructed Milner to obtain an overview of the activities.[135] For Milner, only 'the com-plete control of Delagoa Bay' could stop the trade with the enemy.[136] A secret report from Samuel Evans about the activities in Lourenço Marques sug-gested enforcing 'the most rigorous and stringent Customs Regulations that can be legally applied'. Evans did not trust the Portuguese officials and, thus,

---

[129] Foreign Office (Francis Bertie) to Colonial Office, 10 Nov. 1899 (No. 97), TNA, CO 879/60/5.

[130] Colonial Office (Fred. Graham) to Foreign Office, 11 Nov. 1899 (No. 101), TNA, CO 879/60/5.

[131] Mr Chamberlain to High Commissioner Sir Alfred Milner (Telegram), 16 Nov. 1899 (No. 117), TNA, CO 879/60/5; Foreign Office (Francis Bertie) to Colonial Office, 11 Dec. 1899 (No. 189), TNA, CO 879/60/5.

[132] Denis Judd and Keith Surridge, *The Boer War. A History* (London, 2013), 118–30; John W. Coogan, *The End of Neutrality: The United States, Britain, and Maritime Rights, 1899–1915* (Ithaca, NY, 1981), 35–6.

[133] Admiralty to Commander-in-Chief (Cape of Good Hope), 12 Dec. 1899 (Enclosure in No. 199), TNA, CO 879/60/5.

[134] High Commissioner Sir Alfred Milner to Mr Chamberlain (Secret), 14 Dec. 1899 (No. 243), TNA, CO 879/60/5.

[135] Mr Chamberlain to High Commissioner Sir Alfred Milner (Telegram), 24 Dec. 1899 (No. 225), TNA, CO 879/60/5.

[136] High Commissioner Sir Alfred Milner to Mr Chamberlain (Telegram), 26 Dec. 1899 (No. 229), TNA, CO 879/60/5.

demanded that experienced British customs officials should be sent to Delagoa Bay to oversee the trade.[137]

Britain's measures to control the trade via Lourenço Marques increased the pressure on the Boers but also affected neutrals, which had regularly protested against Britain's measures.[138] The Portuguese complained that foodstuffs and other goods for locals in Lourenço Marques were scarce, and asked that the British let foodstuffs pass to ease the situation. Lord Salisbury signalled the willingness of the British government to loosen the controls and allow British ships to carry foodstuffs to Lourenço Marques on condition that the Portuguese 'co-operate[d]' and took effective control of the local markets.[139] Although Milner objected to the change of policy and thought that the complaint of the Portuguese was 'humbug', Lord Salisbury decided on this policy in order to avoid a confrontation with the neutrals.[140]

The experience as a belligerent in the Boer War illustrated Britain's balancing act between the exercise of belligerent rights, which allowed the control of Delagoa Bay, and the respect of neutral rights. The question of foodstuffs showed that the British government was willing to change its practice if it suited its short-term needs. However, the Law Officers also considered the long-term effects of such a decision. Nor could Salisbury ignore the protests of neutrals, not least because of the wide-ranging effects any decision might have on a future war at sea in which Britain would be neutral.[141] The experience of the Boer War also revealed how incoherently the British government reached decisions on legal matters. At the outbreak of the war, the Foreign Office, the Colonial Office, and the Admiralty were ill-coordinated, so confusing colonial and naval administrators. Instructions on contraband were contradictory and the Foreign Office first needed to clarify the legal framework.[142] Although the Foreign Office was chiefly responsible for the decision-making, it was the man on the spot, Milner as High Commissioner for South Africa, who needed to be tamed as he was

---

[137] Secret Report about Delagoa Bay by Samuel Evans, Cape Town, Cape Colony, 22 Jan. 1900 (Enclosure: No. 538), TNA, CO 879/60/5.

[138] For more details on American and German protests, see: Coogan, *End of Neutrality*, 35–43.

[139] Foreign Office (Francis Bertie) to Colonial Office, 24 Feb. 1900 (No. 620), TNA, CO 879/60/5.

[140] High Commissioner Sir Alfred Milner to Mr Chamberlain (Telegram), 4 Mar. 1900 (No. 653A), TNA, CO 879/60/5; Foreign Office (Francis Bertie) to Colonial Office, 10 Mar. 1900 (No. 674), TNA, CO 879/60/5.

[141] Coogan, *End of Neutrality*, 30–43.

[142] Colonial Office (Fred. Graham) to Foreign Office, 21 Oct. 1899 (No. 29), TNA, CO 879/60/5; Foreign Office (Francis Bertie) to Colonial Office (Secret), 23 Oct. 1899 (No. 31), TNA, CO 879/60/5. See also Coogan, *End of Neutrality*, 37–43.

the readiest to break with existing practice. Chamberlain's role as Colonial Secretary was crucial, and Andrew Porter has highlighted how the relationship between Chamberlain and Lord Salisbury dominated the decision-making process.[143] Yet, the Law Officers restrained Milner's plans, which illustrates their influence on the government vis-à-vis pressure from men on the spot like him.

Arms and Ammunition

There was no doubt that arms and ammunition were to be treated as absolute contraband and were therefore subject to seizure in wartime. In 1870 Prussia accused Britain of un-neutral behaviour because of its delivery of arms and ammunition to France. Indeed, France depended on the import of arms and ammunition from various neutrals including Britain due to its own production shortages.[144] Yet, Britain had no intention of 'prevent[ing] the export or munitions of war to either belligerent'. The government was only obliged to warn its citizens 'of the risk of hostile capture, which they run if they engage in contraband adventures'.[145] After Count Bernstorff, the Prussian Ambassador in London, repeatedly intervened on this matter, the Home Office started an investigation into the truth of the allegations. However, police investigations were not able to substantiate the claims.[146] The Law Officers restated that Britain could not be forced to prohibit the export of arms and ammunition and that its position concurred with the existing practice in international law. Bernstorff demanded changes to international law as there was no 'benevolent neutrality and a neutrality which is not so. A nation is either belligerent or neutral.' Yet, Prussia had pursued the same practice as the British in the past, and, thus, the Law Officers concluded that 'the existing rules and former practice would be maintained'.[147] Only a small number of cases were reported in which British citizens were engaged in contraband trade, and their ships captured at sea

---

[143] Andrew Porter, 'Lord Salisbury, Mr. Chamberlain and South Africa, 1895–9', *The Journal of Imperial and Commonwealth History*, 1 (1972), 3–26.

[144] Michael Howard, *The Franco-Prussian War: The German Invasion of France, 1870–1871* (London, 1961; reprint London, 2000), 246–7.

[145] Law Officers Report, 25 July 1870 (No. 199), TNA, FO 834/9.

[146] Investigation of German Allegations regarding Export of Arms, Sept. 1870, TNA, HO 45/8444.

[147] Law Officers of the Crown (R. P. Collier, J. D. Coleridge, Travers Twiss) to Earl Granville, 5 Sept. 1870 (No. 206), TNA, FO 834/9.

by France or Prussia. In all cases the British government accepted French and Prussian prize court decisions.[148]

The export of arms and ammunition again became an issue during the Sino-French War of 1884–5, when France accused Britain of breaching neutrality by exporting arms and ammunition from neutral Hong Kong to mainland China. France declared this trade to be illegal and demanded Britain prohibit the export of arms.[149] The Law Officers' response stated the French had 'no right…to call upon a neutral Government to prevent the exportation of goods from its territory, on the ground that they may be used for belligerent purposes'. Moreover, the Law Officers remarked that 'the French nation would have had great ground of complaint if this country [Britain] had complied with the request of the German Government in 1870 to prohibit the exportation of arms and munitions of war from this [Britain] territory'.[150] The Governor of Hong Kong had the power under Ordinance No. 3 of 1862, the local adaptation of the Customs Consolidation Act, to independently prohibit the export of arms and ammunition, yet the British government could veto such a decision.

France's only way of stopping the arms trade between Hong Kong and China was to control the waterways by stopping and searching neutral ships destined for Hong Kong. Consequently, France announced on 10 February 1885 that it would exercise such belligerent rights as the right of search of neutral ships.[151] A short notice from the Foreign Office publicly announced the French government's intention and caused uproar among British insurers and shipowners, who were worried about the consequences for their business contracts.[152] Britain condemned the French decision, and the Law Officers argued that 'the geographical position of a neutral port cannot justify a belligerent Power in interfering with its trade'. At the same time, the Law Officers acknowledged France's belligerent rights to 'stop such trading by seizure, in the manner recognized by international law'.[153] However, the

---

[148]   Law Officers of the Crown (R. P. Collier, J. D. Coleridge, Travers Twiss) to Earl Granville, 30 Aug. 1870 (No. 65), TNA, FO 834/9.

[149]   Foreign Office to Colonial Office (Confidential), 5 Feb. 1885 (No. 48), TNA, FO 881/5163.

[150]   Law Officers of the Crown (Henry James, Farrer Herschell) and Dr Deane to Earl Granville, 18 Feb. 1885 (No. 66), TNA, FO 834/15.

[151]   Law Officers of the Crown (Henry James and Farrer Herschell) to Earl Granville, 10 Feb. 1885 (No. 65), TNA, FO 834/15.

[152]   'Foreign Office Note, February 11, 1885', The London Gazette, No. 25441, 13 Feb. 1885, 625; Law Officers of the Crown (Henry James and Farrer Herschell) and Dr Deane to Earl Granville, 20 Feb. 1885 (No. 67), TNA, FO 834/15.

[153]   Law Officers of the Crown (Henry James and Farrer Herschell) and Dr Deane to Earl Granville, 2 Apr. 1885 (No. 83), TNA, FO 834/15.

Lord Chancellor, Lord Selborne, disagreed with the Law Officers' opinion. He acknowledged that 'in strict international law the Law Officers are undoubtedly right, but by our [British] own statute law we have, I conceive, the power to prohibit the exportation of arms, &c., from Hong Kong, and the strong inclination of my own opinion is that it would be the safer and wiser policy *to exercise that power* under the peculiar circumstances and situation of Hong Kong'. He feared that, if Britain insisted on its rights as a neutral, it could end up in a situation similar to that of the American Civil War when it had to pay compensation for un-neutral behaviour. Selborne argued that 'this seems...to be a question, not of international law, but of policy'. To underline his argument, Lord Selborne referred to Lord Stowell, the most famous British prize court judge during the Napoleonic Wars, who had looked 'beyond' the immediate facts and had made decisions based on broader principles.[154] The Law Officers admitted that the question before them was one 'of policy rather than of law'. Their views were based on a meeting of the Cabinet, in which its members were primarily concerned with Britain's economic interests in the region. Accordingly, they formulated a legal opinion, highlighting Britain's consistent practice with regard to the export of arms and ammunition in previous conflicts, for example during the Franco-Prussian War. They said that 'the restriction should only be imposed when, in our own interests, we desired to retain the arms in this country, and not because we wished to prevent their reaching the belligerent State'.[155] Selborne responded that although the Customs Consolidation Act was primarily an instrument of 'our own defence', its use should be considered in this particular case because the trade between Hong Kong and China was only established as a result of the conflict and so could be seen as unlawful. Before the dispute could reach a new level, the Sino-French War came to an end. The matter was adjourned and no further action was taken.[156] The interference of the Lord Chancellor in the matter of contraband trade was a sign that the independent judgement of the Law Officers was at stake. Yet it remained an open question whether this delicate issue should be left to politics alone.

---

[154] Note by the Lord Chancellor (Lord Selborne), 8 Apr. 1885 (No. 86), TNA, FO 834/15.

[155] Law Officers of the Crown (Henry James and Farrer Herschell) and Dr Deane to Earl Granville, 16 Apr. 1885 (No. 87), TNA, FO 834/15.

[156] Memorandum by the Lord Chancellor (Lord Selborne), 1 May 1885 (No. 92), TNA, FO 834/15.

Destruction of Neutral Ships

At the beginning of the twentieth century, the destruction of neutral ships became a new phenomenon in war at sea. According to long-standing practice in international law the destruction of a prize was only allowed in special circumstances. Customs obliged belligerents to bring prizes into a port for a proper prize court procedure, which judged the lawfulness of the prize. However, the Russo-Japanese War marked a departure from this practice. Immediately after its outbreak in February 1904, Russian warships seized numerous British merchant ships and, in many cases, sunk them. A list compiled by T. V. S. Angier illustrating the dramatic increase in the destruction of neutral property was brought to the attention of the Foreign Office.[157]

The destruction of the British merchant ship *Knight Commander* by the Vladivostok squadron in July 1904 became one of the most prominent cases. The British government said the Russian measure was 'unjustified by any accepted principles of international law'. The Russian commander of the ship explained that the *Knight Commander* was seized and sunk because it had been carrying coal, which Russia had declared absolute contraband. The Foreign Secretary, the Marquess of Lansdowne, argued that the destruction of the ship was against Russian prize laws and that, accordingly, a prize court trial was 'the maximum penalty' that could be expected. As the neutral ship had been sunk and all evidence destroyed, no prize court could verify the lawfulness of the prize.[158] Lansdowne further argued that coal should not be treated as absolute contraband, and so the incident constituted an 'unprecedented extension of the doctrine of contraband of war' putting 'the greater part, if not the whole, of the large trade now carried on between Great Britain and the Far East' in danger.[159] Lansdowne's fears of the destruction of neutral property were justified.

The case of the *Knight Commander* alarmed British merchants and the stock market in London reacted swiftly to the new dangers to which British

---

[157] List compiled by T. V. S. Angier of British Steamers Seized, Sunk, Boarded, and Papers Overhauled, or Stopped and Delayed by Russian Cruisers since February 1904, Sept. 1904 (No. 721), TNA, FO 881/8433. See also Sakuyé Takahashi, *International Law Applied to the Russo-Japanese War. With the Decisions of the Japanese Prize Courts* (New York, 1908).

[158] The Marquess of Lansdowne to Sir C. Hardinge, 10 Aug. 1904 (No. 377), TNA, FO 881/8433.

[159] The Marquess of Lansdowne to Sir C. Hardinge, 10 Aug. 1904 (No. 377), TNA, FO 881/8433.

merchants were exposed.[160] The China Association, for instance, complained to the Foreign Office that the current situation 'paralysed' the trade to the Far East, and they criticized the Russian contraband list for its 'most sweeping nature'. The association also pointed out that German- and French-owned ships were less of a target, and thus cargo owners would choose them over British ships for their business in the Far East.[161] There were, however, no exact figures available to verify the claims. The London Chamber of Commerce urged the Foreign Secretary to respond as 'the continuance of the present situation causes irreparable damage to the whole course of Eastern trade'. It demanded the introduction of counter-measures in order 'to place British commerce on the same footing as that of other non-belligerent countries in the treatment of so-called "contraband of war"'.[162] The British Ambassador to Russia, Sir Charles Hardinge, spoke with the Russian Foreign Minister, Count Vladimir Lamsdorff on 27 August 1904, presenting evidence that Russia 'discriminated' against British trade as opposed to French and German. Lamsdorff denied the allegations but promised an inquiry. Hardinge also demanded that the definition of contraband be clarified, not least because of 'the danger of an excited public opinion in England'. A solution, though, would take time. For instance, Hardinge remarked that 'everything in this country [Russia] moves so slowly that I fear some little patience will be required'.[163]

Meanwhile, the Admiralty and the Foreign Office worked on a British proposal. At a meeting at the Admiralty on 6 September 1904, Lord Walter Kerr, Vice-Admiral Sir C. Drury, the Assistant Hydrographer, Mr C. I. Thomas, and Captain Nicholson from the Admiralty discussed the idea of a 'zone outside which neutral vessels should be exempt from stoppage and search for contraband'. In other words, they considered a restriction of

---

[160] For more details, see Gabriela A. Frei, 'How to Wage Economic Warfare in a Globalised Economy? International Jurisdiction between State and Private Interests, 1880–1914', under peer-review.

[161] China Association (Joseph Welch) to Foreign Office, 11 Aug. 1904 (No. 396), TNA, FO 881/8433. The number of cases reported involving French and German ships were much lower than that of British ships: see List compiled by T. V. S. Angier of British Steamers Seized, Sunk, Boarded, and Papers Overhauled, or Stopped and Delayed by Russian Cruisers since February 1904, Sept. 1904 (No. 721), TNA, FO 881/8433.

[162] The London Chamber of Commerce to the Marquess of Lansdowne, 25 Aug. 1904 (No. 497), TNA, FO 881/8433.

[163] Sir C. Hardinge to the Marquess of Lansdowne (Telegraphic), 27 Aug. 1904 (No. 580), TNA, FO 881/8433.

belligerent rights.[164] A memorandum revealed that the Admiralty had installed such a zone during the Boer War: ships could only be stopped and searched within a radius of 3,000 nautical miles from Delagoa Bay. The main reason for the restriction of the right of search and capture was to avoid upsetting neutrals in face of the difficulty of verifying the 'real destination' of goods. Yet, the situation in South Africa differed considerably from that in the Russo-Japanese War. The Russian Navy was operating far from its home ports, and the Japanese would certainly take advantage of the restriction. Given that the theatre of war had already significantly limited the radius of operation for the Russian fleet, any further restriction would hardly be acceptable. After all, the British practice during the Boer War was self-imposed and the Royal Navy did not face a naval enemy.[165] W. Maycock from the Foreign Office admitted that 'British Naval Regulations distinctly lay down that visit, search, and detention may be exercised *anywhere* on the high seas, and Russia would assuredly cite these if we asked them to restrict the area'.[166] After prolonged discussions, the idea of a neutral zone was dropped because the British government feared that it would have a negative impact on Britain in a future maritime conflict. The specific measure during the Boer War was not supposed to serve as a precedent or even become a principle in international law.[167] Discussion about neutral zones shows that Britain seriously considered limiting the right of search and capture for belligerents only in order to avoid antagonizing neutrals.

A list compiled by T. V. S. Angier, which he presented to Prime Minister Balfour on 5 September 1904, showed the scale of Russian naval operations against neutral trade. Particularly striking was the number of British ships seized, detained, or sunk in the period between February and August 1904. Although the list was not complete, the Foreign Office used it to demonstrate the extent to which Russia 'discriminated' against British trade.[168] Ultimately, it was the question of contraband that needed to be settled, as this had been the main reason for the seizure of British

[164] Memorandum by F. A. Campbell (FO) on the Need of a Neutral Zone, 6 Sept. 1904 (No. 687), TNA, FO 881/8433.

[165] Admiralty (C. I. Thomas) to Foreign Office (Confidential), 7 Sept. 1904 (No. 700), TNA, FO 881/8433.

[166] Minute by W. Maycock (FO), 7 Sept. 1904 (No. 700), TNA, FO 881/8433.

[167] B. J. C. McKercher, 'Diplomatic Equipoise: The Lansdowne Foreign Office, the Russo-Japanese War of 1904–1905, and the Global Balance of Power', *Canadian Journal of History/ Annales Canadiennes d'Histoire*, 24 (1989), 299–339, in particular, see 324.

[168] List compiled by T. V. S. Angier of British Steamers Seized, Sunk, Boarded, and Papers Overhauled, or Stopped and Delayed by Russian Cruisers since February 1904, Sept. 1904 (No. 721), TNA, FO 881/8433.

ships. Internal Russian discussions on the topic dragged on, as a confidential source informed the British Ambassador to Russia, Hardinge.[169] After prolonged Russian deliberations, Lamsdorff informed Hardinge of the altered contraband regulations. Foodstuffs were no longer considered absolute contraband in the new Russian instructions. This did not mean that vessels carrying those goods were exempt from seizure but rather that a prize court would decide whether they were considered contraband or not. In the Foreign Office, Maycock did not think that the new Russian instructions went far enough, but his colleague Campbell and the Foreign Secretary, Lansdowne, were satisfied.[170] Maycock's main concern was that 'food-stuffs are only to be considered contraband if intended for the enemy's *fighting forces* as distinguished from the *enemy's country*'. The wording changed the existing practice as it was usually not enough that goods were destined for an 'enemy country'.[171] Cecil J. B. Hurst, the legal adviser to the Foreign Office, concurred with Maycock in principle but was supportive of the new Russian regulations. The Attorney-General, R. B. Finlay, finally approved the Russian regulations and wrote that it was 'a great step in advance, and relates to a point of vital importance to this country'.[172] He particularly highlighted that Russia had agreed that the captor was responsible for providing evidence, which was a key argument in getting the British to accept the new regulations.

While the Russians no longer considered foodstuffs as absolute contraband, coal and cotton were still on the list, and thus the protests of neutrals, in particular Britain and the United States, continued. The Attorney-General supported the British government's protest concerning coal and cotton, but said it was 'of great value' that foodstuffs were no longer on the list.[173] Britain's perseverance in the matter on foodstuffs was a success for British

---

[169] Sir C. Hardinge to the Marquess of Lansdowne (Very Confidential) (Telegraphic), 7 Sept. 1904 (No. 703), TNA, FO 881/8433.

[170] Sir C. Hardinge to the Marquess of Lansdowne (Telegraphic), 16 Sept. 1904 (No. 800), TNA, FO 881/8433; Minute by W. Maycock, 16 Sept. 1904 (No. 800), TNA, FO 881/8433; Minute by F. A. Campbell, 17 Sept. 1904 (No. 800), TNA, FO 881/8433; Minute by Lansdowne, 19 Sept. 1904 (No. 800), TNA, FO 881/8433.

[171] Minute by W. Maycock, 16 Sept. 1904 (No. 800), TNA, FO 881/8433.

[172] The Attorney-General (R. B. Finlay) to the Foreign Office, 22 Sept. 1904 (No. 21), TNA, FO 834/21.

[173] The Marquess of Lansdowne to Sir C. Hardinge, 30 Sept. 1904 (No. 903), TNA, FO 881/8433; Sir C. Hardinge to the Marquess of Lansdowne, 9 Sept. 1904 (No. 723), TNA, FO 881/8433; Sir C. Hardinge to the Marquess of Lansdowne, 21 Sept. 1904 (No. 855), TNA, FO 881/8433; Memorandum by the Attorney-General (R. B. Finlay), 23 Sept. 1904 (No. 856), TNA, FO 881/8433.

diplomacy but the discussion also illustrated the limitations confronting a neutral power, regardless of its standing as a major or minor sea power. For instance, Britain could not demand that a belligerent relinquish parts of its belligerent rights, not least because it feared creating a precedent that might be used against Britain. The destruction of neutral property was a clear breach of customary international law and would become one of the major points of contention at the Hague peace conference in 1907.

Britain's Experience of Neutrality

Between 1856 and 1885 Britain turned from a sceptic to an advocate of neutrality. While parts of the British political elite had seen the country's neutrality policy as a constraint on Britain's capabilities as a sea power, they soon recognized it as an effective instrument to protect Britain's global economic interests, to pressure belligerent powers, to force them to limit their own rights and respect neutral rights. No other power had ever been so successful in negotiating neutral rights as Britain. Britain's diplomatic success in negotiating the law of neutrality with belligerents was based on its predominant economic and strategic position as a sea power. No other power in the world possessed a near monopoly of the world's highest quality steam coal, had more coaling stations, and was the world's largest carrier of commodities. All these factors strengthened Britain's position and gave its neutrality policy clout, a fact which belligerents could not easily ignore.

The cases discussed in this chapter show that, although British businesses had to comply with the provisions of the Foreign Enlistment Act, the British government was careful not to restrain businesses too much. Rather, it used the law of neutrality as an instrument to protect and defend British economic interests. For instance, it successfully negotiated the internationally accepted terms under which neutrals could continue trading with belligerents. Britain also put pressure on belligerents if they disregarded the law of neutrality or the principles of international law, for example when Russia declared coal to be absolute contraband. At the same time, Britain as a belligerent limited the radius of operation of its naval forces.

British state practice considerably strengthened the concept of neutrality both domestically and internationally. Domestically, the revision of the Foreign Enlistment Act in 1870 and its subsequent application in various conflicts demonstrated Britain's willingness to enforce its neutrality policy, even if it affected British businesses. It is notable that no other state had such a stringent domestic neutrality policy in place. The domestic legislation was effective in controlling British citizens and their businesses, even though the British government never prosecuted a British citizen under the Foreign Enlistment Act. Internationally, the principles laid out in the Declaration of Paris of 1856 were put into practice. Britain became an advocate of the principle of 'free ship, free good', to which it had objected for such a long time prior to 1856. Now, the provisions were repeatedly quoted in government documents concerned with the protection of neutral trade. Despite the initial scepticism with regard to the Declaration of Paris, British practice ultimately affirmed its principles throughout the period prior to the First World War. Although Tenterden's hopes in 1868 that the Foreign Enlistment Act would serve as an example for other states were not fulfilled, other states increasingly respected Britain's legislation.[174]

The formulation and execution of Britain's neutrality policy was foremost a Foreign Office responsibility. On the one hand, it communicated with foreign powers about Britain's neutrality status and negotiated in cases of dispute, and on the other, it was also chiefly responsible for enforcing neutrality within Britain's jurisdiction. The revision of the Foreign Enlistment Act in the late 1860s laid the legal basis for Britain's neutrality policy, and allowed the Foreign Office to intervene in any private business if it infringed its provisions. Crucial for the enforcement of the domestic legislation were the many port authorities and customs officials, who collected information and who even had the power to act on behalf of the Foreign Office in suspicious circumstances. The cases discussed in this chapter illustrate that the Foreign Office increasingly gained control over British businesses, and demonstrate how closely it was in contact with them.

The Foreign Office's control also expanded to overseas colonies. The examples of Hong Kong and the Cape Colony, although they were formally under the control of the Colonial Office in matters of neutrality, show that the Foreign Office was primarily responsible for their decision-making. The Foreign Office depended on information from the Colonial Office, which was much better informed about local conditions. The colonial and port authorities, as well as the customs officials around the world, acted as informants and executed Foreign Office decisions. The commanders-in-chief of the overseas stations provided further information, in particular regarding the activities and whereabouts of merchant ships and warships. Although

---

[174] Memorandum by Lord Tenterden on the Analysis of the Report of the Neutrality Laws Commission (Confidential), 10 June 1868, TNA, FO 881/1629.

the commanders often reported to the Admiralty first, decisions were made in the Foreign Office. While the Foreign Office was in charge of the execution of Britain's neutrality policy, the overlapping competences of different branches of government, such as the Admiralty, the Colonial Office, or the Home Office, often led to contradictory information being communicated between the different actors. Confusion often occurred at the outbreak of a conflict, but soon declined once the Foreign Office had gained full control. The Law Officers clarified the competences as early as June 1877, and Lord Tenterden, Permanent Under-Secretary to the Foreign Office, highlighted that all public servants were obliged to cooperate and share information. Another important source of information was Lloyd's of London. As an underwriter, Lloyd's was well informed about global political and business developments. Naturally, it maintained close relations with the Foreign Office and the Admiralty in order to calculate the risks in which it was involved. At the same time, the Foreign Office and the Admiralty profited from this relationship by gaining invaluable information about ships' cargoes and destinations as well as about the concerns of the British insurance market.[175]

Legal advisers to the Foreign Office were crucial in shaping Britain's neutrality policy, and became increasingly important for the British government and its administration in the latter half of the nineteenth century. The Foreign Office had no designated legal department. Julian Pauncefote joined the Foreign Office in 1876 as Legal Assistant Under-Secretary. In 1886, W. Edward Davidson was first appointed as Pauncefote's assistant, and later as legal adviser, and in 1902, Cecil J. B. Hurst joined as the second legal adviser to deal with the increasing demand of legal business in the Foreign Office.[176] The cases discussed in this chapter illustrate how legal advice worked in the Foreign Office. It was principally the legal advisers to the Foreign Office who dealt with legal matters, but experts from the political departments were also involved in the process. The recent literature on the legal advisers describes their principal task as drafting legal documents, but neglects the

---

[175] Lloyd's Act, 1871, 34 VICT.– Ch. xxi. See also Charles Wright and C. Ernest Fayle, *A History of Lloyd's from the Founding of Lloyd's Coffee House to the Present Day* (London, 1928), 378–91.

[176] Gabriela A. Frei, 'Legal Advisers, the Foreign Office and Britain's Neutrality Policy, 1870–1914', in Marcus Payk and Kim Christian Priemel (eds), *Jurists in International Politics: Practice and Practitioners of International Law in the Nineteenth and Twentieth Centuries* (Oxford, forthcoming). See also William Malkin, 'International Law in Practice', *The Law Quarterly Review*, 49 (1933), 489–510.

importance of the Law Officers of the Crown in advising the Foreign Office, whose legal advice was crucial in shaping Britain's neutrality policy.[177]

The Law Officers of the Crown, consisting of the Attorney-General and the Solicitor-General, as well as the Queen's Advocate until 1872, after that replaced by James Parker Deane, the Admiralty Advocate, took all principal decisions regarding Britain's neutrality policy.[178] Usually, the Foreign Office sent all relevant papers to the Law Officers, including a description of the situation and a list of questions. This formed the basis upon which the Law Officers made their decision and wrote a report containing their legal advice. While the report was directly addressed to the Foreign Secretary, the legal adviser as well as other civil servants in the Foreign Office commented on the advice. The extensive correspondence (sometimes several times a day) between the Law Officers and the Foreign Office suggests that they worked together closely. In particular, the legal adviser to the Foreign Office liaised with the Law Officers, who mostly wrote the reports from the Royal Courts of Justice or the Inns of Court. While the Foreign Office prepared the papers and drafted instructions, the Law Officers also checked them. So, the Law Officers were involved in the whole process from the initial decision-making to the final approval of the formulation of the legal instructions and telegrams, which the Foreign Office then sent to other authorities.[179]

The Law Officers' integrity was based on their independence. Yet, as they were working in the field of international law, they could not entirely separate their legal advice from the broader political context. An incident in 1885, when the Law Officers defended the export of arms and ammunition from Hong Kong to China due to interests voiced in Cabinet is a case in point. Despite occasional transgressions, the Law Officers were aware of the delicate nature of their task and usually made it clear when, in their opinion, a question from the Foreign Office crossed the line from law into politics. Their reference to precedents as well as their interpretation of existing laws and practices were central to their legal advice. However, if

---

[177] Kate Jones, 'Marking Foreign Policy by Justice: The Legal Advisers to the Foreign Office, 1876–1953', in Robert McCorquodale and Jean-Pierre Gauci (eds) *British Influences on International Law, 1915–2015* (Leiden, 2016), 28–55; Ronald St. John MacDonald, *The Role of the Legal Adviser of Ministries of Foreign Affairs (Collected Courses of the Hague Academy of International Law, 156)* (Leiden, 1977), 444–9.

[178] John Ll. J. Edwards, *The Law Officers of the Crown: A Study of the Offices of Attorney-General and Solicitor-General of England, with an Account of the Office of the Director of Public Prosecutions of England* (London, 1964).

[179] Ray Jones, *The Nineteenth-Century Foreign Office: An Administrative History* (London, 1971), 65–83; Zara S. Steiner, *The Foreign Office and Foreign Policy, 1898–1914* (Cambridge, 1969).

the matter in question suggested a change in state practice (as happened after the outbreak of the Boer War when the government considered putting foodstuffs on the contraband list), the Law Officers made the government aware of previous practice and the possible implications of such a decision. As such decisions would have to find political support, the Law Officers abstained from giving any concrete legal advice. The Law Officers' main responsibility was to take a broader view instead of narrowly justifying political viewpoints. The Law Officers were aware of the limitations of their legal advice, and drew a clear boundary between giving legal advice and engaging in political decision-making.

In politically delicate matters, the Foreign Office also involved the Lord Chancellor, responsible for the independence of the judiciary. The Lord Chancellor intervened on an ad hoc basis in cases where decisions concerned national security, or when the advice of the Law Officers did not command unanimity. While the Law Officers often tried to distinguish between legal and political advice, the Lord Chancellor always brought the two together. Discussions following interventions by the Lord Chancellor show that the legal advisers were generally well aware of the political significance of their advice, particularly regarding the question of neutrality, where strategic and economic implications were at stake. Most prominently, the Lord Chancellor intervened in the question of foodstuffs as contraband. No other issue attracted so much attention, not least because it brought to light the differences between major and minor sea powers.

The Foreign Enlistment Act became the primary instrument for the British government to implement its neutrality policy. In the 1870s and 1880s, it did not always do so consistently as the act could only be applied after Britain had declared its neutrality in a conflict. Sometimes the Law Officers modified the conditions under which the act could be applied, as the example of the Sino-French War illustrates. From the 1890s onwards, the Foreign Enlistment Act proved to be a robust and flexible tool, which the Foreign Office used to defend Britain's neutrality policy, and the Law Officers reaffirmed the importance of the act in their legal advice. Whether the act was in fact an effective tool can be disputed. With the support of the Law Officers, the Foreign Office opened many investigations on behalf of the Crown, and yet none of the accused was ever prosecuted under the Foreign Enlistment Act. This may be interpreted as a weakness of the act, but it could also be argued that the act served as a deterrent for British citizens and as a reference point for foreign powers, and in that sense, was a successful instrument of British foreign policy.

The Russo-Japanese War marked a turning point for the modus operandi between belligerents and neutrals in war at sea. The sinking of neutral merchant ships became a symbol of the departure from established practices in the laws of naval warfare. Legal conflicts resurfaced after tensions had reached a new level in international diplomacy. Issues such as neutrality, the right of search and capture, the contraband issue, the doctrine of continuous voyage, and blockade needed to be readdressed in the light of modern warfare.

These developments challenged British practices and strained more generally the relationship between neutrals and belligerents. On the one hand, belligerents used their belligerent rights excessively, by expanding the contraband list or sinking neutral merchant ships. On the other hand, neutral powers, which were not bound by domestic legislation, undermined Britain's neutrality policy by continuing to trade with belligerents. For instance, Germany built and sold warships to Russia, while the Foreign Enlistment Act prohibited British shipbuilders from doing the same. France allowed Russian warships to coal and take supplies on board, and so enabled a belligerent to use neutral waters as a base for military operations. In many ways, neutral states continuously undermined the law of neutrality. When Lord Selborne, First Lord of the Admiralty, assessed the latest developments in war at sea, he feared the damaging effect of un-neutral behaviour by other neutrals as well as of the unscrupulous use of belligerent rights. The new century demanded new solutions to each of these questions—solutions that would have considerable impact on future maritime conflicts.[180]

---

[180] Memorandum by Lord Selborne on the Consequences of the Regulations Published by Russia and Japan, 1 June 1904 (No. 701), TNA, FO 881/8404. For a discussion on neutrality, see Memorandum by W. Maycock (FO), 31 Dec. 1904 (No. 518), TNA, FO 881/8512.

4

The Codification of International Maritime Law

At the beginning of the twentieth century politicians, strategists, and international lawyers increasingly dealt with legal questions as part of war-planning and strategic decision-making. The Russo-Japanese War showed that conflicts between neutrals and belligerents had become a highly polit-ical affair, and in many cases the Law Officers urged British politicians to seek a political solution to legal conflicts. Britain was concerned about recent developments in international maritime law and pressure grew from the international community to find a mutually acceptable agreement. The time was ripe to advance the process of the codification of international law for application in future wars. In 1856, the Declaration of Paris had been a first step towards regulating the conflicting interests between neutrals and belligerents at sea, and in limiting naval warfare. This chapter focuses on the period prior to the Hague peace conferences of 1899 and 1907, examining challenges which codification met in this period. The chapter also provides an insight into the interaction of law and politics, focusing on the state as a key actor in shaping the process of codification, and explaining Britain's scepticism towards it. The chapter also addresses the important role of non-governmental organizations, such as the Institut de droit international.

In the nineteenth century, international law was primarily based on customs and treaties. Yet, an increasingly interconnected world needed common rules to govern the international sphere, and thus the codification of international law offered new opportunities. Also influential was the emergence of international law as a discipline.[1] In 1925 Elihu Root, a

---

[1] Martti Koskenniemi, *The Gentle Civilizer of Nations: The Rise and Fall of International Law 1870–1960 (Hersch Lauterpacht Memorial Lectures)* (Cambridge, 2001), 11–97; Luigi Nuzzo and Miloš Vec (eds), *Constructing International Law: The Birth of a Discipline* (Frankfurt/Main, 2012); Ernest Nys, 'Codification et Consolidation', *Revue de droit international et de législation comparée*, 6 (1904), 198–212; Elihu Root, 'The Codification of International Law', *The American Journal of International Law* 19, 4 (1925), 675–84; Verena Ritter-Döring, *Zwischen Normierung und Rüstungswettlauf. Die Entwicklung des Seekriegsrechts, 1856–1914* (Baden-Baden, 2014);

Great Britain, International Law, and the Evolution of Maritime Strategic Thought, 1856–1914. Gabriela A. Frei, Oxford University Press (2020). © Gabriela A. Frei.
DOI: 10.1093/oso/9780198859932.001.0001

prominent US international lawyer, reflected on the process of the codification of international law prior to 1914, arguing that 'we have gradually come into a method of making international law quite different from the slow general acceptance of the rules adopted in particular concrete cases, by which the law was originally created'. He went on that 'the changes in the conditions of civilized life during the past century have been so extensive and so much more rapid than the growth of international law in the old way, that the law has been falling behind and becoming continually less adequate to cover the field of international contacts'.[2]

Governmental Action and the Brussels Declaration

The United States spearheaded the codification of international law in the nineteenth century. Most prominently, US President Abraham Lincoln issued *General Orders No. 100 Instructions for the Government of Armies of the United States in the Field*, also known as the Lieber Code, in 1863. The instructions for the army described the existing customs of war and dealt with issues like the status of prisoners of war, the treatment of the public and private property of the enemy, the status of deserters, hostages, partisans, and spies.[3] Shortly after, in 1864, the International Committee of the Red Cross drafted the Geneva Convention, which concerned the wounded in the field. Both documents regulated the use of force and, thus, limited land warfare by protecting civilians and the wounded. These documents continue to influence the process of codifying the laws of war to this day.[4]

Daniel Marc Segesser, *Recht statt Rache oder Rache durch Recht? Die Ahndung von Kriegsverbrechen in der internationalen wissenschaftlichen Debatte 1872–1945* (Paderborn, 2010), 76–102.

[2] Root, 'Codification', 681–2.
[3] 'Instructions for the Government of Armies of the United States in the Field, 24 April 1863 (Lieber Code)', in Dietrich Schindler and Jiří Toman (eds.), *The Laws of Armed Conflicts. A Collection of Conventions, Resolutions and other Documents*, (Dordrecht, 2004), 3–20. See also John Fabian Witt, *Lincoln's Code: The Laws of War in American History* (New York, 2013).
[4] Geoffrey Best, *Humanity in Warfare: The Modern History of the International Law of Armed Conflicts* (London, 1980), 155–6; James F. Childress, 'Francis Lieber's Interpretation of the Laws of the War: General Orders No. 100 in the Context of his Life and Thought', *American Journal of Jurisprudence*, 21 (1976), 34–70; Theodor Meron, 'Francis Lieber's Code and Principles of Humanity', *Columbia Journal of Transnational Law*, 36 (1998), 269–82.

In April 1874, after the Franco-Prussian War, the president of the Société pour l'Amélioration du Sort des Prisonniers de Guerre (Society for the Improvement of the Condition of Prisoners of War), Comte de Houdetot, suggested an international conference to be held in Paris to deal with the question of prisoners of war.[5] Only a few days later, the Russian government proposed a similar project but with a much broader scope, namely 'of determining the laws and usages of warfare'. The aim of the conference was, according to the Russian invitation, 'to establish by common accord, upon a basis of complete reciprocity, rules which may be made binding on all Governments and their armies'.[6] Given the broad scope of the Russian project, the Society for the Improvement of the Condition of Prisoners of War withdrew their initial proposal, and was not in fact even invited to the conference in Brussels.[7] Britain reluctantly accepted the Russian invitation but made clear that 'Her Majesty's Government are not convinced of the practical necessity of such a scheme'. At the same time, the British government also stated that Britain would only attend under the condition that 'naval matters' were not discussed, and sought the reassurance of all participating states to that effect.[8] Public opinion in Britain was opposed to the conference, and international affairs clubs and societies from all over the country sent petitions to the Queen urging her to abstain from the conference because they feared a further limitation of belligerent rights. The petitioners even went a step further and demanded Britain's withdrawal from the Declaration of Paris of 1856.[9] In light of the situation, the Foreign Secretary, the Earl of Derby, instructed the delegates at the Brussels conference 'not to

---

[5] 'Lord Lyons to the Earl of Derby, 11 Apr. 1874 (No. 1)', in P.P. Misc. 1 (1874): Correspondence Respecting the Proposed Conference at Brussels on the Rules of Military Warfare, [C. 1010].

[6] 'Prince Gortchakow to Count Brunnow (communicated to the Early of Derby), 17 Apr. 1874 (No. 7)', in P.P. Misc. 1 (1874): Correspondence Respecting the Proposed Conference at Brussels on the Rules of Military Warfare, [C. 1010].

[7] 'The Universal Alliance, London Branch (Henry Dunant) to the Earl of Derby, 16 May 1874 (No. 12)', in P.P. Misc. 1 (1874): Correspondence Respecting the Proposed Conference at Brussels on the Rules of Military Warfare, [C. 1010]; 'Conférence de Bruxelles-Historique', *Revue de droit international et de législation comparée*, 7 (1875), 86–92. See also Tracey L. Dowdeswell, 'The Brussels Peace Conference of 1874 and the Modern Laws of Belligerent Qualification', Special Issue: Law, Authority and History: A Tribute to Douglas Hay. *Osgoode Hall Law Journal*, 54, 3 (2017), 805–850, here: 827.

[8] 'The Earl of Derby to Lord A. Loftus (British Ambassador to Russia), 4 July 1874 (No. 28)', in P.P. Misc. 1 (1874): Correspondence Respecting the Proposed Conference at Brussels on the Rules of Military Warfare, [C. 1010]; 'The Earl of Derby to Her Majesty's Representatives in Countries invited to take part in the Brussels Conference, 4 July 1874 (No. 29)', in P.P. Misc. 1 (1874): Correspondence Respecting the Proposed Conference at Brussels on the Rules of Military Warfare, [C. 1010].

[9] Petitions against the Declaration of Paris, 1874–75, TNA, HO 45/9363.

enter into any discussion of the rules of international law by which the relations of belligerents are guided, or to undertake any new obligations or engagements of any kind in regard to general principles'.[10] He further stated that, 'it will be your duty to guard carefully against being led, in the course of deliberations on other matters, into any discussions which may, however remotely, affect the subject of maritime warfare which Her Majesty's Government have thus agreed with other Governments should be formally excluded'.[11] The instructions demonstrated Britain's hesitant position towards the project as a whole, and limited the scope of the discussions. Nevertheless, the conference programme addressed major issues concerning the laws of war, such as the status of prisoners of war, the recognition of combatants, spies, sieges and bombardments, and the treatment of the sick and wounded.[12] The participants signed the Final Protocol on 27 August 1874.[13] In the aftermath of the conference, the Russian government wanted the participants to agree to a binding convention based on the declaration but no state was willing to commit to it. Derby told the British ambassador in Russia, Lord Loftus, that the British government had 'to repudiate...any project for altering the principles of international law upon which this country [Britain] has hitherto acted'.[14] Thus, the conference failed in its mission to produce an authoritative text of existing customary law.

The Chichele Professor of International Law and Diplomacy at All Souls College, Oxford, Thomas E. Holland, remarked that 'the time was not yet ripe for the codification of the laws and usages of war'.[15] In Holland's opinion, the conference failed because it tried to achieve too much, instead of just focusing on the status of prisoners of war. Only the United States had issued clear instructions as to the laws governing the conduct of war.

---

[10] 'The Earl of Derby to Sir A. Horsford, 25 July 1874 (No. 1)', in P.P. Misc. 1 (1875): Correspondence Respecting the Brussels Conference on the Rules of Military Warfare, [Cd. 1128].
[11] 'The Earl of Derby to Sir A. Horsford, 25 July 1874 (No. 1)', in P.P. Misc. 1 (1875): Correspondence Respecting the Brussels Conference on the Rules of Military Warfare, [Cd. 1128].
[12] See correspondence in P.P. Misc. 1 (1875): Correspondence Respecting the Brussels Conference on the Rules of Military Warfare, [Cd. 1128]. For an overview, see Dowdeswell, 'The Brussels Peace Conference', 824–41.
[13] Correspondence of Brussels Conference. Military Warfare. Opinions of Foreign Powers, 1874–75, TNA, FO 881/2579; 'Project of an International Declaration concerning the Laws and Customs of War. Brussels, 27 August 1874', in Dietrich Schindler and Jiří Toman (eds.), The Laws of Armed Conflicts: A Collection of Conventions, Resolutions and other Documents (Dordrecht, 2004), 25–8.
[14] The Earl of Derby to Lord A. Loftus, 20 Jan. 1875 (No. 20), TNA, FO 881/2579.
[15] Thomas E. Holland, Brussels Conference of 1874, and other Diplomatic Attempts to Mitigate the Rigour of Warfare, Delivered at All Souls College, May 10, 1876 (Oxford, 1876), 22.

Holland therefore demanded that states should first prepare a similar code to that issued by the United States, and introduce these instructions into officers' education before attempting to codify the laws of war on an international platform.[16]

More generally, Holland reflected on the importance of codification for the continental school of law arguing that 'the English mind, by nature averse to definition and careless of method, is in danger of treating as pedantic what on the other side of the Channel is the universally accepted mode of discussion. We do not sufficiently consider that the statesmen and jurists of the rest of Europe are accustomed to live under codes, are fond of abstract statements, and employ, as a matter of course, a terminology adopted from Roman law, which is convenient because at once precise and generally intelligible.'[17] Holland's appreciation for the continental school was a critique of the British attitude. From the outset, the British government had expressed its doubts as to the Russian project. It avoided entering any discussions on the codification of international law until the turn of the century. In the interim other actors shaped the discussion.

Non-Governmental Action and the Process of Codification

Due to a lack of political will, non-governmental organizations such as the American Peace Society or the British Association for the Promotion of Social Science advanced the process of codification.[18] The American jurist, David Dudley Field of New York, an early proponent of the codification of international law, suggested in a talk in 1866 that a committee of jurists from different countries prepare an 'international code'. Their work would be important 'in promoting beneficial intercourse, protecting individual rights, settling disputes and [would] lessen the chances of war'.[19] Field believed that the sort of code he had in mind was 'capable of binding all

---

[16] Holland, *Brussels Conference of 1874*. See also Thomas E. Holland, *Studies in International Law* (Oxford, 1898), 77.

[17] Holland, *Brussels Conference of 1874*, 23.

[18] Ernest Nys, 'The Codification of International Law', *American Journal of International Law*, 5, 4 (1911), 885–6. See also Ramaa Prasad Dhokalia, *The Codification of Public International Law* (Manchester, 1970), 37–75.

[19] David Dudley Field, 'First Project of an International Code', in A. P. Sprague (ed.), *Speeches, Arguments, and Miscellaneous Papers of David Dudley Field*, 2 vols (New York, 1884), vol. 1, 394.

nations and all races' together. It was 'a uniform system of rules for the guidance of nations and their citizens'. Above all, he argued that the code 'will prove a gentle but all-constraining bond of nations, self-imposed, and binding them together to abstain from war, except in the last extremity, and in peace to help each other, making the weak strong and the strong just'.[20] These ideals guided Dudley's work, which resulted in the 1872 publication of *Draft Outlines of an International Code*, describing the laws of peace. A second volume appeared in 1876 which concerned the laws of war.[21] The work was intended to initiate a much broader discussion on codification with colleagues from around the world. Other international jurists, among them the Swiss Johann Caspar Bluntschli, had published similar works, and endorsed Dudley's plea.[22]

The Institut de Droit International

The various codification projects brought forward by peace societies, organizations for the advancement of social sciences, juridical clubs, and international jurists, finally led to the foundation of two professional organizations in 1873, the International Association for the Reform and Codification of the Laws of England (later known as the International Law Association) and the Institut de droit international. Both organizations were founded in Belgium with the aim of advancing the codification of international law. Among the initiators were many leading international jurists and philanthropists, including David Dudley Field, Henry Dunant, Pasquale S. Mancini, and Gustave Rolin-Jaequemyns. All of them were convinced that private initiative would be more fruitful in achieving the task of codifying international law than political or diplomatic efforts. Their belief in the scientific approach reflected the trend to professionalization. The foundation of those international bodies can also be understood as a manifestation both of their will and their optimism.[23]

---

[20] Field, 'First Project of an International Code', 396.
[21] David Dudley Field, *Draft Outline of an International Code* (New York, 1872); David Dudley Field, *Outlines of an International Code*, 2nd edn (New York, 1876). See also Dhokalia, *Codification*, 51–3.
[22] Nys, 'Codification of International Law', 886–8.
[23] Nys, 'Codification of International Law', 889–91; Koskenniemi, *Gentle Civilizer*, 11–97; Nuzzo and Vec, *Constructing International Law*.

While the International Law Association and the Institut de droit international both pursued the same goal and recognized each other as complementary bodies, they were quite different in set-up and in the composition of their member bases. The latter was effectively an exclusive club of senior international jurists with a strict limitation on the number of members, while the former was open to anyone interested in the matter. Thus, the International Law Association was a much more heterogeneous organization, including economists, philanthropists, peace activists, and other intellectuals. Consequently, the International Law Association was much closer to the peace movement than the Institut de droit international, which regarded itself as the 'conscience of the civilized world'. The statutes of the Institut outlined the aims of the 'strictly scientific' organization, such as the advancement of international law, finding concrete solutions to 'controversial issues' and, above all, 'formulating principles from which rules could be deduced'.[24]

The Institut de droit international continued the work of the Brussels conference of 1874. Its members met annually at different places to discuss the most complicated problems in international law. They formed expert committees which presented their results at the annual meeting, and the members usually adopted a resolution. It was hoped that these resolutions would lead to a wider political discussion of the subjects. At their annual meeting in The Hague in 1875, the members of the Institut agreed to examine the Brussels Declaration more closely. For them the work had just begun, and the declaration was seen as a good starting point. Gustave Rolin-Jaequemyns explained that 'the draft Declaration gives a glimpse of important progress, the results of which appear to be all the more lasting from the very fact that we refrained from formulating Utopian *voeux*, and imposing upon armies, in the name of misunderstood philanthropy, requirements which are incompatible with their security and with the pursuit of military operations'.[25] Rolin-Jaequemyns argued that the Institut was not merely an academic or philanthropic institution but a body to find solutions to real-world problems—problems that were too difficult for states to

---

[24] 'Statuts votes par la Conférence Juridique international de Gand, le 10 Sept. 1873', *Annuaire de l'Institut de droit international*, 1 (1877), 1–2. See also Gabriela A. Frei, 'The Institut de Droit International and the Making of Law for Peace (1899–1917)', in Rémi Fabre (ed.), *Les défenseurs de la paix (1899–1917)* (Rennes, 2018), 127–38.

[25] 'Laws and Customs of War on Land-Examination of the Declaration of Brussels of 1874', in James Brown Scott (ed.), *Resolutions of the Institute of International Law Dealing with the Law of Nations. With an Historical Introduction and Explanatory Notes* (New York, 1916), 9.

solve, as the Brussels conference had shown. The members of the Institut made up a who's who in international law, including Gustave Moynier, Swiss jurist and president of the International Committee of the Red Cross; Tobias Asser, law professor at Amsterdam and legal adviser to the Dutch Foreign Ministry; August von Bulmerincq, law professor at Heidelberg and former Secretary of State in Russia; James Lorimer, Regius Professor of Public Law in Edinburgh; Feodor Martens, law professor at St Petersburg; and Theodor D. Woolsey, former president of Yale College.[26]

The members of the Institut agreed to form a committee to discuss the Brussels Declaration. The committee consisted of Johann Caspar Bluntschli, professor of international law at the University of Zürich, and later in Munich and Heidelberg; Moynier; Martens; Mountague Bernard, Chichele Professor of International Law and Diplomacy at All Souls College, Oxford; and Travers Twiss, Regius Professor of Civil Law in Oxford, later law professor at King's College in London, Advocate-General to the Admiralty, and Queen's Advocate-General. They started their work with a critical analysis of the Brussels Declaration of 1874, remarking that the declaration did not consider all aspects of the laws of war.[27] Rolin-Jaequemyns then designed a questionnaire for the committee.[28] The most controversial question was whether 'it was desirable to regulate the laws and customs of war by an international convention between different civilised states'.[29] Lawyers were divided between the common law and the Roman law traditions. The British international jurist Mountague Bernard argued from a common law point of view, expressing his scepticism of codification, and stating that 'although such a convention might at some time be found practicable and useful, the time for it had not yet arrived'.[30] His colleague, Travers Twiss, underscored Bernard's position, and argued that practice would gradually advance the law while codification would only slow it down. However, most colleagues from the European continent, whose legal systems were based on the Roman law tradition, were generally very supportive of the codification.[31]

---

[26] 'Members' List, Nov. 1876', *Annuaire de l'Institut de droit international*, 1 (1877), xiii–xv.

[27] 'Examen critique des traveaux de la conférence de Bruxelles', *Revue de droit international et de législation comparée*, 7 (1875), 95–111.

[28] Gustave Rolin-Jaequemyns, 'Examen de la declaration de Bruxelles', *Revue de droit international et de législation comparée*, 7 (1875), 438–47.

[29] Original: 'Est-il désirable de réglementer, par voie de convention international entre les différents Etats civilisés, les lois et coutumes de la guerre', in Rolin-Jaequemyns, 'Examen', 438.

[30] 'Rapport de M. Rolin-Jaequemyns', *Revue de droit international et de législation comparée*, 7 (1875), 449.

[31] 'Rapport de M. Rolin-Jaequemyns', *Revue de droit international et de législation comparée*, 7 (1875), 452–6.

At the same time, Moynier reminded his listeners that a 'regulation is desirable only as far as it can be useful, that is to say, as far as it is able to make humanity a larger part in the laws and customs of the war than in the past'.[32] And Bluntschli added that 'the codification is very desirable, under the condition that it strives to end the abuse [of law], and, at the same time, formulate the humanitarian legal consciousness and as far as possible implement it and advance the law accordingly'.[33] The conditions which Moynier and Bluntschli attached to the process of codification showed pragmatism rather than idealism. The positions were irreconcilable and the concluding resolutions with regard to the Brussels Declaration were not unanimously carried.[34] Bernard and Twiss published two separate notes in which they reiterated their reservations.[35] Despite the dissenting views on the importance of codification, the Institut started on its task, and in 1880, at its annual conference in Oxford, Moynier presented a draft manual which regulated all aspects of the laws of war on land. The Oxford Manual was celebrated as a milestone for the Institut.[36]

At their annual meetings, the members of the Institut also discussed the laws of naval warfare, and formed several committees to deal with the law of neutrality, the treatment of the immunity of private property in a maritime conflict, the foundation of an international prize court, and the definition of contraband of war. These topics reflected the conflicting interests of neutrals and belligerents in war at sea.[37] The law of neutrality, for instance, was one of the subjects that occupied the Institut from its very beginning. At the annual meeting in 1875, the 'three rules' adopted in the Treaty of Washington in 1871, were recommended as international duties incumbent on neutral states, so the Institut pleaded for international recognition of the content of

---

[32] 'Rapport de M. Rolin-Jaequemyns', *Revue de droit international et de législation comparée*, 7 (1875), 454.

[33] Original: 'Ich halte die Codification für sehr wünschenswerth, unter der Voraussetzung dass sie sich bemüht, Missbräuche abzustellen und das humane Rechtsbewusstsein zeitgemäss, soweit dessen Durchführung möglich ist, auszusprechen und das Recht demgemäss fortzubilden', in Rolin-Jaequemyns, 'Conférence de Bruxelles', 456.

[34] 'Conclusions adoptées par l'Institut', *Revue de droit international et de législation comparée*, 7 (1875), 284–7.

[35] '4th Commission—Déclaration de Bruxelles', *Revue de droit international et de législation comparée*, 7 (1875), 674–5.

[36] 'The Laws of War on Land. Oxford, 9 Sept. 1880 (Oxford Manual)', in Dietrich Schindler and Jiří Toman (eds), *The Laws of Armed Conflicts: A Collection of Conventions, Resolutions and other Documents* (Dordrecht, 2004), 29–40.

[37] Scott, *Resolutions of the Institute of International Law*. See also Koskenniemi, *Gentle Civilizer*, 61–2.

the bilateral treaty between Britain and the United States.[38] In 1904, the violation of neutral rights during the Russo-Japanese War made headlines. The Belgian international jurist and politician, Edouard Descamps, demanded at the annual meeting of the Institut in Edinburgh that it reconsider the role of neutrality in the context of 'the intensity of international life, the solidarity of economic relations, the character of modern armed conflicts, the needs of our time'.[39] He even coined the term 'pacigérat' in French, meaning 'to coordinate the rights of neutrals'.[40] In the plenary discussion the members were not particularly enthused about either the terminology, which Holland described as 'barbaric', or a general reconsideration of neutrality. For Holland and others, the contemporary practice of the law of neutrality was sufficient. At the same time, the French professor, Antoine Pillet, argued that, in light of another peace conference at The Hague and a recent speech by US President Roosevelt, who wished to adapt neutrality to present conditions, the Institut should enquire into a new regulation of neutrality. Finally, the members agreed to form a committee with Descamps and Swedish international jurist and diplomat, Richard Kleen, as rapporteurs.[41] In 1905, Kleen circulated a comprehensive draft code on the rights and duties of neutrals, which consisted of 71 Articles and dealt with all aspects of neutrality.[42] For most committee members, the draft was not acceptable as most articles touched on controversial practices.[43] At the annual meeting in 1906, the project was put on the agenda. After much deliberation on whether or not to discuss the project at the plenary meeting, the members finally agreed to examine the draft.[44]

---

[38] Johann Caspar Bluntschli (Rapporteur), 'Projet de redaction nouvelle des trois règles de Washington, adopté par l'Institut', *Revue de droit international et de législation comparée*, 7 (1875), 282–3.

[39] Original: 'L'intensité de la vie internationale, la solidarité des relations économiques, le caractère moderne des conflicts armés, les besoins nouveaux de notre temps', in Edouard Descamps, 'Thèses sur Pacigérat', *Annuaire de l'Institut de droit international*, 20 (1904), 61. See also Edouard Descamps, *Le droit de la paix et de la guerre. Essai sur l'évolution de la neutralité et sur la constitution du pacigérat* (Paris, 1898); Edouard Descamps, 'Le pacigérat ou régime juridique de la paix en temps de guerre', *Revue générale de droit international public*, 7 (1900), 629–704.

[40] Descamps, 'Thèses sur Pacigérat', 61–3.

[41] 'Séance plénièrès—La regime de la neutralité', *Annuaire de l'Institut de droit international*, 20 (1904), 211–20.

[42] Richard Kleen, 'Avant-Projet de Règlement concernant les lois et coutumes de la neutralité', *Annuaire de l'Institut de droit international*, 22 (1906), 100–21.

[43] 'Observations of various committee members', *Annuaire de l'Institut de droit international*, 22 (1906), 121–88.

[44] 'Séance plénièrès—La regime de la neutralité', *Annuaire de l'Institut de droit international*, 22 (1906), 345–409.

Another controversial issue was the question of contraband. No other matter caused more conflicts between neutrals and belligerents. In 1892, the Institut formed a committee to examine the issue with Richard Kleen and Emilio Brusa, a law professor at the University of Torino, as rapporteurs. The former published a comprehensive book on the issue in 1893, which served as a basis for the discussion at the annual meeting the year after.[45] The project was innovative, and yet committee members expressed doubts as to whether the concept of contraband could be extended to land warfare, and whether belligerents would ever agree on the contraband issue. Kleen and Brusa were convinced that only a comprehensive approach could solve it.[46] In the end, the committee chose the concise draft proposal of Ferdinand Perels, a German honorary law professor at the Friedrich Wilhelms University of Berlin and director of the civil department of the German Imperial Naval Office, as a working paper.[47] The regulations, which the Institut adopted in 1896, differed considerably from the first comprehensive draft. They distinguished between absolute and conditional contraband. Arms, munitions, explosives, and military materiel, such as uniforms, warships, and instruments used for the production of munitions, were generally contraband goods if they were transported to an enemy port. The regulations avoided giving a precise definition of what constituted conditional contraband, and only indirectly acknowledged the doctrine of continuous voyage, according to which the final destination of the cargo decided the nature of the good.[48] The rapporteurs were not fully satisfied with the result. While the regulations were short and uncontroversial, the rapporteurs had hoped to create 'a new system' based on a 'comprehensive regulation'.[49] The issues of conditional contraband, confiscation, and repression of a neutral state were controversial. The latter in particular concerned

---

[45] Richard Kleen, *De la contrabande de guerre et des transports interdits aux neutres* (Paris, 1893).

[46] Richard Kleen and Emilio Brusa (Rapporteurs), 'Contrebande de guerre et transports interdits', *Annuaire de l'Institut de droit international*, 13 (1894), 50–124; Richard Kleen and Emilio Brusa (Rapporteurs), 'Avant-projet de règlement international sur la contrebande de guerre et des transports interdits aux neutres, 30 Mar. 1894', *Annuaire de l'Institut de droit international*, 14 (1895), 33–43. For further observations and proposals from committee members, see *Annuaire de l'Institut de droit international*, 14 (1895), 43–66.

[47] 'Conclusions adoptees à Cambridge par la huitième commission, Aug. 1895', *Annuaire de l'Institut de droit international*, 14 (1895), 191–3.

[48] 'Règlementation internationale de la contrebande de guerre, 29 Sept. 1896', *Annuaire de l'Institut de droit international*, 15 (1896), 230–3.

[49] Richard Kleen and Emilio Brusa (Rapporteurs), 'Rapport final et projet transactionnel presents au nom de la commission, 30 Apr. 1896', *Annuaire de l'Institut de droit international*, 15 (1896), 99.

the question 'why contraband trade was not subject to international repression as it contradicted neutrality'.[50] For Kleen and Brusa, neutrality was 'essentially an international institution', which demanded international rules.[51] These ideas, though, were too radical to be acceptable to the international community.

Closely linked to the contraband issue was the matter of prizes. Belligerents and neutrals often disputed the legitimacy of prizes and national prize court procedures. The examples in Chapter 3 have shown the increasing discontent among neutrals with regard to the treatment of prizes by belligerents. The destruction of prizes during the Russo-Japanese War marked the culmination of those developments. The Institut had looked into this issue as early as 1877 when the British international jurist, John Westlake, suggested the creation of an international prize court.[52] While the project was enthusiastically embraced, obstacles to its creation were evident in subsequent discussions. They revolved around the composition of the court, whether the court should act only as a court of appeals or, more radically, whether national courts should be abolished and a new international court created to consider all prize cases in the first instance. August von Bulmerincq criticized the project for the reason that an international court would be 'ineffective' without the necessary legal basis. Thus, he argued, a second project should 'prepare a code, formulating the international prize laws'.[53] The British international jurist, Mountague Bernard, rejected Westlake's proposal because he feared that an international prize court would strengthen neutrals to the extent that belligerents would be disadvantaged of the exercise of their rights. He reminded his colleagues that 'the right of maritime capture…has arisen out of the necessities of maritime war which continue to exist and must be respected, and is a recognized compromise between those necessities and the antecedent rights of neutrals'.[54] The Institut finally agreed to examine the 'principles of international prize laws', as well as the

---

[50] Kleen and Brusa (Rapporteurs), 'Rapport final, 30 Apr. 1896', 106.

[51] Kleen and Brusa (Rapporteurs), 'Rapport final, 30 Apr. 1896', 107.

[52] August von Bulmerincq, 'Rapport sur les délibérations et les résolutions de l'Institut relatives au projet d'organisation d'un tribunal international des prises maritimes, présenté par M. Westlake', *Annuaire de l'Institut de droit international*, 2 (1878), 113–21. See also Gabriela A. Frei, 'How to Wage Economic Warfare in a Globalised Economy? International Jurisdiction between State and Private Interests, 1880–1914', under peer-review.

[53] Bulmerincq, 'Rapport sur les délibérations et les résolutions de l'Institut', 118.

[54] Mountague Bernard, 'Oberservations', *Annuaire de l'Institut de droit international*, 2 (1878), 130.

organization and procedure of an international prize court.[55] In 1880, a new commission was formed, and Bulmerincq circulated a comprehensive draft code consisting of 131 Articles dealing with all aspects of maritime capture, the procedures following the capture, and the organization of an international prize court.[56] For many members, the draft went too far, and Bluntschli argued that on certain matters it left no 'freedom to the court' to decide. Thus, the project was split in two parts. Part one considered maritime capture, while part two dealt with the creation of an international prize court.[57] After much deliberation, the Institut at its annual meeting in Torino in 1882 accepted the *Règlement international des prises maritimes*, which only dealt with maritime capture.[58] The commission continued its work and examined the various prize courts of different states as a basis for its draft regulation.[59] Finally, the Institut agreed to an international prize court of appeal in 1887.[60] Bulmerincq, amongst others, had argued for an international court only, while Perels, Holland, and Martens had opposed an international jurisdiction altogether.[61] Only the British and German members were opposed because they considered the rules in light of their own state interests, with Britain as the dominant and Germany as an aspiring sea power. Although the Institut tried to discuss international law detached from the political context, the question of an international prize court demonstrated that this was impossible.[62]

The Institut had shaped international law like no other organization. It was rigorous in collecting practices and rules from different states, comparing

[55] Bernard, 'Oberservations', 122. See also 'Extrait du procès-verbal de la première séance du 12 Sept. 1877', *Annuaire de l'Institut de droit international*, 2 (1878), 112–25.

[56] August von Bulmerincq, 'Projet de règlement international des prises maritimes', *Annuaire de l'Institut de droit international*, 6 (1883), 129–38.

[57] 'Extrait du procès-verbal de la première séance de la Commission des prises maritimes, tenue à Wiesbaden, 5 Sept. 1881, sous la présidence de M. de Bulmerincq, *Annuaire de l'Institut de droit international*, 6 (1883), 139; 'Extrait du procès-verbal de la 4e séance plénière, tenue à Turin, 13 Sept. 1882, sous la présidence de M. de Pierantoni, *Annuaire de l'Institut de droit international*, 6 (1883), 177–212.

[58] 'Règlement international des prises maritimes, voté à Turin, 13–15 Sept. 1882', *Annuaire de l'Institut de droit international*, 6 (1883), 213–23.

[59] August von Bulmerincq, 'Rapport', *Annuaire de l'Institut de droit international*, 7 (1885), 163–9; 'Résolutions votées dans la séances, 6–7 Sept. 1883', *Annuaire de l'Institut de droit international*, 7 (1885), 185–9.

[60] 'Règlement international des prises maritimes, voté à Heidelberg, 8 Sept. 1887', *Annuaire de l'Institut de droit international*, 9 (1887), 218–43.

[61] August von Bulmerincq (Rapporteur), 'Troisième commission d'études-Droit matériel et formel en matière des prises maritimes', *Annuaire de l'Institut de droit international*, 9 (1887), 188–210, here: 197, 203–4.

[62] Frei, 'Economic Warfare'.

them with each other, and adopting resolutions which they thought would prepare the foundation for further political discussions and the final adoption of international legislation. When the first Hague peace conference was held in 1899, the Institut achieved a central objective of its labours. The US international jurist David Dudley Field had already highlighted the importance of the states and the public in the process of the adoption of an international code.[63] The Hague peace conferences of 1899 and 1907 opened a new chapter in international relations, one in which the international community met to discuss the rules which should govern them in the future, and in which the resolutions and examinations of the Institut provided an indispensable basis.[64] For instance, the delegates often referred to the Institut's resolutions and discussions in their presentations on the contraband issue at the second Hague peace conference in 1907.[65] Many members of the Institut were present as delegates of their respective states, guaranteeing continuity between the Institut's discussions and those at the new political platform.[66]

The US Naval War Code

At the turn of century, the US Navy became the first in the world to adopt a comprehensive Naval War Code, following the example of the Lieber Code adopted by the US Army in 1863. The Naval War Code codified the customs and practices of the laws of naval warfare and was intended to instruct and guide American naval officers in their naval operations. The United States Naval War College, founded in 1884, was

---

[63] Field, *Outlines of an International Code*, 393–4.

[64] Friedrich August Freiherr von der Heydte, 'Die Auswirkungen der Resolutionen des Institut de Droit International im Bereich des Kriegsrechts auf die Fortentwicklung des Kriegsvölkerrechts', in Wilhelm Wengler (ed.), *Justitia et Pace. Festschrift zum 100 jährigen Bestehen des Institut de Droit International* (Berlin, 1974), 31–62; Alexander N. Makarov, 'Beiträge des "Institut de Droit International" zu den Problemen der internationalen Organisationen bis 1914', in Walter Schätzel (ed.) *Rechtsfragen der internationalen Organisation* (Frankfurt/Main, 1956), 257–72; Charles de Visscher, 'La contribution de l'Institut de droit international au développement du droit international (Rapport spécial)', in L'Institut de Droit International (ed.), *Livre du Centenaire 1873-1973. Evolution et perspectives du droit international* (Basel, 1973), 128–61.

[65] James Brown Scott (ed.), *The Proceedings of the Hague Peace Conferences. Translation of the Original Texts. Thje Conference of 1907, Vol. III: Meetings of the Second, Third and Fourth Commissions*, Carnegie Endowment for International Peace, Division of International Law (New York, 1921), 845, 1091–109.

[66] Frei, 'Institut de Droit International', 130–3.

chiefly responsible for the drafting of the Naval War Code. Its curriculum was built on the pillars of naval tactics, strategy, history, and international law, in order to aid the study and understanding of naval warfare.[67] International law courses revolved around case studies, which were designed to enable the officers to study a particular situation, a method introduced by Freeman Snow, professor of law at Harvard Law School.[68] In 1901, the Naval War College started an annual publication entitled *International Law Discussions* (later renamed *International Law Studies*, or the 'blue book series', which is still running today). Each volume dealt with a particular situation addressing a specific topic of international law and discussed the laws applicable to the US Navy. Additionally, the books included notes with references to the various practices of foreign navies and other relevant interpretations of international law. No other naval service published as extensively on international law before the First World War as did the US Navy. The case studies also reflected on the strategic impact of those legal considerations, so elucidating the relationship between law and strategy.

A key figure in the drafting of the Naval War Code was Captain Charles H. Stockton, a lecturer in international law at the United States Naval War College. Stockton was a naval officer rather than a jurist by training, and so he stood out from the crowd of many distinguished international jurists who taught at the college, including John Bassett Moore, professor of international law at Columbia University, and George Grafton Wilson, professor of social and political science at Brown University, and later professor of international law at Harvard University. Stockton entered the navy during the American Civil War and his assignments at sea, combined with an interest in law, led him to advocate the study of international law as part of naval officer education. When Stockton was president of the Naval War College in 1893, he promoted the study of international law, and regularly corresponded with Freeman Snow, who had introduced international law lectures at the college. In 1895, the college published its first book on international law and in the same year Stockton started to lecture on

---

[67] Freeman Snow, *Cases and Opinions on International Law with Notes and a Syllabus* (Boston, MA, 1893). See also John B. Hattendorf, B. Mitchell Simpson III, and John R. Wadleigh, *Sailors and Scholars: The Centennial History of the U.S. Naval War College* (Newport, RI, 1985), 1–111; Ronald Spector, *Professors of War: The Naval War College and the Development of the Naval Profession* (Newport, RI, 1977).

[68] John B. Hattendorf, 'Rear Admiral Charles H. Stockton, the Naval War College, and the Law of Naval Warfare', in Michael N. Schmitt and Leslie C. Green (eds), *The Law of Armed Conflict: Into the Next Millennium* (Newport, RI, 1998), xxxv.

the subject.[69] In 1899, Stockton convinced US Secretary of the Navy, John D. Long, of the need for a code of naval warfare similar to that of the Lieber Code.[70]

US President Theodore Roosevelt approved Stockton's draft code, sent to the US Secretary of the Navy in May 1900, and it was issued as General Orders No. 551 on 27 June 1900. The Naval War Code was comprehensive in its approach and reflected the American position on the laws of naval warfare. The code consisted of nine sections, all of which dealt with a specific aspect of the laws of naval warfare. Section 1, Article 1 defined the 'object of war' as 'the capture or destruction of the military and naval forces of the enemy;... of his maritime commerce;... to protect and defend the national territory, property, and sea-borne trade'. More generally, the objective of war was 'to procure the complete submission of the enemy at the earliest possible period with the least expenditure of life and property'. Article 2 described the scope of naval operations, where the navy could exercise belligerent rights, and acknowledged the rights of neutrals. Article 3 dealt with military necessity—a delicate subject, which was defined as 'measures that are indispensable for securing the ends of the war and that are in accordance with modern laws and usages of war'. Article 6 specified that 'neutral vessels found within the limits of belligerent authority may be seized and destroyed or otherwise utilized for military purposes' while neutrals were compensated for any such act. Article 8 mentioned another sensitive topic, namely that of reprisals. In cases where an enemy breached international law, reprisals were allowed as part of 'necessity'; yet, it stated, the measure should always be within 'the duties of humanity'. Section 2 elaborated on who was considered a combatant, and what should happen to those who were captured. Since the United States had not renounced privateering, the treatment of privateers was regulated under Section 3, Article 9. Section 3, Articles 13–20 were concerned with lawful capture and Article 19 affirmed the principle of 'free ship, free good' as outlined in the Declaration of Paris. The section also described the rights of belligerent ships with regard to neutral ports. The code also adopted the rules for naval warfare deduced from the Hague conventions of 1899 and the Geneva Convention in Section 4, Articles 21–9. Section 5, Articles 30–3 regulated the right of search and

---

[69] Charles H. Stockton, Memoranda of Subjects etc. for Proposed Lectures upon International Law at the Naval War College—Drawn up as Suggestions to Professor Freeman Snow, 1894, United States Naval War College, Record Group 28 (President's Files).

[70] Charles H. Stockton, 'Naval War Code Memorandum, May 1900', *International Law Discussions, 1903: The United States Naval War Code of 1900* (Washington, DC, 1904), 5–7.

capture, with Article 30 stressing that neutral convoys were exempt from the right of search and capture. Section 6, Article 36 distinguished between absolute and conditional contraband of war, treating foodstuffs and coal as conditional contraband. Section 7 dealt with the law of blockade, restating the provision of the Declaration of Paris in Article 37 and the issue of the liability of blockade runners was defined in Article 44. Section 8 was concerned with prizes and the lawful procedures in prize courts. Finally, Section 9 addressed broader issues, such as armistice agreements.[71]

The Naval War Code received favourable reviews in international law circles in the United States and Britain. The American international jurist, Theodore S. Woolsey, praised the code as an 'enlightened and specific' document, which 'like Lieber's Code, in scope and comprehensiveness is the first in the field'.[72] In Britain, two articles appeared in *The Times*. The first was published anonymously by a 'naval correspondent', who praised the work as 'another product of the United States Naval War College, to which we owe Captain Mahan's work on Sea Power'. The author highlighted the United States' decided views on conflicting practices, such as military necessity, the neutrality of submarine cables, the definition of contraband of war, the capture of merchant vessels, the definition of neutral vessels, and the right of search and capture. In contrast, the author argued that nothing like the Naval War Code could be produced in Britain because too little money was spent on the education of officers.[73]

Thomas E. Holland wrote the second article. He also praised the code as a clear and frank statement of the United States' position towards the laws and customs of war at sea, pointing out that it dealt with delicate issues such as reprisals and military necessity, which were not discussed at the international conferences in Brussels and The Hague, nor considered by the British government. He admired the United States' firm position on the questions of international law, and contemplated whether 'it is worth considering whether something resembling the United States code would not be found useful in the British Navy'. Holland's ambition was to adopt a code which 'resemble[d] it [Naval War Code] in clearness of expression, in brevity, and, above all things, in frank acceptance of responsibility'. Holland emphasized the benefits for naval officers, and argued that 'what our naval

---

[71] 'The United States Naval War Code of 1900. The Laws and Usages of War at Sea', *International Law Discussions, 1903: The United States Naval War Code of 1900* (Washington, DC, 1904), 103–14.

[72] Theodore S. Woolsey, 'The Naval War Code', *Columbia Law Review*, 1 (1901), 298.

[73] Anonymous, 'A Naval War Code from a Naval Correspondent', *The Times*, 5 Apr. 1901.

men most want is definite guidance, in categorical language, upon those points of maritime international law upon which their Government has made up its own mind'.[74]

His hopes were not met. Neither the Royal Navy nor the navies of France, Russia, Germany, Italy, Japan, and Austria-Hungary adopted a code of naval warfare prior to the First World War. Instead, the Royal Navy relied on a body of instructions, regulations, and manuals to guide its naval officers and commanders when it came to the question of international law. As shown in Chapter 3, commanding officers needed to make frequent contact with the Admiralty and the Foreign Office to clarify uncertain situations.

A Royal Navy intelligence report from 1901 contained a survey of international law books used by other navies. Apart from the Naval War Code, the report also mentioned the Prize Law of Japan as a comprehensive guide to how the Japanese Navy operated. No other navy had issued similar instructions.[75] Interestingly though, Austria-Hungary, France, and Japan had issued international law textbooks to guide commanding officers. The Austrian naval officer Ferdinand Attlmayr first published his textbook, *Die Elemente des Internationalen Seerechtes* (*Elements of International Law of the Sea*), in 1872, in which he dealt with all matters concerning law of the sea, including reprisals, blockade, and the right of search and capture. He also added a comprehensive list of all relevant treaties, such as the Declaration of Paris, the treaties to supress the slave trade, and others. Attlmayr pointed out that the book was written by a naval officer for naval officers, and that he had based it on the work of the French naval officer, Théodore Ortolan, who had published *Diplomatie de la mer* (*Diplomacy at Sea*) back in 1845.[76] Another French Commander, Eugène Marie Henri Rosse, issued a book in 1891, used as a manual in the French navy, which described the rights and duties of the commanding officer of a warship.[77] Japan gained substantive experience in naval warfare in the Sino-Japanese War as well as in the Russo-Japanese War, and published extensive instructions to their officers. The work of Sakuyé Takahashi provides a good example. He was a law professor at the Imperial Naval Staff College of Japan, and advised the Imperial

---

[74] Thomas E. Holland, 'The United States Naval War Code', *The Times*, 10 Apr. 1901.
[75] Naval War Code of the United States and Prize Law of Japan, Nov. 1901, TNA, ADM 231/35.
[76] Ferdinand Attlmayr, *Die Elemente des Internationalen Seerechtes und Sammlung von Verträgen. Ein Handbuch für die kais. und kön. österr. See-Officiere*, 2 vols (Vienna, 1872 and 1873); Théodore Ortolan, *Règles internationales et diplomatie de la mer*, 2 vols (Paris, 1845).
[77] Eugène Marie Henri Rosse, *Guide international du commandant de batiment de guerre–du droit de la force* (Paris, 1891).

Japanese Navy during the wars. The English version of his first book was published in 1899 and appeared thanks to Takahashi's friendship with Thomas E. Holland and John Westlake.[78]

While the French, Austrians, and Japanese did not adopt a comprehensive code of naval warfare comparable to that of the United States, those works treated the subject exhaustively, dealing with case studies and discussing different state practices. All authors except Takahashi were naval officers rather than jurists. In this context, Stockton's work stands in a much longer tradition, that of naval officers writing for naval officers on issues concerning the laws of naval warfare. Going back to Ortolan, all those works highlighted the importance of understanding naval warfare in the context of diplomacy and international relations. Thus, their works not only dealt with war but also with the role of the navy in peacetime. As Ortolan observed poetically, 'a mariner far away from his country, had always his ship with him, which carries everywhere his homeland'. More precisely, the commander of a ship was always a representative of his respective state.[79] Similar expressions can be found elsewhere in the works discussed above.[80]

The authors of the reviews in *The Times* demanded an improvement in the education of British naval officers with regard to the study of international law. At the Royal Naval College, the curriculum included a course taught by eminent British international jurists such as William E. Hall and Thomas J. Lawrence, professor of international law at the University of Cambridge. However, naval officers were doubtful as to the usefulness of the course.[81] During a lecture delivered by Lawrence at the Royal United Services Institution on the subject of belligerency, the officers admitted that they were not well acquainted with the subject. Most striking was the response of the eminent naval strategist and historian, Philip H. Colomb, who declared that 'I never myself had much to do with questions of international law, as dealing with the status of ships, but I have had rough and ready

---

[78] Sakuyé Takahashi, *Cases on International Law during the Chino-Japanese War* (Cambridge, 1899); Sakuyé Takahashi, *International Law Applied to the Russo-Japanese War with Decisions of the Japanese Prize Courts* (New York, 1908).

[79] Ortolan, *Règles international*, viii–ix.   [80] Rosse, *Guide international*, 1.

[81] Christian Jentzsch, *Vom Kadetten bis zum Admiral. Das britische und das deutsche Seeoffizierskorps 1871–1914* (Oldenburg, 2018); Andrew D. Lambert, 'The Naval War Course, Some Principles of Maritime Strategy and the Origins of "The British Way in Warfare"', in Keith Neilson and Greg Kennedy (eds), *The British Way in Warfare: Power and the International System, 1856–1956* (Farnham, 2010), 219–53.

work where international law did not much come in.'[82] Colomb's statement seems astonishing given his active engagement in the suppression of the slave trade in the Indian Ocean—missions based on international legal agreements.[83]

Vice-Admiral Sir Edmund Fremantle, on the other hand, remarked on the study of international law for naval officers that 'the writers on the subject are very voluminous, and many of them are very clear, at the same time they refer us to a great many cases—cases, no doubt, of great interest—but there are "ifs" and "buts," which, though I dare say they are quite intelligible to lawyers, are not always equally clear to the naval officer'.[84] As Commander-in-Chief of the China Station (1892–5), Fremantle had first-hand experience of the daily use and application of international law during the Sino-Japanese War of 1894–5. The correspondence between him, the Admiralty, and the Foreign Office gives good insight into how a commanding naval officer received, used, and applied international law in this particular situation. Fremantle received instructions directly from the Admiralty. Yet, whenever he needed clarification he contacted the Foreign Office to receive further instructions. It could take some time for the Foreign Office to gain an overview of the situation, which meant that the commander could be left in doubt at crucial moments in his decision-making.[85] In Fremantle's opinion, the officers' education did not prepare them well for these situations but thought that it was 'necessary and right that the naval officer should have a pretty clear idea in his mind of what international law consists, and he will then be better prepared to appreciate the arguments of Hall, Phillimore, Wharton, Hallett, or any other of the recognised authorities whose books are provided by the Admiralty for the naval officer's use. Having a clear idea in his mind, the naval officer will be more fully prepared to go into details.'[86] Fremantle believed that, rather than a lack of resources and books, the teaching methods were insufficient. The international law textbooks were simply not compiled for the purposes of naval officers.

---

[82] Philip H. Colomb in discussion of Thomas J. Lawrence, 'Recognition of Belligerency Considered in Relation to Naval Warfare', *Journal of Royal United Service Institution*, 41, 1 (1897), 20.

[83] Philip H. Colomb, *Slave Catching in the Indian Ocean. A Record of Naval Experiences* (London, 1873).

[84] Vice-Admiral Edmund Fremantle in discussion of Lawrence, 'Recognition of Belligerency', 19.

[85] Foreign Office to Admiralty, 16 Aug. 1894 (No. 96), TNA, FO 881/6692; Admiralty to Foreign Office, 18 Aug. 1894 (No. 105), TNA, FO 881/6692.

[86] Vice-Admiral Edmund Fremantle in discussion of Lawrence, 'Recognition of Belligerency', 19.

Here a stark contrast can be noted in the education of naval officers in the United States, whose methods were based on case studies rather than on a compilation of textbooks.

The Naval War Code marked a significant step towards the codification of international maritime law even though the code was a unilateral commitment by the United States to restrain its own forces. Stockton had 'hoped that this code will tend toward the amelioration of the hardships of naval warfare in general'.[87] He proposed to prepare a modified draft without the controversial clauses of the original version, for instance the clause on reprisals. This proposal, he believed, would facilitate an open debate at an international conference of sea powers.[88] In the spring of 1903, US Naval Intelligence gathered information from all major sea powers except Japan regarding their position towards the Naval War Code on Stockton's behalf.

The survey report gives good insight into the nations' opinions on the codification of the laws of naval warfare. Austria-Hungary welcomed the international project and Ferdinand Attlmayr from the Austrian Naval Academy wrote a detailed criticism with suggestions and modifications. The French reply contained no comments regarding the code but mentioned a book used by naval officers discussing the *guerre de course* strategy. Similarly, Britain issued no direct comment. The German response was short—their officers were familiar with the Naval War Code but the German navy had no 'intention of publishing a book of like character'. An official of Venezuela replied that his country did not know the Naval War Code, nor had it access to the book or an 'officer competent' in this subject matter.[89]

The information served as preparatory work for the planned conference at the United States Naval War College, the aim of which was to discuss the effects of the Naval War Code in the event of war. Two results were noticeable, as George Grafton Wilson, professor of social and political science at Brown University, who also taught at the college, highlighted in his report. First, the creation of an internationally binding code of international maritime law was generally welcomed, and the Naval War Code could serve as a starting point. Second, the Naval War Code should be withdrawn and

---

[87] Stockton, 'Naval War Code Memorandum, May 1900', 5–7, here: 6. See also Hattendorf, 'Stockton', xvii–lxviii.

[88] Charles H. Stockton to Secretary of the Navy, 19 May 1900, United States War College, Record Group 28 (President's Files).

[89] Criticism of U.S. Naval War Code received through the Naval Attachées to Austria, Great Britain, France, Germany, and Venezuela, 1903, Navy Department, Office of Naval Intelligence, United States Naval War College, Record Group 28 (President's Files).

reissued as 'a statement of the rules which may be expected to prevail in case of war upon the sea', rather than as an official order. The reason for this change was to free the delegates at international conferences for the negotiation of international agreements. More importantly, though, the US Navy would no longer be constrained in wartime.[90]

The American government withdrew the Naval War Code in February 1904 for the reasons mentioned above.[91] As long as there was no internationally binding consensus on the laws and customs of naval warfare, a unilaterally binding code could be disadvantageous in future maritime conflict, particularly if the enemy were not bound by the same laws. Britain found itself in a similar situation in 1904 when it considered giving up the restrictions of the Foreign Enlistment Act because no other state had adopted similar laws. Both cases illustrate the importance of reciprocity in international law. Britain and the United States had hoped that their self-imposed legislation would lead to a broad recognition and subsequent adoption of similar national laws by other states. The codification of international law could only work effectively if all agreed on the same rules. This, however, was a long and difficult process.

The Naval War Code was remarkably far-sighted, progressive, and a lasting example for a comprehensive code of naval warfare. In fact, the United States used the Naval War Code as a basis for their preparatory work for the Hague and London conferences. Stockton himself would be the first delegate of the United States at the London conference of 1909. When he was asked in 1912 to give a lecture at the annual meeting of the American Society of International Law, he opened his speech with the words: 'the laws, codes and customs concerning sea warfare should be collected, codified and stamped with international authority'.[92]

In conclusion, the codification projects of the nineteenth and early twentieth centuries originating from the United States and the Institut de droit international were innovative attempts to codify international maritime law. In both cases, the drafters wanted to create a comprehensive code that considered all aspects of naval warfare, and saw their work as a basis for an international agreement. While the Naval War Code represented the United

---

[90] George Grafton Wilson, 'General Conclusions', *International Law Discussions, 1903: The United States Naval War Code of 1900* (Washington, DC, 1904), 89–91.

[91] Hattendorf, Simpson, and Wadleigh, *Sailors and Scholars*, 55.

[92] Charles H. Stockton, 'The Codification of the Laws of Naval Warfare', in *Proceedings of the American Society of International Law at its Sixth Annual Meeting held at Washington, DC* (Washington, DC, 1912), 115.

States' perspective, the Institut wanted to produce resolutions, which were supposed to go a step further by harmonizing different state practices. Yet, there were limitations to the Institut's efforts. Various projects started out as complex multi-layered endeavours but ended in a simple resolution that only dealt with one particular issue. Despite their limitations, these projects all served as an invaluable basis for the Hague peace conference in 1907 and the London naval conference in 1909.

5

The Hague and London Conferences and the Rise of an International Legal Order

The Russo-Japanese War had shown that legal disputes, which had arisen during the war, needed urgent political solution. This chapter explores the Hague peace conference in 1907 as well as the London naval conference in 1909 with regard to the codification of international maritime law, and examines the role of state practice in this process. The chapter also addresses the role of Britain, and explains its change from a sceptic of codification in 1874 to its advocate. Both conferences were celebrated as milestones for the codification of international maritime law. While much has been written on attempts to limit and control arms, this chapter focuses on how state practice and custom shaped the results of the conferences. The conferences achieved more than previous literature generally acknowledges because it has neglected the consideration of state practice and custom to the process of codification.[1]

---

[1] Maartje Abbenhuis, Christopher Ernest Barber, and Annalise R. Higgins (eds), *War, Peace and International Order? The Legacies of the Hague Conferences of 1899 and 1907* (London, 2017); Maartje Abbenhuis, *The Hague Conferences and International Politics, 1898–1915* (London, 2018); Jost Dülffer, 'Chances and Limits of Armament Control 1898–1914', in Holger Afflerbach and David Stevenson (eds), *An Improbable War: The Outbreak of World War I and European Political Culture before 1914* (New York, 2007), 95–112; Jost Dülffer, *Regeln gegen den Krieg? Die Haager Friedenskonferenzen von 1899 und 1907 in der internationalen Politik* (Berlin, 1981), 205–99; Scott A. Keefer, 'Building the Palace of Peace: The Hague Conference of 1907 and Arms Control before the World War', *Journal of the History of International Law*, 9, 1 (2007), 35–81; Scott A. Keefer, *The Law of Nations and Britain's Quest for Naval Security: International Law and Arms Control, 1898–1914* (Cham, 2016); Christopher Martin, 'The 1907 Naval War Plans and the Second Hague Peace Conference: A Case of Propaganda', *Journal of Strategic Studies* 28, 5 (2005), 833–56; B. J. C. McKercher (ed.), *Arms Limitation and Disarmament: Restraints on War, 1899–1939* (Westport, CT, 1992).

Great Britain, International Law, and the Evolution of Maritime Strategic Thought, 1856–1914. Gabriela A. Frei,
Oxford University Press (2020). © Gabriela A. Frei.
DOI: 10.1093/oso/9780198859932.001.0001

Preparations for the Second Hague
Peace Conference

In September 1904, the Inter-Parliamentary Union, an international organization which advocated peace and arbitration, urged US President Theodore Roosevelt to support another Hague peace conference.[2] The State Department under Secretary of State John Hay informed foreign governments of its intention to do so on 21 October 1904.[3] When the United States received favourable replies, Roosevelt announced in his Fourth Annual Message, on 6 December 1904, in the midst of the ongoing Russo-Japanese War, that he would invite other states to hold a second Hague peace conference. The Russians were reluctant because they thought it inopportune to hold a conference during an ongoing conflict.[4] Yet, the United States had gained political strength and influence in international politics, and was prospering economically. Its firm belief in a new world order based on international law was demonstrated when it was the first country to submit a case to the newly founded Permanent Court of Arbitration in 1902.[5] At the same time, the role of the American peace and arbitration societies should not be underestimated. They had lobbied for the establishment of a world order based on the rule of international law for a long time. Among the many prominent supporters of the peace movements were renowned international jurists, such as John Bassett Moore, vice-president of the American Peace Society from 1907 to 1919, and James Brown Scott, its vice-president since 1908 and secretary of the Carnegie Endowment for International Peace since 1910.[6]

---

[2] James L. Tyron, *The Inter-Parliamentary Union and its Work* (Boston, MA, 1910). See also Calvin DeArmond Davis, *The United States and the Second Hague Peace Conference: American Diplomacy and International Organization 1899–1914* (Durham, NC, 1975), 103–10.

[3] 'Memorandum by Beilby Alston on Origin of Proposal, Foreign Office, 23 Sept. 1905 (No. 157)', in G. P. Gooch and Harold Temperley (eds), *British Documents on the Origins of the War 1898–1914, Vol. VIII: Arbitration, Neutrality and Security* (London, 1932), 185–8.

[4] Theodore Roosevelt, 'Fourth Annual Message, 6 Dec. 1904', in John T. Woolley and Gerhard Peters, *The American Presidency Project*, https://www.presidency.ucsb.edu/documents/fourth-annual-message-15 (accessed 19 Oct. 2018).

[5] Benjamin Allen Coates, *Legalist Empire: International Law and American Foreign Relations in the Early Twentieth Century* (Oxford, 2016), 89–95.

[6] Charles Chatfield, *The American Peace Movement: Ideals and Activism* (New York, 1992); David S. Patterson, *Toward a Warless World: The Travail of the American Peace Movement 1887–1914* (Bloomington, IN, 1976); Edson Leone Whitney, *The American Peace Society: A Centennial History* (Washington, 1928), 257; Lawrence S. Wittner, 'Peace Movements and Foreign Policy: The Challenge to Diplomatic Historians', *Diplomatic History*, 11 (1987), 355–70.

Although the United States initiated the Hague peace conference, it was Russia that was given the role of organizing it. The Russian programme first outlined in April 1906, focused heavily on international maritime law. No other country had gained more experience in modern naval warfare than the Russians, and the recent war had shown that the regulation of international maritime law was urgent. Among the issues which the Russians put on the programme were the questions of contraband, the law of neutrality, prize laws, the transformation of merchant ships into warships, and the immunity of private property from capture at sea (see Chapter 7). It was also hoped that the conference would adapt the rules concerning land warfare, such as the Geneva Convention of 1864 and the Hague conventions of 1899, to the context of naval warfare.[7]

The British Foreign Secretary, Sir Edward Grey, accepted the Russian programme on behalf of his government with the reservation that it would 'abstain from taking part in the discussion' in case it would not 'lead to any useful result'.[8] This cautionary language shows British government scepticism about the direction of the discussion and the likely outcome of the conference.

The political climate had changed considerably since 1899, when the first Hague peace conference had taken place. With an ongoing naval arms race between Britain and Germany, as well as the rise of Germany and the United States as land powers, Britain's position was now less secure than it had been before 1900, a point reflected in the preparatory work for the second Hague peace conference.[9] The Russian programme did not directly address broader aspects of maritime war, such as the objectives of war at sea, but many of the topics dealt indirectly with the nature of a future maritime war. In preliminary exchanges with other states,

[7] Memorandum by W. Maycock Showing the Attitude of His Majesty's Government and that of Other Powers, with a Summary of the Recommendations of the Inter-Departmental Committee on the Principal Topics in the Russian Programme, 27 Apr. 1907, TNA, FO 881/10082.

[8] Sir Edward Grey to Russian Ambassador, 23 July 1906, Memorandum by W. Maycock Showing the Attitude of His Majesty's Government and that of Other Powers, with a Summary of the Recommendations of the Inter-Departmental Committee on the Principal Topics in the Russian Programme, 27 Apr. 1907, TNA, FO 881/10082; 'Sir Edward Grey to Sir A. Nicolson, 15 Feb. 1907 (No. 178)', in Gooch and Temperley, *British Documents on the Origins of the War 1898–1914, Vol. VIII*, 207–9.

[9] Geoffrey Best, 'Peace Conferences and the Century of Total War: The 1899 Hague Conference and What Came After', *International Affairs*, 75, 3 (1999), 619–34; Dülffer, *Regeln gegen den Krieg?*, 205–99; Matthew S. Seligmann, Frank Nägler, and Michael Epkenhans (eds), *The Naval Route to the Abyss: The Anglo-German Naval Race 1895–1914* (Farnham, 2015).

both formal and informal, the British government was anxious to ascertain its position with regard to the Russian programme.[10]

In October 1906, an Inter-Departmental Committee of experts examined the positions of other states and, most importantly, defined Britain's position in relation to the Russian programme. Sir John Lawson Walton, the Attorney-General, chaired the committee, which consisted of Lord Desart, director of public prosecutions; Charles L. Ottley, director of Naval Intelligence; George S. Clarke, secretary to the Committee of Imperial Defence; Walter J. Howell, marine secretary to the Board of Trade; a lawyer, John S. Risley, a Colonial Office legal assistant; Cecil J. B. Hurst, assistant legal adviser to the Foreign Office; W. E. Davidson, legal adviser to the Foreign Office; Eyre A. Crowe, senior clerk to the Foreign Office; Major George K. Cockerill, a member of the general staff of the War Office; and E. G. Wetherall, secretary to the Foreign Office. All committee members were senior civil or military servants, and many had legal backgrounds and would later serve as delegates at the Hague and London conferences.

New players were involved in defining Britain's legal position. The Foreign Office was no longer solely responsible, and consequently became less influential in the preparatory work.[11] While Hurst and Davidson were actively involved in the formulation of Britain's position towards the codification of international law, the Attorney-General and the Solicitor-General, who both regularly advised the Foreign Office, were not as prominently represented on the committee as had been expected. Walton was head of the committee but ill health prevented him from active engagement, so Lord Desart, who was the most senior legal expert but with no close connection to the Foreign Office, chaired the committee.[12]

The committee published its report on 17 March 1907. It is an extraordinary document outlining Britain's views on international maritime law, and

---

[10] 'Sir Edward Grey to Sir M. Durand (British Ambassador to the United States), 17 Oct. 1906 (No. 166)', in Gooch and Temperley, *British Documents on the Origins of the War 1898–1914, Vol. VIII*, 196–7; 'Sir Edward Grey to Sir M. Durand (British Ambassador to the United States), 6 Nov. 1906 (No. 167)', in Gooch and Temperley, *British Documents on the Origins of the War 1898–1914, Vol. VIII*, 197. A summary of the views of other states in response to the Russian programme can be found in Memorandum by W. Maycock showing the Attitude of His Majesty's Government and that of other Powers, with a Summary of the Recommendations of the Inter-Departmental Committee on the Principal Topics in the Russian Programme, 27 Apr. 1907, TNA, FO 881/10082.

[11] T. G. Otte, 'The Foreign Office and Defence of Empire, 1856–1914', in Greg Kennedy (ed.), *Imperial Defence: The Old World Order, 1856–1956* (Abingdon, 2008), 18–24.

[12] Clive Parry, 'Foreign Policy and International Law', in Francis H. Hinsley (ed.), *British Foreign Policy under Sir Edward Grey* (Cambridge, 1977), 89–110.

providing, for the first time, a systematic analysis of the country's understanding of important aspects such as the right of search and capture of private property at sea, contraband of war, the creation of an international prize court, and the law of neutrality.[13] Each subject was carefully examined. First, the committee looked at the historic background, then it analysed the deficiencies and problems with existing practices, and, finally, it made a proposal explaining the possible resistance from other states and outlining Britain's likely benefits. The report was remarkable in that it examined international law in relation to a future war at sea, and thus gives an invaluable insight into Britain's position on international maritime law, its vision of a future maritime war, and its strategic position. The scenarios outlined in the report not only identified the possibilities but also showed the limitations of the topics in the Russian programme. Moreover, the topics were examined in the context of international politics, evaluating other countries' acceptance of the proposed international maritime law.

Central to the report was the question of contraband, an issue that had caused many disputes between neutrals and belligerents in the past. The committee suggested the abolition of contraband altogether—existing practices had distinguished between absolute and conditional contraband.[14]

The committee argued that 'the lists of contraband published after the outbreak of modern wars can scarcely be harmonized with any principle, or explained upon [sic] any other theory than the intention of inflicting the maximum of loss upon an enemy by restricting to the utmost extent considered practicable his trade with a neutral'. A neutral power was undoubtedly exposed to a belligerent's decision on contraband, and Britain, as the world's leading trading nation, was hit particularly hard. In the committee's view, modern maritime wars were led with 'the intention of the maximum of loss' for neutrals, but such a strategy ran the 'risk of converting a neutral into a belligerent'. For the committee the 'present system creates, in short, a breach of the spirit of the Declaration of Paris by an undue extension of the right to cripple a neutral's trade by treating as contraband articles that could not in 1856, nor can now, be properly considered to possess that character'.

---

[13] Report of the Inter-Departmental Committee Appointed to Consider the Subjects which may Arise for Discussion at the Second Peace Conference (Confidential), 21 Mar. 1907, TNA, FO 881/9041X.
[14] Report of the Inter-Departmental Committee Appointed to Consider the Subjects which may Arise for Discussion at the Second Peace Conference (Confidential), 21 Mar. 1907, TNA, FO 881/9041X. For a broader debate, see Gabriela A. Frei, 'Great Britain, Contraband and Future Maritime Conflict (1885–1916)', Francia. Forschungen zur Westeuropäischen Geschichte, 40 (2013), 409–18.

With their reference to the Declaration of Paris, the committee hoped to gain the maximum attention from other states as most of them, except the United States, were signatories.[15]

The principles laid out in the Declaration of Paris formed part of the basis for Britain's neutrality policy in the latter half of the nineteenth century. Britain particularly acknowledged the principle of 'free ship, free good'—a principle that had been internationally recognized as a right of neutrals. The committee's report therefore emphasized the rights of neutrals to transport goods freely to any port, even to a belligerent one, unless the latter was blockaded, in which case a neutral ship would be subject to capture.[16]

George S. Clarke, a committee member and secretary of the Committee of Imperial Defence, examined the benefits to Britain of the proposed new contraband regime, considering both the total abolition of contraband and a restricted list of contraband, similar to that of absolute contraband. If Britain were a belligerent and blockaded by an enemy, it 'will be at the mercy of an enemy, whatever may be the definition of contraband'. In the event that no enemy blockade could be established, 'the island Powers [referring here to Britain and Japan] will be able to obtain any articles falling within the scope of a restricted definition of contraband', assuming that they only 'form a very small proportion of the total imports'. If Britain stayed neutral in a conflict, it 'would gain by the adoption' of this new contraband regime, compared with the existing regulation under which 'a neutral island Power is placed at a disadvantage as regards the supply of contraband, as compared with a continental Power'. However, Clarke warned that, for Britain as a neutral, the new regime might 'lead to large exports of material of war to a belligerent, and that the other belligerent would thus be furnished with a serious grievance against us, leading to strong diplomatic protests, and possibly involving us in war'.[17]

Clarke's memorandum looked at the broader implications of such a radical change in state practice. His analysis was particularly concerned with

[15] Report of the Inter-Departmental Committee Appointed to Consider the Subjects which may Arise for Discussion at the Second Peace Conference (Confidential), 21 Mar. 1907, TNA, FO 881/9041X, 13.

[16] Report of the Inter-Departmental Committee Appointed to Consider the Subjects which may Arise for Discussion at the Second Peace Conference (Confidential), 21 Mar. 1907, TNA, FO 881/9041X, 13.

[17] Memorandum by George S. Clarke on the Law of Contraband (Appendix 10), n.d., in Report of the Inter-Departmental Committee Appointed to Consider the Subjects which may Arise for Discussion at the Second Peace Conference (Confidential), 21 Mar. 1907, TNA, FO 881/9041X, 78–9.

the strategic and economic impacts of such a proposal for Britain, drawing attention to sea powers' heightened vulnerability in regard to contraband compared to land powers which would be much less affected. Clarke supported the abolition of contraband for the reason that it would balance the advantages and disadvantages of sea powers and land powers. In his opinion, land powers could easily import contraband goods overland, whereas sea powers, which were exposed to the potential enemy capture of contraband goods at sea, could not. Interestingly, Clarke considered only Britain and Japan as major sea powers, as they were the two countries with strong navies that were also 'island powers'. For these 'island powers', the ability to control the sea and the capability of installing and upholding an effective blockade was absolutely essential for their security, and thus the law of blockade needed to be strengthened. Minor sea powers, on the other hand, lacked the capability of an effective blockade and rather favoured a *guerre de course* strategy by attacking enemy trade, which needed to be limited.[18]

Clarke concluded that the abolition of contraband of war was desirable. If this goal could not be achieved, the British government should aim for a restricted definition of contraband. Furthermore, he advised the government to ensure that contraband lists were agreed to in peace time so that 'differences of opinion' could be settled before an armed conflict broke out. The British government should take 'every effective measure necessary to protect the importation of food supplies and raw materials for peaceful industries' and should make use of 'all the sanction which the Law of Nations can supply'. Finally, Clarke advocated 'that the right of search be limited in every practicable way, e.g. by the adoption of a system of Consular certificates of the absence of contraband from the cargo'.[19]

The proposed change of policy was based on earlier discussions, which had taken place within the Committee of Imperial Defence (CID), the body founded in 1902 to coordinate war planning and act as an advisory board to the Cabinet.[20] During the Russo-Japanese War the CID held several meetings

[18] Memorandum by George S. Clarke on the Law of Contraband (Appendix 10), n.d., in Report of the Inter-Departmental Committee Appointed to Consider the Subjects which may Arise for Discussion at the Second Peace Conference (Confidential), 21 Mar. 1907, TNA, FO 881/9041X.

[19] Memorandum by George S. Clarke on the Law of Contraband (Appendix 10), n.d., in Report of the Inter-Departmental Committee Appointed to Consider the Subjects which may Arise for Discussion at the Second Peace Conference (Confidential), 21 Mar. 1907, TNA, FO 881/9041X.

[20] David French, *British Economic and Strategic Planning 1905–1915* (London, 1982); John Gooch, 'The Weary Titan: Strategy and Policy in Great Britain, 1890–1918', in Williamson Murray, MacGregor Knox and Alvin Bernstein (eds), *The Making of Strategy: Rulers, States,*

that dealt with the practices of international law, mostly concerning the question of contraband and the 'value' of the right to search and capture neutral vessels for Britain.[21] For the CID, these issues were closely linked and needed thorough consideration. It argued that defining 'contraband is of supreme importance to neutrals, and existing international custom leaves this question to be settled by the belligerents'. The British experience of the Russo-Japanese War had shown that in a future major war, neutral Britain would be at the mercy of the belligerents, and the CID argued that 'so long as contraband of war is not defined by International Agreement this evil will remain'. Britain's position towards contraband of war had been formed during the Boer War, and the CID concluded that Britain as a belligerent 'would probably adopt a much less comprehensive definition of contraband' than Russia, not least because 'powerful neutrals' could object to Britain's definition and would demand 'heavy compensation' as Germany had in the Boer War when it objected to Britain's definition of contraband.[22]

Reflecting on Britain's experiences as both a neutral and a belligerent power in the nineteenth century, the CID weighed the advantages and disadvantages of the right of search and capture. It examined how many potentially contraband goods could be seized in case of a war against Germany, France, Russia, the United States, and other European powers. Using the Board of Trade's import figures for grain, flour, meat, fuel, and raw cotton from these countries, it showed that no significant harm would be inflicted upon these countries, as most of them were able to obtain contraband goods via neutral ports, such as Antwerp or Dunkirk.[23]

---

and War (Cambridge, 1994), 278–306; Franklyn A. Johnson, *Defence by Committee: The British Committee of Imperial Defence, 1885–1959* (Oxford, 1960); Robert S. Jordan, 'The Influence of the British Secretariat Tradition on Twentieth-Century International Peace-Keeping', in John B. Hattendorf and Robert S. Jordan (eds.), *Maritime Strategy and the Balance of Power: Britain and American in the Twentieth Century* (Basingstoke, 1989), 56–60; Andrew D. Lambert, 'The Royal Navy, 1856–1914: Deterrence and the Strategy of World Power', in Keith Neilson and Elizabeth J. Errington (eds.), *Navies and Global Defence: Theories and Strategy* (Newport, CT, 1996), 69–92; David G. Morgan-Owen, *The Fear of Invasion: Strategy, Politics, and British War Planning, 1880–1914* (Oxford, 2017), 87–130; John Tetsuro Sumida, *In Defence of Naval Supremacy: Finance, Technology and British Naval Policy, 1889–1914* (London, 1989).

[21] Note on the Conclusions Arrived at by the Sub-Committee Appointed to Consider Certain Questions of International Law Arising out of the Russo-Japanese War (Secret), June 1904, TNA, CAB 38/5/68.

[22] Memorandum by George S. Clarke on the Value to Great Britain of the Right of Capture of Neutral Vessels (Secret), 12 Dec. 1904, TNA, CAB 38/6/120, 1.

[23] Memorandum by George S. Clarke on the Value to Great Britain of the Right of Capture of Neutral Vessels (Secret), 12 Dec. 1904, TNA, CAB 38/6/120, 2–4.

The CID concluded that the right of search and capture 'has not the value which is commonly assumed to this country [Britain] as a belligerent'. Rather, it feared that its exercise 'involved risks, and might inflict considerable injury on British interests'. The recent experience of the Boer War, in which Britain was a belligerent, had shown that 'the results of our [Britain's] action were distinctly discouraging'. If Britain stayed neutral it would 'prove a serious inconvenience to our trade' and more generally 'be a danger to our peace'. The CID's evaluation of the Russo-Japanese War, in which Britain stayed neutral, concluded that the right of search had no 'real influence upon the course of the events'.[24]

The results of the CID were sobering, as 'the sea pressure that can be brought to bear on a Continental Power appears, therefore, to be far less effective now than formerly'. It feared that 'the advantage a belligerent State possesses from the right to capture contraband on the high seas, on the plea of "continuous voyage", must seem to be illusionary'. The CID feared that, in a war with a European state, Britain had more to lose than to gain by retaining this right. The report drew attention to the fact that British interests not only concerned British overseas trade, but also included British trade under foreign flags, for which the CID had no data. Finally, the CID remarked that Britain had 'not been engaged in a war which threatened the movements of our [Britain's] commerce', while Russia had faced such a scenario three times in the recent past. In light of these broader conclusions, the CID summarized that the right of search and capture could not 'compensate for the restriction of our rights as neutrals'.[25] Although the Admiralty generally concurred with the view expressed by the CID, Charles L. Ottley, a former naval attaché and director of Naval Intelligence since 1905, argued that unless 'clear evidence exists that we do lose as a neutral more than we gain, which is at least doubtful, it would appear undesirable to relinquish a right whose effects may be at times very beneficial'.[26]

When the Inter-Departmental Committee put forward the bold proposal of the abolition of contraband it also showed how best to present it for discussion at the conference. Since Britain would be a beneficiary of the proposal, the committee hoped that the United States or Japan would

[24] Memorandum by George S. Clarke on the Value to Great Britain of the Right of Capture of Neutral Vessels (Secret), 12 Dec. 1904, TNA, CAB 38/6/120, 5.

[25] Memorandum by George S. Clarke on the Value to Great Britain of the Right of Capture of Neutral Vessels (Secret), 12 Dec. 1904, TNA, CAB 38/6/120, 6.

[26] Minute by Charles L. Ottley, 12 Apr. 1905, TNA, ADM 1/7846. These views were again stated in Admiralty (Evan MacGregor) to CID, 10 June 1905, TNA, ADM 1/7846.

support it and take the initiative that, if the committee rejected the proposal, Britain should propose a restricted definition of contraband.[27]

Apart from the regulation of the right of search and capture in conjunction with the question of contraband, the committee reconsidered the existing prize court regime. Prize courts had always played an important part in naval warfare as they decided upon the lawful capture of prizes. Although prize courts were national institutions and their decisions reflected national practice, their decisions interpreted and also shaped international law. The impartiality of these courts, however, was never beyond doubt and the Russo-Japanese War had given the committee 'good ground for dissatisfaction'. The committee questioned whether foreign prize courts could treat cases impartially and feared that the courts were used to legitimize breaches of international law. Therefore, the committee proposed the establishment of an international prize court of appeal where earlier national prize court rulings could be decided in the last instance in front of 'a body composed of jurists of eminence drawn from all nations'. This, they suggested, would guarantee 'the most rapid and efficient machinery which the world has yet known for giving form and authority to the canons of international law'.[28] The novelty in this proposal lay in the creation of an international judicial institution that produced precedents, which were to guide national courts in their rulings. Britain wanted to create an additional instrument to protect neutral rights. The committee was convinced that 'if The Hague Conference accomplishes no other object than the constitution of this Tribunal, it will still, in our opinion, have rendered an inestimable service to civilization and mankind'.[29]

The law of neutrality played a relatively insignificant role in the Inter-Departmental Report and was only treated in a section on minor points, surprisingly given that Britain had mostly been a neutral rather than a belligerent since 1856. The committee stressed the 'great divergence in the standard of obligations' in terms of the rights and duties of neutrals, and advocated the adoption of the 'three rules' on neutrality, outlined in Article

[27] Report of the Inter-Departmental Committee Appointed to Consider the Subjects which may Arise for Discussion at the Second Peace Conference (Confidential), 21 Mar. 1907, TNA, FO 881/9041X, 13–14.
[28] Report of the Inter-Departmental Committee Appointed to Consider the Subjects which may Arise for Discussion at the Second Peace Conference (Confidential), 21 Mar. 1907, TNA, FO 881/9041X, 17.
[29] Report of the Inter-Departmental Committee Appointed to Consider the Subjects which may Arise for Discussion at the Second Peace Conference (Confidential), 21 Mar. 1907, TNA, FO 881/9041X, 17–18.

6 of the Washington Treaty of 1871. In addition, it stated that neutrals should ensure that belligerents did not use their territorial waters or territories as operational bases. Second, neutrals should grant access to their ports as an act of 'hospitality' to belligerents in distress. Third, neutrals did not have to prohibit contraband trade but were not allowed to encourage their subjects to engage in it. Fourth, prizes were not allowed to be brought into neutral ports.[30] The adoption of an internationally binding law of neutrality would be of considerable benefit to Britain and the committee argued that, if Britain were a belligerent, it would 'not depend on the assistance of neutrals in the direct carrying out of operations of war'. However, Britain as a neutral would 'require uniformity of procedure'.[31]

The law of neutrality was mostly examined from the belligerent point of view. Only in the sale of warships to a belligerent did the committee look at neutrality from the position of a neutral, not least because this was the core of the revised Foreign Enlistment Act of 1870, and the basis of the Treaty of Washington of 1871. Charles L. Ottley argued that 'it is the duty of neutrals to prevent the sale of such vessels during hostilities to any persons other than *bona fide* neutrals'. He supported strict adherence to the law of neutrality and argued that neutrals should be responsible if a ship left its 'ports for an unknown destination' because it would then be 'guilty of culpable negligence'.[32] Britain wanted other powers to adhere to the same strict law of neutrality, but whether they would, was uncertain. Ottley concluded that 'it is highly undesirable that Great Britain should continue to harass shipbuilders and others by the present onerous restrictions of the Foreign Enlistment Act of 1870 in all cases where the belligerents are *not* prepared to act reciprocally when the position of neutral and belligerent is reversed'.[33] In other words Ottley proposed loosening the strict domestic legislation

---

[30] Report of the Inter-Departmental Committee Appointed to Consider the Subjects which may Arise for Discussion at the Second Peace Conference (Confidential), 21 Mar. 1907, TNA, FO 881/9041X, 23.

[31] Report of the Inter-Departmental Committee Appointed to Consider the Subjects which may Arise for Discussion at the Second Peace Conference (Confidential), 21 Mar. 1907, TNA, FO 881/9041X, 23.

[32] 'Memorandum by Captain Charles Ottley on the Question of Contraband of War in its Relation to Ships sold by a Neutral to a Belligerent (Appendix 11), n.d.', in Report of the Inter-Departmental Committee Appointed to Consider the Subjects which may Arise for Discussion at the Second Peace Conference (Confidential), 21 Mar. 1907, TNA, FO 881/9041X, 81.

[33] 'Memorandum by Captain Charles Ottley on the Question of Contraband of War in its Relation to Ships sold by a Neutral to a Belligerent (Appendix 11), n.d.', in Report of the Inter-Departmental Committee Appointed to Consider the Subjects which may Arise for Discussion at the Second Peace Conference (Confidential), 21 Mar. 1907, TNA, FO 881/9041X, 83.

unless other states were also willing to enforce the same laws. The argument of reciprocity had often been brought up after the Russo-Japanese War. Reciprocity was important in international law, and in the absence of a higher legal authority, the responsibility rested solely on the individual state. As a result, the primary aim in the discussion on neutrality was to make states accountable for their decisions.

Another difficulty, which Ottley addressed, was that of how international law differentiated between ships built 'for fighting purposes' and others built 'for peaceful purposes'. Hence, he produced a list with distinctive features for warships or potential warships, which was intended to help port officials identify the different ship types more easily and at the same time to offer some clarification for the shipbuilding industry.[34] The committee took up this point, and pushed the matter further, recommending a definition of what constituted a ship of war, and what was an auxiliary ship, which had hitherto been a grey area.[35]

The committee took a clear position with regard to the destruction of neutral property and reiterated Britain's long-held opinion that such behaviour was intolerable. Only prizes of belligerent vessels might be destroyed. The prizes of neutrals had to be released if they could not be brought into a port for a proper prize court procedure. This reflected what had been British practice 'for at least 200 years'.[36]

An undated report comprehensively summarized the committee's discussion on the law of neutrality. It said that the principle of neutrality was 'habitually violated' and more generally that the 'interests of neutrals have hitherto been inadequately considered'. Due to the 'present condition of commerce and the growing inter-dependence of nations', belligerents could not assume 'that the rights of belligerents are to take precedent', and that 'neutrals should have means of obtaining prompt and adequate redress'. The committee suggested a reversal of Britain's 'dominant policy', which consisted

[34] 'Memorandum by Captain Charles Ottley on the Question of Contraband of War in its Relation to Ships sold by a Neutral to a Belligerent (Appendix 11), n.d.', in Report of the Inter-Departmental Committee Appointed to Consider the Subjects which may Arise for Discussion at the Second Peace Conference (Confidential), 21 Mar. 1907, TNA, FO 881/9041X, 82.

[35] 'Memorandum by Captain Charles Ottley on the Question of Contraband of War in its Relation to Ships sold by a Neutral to a Belligerent (Appendix 11), n.d.', in Report of the Inter-Departmental Committee Appointed to Consider the Subjects which may Arise for Discussion at the Second Peace Conference (Confidential), 21 Mar. 1907, TNA, FO 881/9041X, 25–6.

[36] 'Memorandum by Captain Charles Ottley on the Question of Contraband of War in its Relation to Ships sold by a Neutral to a Belligerent (Appendix 11), n.d.', in Report of the Inter-Departmental Committee Appointed to Consider the Subjects which may Arise for Discussion at the Second Peace Conference (Confidential), 21 Mar. 1907, TNA, FO 881/9041X, 26.

of 'the maintenance and enlargement of belligerent rights', and instead strengthen neutral rights.[37] Its view had been reinforced by the experience of the Russo-Japanese War, which had seen 'a tendency to trespass upon or impair the recognised rights of neutrals'.[38] Consequently, the committee suggested that contraband be specified more clearly, that convoys should be exempt from capture, that a new prize court system should be created, and that it be forbidden to sink neutral prizes. All these issues indirectly dealt with the rights of neutrals, and thus formed an integral part of Britain's position, which it had based on its practice throughout the latter half of the nineteenth century. Clearly, Britain saw itself as an example to others. With its strict adherence to the law of neutrality, as well as its consistency in its neutrality policy, Britain hoped for reciprocity in a future conflict. The committee saw the conference as an opportunity to internationalize British practice on neutrality but it was also aware that not all points were acceptable and enforceable.[39]

According to the recommendations of the Inter-Departmental Committee, Britain had more to gain than to lose, strategically and economically: Strategically, the proposals favoured a major sea power by emphasizing the effective control of the sea, with a strong law of blockade as the only means to seize enemy and neutral ships. Economically, the abolition of contraband and the limitation of the right of search and capture would be beneficial to Britain's economic interests. No matter whether Britain was a neutral or a belligerent in a future maritime conflict, its economic interests would be effectively protected. The report presented a balanced view on belligerent and neutral rights, although the final report examined the Russian programme mainly from the perspective of a belligerent. The committee's stance aimed to strengthen neutral rights and accepted limitations on the exercise of belligerent rights.

The preparatory work for the Hague peace conference was shaped not only by the Foreign Office, whose domain such preparations had always been, but also by other offices, for instance from the Committee of Imperial Defence, the Admiralty, the War Office, the Colonial Office, and the Board of Trade. This reflected the complexity of the task, and the different perspectives from which the legal aspects were examined. Most committee members were jurists by training, such as Cecil J. B. Hurst from the Foreign Office.

---

[37] Draft Report as to Rights of Neutrals, n.d., TNA, CAB 17/85, 71.
[38] Draft Report as to Rights of Neutrals, n.d., TNA, CAB 17/85, 72.
[39] Draft Report as to Rights of Neutrals, n.d., TNA, CAB 17/85, 70–84.

Yet, two non-jurists dominated the discussion, George S. Clarke and Charles L. Ottley, whose memoranda formed the basis for the report's recommendations. Clarke as secretary of the CID had access to the highest echelons in politics and was well informed about the government's war planning and strategic decision-making.[40] He saw the conference as a chance 'to educate opinion throughout the world in regard to certain subjects of supreme importance to humanity as a whole'. This rather idealistic goal was more important than 'the settlement of specific questions that we should endeavour to promote'. He was convinced that 'the fruits of such endeavours will be reaped in the future'.[41] Realism kicked in when Clarke added that although 'the mutual interests of nations are steadily increasing', 'the blessings of peace...are visibly restricted by the vast expenditure on preparation for war'.[42]

The second non-jurist was the director of Naval Intelligence, Charles L. Ottley. He was involved in war planning, and had spent several years as a naval attaché in Paris. Although Ottley was not part of Sir John Fisher's inner circle, the First Sea Lord sent him to the Hague and London conferences as naval delegate. Ottley would later succeed Clarke as secretary of the CID in 1907. The interest of the CID and the Admiralty in questions of international law suggests that the complexity of naval operations and their legal challenges was of the highest importance for them, and thus became an important factor in the war planning and strategic decision-making processes for the British government prior to the First World War.[43]

The Admiralty was consistently ambivalent about international law prior to 1914. When the Royal Commission on Food Supply asked the Admiralty in 1903 about international law in relation to the protection of trade, the Admiralty replied that 'the interests of Great Britain in regard to these matters are so widely different to those of the other powers that it is hardly advisable for her [Britain] to raise any question with regard to them at the

---

[40] Morgan-Owen, *The Fear of Invasion*, 112–14, 145–8; Nicholas d'Ombrain, *War Machinery and High Policy: Defence Administration in Peacetime Britain 1902–1914* (Oxford, 1973), 14–15; John Gooch, 'Sir George Clarke's Career at the Committee of Imperial Defence 1904–1907', *The Historical Journal* 18, 3 (1975), 555–69.

[41] Memorandum by George S. Clarke on the Hague Conference (Secret), 20 Apr. 1906, TNA, CAB 17/85, 258.

[42] Memorandum by George S. Clarke on the Hague Conference (Secret), 20 Apr. 1906, TNA, CAB 17/85, 251–2.

[43] Christopher Martin, 'The Declaration of London: A Matter of Operational Capability', *Historical Research*, 82, 218 (2009), 731–55; Avner Offer, 'Morality and Admiralty: "Jacky" Fisher, Economic Warfare and the Laws of War', *Journal of Contemporary History*, 23 (1988), 99–118.

present time'. In fact, the Admiralty only wanted to deal with international law when 'the circumstances...arise'.[44] The Admiralty's indecisive reply indicates that it was not primarily involved in defining Britain's legal position, nor was it greatly interested in the question. Despite the Admiralty's ambiguous position towards international law under Fisher, two very different personalities, Ottley and Edmond J. W. Slade, became influential on the Inter-Departmental Committee. Their memoranda on law and strategy were widely respected, and showed how a legal framework could be constructed to fit Britain's maritime strategy.[45]

The Inter-Departmental Report was intended for circulation within wider government circles, and was also sent to Edmond Slade, who acted as director of the Royal Naval War College in Portsmouth. On the question of contraband, Slade was rather pessimistic about the conference reaching a viable compromise. He thought that, if the conference could agree that 'the destination of the cargo' was the criterion upon which the nature of the cargo was to be decided, then a lot would have been achieved. He was against curtailing the right of search and capture because he feared that Britain could 'lose a weapon'. Hence, he hoped that Britain could 'retain it without raising too much opposition'. On the other hand, Slade suggested that the right of search and capture could be used to 'bargain it against the question of the "obligations of neutrals"'. It was clear to him that 'whatever we [Britain] do we must remember that we possess a valuable asset and if we part with it, we must do so at the highest price'.[46]

The report of the Inter-Departmental Committee was also circulated amongst members of the Cabinet, and, at the same time, served as the basis for the instructions to the British delegates. The report itself, however, was 'too confidential' to be presented to parliament.[47] Willoughby Maycock

---

[44] Memorandum by the Admiralty on the Protection of Ocean Trade in War Time, Oct. 1903, TNA, CAB 17/3, 27.

[45] Nicholas A. Lambert, *Planning Armageddon: British Economic Warfare and the First World War* (Cambridge, MA, 2012), 85–101; Martin, 'Declaration of London', 731–55; Offer, 'Morality and Admiralty', 99–118. For an appreciation of Slade's role, see Matthew S. Seligmann, *The Royal Navy and the German Threat, 1901–1914: Admiralty Plans to Protect British Trade in a War Against Germany* (Oxford, 2012), 91–107. For a critical reflection on Lambert's book, see John W. Coogan, 'The Short-War Illusion Resurrected: The Myth of Economic Warfare as the British Schlieffen Plan', *The Journal of Strategic Studies*, 38 (2015), 1045–64.

[46] Edmond J. W. Slade to William Nicholson, 20 June 1906, TNA, CAB 17/85, 259–69.

[47] Memorandum by W. Maycock showing the Attitude of His Majesty's Government and that of other Powers, with a Summary of the Recommendations of the Inter-Departmental Committee on the Principal Topics in the Russian Programme, 27 Apr. 1907, TNA, FO 881/10082, 5.

from the treaty department of the Foreign Office summarized the committee's main points in response to the Russian programme. Most prominently, the memorandum mentioned the creation of an international prize court under the first point, followed by proposals for the regulation of naval warfare. Amongst the points discussed were the right of search and capture, the law of neutrality, contraband of war, the treatment of belligerent vessels in neutral ports, and the sinking of neutral prizes.[48]

The 1907 Hague Peace Conference

The Cabinet approved the report with some minor corrections. The instructions to the delegates to The Hague were compared with the final report of the Inter-Departmental Committee formulated rather vaguely.[49] The head of the British delegation was Sir Edward Fry, a former judge of the Court of Appeal and legal assessor on various international commissions, who had settled the California dispute between the United States and Mexico in 1902–3 and the Dogger Bank incident of 1904. Other members were Sir Ernest Satow, senior diplomat with expertise in the Far East; Lord Reay, former Governor of Bombay and Under-Secretary for India, and president of the Institut de droit international in 1904; Sir Henry Howard, an attaché in the diplomatic service; Sir Edmond R. Elles, military delegate; and Charles L. Ottley, naval delegate. The composition of the delegation was rather unusual. Fry had only rather reluctantly accepted the position as its head, since in his opinion he was ignorant of 'international law, of diplomatic forms, and of the French language'.[50] He was also 80 years old. Although two senior jurists were part of the delegation, neither of them was associated with the Foreign Office, which had sent Ernest Satow instead. The announcement of the membership was closely watched abroad. The German government concluded that Fry was an 'able and formidable' jurist

---

[48] Memorandum by W. Maycock showing the Attitude of His Majesty's Government and that of other Powers, with a Summary of the Recommendations of the Inter-Departmental Committee on the Principal Topics in the Russian Programme, 27 Apr. 1907, TNA, FO 881/10082, 5.

[49] 'Sir Edward Grey to Sir E. Fry, 12 June 1907 (No. 206)', in Gooch and Temperley, *British Documents on the Origins of the War 1898–1914, Vol. VIII*, 242–50.

[50] Agnes Fry, *A Memoir of the Right Honourable Sir Edward Fry, G.C.B., 1827–1918* (Oxford, 1921), 194.

but quite old. Ottley, on the other hand, was a 'lucky' appointment as the German government regarded him as a 'very educated' naval officer.[51]

The Foreign Secretary, Sir Edward Grey, reminded Fry in private that for Britain the protection of neutral rights was invaluable for its economic and strategic interests, and instructed him to free 'neutral commerce to the utmost extent possible from interference by belligerent Powers'. At the same time, however, Grey instructed Fry not to take the initiative in the contraband issue. He feared that 'a novel proposal of a far-reaching character coming from ourselves, may arouse more suspicion in the minds of one of our European neighbours than if it was proposed by some other Power who could not be regarded as a rival'.[52] Grey favoured the United States as an option, but when the conference started, it was the British delegate, Lord Reay, who presented the proposal at the meeting of the Fourth Commission on 24 June 1907. The proposal was postponed due to its novelty, and to allow the members of the commission to give it careful consideration.[53]

The Fourth Commission discussed it a month later. After presenting the main arguments which had been outlined in the Inter-Departmental Report, Reay explained the shortcomings of the existing law of contraband. Neutrals and neutral commerce were hit hard under the conditions of modern warfare, which ultimately undermined the then current practice of the principles of the Declaration of Paris of 1856. With the advance in technology and the mechanization of warfare, the list of conditional goods expanded steadily, and hence all goods could serve civilian as well as military purposes.[54] Railway transport, in particular, allowed land powers to gain access to contraband goods more easily and quickly than before, which put them at an advantage in comparison to island nations. Therefore, the doctrine of continuous voyage became more relevant as new modes of

---

[51] German Embassy to Count v. Bülow, London, 26 Apr. 1907, BA [Bundesarchiv, Berlin-Lichterfelde], R 901, 121–2; Naval Attaché to Reichsmarineamt (German Imperial Naval Office), London, 3 May 1907, BA, R 901, 73.

[52] 'Sir Edward Grey to Sir E. Fry (Private and Confidential), 12 June 1907 (No. 207)', in Gooch and Temperley, *British Documents of the Origins of the War 1898–1914, Vol. VIII*, 242–51.

[53] Fourth Commission, First Meeting, 24 June 1907, in James Brown Scott (ed.), *The Proceedings of the Hague Peace Conferences. Translation of the Original Texts. The Conference of 1907, Vol. III: Meetings of the Second, Third and Fourth Commissions* (New York, 1921), 744. See also Appendix 27: Declaration Read by His Excellency Lord Reay in the Name of the British Delegation, Concerning Contraband of War, in Scott (ed.), *Proceedings. The Conference of 1907, Vol. III: Meetings of the Second, Third and Fourth Commissions*, 1136.

[54] Fourth Commission, Eighth Meeting, 24 July 1907, in Scott (ed.), *Proceedings. The Conference of 1907, Vol. III: Meetings of the Second, Third and Fourth Commissions*, 845.

transport allowed goods to be transported more easily from ports to destinations inland. During the American Civil War, the United States had expanded the doctrine of continuous voyage in order to stop neutral commerce destined for the Confederates, which were consigned to neutral islands in the Caribbean. With the improvement of infrastructure on land, the application of the rule became more difficult, in particular proving the ultimate destination of goods. At the same time, the liability of contraband goods was not settled. While the 'burden of proof' lay with the captor of the ship, Britain suggested that the owner of the ship should prove the 'innocent destination'.[55] In principle, Britain made cargo owners liable for the nature of their goods, while continental practice made shipowners responsible. Lord Reay concluded 'that in the present condition of world commerce and of human knowledge the exercise of the right of seizure results only in hampering neutral commerce without giving belligerents compensating advantages and in bringing the former eventually into the war'. Thus, Britain proposed the abolition of contraband to 'remove a frequent cause of international differences'.[56]

The British proposal met with strong opposition. The German delegate, Johannes Kriege, the head of the legal department at the German Foreign Office, replied that Germany would not abstain from its right of search and capture, which was in his opinion a 'principle of legitimate self-defence'.[57] Kriege presented Germany's own proposal, which basically aimed at limiting 'the area of the right of control and suppression exercised by belligerents' by which Kriege meant that neutral ships were only liable for capture if they were sailing for an enemy port, and that 'regular mail' steamers would be exempt from capture.[58] France, Brazil, and the United States also prepared their own proposals.[59] They all favoured the existing practice of

---

[55] Fourth Commission, Eighth Meeting, 24 July 1907, in Scott (ed.), *Proceedings. The Conference of 1907, Vol. III: Meetings of the Second, Third and Fourth Commissions*, 845.

[56] Fourth Commission, Eighth Meeting, 24 July 1907, in Scott (ed.), *Proceedings. The Conference of 1907, Vol. III: Meetings of the Second, Third and Fourth Commissions*, 849.

[57] Fourth Commission, Eighth Meeting, 24 July 1907, in Scott (ed.), *Proceedings. The Conference of 1907, Vol. III: Meetings of the Second, Third and Fourth Commissions*, 849.

[58] Fourth Commission, Eighth Meeting, 24 July 1907, in Scott (ed.), *Proceedings. The Conference of 1907, Vol. III: Meetings of the Second, Third and Fourth Commissions*, 850–1. See Annex 28: Proposition of the German Delegation, Contraband of War, in Scott (ed.), *Proceedings. The Conference of 1907, Vol. III: Meetings of the Second, Third and Fourth Commissions*, 1136–7.

[59] Fourth Commission, First Meeting, 12 Aug. 1907, in Scott (ed.), *Proceedings. The Conference of 1907, Vol. III: Meetings of the Second, Third and Fourth Commissions*, 1091–2. See Annex 29: Proposition of the French Delegation, Drafts Regulations on Contraband of War, in Scott (ed.), *Proceedings. The Conference of 1907, Vol. III: Meetings of the Second, Third and*

distinguishing between conditional and absolute contraband.[60] An initial vote on the abolition of contraband was to give an indication of the further debate on the issue. In principle, Austria-Hungary and the United States favoured the abolition of contraband, but were hesitant in supporting the British proposal, preferring any proposal with a restricted list of contraband. Before the delegates voted, the president of the Fourth Commission declared that 'no one disputes the belligerent's right of legitimate self-defence; nor does anyone dispute the fact that it is the duty of neutrals not to intervene in hostilities'. Effectively, belligerents had 'the right to take measures against the hostile commerce of neutrals'. Yet, reforms were necessary in order to avoid conflicts between neutrals and belligerents in a future war at sea. Twenty-six states, including Britain, Austria-Hungary, Brazil, Belgium, Switzerland, and Italy, approved abolition; Germany, the United States, Russia, France, and Montenegro voted against; and Japan, Spain, Turkey, Romania, and Panama abstained. Given the lack of unanimity, a committee was formed to harmonize the different proposals.[61]

The committee's discussions showed that members agreed in principle on a list of absolute contraband, but they disagreed on how to treat conditional contraband. Britain, Brazil, Chile, and the United States favoured the abolition of conditional contraband altogether. Germany, France, and Russia insisted on a list of conditional contraband.[62] The divide among the major sea powers on this question prompted France to offer to negotiate with Britain in order to reach an agreement.[63] The offer was met favourably and Cecil J. B. Hurst, the assistant legal adviser to the Foreign Office, explained that 'from a strategic point of view...a satisfactory agreement with France as to contraband is much more important than an agreement with Germany'.

Fourth Commissions, 1138–9; Annex 30: Proposition of the Brazilian Delegation, Contraband of War, in Scott (ed.), *Proceedings. The Conference of 1907, Vol. III: Meetings of the Second, Third and Fourth Commissions*, 1139–40; Annex 31: Proposition of the Delegation of the United States, Contraband of War, in Scott (ed.), *Proceedings. The Conference of 1907, Vol. III: Meetings of the Second, Third and Fourth Commissions*, 1140.

[60] A summary of all proposals can be found under Annex 32: Table of Proposals Relative to Contraband of War, in Scott (ed.), *Proceedings. The Conference of 1907, Vol. III: Meetings of the Second, Third and Fourth Commissions*, 1141–7.
[61] Fourth Commission, Tenth Meeting, 31 July 1907, in Scott (ed.), *Proceedings. The Conference of 1907, Vol. III: Meetings of the Second, Third and Fourth Commissions*, 872.
[62] Fourth Commission, First Meeting, 12 Aug. 1907, Second Meeting, 15 Aug. 1907, Third Meeting, 21 Aug. 1907, in Scott (ed.), *Proceedings. The Conference of 1907, Vol. III: Meetings of the Second, Third and Fourth Commissions*, 1093–104.
[63] 'Sir E. Fry to Sir Edward Grey, 2 Sept. 1907 (No. 245)', in Gooch and Temperley, *British Documents of the Origins of the War 1898–1914, Vol. VIII*, 274–5.

The thinking behind this decision was that Germany was less likely 'to interfere materially with the sea-borne trade of Great Britain and would therefore not be able to intercept the cargoes of corn and cotton *en route* for British ports'. Hurst feared that, if Britain was at war with France, the French would take 'the advantage of the geographical situation,...and intercept a certain number of cargoes intended for Great Britain'.[64] While Hurst reckoned that an agreement with the Germans was unlikely, he underlined the importance of getting the United States on board. The American delegate, Rear Admiral Charles S. Sperry, had signalled that his country would consider a 'restricted list' for conditional and absolute contraband.[65] Despite the efforts of the committee, no agreement could be reached on a list of conditional contraband. The list of absolute contraband was never ratified. Hence, no resolution was achieved at the Hague peace conference. A radical departure from existing practice was a hopeless endeavour without the prior agreement of the major sea powers. The result reflected the political climate, which was much more confrontational than at the first Hague peace conference in 1899. Negotiating the rules for a future maritime war was therefore a difficult venture.[66]

The question of contraband was linked to the law of neutrality. The second sub-committee of the Third Commission had received four drafts for discussion, one each from Japan, Spain, Russia, and Britain. The British draft treated the subject most exhaustively and formed the basis for the discussion.[67] Sir Ernest Satow explained that the rules presented 'a summary of the rules which the British Government, as a neutral, considers itself bound to observe in time of war'. Satow hoped that Britain's experience as a neutral would 'produce satisfactory results', not least because Britain had also experience as a belligerent.[68]

---

[64] 'Memorandum by Cecil Hurst on Contraband, 31 Aug. 1907 (Enclosure 1 in No. 245)', in Gooch and Temperley, *British Documents on the Origins of the War 1898–1914, Vol. VIII*, 274–279, here: 275.

[65] 'Minute by Mr. F. A. Campbell on the Attitude of United States in the Matter of Contraband, 7 Sept. 1907 (No. 248)', in Gooch and Temperley, *British Documents of the Origins of the First World War 1898–1914, Vol. VIII*, 281–2.

[66] Seventh Plenary Meeting, 27 Sept. 1907, in James Brown Scott (ed.), *The Proceedings of the Hague Peace Conferences. Translation of the Original Texts. The Conference of 1907, Vol. I: Plenary Meetings of the Conference* (New York, 1920), 250–4.

[67] Third Commission: Second Subcommission, Third Meeting, 27 July 1907, in Scott, (ed.), *Proceedings. The Conference of 1907, Vol. III: Meetings of the Second, Third and Fourth Commissions*, 573–4.

[68] Third Commission: Second Subcommission, Third Meeting, 27 July 1907, in Scott, (ed.), *Proceedings. The Conference of 1907, Vol. III: Meetings of the Second, Third and Fourth Commissions*, 575.

The draft Convention (XIII) consisted of 32 Articles.[69] Paramount for a neutral was the recognition of its sovereignty. Article 1 stated that a belligerent had 'to respect the sovereign rights of neutral Powers'.[70] Articles 2 to 4 forbade belligerents from using neutral waters for their operations. Articles 5 to 8 reflected the 'Three Rules' of Article 6 of the Treaty of Washington of 1871. Article 8, which dealt with the building, equipping and dispatching of warships, was formulated less restrictively in order to give greater freedom to shipbuilders.[71]

Article 12 of the draft Convention (XIII), which dealt with the twenty-four hours rule—the time within which belligerent ships were required to leave neutral ports—proved controversial. Russia and Germany opposed such a regulation and proposed an indefinite length of stay. This was not acceptable to Britain or Japan, which had been enforcing the twenty-four hours rule. Russia and Germany suggested limiting the indefinite stay to neutral ports far away from the theatre of war, but Britain and Japan rejected this proposal on the grounds that the term 'theatre of war' was imprecise and would fail to account for fast-moving modern naval warfare. Finally, the delegates settled the issue by adding a clause that the twenty-four-hours rule should apply in the absence of any other domestic regulation. Effectively, no compromise was achieved.[72]

Article 19 dealt with the resupplying of belligerent ships in neutral ports, in particular in regard to re-coaling. The British practice limited the amount of coal to what was needed to reach the nearest home port or a nearer neutral destination. The Russians, on the other hand, wanted as much as 'necessary' for the ship to continue its voyage. Pressure also came from several minor sea powers which relied on supplies in neutral ports. The delegates agreed that 'vessels may only ship sufficient fuel to enable them to reach the

[69] Third Commission: Second Subcommission, Third Meeting, 27 July 1907, in Scott, (ed.), *Proceedings. The Conference of 1907, Vol. III: Meetings of the Second, Third and Fourth Commissions*, 575. See also Annex 44: Rights and Duties of Neutral Powers in Naval War, Proposal of the British Delegation, in Scott, (ed.), *Proceedings. The Conference of 1907, Vol. III: Meetings of the Second, Third and Fourth Commissions*, 698–701.
[70] Annex: Draft Convention Regarding the Rights and Duties of Neutral Powers in Naval War. Report to the Commission, in Scott, (ed.), *Proceedings. The Conference of 1907, Vol. III: Meetings of the Second, Third and Fourth Commissions*, 489–518, here: 492.
[71] Annex: Draft Convention Regarding the Rights and Duties of Neutral Powers in Naval War. Report to the Commission, in Scott, (ed.), *Proceedings. The Conference of 1907, Vol. III: Meetings of the Second, Third and Fourth Commissions*, 489–518, here: 496–7.
[72] Annex: Draft Convention Regarding the Rights and Duties of Neutral Powers in Naval War. Report to the Commission, in Scott, (ed.), *Proceedings. The Conference of 1907, Vol. III: Meetings of the Second, Third and Fourth Commissions*, 489–518, here: 500–5.

nearest port in their own country', but also conceded that belligerents were allowed 'to bring up their supplies to the peace standard'. The wording described a significant departure from the strict rules Britain had practised in the Russo-Japanese War. Consequently, Britain, the United States, and Japan expressed their reservations and abstained from voting.[73]

Article 20 of the draft Convention (XIII) dealt with the length of time during which a belligerent was not allowed to enter another neutral port of the same country after resupplying. Britain had controversially introduced the three months rule during the American Civil War. Alternative rules, such as mileage, radius or a second resupplying were discussed but none of them gained a unanimous vote. No compromise was found, which was also reflected in the vote for Article 20, which received five votes in favour, three rejections, and six abstentions.[74]

The fierce discussion of the draft Convention (XIII) illustrated how divided the major powers were on the question of the law of neutrality. When the Third Commission met on 4 October 1907, several states entered reservations with regard to Article 12, and, in the case of Britain, Sir Ernest Satow stated that his government would need to examine carefully the draft convention before accepting it because it differed 'seriously from the original proposals put forward'.[75] Nevertheless, the delegates approved Convention (XIII) concerning the Rights and Duties of Neutral Powers in Naval War with minor reservations.[76] The creation of an internationally binding law of neutrality attracted a great deal of discussion at The Hague, and, although the British draft was amended as a result, Convention (XIII) was based principally on British state practice.

The report, which the rapporteur and French jurist, Louis Renault, submitted to the Third Commission, highlighted the importance of the convention as 'the neutral states urgently demand such precise rules as will, if

---

[73] Annex: Draft Convention Regarding the Rights and Duties of Neutral Powers in Naval War. Report to the Commission, in Scott, (ed.), *Proceedings. The Conference of 1907, Vol. III: Meetings of the Second, Third and Fourth Commissions*, 489–518, here: 510–11.

[74] Annex: Draft Convention Regarding the Rights and Duties of Neutral Powers in Naval War. Report to the Commission, in Scott, (ed.), *Proceedings. The Conference of 1907, Vol. III: Meetings of the Second, Third and Fourth Commissions*, 489–518, here: 511–13.

[75] For a full discussion on the Draft Convention (XIII), see Third Commission, Eighth Meeting, 4 Oct. 1907, in Scott, (ed.), *Proceedings. The Conference of 1907, Vol. III: Meetings of the Second, Third and Fourth Commissions*, 463–489, here: 467.

[76] 'Convention (XIII) Concerning the Rights and Duties of Neutral Powers in Naval War. The Hague, 18 Oct. 1907', in Dietrich Schindler and Jiří Toman (eds), *The Laws of Armed Conflicts: A Collection of Conventions, Resolutions and other Documents* (Dordrecht, 2004), 1407–16.

observed, shelter them from accusations on part of either belligerent'. Yet, Renault reminded his colleagues that 'neutrality is not viewed in the same light by everybody'. It was important that the project dealt with concrete examples so as to remove uncertainties for neutrals as much as belligerents in particular situations.[77] Naturally, according to Renault, Convention (XIII) also had to be examined in relation to the creation of an international prize court, where, ultimately, disputes between neutrals and belligerents would be settled. Thus, the work of the Third Commission also had to be viewed in this context, and 'at a time when an International Prize Court is being created, it would be wise to develop to as great a degree as possible a codification of international maritime law in time of war'.[78]

The First Commission dealt with the creation of an international prize court—a subject that had not been on the agenda but for which Germany and Britain each presented a draft.[79] The drafts differed substantially in regard to the nature of the court and the composition of the judges. The German draft proposed an ad hoc court, consisting of admirals of both belligerent and neutral parties. On the other hand, Britain's proposal envisaged a permanent court of appeal composed of jurists, who would be nominated by a rota system, and operated by states with a navy larger than 800,000 tons. Both drafts reflected their states' national interests in a future war at sea, and a sub-committee was appointed to prepare a joint draft.[80]

Renault again acted as rapporteur and presented a joint draft on 21 September 1907. His report argued that 'prize courts really are national courts passing judgements on international questions'. Yet, the judges had to 'apply the laws of their country without inquiring whether these laws are in

---

[77] Annex: Draft Convention Regarding the Rights and Duties of Neutral Powers in Naval War. Report to the Commission, in Scott, (ed.), *Proceedings. The Conference of 1907, Vol. III: Meetings of the Second, Third and Fourth Commissions*, 489–518, here: 491.

[78] Annex: Draft Convention Regarding the Rights and Duties of Neutral Powers in Naval War. Report to the Commission, in Scott, (ed.), *Proceedings. The Conference of 1907, Vol. III: Meetings of the Second, Third and Fourth Commissions*, 489–518, here: 490.

[79] Second Plenary Meeting, 19 June 1907, in Scott (ed.), *Proceedings. The Conference of 1907, Vol. I: Plenary Meetings of the Conference*, 55.

[80] Annex 88: Proposition of the German Delegation Regarding the Prize Court, in James Brown Scott (ed.), *The Proceedings of the Hague Peace Conferences. Translation of the Original Texts. The Conference of 1907, Vol. II: Meetings of the First Commission* (New York, 1920), 1051–6; Annex 89: Proposition of the British Delegation, in Scott (ed.), *Proceedings. The Conference of 1907, Vol. II: Meetings of the First Commission*, 1056–8. For a detailed analysis, see Gabriela A. Frei, 'How to Wage Economic Warfare in a Globalised Economy? International Jurisdiction between State and Private Interests', under peer-review.

harmony with international law or not'.[81] This was the reason for disputes between neutrals and belligerents, and, although it seemed impossible to dream of an international prize court for many decades, the conference opened the opportunity to initiate such a proposal. Renault emphatically stated that the court was 'also distinctly a work of peace, introducing law into a subject hitherto left to arbitrariness and violence'.[82] Convention (XII) relative to the Creation of an International Prize Court,[83] which resulted from the discussions, outlined how such an international court could operate. The international prize court would be a permanent court of appeal only, to consider neutral and, in certain cases, enemy property. Individuals and states would have access to the court, which would be composed of eight permanent judges and seven judges chosen from a rota system. The legal basis was treaty law, or 'the rules of international law'.[84]

Belligerent rights had not been part of the official Russian programme, although many issues touched upon them directly or indirectly. For instance, the discussion on contraband sparked a discussion on blockade. The Fourth Commission, presided over by the Russian international jurist, Feodor Martens, had prepared a general questionnaire, which also addressed the question of blockade.[85] The Italian delegate, Guido Fusinato, stated that 'contraband and blockade are the two great restrictions which war placed upon the commerce of neutrals in the present state of positive international law'.[86] The Declaration of Paris of 1856 had defined what constituted a lawful blockade, and yet the development of technology questioned its principles.

---

[81]   Sixth Plenary Meeting, 21 Sept. 1907, in Scott (ed.), *Proceedings. The Conference of 1907, Vol. I: Plenary Meetings of the Conference*, 181.

[82]   Sixth Plenary Meeting, 21 Sept. 1907, in Scott (ed.), *Proceedings. The Conference of 1907, Vol. I: Plenary Meetings of the Conference*, 183.

[83]   'Convention (XII) Relative to the Creation of an International Prize Court. The Hague, 18 Oct. 1907', in Dietrich Schindler and Jiří Toman (eds.), *The Laws of Armed Conflicts. A Collection of Conventions, Resolutions and other Documents* (Dordrecht, 2004), 1093–105.

[84]   First Commission, Second Meeting, 10 Sept. 1907 in Scott (ed.), *Proceedings. The Conference of 1907, Vol. II: Meetings of the First Commission*, 9–31, here: 22. For a detailed discussion, see First Commission: Second Subcommission, First Meeting, 25 June 1907, Second Meeting, 4 July 1907, Third Meeting, 11 July 1907, in Scott (ed.), *Proceedings. The Conference of 1907, Vol. II: Meetings of the First Commission*, 781–809; First Commission: Second Subcommission, Committee of Examination, First Meeting, 12 Aug. 1907, Second Meeting, 17 Aug. 1907, Third Meeting, 22 Aug. 1907, in Scott (ed.), *Proceedings. The Conference of 1907, Vol. II: Meetings of the First Commission*, 817–48; Sixth Plenary Meeting, 21 Sept. 1907, in Scott (ed.), *Proceedings. The Conference of 1907, Vol. I: Plenary Meetings of the Conference*, 164–9.

[85]   Annex 1: Questionnaire, Prepared by His Excellency, Mr Martens, President of the Fourth Commission, to Serve as a Basis for the Discussions of that Commission, in Scott (ed.), *Proceedings. The Conference of 1907, Vol. III: Meetings of the Second, Third and Fourth Commissions*, 1115–16.

[86]   Fourth Commission, Tenth Meeting, 31 July 1907, in Scott (ed.), *Proceedings. The Conference of 1907, Vol. III: Meetings of the Second, Third and Fourth Commissions*, 878.

The Italian proposal defined what constituted an 'effective blockade' more precisely. This particularly concerned the terms of notification, as well as the beginning and the end of blockade.[87] Fusinato argued that a blockade was only effective when 'military power is established'. For him the aim was to 'confine blockade within its true limits' as it 'was one of the most serious attacks on the rights of peaceful commerce'.[88] The debate of the Fourth Commission touched upon a sensitive aspect of naval warfare, which was why the British delegation urged its postponement to a later conference.[89] Without a discussion on belligerent rights, however, none of the conflicts between neutrals and belligerents could be resolved.

Sir Edward Fry, the head of the British delegation, was content with the results of the Hague peace conference. He particularly highlighted the success of Convention (XII) relative to the Creation of an International Prize Court, which had been one of Britain's primary goals. On the question of contraband, he was optimistic about achieving an agreement between Britain and the United States 'in the near future', despite the rather disappointing result. On a more general note, Fry urged the government to organize a separate conference to address the open questions with regard to belligerent rights.[90] Another British delegate, Eyre Crowe of the Foreign Office, offered a more personal opinion on the work and outcome of the conference, describing it as 'a state of perpetual flurry and tedious and invariably useless work. Nothing is to come out of all our labours, everything is to be thrown into limbo. It seems a needlessly lengthy funeral of 4 months duration!' As head of the Western Department, he seemed to be more worried that he had 'been quite unable to keep the FO "au courant".... Nothing really important depends on what goes on here. The interesting thing is the political grouping.'[91] Lord Reay shared the general impression that the conference

---

[87] Annex 34: Proposition of the Italian Delegation: Blockade, in Scott (ed.), *Proceedings. The Conference of 1907, Vol. III: Meetings of the Second, Third and Fourth Commissions*, 1149.

[88] Fourth Commission, Tenth Meeting, 31 July 1907, in Scott (ed.), *Proceedings. The Conference of 1907, Vol. III: Meetings of the Second, Third and Fourth Commissions*, 877–887, here: 879.

[89] Fourth Commission: Committee of Examination, Fifth Meeting, 16 Aug. 1907, in Scott (ed.), *Proceedings. The Conference of 1907, Vol. III: Meetings of the Second, Third and Fourth Commissions*, 954. For a summary of the discussion on blockade, see Seventh Plenary Meeting, 27 Sept. 1907, in Scott (ed.), *Proceedings. The Conference of 1907, Vol. I: Plenary Meetings of the Conference*, 255–7.

[90] 'Sir E. Fry to Sir Edward Grey, 16 Oct. 1907 (No. 256)', in Gooch and Temperley, *British Documents on the Origins of the War 1898–1914, Vol. VIII*, 295–7.

[91] 'Eyre Crowe to W. G. Tyrrell, 11 Oct. 1907 (No. 254)', in Gooch and Temperley, *British Documents of the Origins of the First World War 1898–1914, Vol. VIII*, 287. See also Lambert, *Planning Armageddon*, 90–100. For an analysis of Eyre Crowe, see Keith Neilson and T. G. Otte, *The Permanent Under-Secretary for Foreign Affairs, 1854–1946* (New York, 2009), 161–7.

'has not given a greater sense of security, but rather the reverse and outsiders are dissatisfied with the scanty harvest'. Nevertheless, he thought that none of the proposals were contrary to the interests of Britain.[92]

In many ways, the results of the Hague peace conference of 1907 were disappointing. The conventions were the result of considerable compromise, and it remained to be seen to what extent the newly agreed rules would pass the test in war.[93] The Russian diplomat, Aleksandr Nelidow, president of the second Hague peace conference, remarked in his closing address that, 'when strangers to our labours pass judgment on the activity of the Conference, they often lose sight of the fact that we are not called upon to elaborate abstract theories, to seek, by means of mental speculation, ideal solutions for the problems submitted to us'. Rather, Nelidow defended the work of the delegates, arguing that 'we are the agents of our Governments and act by virtue of special instructions, based before all other considerations upon the interest of our respective countries'.[94] Nedilow's remarks could be interpreted as an apology for the limited achievements at The Hague. On the other hand, they highlighted the constraints on the delegates, compared with private non-governmental organizations, such as the Institut de droit international, whose members were much freer in their deliberations on international law.

The Aftermath of the Hague Peace Conference

The negotiations at The Hague provided the basis for an international legal framework, governing the laws of war. Now, the governments had to approve its work. The Dutch delegate, Willem Hendrik de Beaufort, a former foreign minister and vice-president of the Hague peace conference, appealed to his colleagues that 'they should actively lobby for the work of The Hague'.[95]

The British government critically assessed the results of the conference and the Inter-Departmental Committee, which had already drawn up the

---

[92] 'Memorandum by Lord Reay (Confidential), n.d., (No. 258)', in Gooch and Temperley, *British Documents on the Origins of the War 1898–1914, Vol. VIII*, 299–800.

[93] Best, 'Peace Conferences', 619–34.

[94] Aleksandr Nedilow, 'Closing Speech, 18 Oct. 1907', in Scott (ed.), *Proceedings. The Conference of 1907, Vol. I: Plenary Meetings of the Conference*, 581.

[95] Willem Hendrik de Beaufort, 'Closing Speech, 18 Oct. 1907', in Scott (ed.), *Proceedings. The Conference of 1907, Vol. I: Plenary Meetings of the Conference*, 585. See also R. P. Dhokalia, *The Codification of Public International Law* (Manchester, 1970), 104–9.

agenda, evaluated the conventions and made recommendations as to their adoption.[96] The committee, chaired by the Earl of Desart (replacing Sir J. Lawson Walton who had died in January 1908), met from February to May 1908, examining each convention. Convention (XIII) on the law of neutrality took up most of their time because it had been 'of great interest and importance' for Britain as a neutral and as a belligerent. The committee highlighted that, compared with 'the absence of any general understanding as to the obligations or rights of neutral nations' during the Russo-Japanese War, which had caused 'inconvenience and uncertainty', the convention was a significant improvement. The committee was aware that finding a common understanding of the law of neutrality was difficult because the interests of states 'diverge[d] so seriously'. Britain's 'strength at sea has enabled her, generally speaking, to insist on her own rules'. Thus, it was clear to the committee that Britain's rules would hardly 'obtain general acceptance' and compromises were necessary.[97]

The committee carefully considered Articles 12, 19, and 23 of Convention (XIII). Article 12 concerned the twenty-four hours rule, and the committee decided that 'it would be better to accept the article' hoping that it would 'lead neutral nations to adopt some similar rule in the future'. If not, then Britain would also not be bound by the provision. Moreover, the committee was concerned with the opinion of minor states, which were 'anxious to see some rule adopted'. Ultimately the benefits outweighed the disadvantages and the committee advised the adoption of Article 12, also for the sake of 'uniformity of practice'.[98]

Article 19, which dealt with resupplies, including coaling, received careful examination. Britain's position in the matter of re-coaling was hardly tenable as minor states 'were very averse', and, hence, the committee advised that Britain should not 'stand out alone against the acceptance' of Article 19. Yet, if other states declared reservations, then Britain should also follow suit.

Article 23 allowed bringing prizes into neutral ports and had been created as a measure to avoid the sinking of prizes. Yet, the committee was against Article 23, arguing that it was 'detrimental to the interests of Great

---

[96] Final Report by the Inter-Departmental Committee on the Second Peace Conference, 28 May 1908, TNA, FO 881/9325X.
[97] Final Report by the Inter-Departmental Committee on the Second Peace Conference, 28 May 1908, TNA, FO 881/9325X.
[98] Final Report by the Inter-Departmental Committee on the Second Peace Conference, 28 May 1908, TNA, FO 881/9325X.

Britain'. If Britain were a belligerent, prizes could be hidden in neutral ports, and 'the chance of their recapture would be gone'. If Britain were neutral, the committee doubted whether a belligerent prize court could act speedily and competently if a prize was in a neutral port.

Despite the reservations with regard to Convention (XIII), the committee recommended its adoption as long as other states also committed to it. Japan had already signalled its acceptance (except of Articles 19 and 23) and the committee advised the government to enquire about the American and Spanish positions, and to 'persuade them to adopt the same course' as Britain.[99]

Britain's willingness to accept Convention (XIII) sent a strong signal to the other states. 'Uniformity of practice' was paramount in the committee's thinking and underscored Britain's long-standing commitment to neutrality. Many other Hague conventions had the object of defining neutrality more precisely, such as Convention (V) respecting the Rights and Duties of Neutral Powers and Persons in the Case of War on Land, or Convention (XI) relative to Certain Restrictions with Regard to the Exercise of the Right of Capture in Naval War.[100]

Another safeguard for neutral rights was provided by Convention (XII), which dealt with the creation of an international prize court. The Inter-Departmental Committee discussed this matter favourably, celebrating the convention 'as one of the most important agreements' of the conference. They hoped that the new court would secure 'in a naval war the great private interests bound up with shipping against unlawful prejudice by belligerents' and would provide 'an impartial judgment', which national prize courts could not guarantee. The creation of an international jurisdiction, which was concerned with one of the most controversial aspects of war at sea, was a significant step in holding states accountable for their violations of international law.[101]

---

[99] Final Report by the Inter-Departmental Committee on the Second Peace Conference, 28 May 1908, TNA, FO 881/9325X.

[100] 'Convention (V) Respecting the Rights and Duties of Neutral Powers and Persons in the Case of War on Land, The Hague, 18 Oct. 1907', in Dietrich Schindler and Jiří Toman (eds), *The Laws of Armed Conflicts: A Collection of Conventions, Resolutions and other Documents* (Dordrecht, 2004), 1399–406; 'Convention (XI) Relative to Certain Restrictions with Regard to the Exercise of the Right of Capture in Naval War, The Hague, 18 Oct. 1907', in Dietrich Schindler and Jiří Toman (eds), *The Laws of Armed Conflicts: A Collection of Conventions, Resolutions and other Documents* (Dordrecht, 2004), 1087–92.

[101] Final Report by the Inter-Departmental Committee on the Second Peace Conference, 28 May 1908, TNA, FO 881/9325X. See also Frei, 'Economic Warfare'.

Despite the Inter-Departmental Committee's enthusiasm for the establishment of an international prize court of appeal, it was concerned about the legal basis upon which the future court should operate. Article 7 stated that, in the absence of particular rules, 'the court shall apply the rules of international law'.[102] The vague formulation of Article 7 had already caused discussions between the Foreign Office and the Admiralty during the negotiations at The Hague because the Admiralty feared that the new court might rule against Britain's interests. However, the Foreign Office decided not to reopen the negotiations in spite of the Admiralty's concerns. Internally, the Foreign Office had concluded that, should the situation occur, it could amend unfavourable decisions by Orders in Council.[103] For the delegates at The Hague it was clear that an international prize court would only be operable if a legal framework was in place, and thus the British delegation had confidentially informed the German delegation during the Hague peace conference that it would organize another conference, inviting sea powers only, to discuss the open questions.[104]

The 1909 London Naval Conference

In February 1908, the British government invited the major sea powers, France, Germany, Russia, Italy, Austria-Hungary, Spain, and the United States, to a conference in London to discuss future development with regard to international maritime law. The agenda of the London naval conference addressed all major areas of conflict between neutrals and belligerents— areas which would be of particular importance for the rulings of a future international prize court. While the law of blockade and the contraband question were the primary focus of the conference, related issues were also considered, such as the doctrine of continuous voyage, the destruction of neutral vessels, un-neutral services, the legality of the conversion of merchant ships into warships, the transfer of vessels from belligerent to neutral flags, and the definition of enemy property. The Netherlands and Norway

---

[102] 'Convention (XII)', 1096.
[103] Memorandum by G. H. B. K. as to the Legislative Changes Necessary to Give Effect to the Convention for the Establishment of an International Prize Court of Appeal, London, 9 Sept. 1907, TNA, FO 95/800.
[104] Alfred von Tirpitz to Commissioners of the London Conference (Strictly Confidential), Berlin, 19 June 1908, BA–MA [Bundesarchiv, Militärarchiv, Freiburg / Brsg.], RM 3/4921, 139. For a detailed analysis, see Frei, 'Economic Warfare'.

protested against Britain's list of participants as both thought they deserved a seat at the conference table due to the size of their navies. Britain finally invited the Netherlands for the reason that The Hague would be the seat of the new international prize court.[105]

The British government appointed another Inter-Departmental Committee, chaired once again by Lord Desart, to prepare for the conference. On the committee were Edmond J. W. Slade, new director of Naval Intelligence; W. Graham Greene, assistant secretary of the Admiralty; Eyre Crowe and Cecil J. B. Hurst from the Foreign Office; as well as Charles L. Ottley, new at the CID. In the run-up to the conference, participating states were asked to exchange written statements outlining their positions with regard to the agenda. The British memorandum only listed British court decisions and state practice.[106]

When the British government received the memoranda of other states, the committee evaluated them in the context of Britain's own position.[107] From the outset, the committee declared its commitment to the idea of an international prize court, on the assumption that such a court would be more favourable to neutrals than to belligerents. In any case, the committee assumed that, due to Britain's 'enormous commercial interests...and its vast carrying trade, as well as to the fact that it must more often be neutral than belligerent', the court would offer a safeguard for British interests.[108]

The committee focused on two subjects: the question of contraband and that of blockade. The latter was one of the most important points on the agenda. The terms of liability of capture needed to be addressed as British and continental practice differed in this regard. While the former made a ship liable for capture from the beginning to the end of the ship's journey when destined for a blockaded port, the latter only made the ship liable if it actually breached the blockade. The committee had examined the cases carefully but did not find any cases where capture had occurred far away from the blockade. Thus, the committee suggested that Britain might

---

[105] 'Sir Edward Grey to His Majesty's Representatives at Paris, Berlin, St. Petersburgh, Rome, Vienna, Madrid, Washington, and Tokio, 27 Feb. 1908 (No. 263)', in Gooch and Temperley, *British Documents on the Origins of the War 1898–1914, Vol. VIII*, 306–7.

[106] Naval Conference. Memorandum Setting Out the Views of His Majesty's Government, Founded Upon the Decisions in the British Courts, as to the Rules of International Law on the Points Enumerated in the Programme of the Conference, n.d., TNA, FO 881/9753X.

[107] 'Exposés des vues exprimées par les Mémorandums et observations destinées à servir de base aux délibérations de la Conférence, soumis par le Gouvernement britannique, 14 Nov. 1908', in P.P. Misc. 5 (1909): Proceedings of the International Naval Conference, held in London, Dec. 1908–Feb. 1909, [Cd. 4555], 57–122.

[108] Naval Conference Committee. Further Report, 26 Oct. 1908, TNA, FO 881/9753X, 2.

abandon the existing practice and accept a *rayon d'action*, which defined an 'area within which the blockading forces' could operate.[109] The reasoning behind this was that it would 'not often be of material injury to the interests of this country' and, therefore, it would 'not be necessary to insist on the adoption of the British principle'.[110]

Generally, a ship destined for a blockaded port could be condemned, while a ship destined for a neutral port could not. The Americans had expanded the doctrine of continuous voyage during the American Civil War, which made a ship liable to capture when it carried contraband goods ultimately destined for a blockaded port, despite the fact that the ship itself was destined for a neutral port. The British wanted to undo the expansion of the doctrine of continuous voyage in conjunction with blockade.[111] In no case, however, should a neutral prize be destroyed, as British practice demanded the release of the ship if it could not be brought into port.[112] The committee signalled its willingness to compromise on many points but advised approaching Japan and the United States first to find prior agreement on disputed questions.[113]

Slade, as director of Naval Intelligence, had examined the memoranda and Britain's position from the perspective of the navy. He identified areas which were negotiable, such as immunity from capture of neutral vessels in convoy, or the limitation of the radius for seizure of ships that breached a blockade. Other issues, however, were non-negotiable in his opinion, such as compensation for neutral property which had been sunk, the restriction of the contraband list, the prohibition on the sinking of neutral prizes, or the prohibition of the conversion of merchant ships into warships on the high seas.[114] Slade's willingness to compromise on the law of blockade resulted from his understanding that, 'under modern conditions' warships would operate 'at a considerable distance from the port'. Hence, accepting a *rayon d'action* would be favourable for Britain.[115] Slade had actively promoted the codification of international maritime law in order to limit

---

[109] Naval Conference Committee. Further Report, 26 Oct. 1908, TNA, FO 881/9753X, 9.

[110] Naval Conference Committee. Further Report, 26 Oct. 1908, TNA, FO 881/9753X, 10.

[111] Naval Conference Committee. Further Report, 26 Oct. 1908, TNA, FO 881/9753X, 11.

[112] Naval Conference Committee. Further Report, 26 Oct. 1908, TNA, FO 881/9753X, 12–17.

[113] Naval Conference Committee. Further Report, 26 Oct. 1908, TNA, FO 881/9753X, 25–6.

[114] Naval Conference Committee. Memorandum by Edmond J. W. Slade (Confidential), 29 Sept. 1908, TNA, FO 881/9753X, 24–6.

[115] Naval Conference Committee. Memorandum by Edmond J. W. Slade (Confidential), 29 Sept. 1908, TNA, FO 881/9753X, 6–12, here: 7.

belligerent rights.[116] He presented a balanced view on international maritime law, examining it from the perspective of Britain's interests as a neutral as well as that of a belligerent.

Belligerent rights were Britain's key assets as a sea power. At the same time, the protection of trade was vital for Britain, as all reports had highlighted. As a result, the right of search and capture needed to be defined as precisely as possible. Hurst from the Foreign Office argued that the principle of 'free ship, free good' as defined in the Declaration of Paris was taken up again at the Hague peace conference in 1907. While the capture of enemy property was undisputed, the question was whether nationality or domicile determined a good as enemy property. Britain, Japan, and the United States pursued the practice of domicile, while continental powers regarded nationality as the decisive attribute. The positions were irreconcilable, and there was little hope that Britain would be able to persuade others to adopt its practice because, as Hurst argued, 'the principle of regarding nationality as the test of enemy property has never stood the test of a war where the fighting on sea played a material part in the result.'[117] Hurst expected that as long as Britain controlled the sea, the definition of enemy property did not 'matter' because the capture of enemy property was likely to be 'small'.[118]

To protect neutral property more effectively, the question of contraband needed to be settled. The negotiations at The Hague had ended in deadlock, and the London naval conference had to find a solution not least because this would be one of the key areas for the future international prize court. Britain's position towards contraband had been discussed at length prior to the Hague peace conference. After Britain had failed to gain a majority for its proposal to abolish contraband altogether, it aimed to restrict the list of contraband, and, at the same time, agree on a list of goods that could never be declared contraband—this was termed a free list. It was also planned that those lists be published in peacetime, and that no changes would be allowed in wartime.[119] For the committee it was clear that 'the

---

[116] Keith Neilson, '"The British Empire Floats on the British Navy": British Naval Policy, Belligerent Rights, and Disarmament, 1902–1909', in B. J. C. McKercher (ed.), *Arms Limitation and Disarmament. Restraints on War, 1899–1939*, (Westport, CT, 1992), 21–41; Seligmann, *Royal Navy and the German Threat*, 89–108.

[117] Naval Conference Committee. Memorandum by Cecil J. B. Hurst on Enemy Property (Confidential), n.d., TNA, FO 881/9753X, 3.

[118] Naval Conference Committee. Memorandum by Cecil J. B. Hurst on Enemy Property (Confidential), n.d., TNA, FO 881/9753X, 5.

[119] Joint Memorandum by Captain Charles L. Ottley and Cecil J. B. Hurst on Contraband (Confidential), 10 Sept. 1907, TNA, FO 881/9753X.

commerce of the whole world desires certainty', which could only be achieved with definite lists.[120]

The ship's liability to condemnation was not clearly regulated. In British practice, cargo owners were generally liable unless a ship provided false papers, whereas in the continental practice shipowners were liable to condemnation if contraband exceeded a certain value or was the bulk of the cargo. Britain was willing to compromise and the committee argued that shipowners could not be ignorant about the cargo they were carrying.[121] On the question of convoy, the British were equally willing to accept the continental rule in which ships were not liable for capture if they were sailing in convoy.[122]

Overall, the committee report showed not only each country's legal position but also revealed its understanding of the process of codification. For Britain, custom and state practice provided the basis for codification, and although some rules would 'appear...new', they were 'in fact only the adaptation of the general principles of international law to existing conditions', and 'such rules may well be formulated under the name of existing rules of international law'.[123] Russia and Germany criticized the British agenda because it dealt exclusively with the 'existing rules of international law'. Rather than reflecting on the past, they demanded that the conference should deal with rules 'for the future, without reference to the divergent practices of the past'.[124] Supporters of the German and Russian view argued that customary international law was too slow to adapt to a fast-paced modern world and, therefore, international law should be advanced without reference to custom. Others disagreed and emphasized the customary law tradition of international law. The results of the Hague peace conference of 1907 suggested that the codification of international law was primarily based on customary international law. Novel proposals without customary basis, such as the British suggestion for the abolition of contraband, had little chance of acceptance. Despite the different views on codification, the committee was strictly concerned with British practice, avoiding the introduction of new rules.

This position was reiterated in the instructions for the London naval conference, in which Sir Edward Grey stated that the aim of the conference was

---

[120] Naval Conference Committee. Further Report, 26 Oct. 1908, TNA, FO 881/9753X, 5.
[121] Naval Conference Committee. Further Report, 26 Oct. 1908, TNA, FO 881/9753X, 6–7.
[122] Naval Conference Committee. Further Report, 26 Oct. 1908, TNA, FO 881/9753X, 7.
[123] Naval Conference Committee. Further Report, 26 Oct. 1908, TNA, FO 881/9753X.
[124] Sir Edward Grey to His Majesty's Representatives at Paris, Berlin, Vienna, St. Petersburg, Rome, Madrid, The Hague, Washington, and Tokio, 14 Sept. 1908 (No. 77), TNA, FO 881/9668.

to 'harmonize as far as possible the views and interpretations of the accepted law of nations to which the several governments had given expression'. The British government was aware that most existing rules dated from the age of sail and that many rules had 'become practically meaningless and inapplicable'. It was therefore necessary to have 'a restatement of the underlying principles, in words adapted to present-day circumstances', and hoped that the conference would find a 'uniform definition of the main principles of the existing laws'.[125] For Grey, the negotiations should be informed by 'the double object', namely to maintain 'belligerent rights in their integrity, and the widest possible freedom for neutrals in the unhindered navigation of the seas'. The international prize court was expected to ensure 'an impartial and effective international jurisdiction' for Britain whether a neutral or a belligerent.[126]

The London naval conference took place from 4 December 1908 to 26 February 1909. Lord Desart acted as its president, but was later succeeded by the renowned French international jurist and naval expert Louis Renault. The British delegation consisted of all members of the Inter-Departmental Committee with the exception of W. Graham Greene from the Admiralty. This guaranteed continuity in the negotiations on the complex legal matters. The circulation of the memoranda of all participating states anticipated much of the result, and thus many issues had already been settled by the time the conference started.[127]

The 1909 Declaration of London consisted of 71 Articles, of which twenty-one dealt with the law of blockade, and another twenty-three with the question of contraband, which highlighted the importance of the two subjects.[128] A detailed analysis of the declaration provided a report, which Louis Renault produced as a commentary.[129] Although the report was not

---

[125] 'Sir Edward Grey to Lord Desart, 1 Dec. 1908', in P.P. Misc. 4 (1909): Correspondence and Documents respecting the International Naval Conference, held in London, Dec. 1908–Feb. 1909, [Cd. 4554], 22.

[126] 'Sir Edward Grey to Lord Desart, 1 Dec. 1908', in P.P. Misc. 4 (1909): Correspondence and Documents respecting the International Naval Conference, held in London, Dec. 1908–Feb. 1909, [Cd. 4554], 32.

[127] The protocols of the sessions can be found under: 'Séances de la Conférence Navale', in P.P. Misc. 5 (1909): Proceedings of the International Naval Conference, held in London, Dec. 1908–Feb. 1909, [Cd. 4555], 126–230.

[128] 'Declaration concerning the Laws of Naval War. London, 26 Feb. 1909', in Dietrich Schindler and Jiří Toman (eds), *The Laws of Armed Conflicts: A Collection of Conventions, Resolutions and other Documents* (Dordrecht, 2004), 1111–22.

[129] 'Rapport général présenté à la Conférence Navale au nom du Comité de Rédaction, 26 Feb. 1908', in P.P. Misc. 5 (1909): Proceedings of the International Naval Conference, held in London, Dec. 1908–Feb. 1909, [Cd. 4555], 342–77.

an integral part of the declaration it contained useful explanations and definitions, and the British delegates remarked that 'in accordance with the principles and practices of continental jurisprudence, such a report is considered an authoritative statement of the meaning and intention of the instrument which it explains'. The future international prize court would use the commentary as guidance for its rulings.[130]

The law of blockade was one of the most powerful weapons for a sea power. Yet, it was often disputed whether a particular blockade was effective, and Renault pointed out in his report that depending on 'the geographical conditions' the terms of the application of blockade could be very different.[131] Article 17 limited the radius within which a neutral ship could be pursued and captured to 'the area of operations of the warships'. While the formulation in the declaration did not specify this more precisely, the report gave a lengthy definition of *rayon d'action*. The radius of operation depended on the 'effectiveness' of the blockade, which meant that the radius of operation was 'limited' by 'the number of ships which could maintain a blockade' while pursuing the ship. Yet, the radius of operation could never extend to 'distant seas' where merchant ships sailed freely.[132] Article 20 stated that a ship that had breached a blockade inwards or outwards, 'is liable to capture so long as she is pursued by a ship of the blockading force'. However, as soon as 'the pursuit is abandoned, or if the blockade is raised', a ship could no longer be captured.[133] Generally, a ship was liable to condemnation if it had breached a blockade, and so too was the cargo owner unless he did not know about the 'intention to break the blockade'.[134]

The question of contraband was one of the 'most important, if not the most important issue of the Declaration', as Renault highlighted in his

---

[130] 'The British Delegates at the Naval Conference to Sir Edward Grey, 1 Mar. 1909', in P.P. Misc. 4 (1909): Correspondence and Documents respecting the International Naval Conference, held in London, Dec. 1908–Feb. 1909, [Cd. 4554], 94.

[131] 'Rapport général présenté à la Conférence Navale au nom du Comité de Rédaction', in P.P. Misc. 5 (1909): Proceedings of the International Naval Conference, held in London, Dec. 1908–Feb. 1909, [Cd. 4555], 345.

[132] 'Rapport général présenté à la Conférence Navale au nom du Comité de Rédaction', in P.P. Misc. 5 (1909): Proceedings of the International Naval Conference, held in London, Dec. 1908–Feb. 1909, [Cd. 4555], 351.

[133] 'Rapport général présenté à la Conférence Navale au nom du Comité de Rédaction', in P.P. Misc. 5 (1909): Proceedings of the International Naval Conference, held in London, Dec. 1908–Feb. 1909, [Cd. 4555], 345–52.

[134] 'Rapport général présenté à la Conférence Navale au nom du Comité de Rédaction', in P.P. Misc. 5 (1909): Proceedings of the International Naval Conference, held in London, Dec. 1908–Feb. 1909, [Cd. 4555], 352.

report.[135] The subject was treated in two parts. The first part defined contraband, and part two dealt with the right of search and capture of contraband. For the definition of contraband, the delegates created three lists: one for absolute contraband (Article 22), one for conditional contraband (Article 24), and one free list (Articles 28 and 29), for goods which could not be declared contraband. The lists for absolute and conditional contraband goods were identical to the lists agreed at the Hague peace conference of 1907. The free list included articles such as raw cotton, rubber, different kinds of earths, and other materials. Principal alterations to the lists had to be notified (Articles 23, 25, and 26).[136]

The list of conditional contraband was controversial, not least in conjunction with the doctrine of continuous voyage. Renault remarked in his report that the doctrine of continuous voyage had been 'often fought or invoked without realising its exact meaning'. The London Declaration more specifically defined which destinations made goods contraband, and therefore subject to lawful capture. In this context, absolute and conditional contraband were treated separately. The former was subject to capture as soon as the cargo, not the ship, was destined for enemy territory (Articles 30 and 31). Conditional contraband, however, was only subject to capture if the goods were 'destined for the use of the armed forces or of a government department of the enemy State', or the goods were transported on an enemy ship (Article 33), or were destined for an enemy port (Article 34). If goods were destined for a neutral destination, however, they could not be treated as contraband, and the doctrine of continuous voyage did not apply in these cases (Article 35). Other articles specified the conditions under which ships were liable to capture. Generally a ship was liable for capture throughout its journey when carrying contraband (Article 37). The ship, not only the cargo, could be condemned if more than half of the cargo was contraband (Article 40); otherwise a fine had to be paid as a deterrent (Article 41). These articles outlined in which cases contraband goods could be captured, and hence defined the right of search and capture.[137]

---

[135] 'Rapport général présenté à la Conférence Navale au nom du Comité de Rédaction', in P.P. Misc. 5 (1909): Proceedings of the International Naval Conference, held in London, Dec. 1908–Feb. 1909, [Cd. 4555], 352.

[136] 'Rapport général présenté à la Conférence Navale au nom du Comité de Rédaction', in P.P. Misc. 5 (1909): Proceedings of the International Naval Conference, held in London, Dec. 1908–Feb. 1909, [Cd. 4555], 353–6.

[137] 'Rapport général présenté à la Conférence Navale au nom du Comité de Rédaction', in P.P. Misc. 5 (1909): Proceedings of the International Naval Conference, held in London, Dec. 1908–Feb. 1909, [Cd. 4555], 352–62.

Despite all efforts, the delegates could not agree on the question of the conversion of merchant ships into warships on the high seas, or on the question of domicile or nationality with regard to enemy property. In the first instance, Britain did not concede, and in the latter case the United States was not willing to give up its position. The failure to find a compromise on these questions illustrates the difficulty of harmonizing different state practices.[138]

The Aftermath of the London Naval Conference

When the London naval conference ended, Louis Renault as president summarized its achievements. The Declaration of London was 'a work of transaction [and] mutual concessions'. It 'substituted uniformity and stability for diversity and obscurity from which international relations had suffered too long'.[139] Compared with the principles laid out in the Declaration of Paris of 1856 some fifty years earlier, the Declaration of London was far more detailed and addressed delicate issues, such as the question of contraband, the law of blockade, and the right of search and capture. For the first time, an international code of naval warfare had been created. The result disappointed those who had hoped to resolve all the different practices of the past. It also disappointed those who thought that the declaration would limit war at sea. The Declaration of London had continued the work which had started with the Declaration of Paris. Renault called the result a '*media sententia*', and argued that the declaration should 'be examined as a whole' as the study of individual rules would otherwise be 'misleading'. Only if the declaration was examined from the perspective of a neutral as well as from that of a belligerent could the rules be appreciated.[140]

The British delegates were content with the results the conference. They had successfully defended Britain's position in the two most important matters, namely blockade and contraband. The law of blockade was modified

---

[138] 'Rapport général présenté à la Conférence Navale au nom du Comité de Rédaction', in P.P. Misc. 5 (1909): Proceedings of the International Naval Conference, held in London, Dec. 1908–Feb. 1909, [Cd. 4555], 344.

[139] 'Rapport général présenté à la Conférence Navale au nom du Comité de Rédaction', in P.P. Misc. 5 (1909): Proceedings of the International Naval Conference, held in London, Dec. 1908–Feb. 1909, [Cd. 4555], 343.

[140] 'Rapport général présenté à la Conférence Navale au nom du Comité de Rédaction', in P.P. Misc. 5 (1909): Proceedings of the International Naval Conference, held in London, Dec. 1908–Feb. 1909, [Cd. 4555], 343.

according to the British view, and the British delegates highlighted that they were 'able to secure full recognition of the principles'.[141] On the question of contraband, the results could 'not merely [be] satisfactory from the British point of view'. The introduction of a free list was seen as a success as it included many goods which were important to the British economy, for example raw cotton. Yet, it was still disputed whether certain goods, such as horses and mules, should be treated as absolute or conditional contraband. Although Britain aimed at limiting those lists, the delegates agreed that belligerents could add goods to them via notification, and the British delegates stated that 'there was a general desire to preserve in this respect the rights of belligerents in future'.[142] In return for the acceptance of the lists, the doctrine of continuous voyage was restricted to absolute contraband only.[143] Britain also consented to the destruction of neutral prizes under special circumstances (Article 49) or after a court ruling (Article 48).[144]

Overall, the British delegates appraised the Declaration of London as an 'effective safeguard of the best interests of neutrals in general, whilst preserving all legitimate rights of belligerents'.[145] On a more general note, the British delegates observed that the continental tradition 'seem[ed] inconveniently rigid' and its 'view of international law takes little account of any but their own national regulations'. In the common law tradition, on the other hand, international law was 'as a living thing, capable of development and adaptation from time to time to new conditions'.[146] In an attempt to reconcile the two views, the preamble of the declaration declared that the rules 'correspond in substance with the generally recognised principles of international law'. This broad statement gave the future international prize

[141] 'The British Delegates of the Naval Conference to Sir Edward Grey, 1 Mar. 1909', in P.P. Misc. 4 (1909): Correspondence and Documents respecting the International Naval Conference, held in London, Dec. 1908–Feb. 1909, [Cd. 4554], 94.

[142] 'The British Delegates of the Naval Conference to Sir Edward Grey, 1 Mar. 1909', in P.P. Misc. 4 (1909): Correspondence and Documents respecting the International Naval Conference, held in London, Dec. 1908–Feb. 1909, [Cd. 4554], 94–5, here: 95.

[143] 'The British Delegates of the Naval Conference to Sir Edward Grey, 1 Mar. 1909', in P.P. Misc. 4 (1909): Correspondence and Documents respecting the International Naval Conference, held in London, Dec. 1908–Feb. 1909, [Cd. 4554], 95–6.

[144] 'The British Delegates of the Naval Conference to Sir Edward Grey, 1 Mar. 1909', in P.P. Misc. 4 (1909): Correspondence and Documents respecting the International Naval Conference, held in London, Dec. 1908–Feb. 1909, [Cd. 4554], 98–9.

[145] 'The British Delegates of the Naval Conference to Sir Edward Grey, 1 Mar. 1909', in P.P. Misc. 4 (1909): Correspondence and Documents respecting the International Naval Conference, held in London, Dec. 1908–Feb. 1909, [Cd. 4554], 94.

[146] 'The British Delegates of the Naval Conference to Sir Edward Grey, 1 Mar. 1909', in P.P. Misc. 4 (1909): Correspondence and Documents respecting the International Naval Conference, held in London, Dec. 1908–Feb. 1909, [Cd. 4554], 102.

court significance beyond the mere application of the declaration because it 'will have authority to apply the rules generally, as being in conformity with the accepted principles of international law'.[147]

International law circles closely watched the London naval conference and praised its achievements. Among the drafters of the declaration were many jurists, and Charles H. Stockton from the American delegation and author of the US Naval War Code remarked that 'for the first time in history[,] the great sea powers...have agreed upon a code formulated with very considerable detail and precision'.[148] At the annual meeting of the Institut de droit international in Paris in 1910, the French jurist and president of the Institut, Charles Lyon-Caen, celebrated the advancement of the codification of international maritime law at the London naval conference, and his colleague Léon Bourgeois underscored the role of the Institut in facilitating and preparing the work of the codification.[149] The British international lawyer, Lassa Oppenheim, equally applauded the declaration as 'the most important law-making treaty', providing the basis for the 'establishment of an International Prize Court'.[150] The International Law Association, one of the leading organizations for promoting the codification of international law, examined the declaration and in particular praised the work on blockade and contraband. Yet, there were also some critical voices, which argued that important issues were still not settled, as Sir Robert Phillimore, judge at the high court in London, remarked in his analysis of the declaration.[151] While some interpreted the vagueness of the Declaration of London as a weakness, others argued that the codification needed to strike a balance between precision and vagueness in order to allow further development of the law.[152]

---

[147] 'The British Delegates of the Naval Conference to Sir Edward Grey, 1 Mar. 1909', in P.P. Misc. 4 (1909): Correspondence and Documents respecting the International Naval Conference, held in London, Dec. 1908–Feb. 1909, [Cd. 4554], 102.

[148] Charles H. Stockton, 'The International Naval Conference of London, 1908–1909', *The American Journal of International Law*, 3, 3 (1909), 614.

[149] 'Discours de M. Lyon-Caen', *Annuaire de l'Institut de droit international*, 23 (1910), 357–65; 'Discours de M. Léon Bourgeois', *Annuaire de l'Institut de droit international*, 23 (1910), 365–73.

[150] Lassa Oppenheim, *International Law. A Treaise*, 2 vols (London, 1912), vol. 1, 40.

[151] Robert Phillimore, 'Declaration of London', *International Law Association. Report of the Twenty-Sixth Conference held at The Guildhall London, 2–5 Aug. 1910* (1910), 67–88.

[152] Arthur Cohen, 'The Declaration of London', *International Law Association. Report of the Twenty-Sixth Conference held at The Guildhall London, 2–5 Aug. 1910* (1910), 71–2; John Macdonell, 'The Declaration of London', *International Law Association. Report of the Twenty-Sixth Conference held at The Guildhall London, 2–5 Aug. 1910* (1910), 91.

The fate of the Declaration of London is well known and will not be revisited here.[153] However, what is of interest in this context is Britain's position towards the codification of international maritime law. Britain played a major role in the London naval conference, and more than any other power shaped its results. This marked a significant change compared to Britain's position some forty years earlier at the Brussels conference in 1874. Charles H. Stockton, who had been the first delegate of the United States for the London naval conference and was a former naval attaché of the United States in Britain (1903–5), poignantly explained Britain's motives behind its change from scepticism to advocacy of the codification of international maritime law. Britain was 'most concerned' as it was 'the possessor not only of the greatest navy in the world, but also of the largest mercantile marine and seaborne trade'. Without its 'sea power and commerce' Britain's influence 'would shrink from a world-wide empire to an unimportant group of islands on the western face of Europe with detached, heterogeneous and widely separated dependencies'.[154] Stockton illustrated Britain's dilemma in balancing the conflicting interests of a leading sea power with those of a leading economic power.

Britain's experience as a neutral in the conflicts in the latter half of the nineteenth century turned it into an ardent defender of neutral rights. Paired with its clout as the major sea power, neutrality had become an important instrument in British foreign policy. The codification of international maritime law at the beginning of the twentieth century showed that the British government had carefully weighed up how to define belligerent and neutral rights so as to protect Britain's strategic and economic interests.

In conclusion, from the mid-nineteenth century to the beginning of the twentieth century, Britain had turned from a sceptic to an advocate of codification. This transformation had become necessary in order to protect Britain's economic and strategic interests, and international law helped in balancing Britain's competing interests. New actors shaped the codification process, among them the two non-jurists, Ottley and Slade, who

---

[153] For a detailed analysis, see John W. Coogan, *The End of Neutrality: The United States, Britain, and Maritime Rights, 1899–1915* (Ithaca, NY, 1981), 125–47; Hersch Lauterpacht and R. Y. Jennings, 'International Law and Colonial Questions, 1870–1914', in *Cambridge History of the British Empire, Vol. III: The Empire-Commonwealth 1870–1919* (Cambridge, 1959), 707–10. For a broader context of blockade and contraband in war planning, see Matthew S. Seligmann, 'Failing to Prepare for the Great War? The Absence of Grand Strategy in British War Planning before 1914', *War in History*, 24, 4 (2017), 414–37.

[154] Stockton, 'International Naval Conference', 596–7.

demonstrated the impact of the codification of international law on British maritime strategy, so illustrating the interaction between law and strategy. Significantly, Britain's legal position in a future war was not only considered from a belligerent point of view but also from that of a neutral.

The codification of international maritime law at the Hague and London conferences demonstrated the importance of state practice and custom. They constrained strategic and political ambitions. The best example may have been Britain's proposal to abolish contraband. It was a political ambition based on strategic and economic considerations. Yet, it failed to convince other states because it lacked precedent, and because it was not in the interests of other states. As a result, the Hague and London conferences were more successful in harmonizing existing and diverging practices of international maritime law, than in creating new rules which lacked any reference to practice. At the same time, the newly agreed legal framework was intended to provide the basis for the future international prize court. This was an ambitious project, proposed by the two competing sea powers, Britain and Germany. With their initiative, they went far beyond the agreement of specific rules to lay the basis for an international jurisdiction, hoping that international law would not only settle international legal disputes impartially but also protect state interests, and to do that, they were prepared to limit their sovereign rights by creating a truly international legal order.

6

Maritime Strategic Thought and International Law

The practice and codification of international law provided the legal framework around which the British government could act. The previous chapters have shown that both British state practice and Britain's position at the Hague and London conferences reflected its strategic concerns about a future war at sea. This chapter examines how the debate on British maritime strategic thought evolved alongside international law. Matters of defence and strategy were discussed in many places.[1] This chapter focuses on the Royal United Service Institution (RUSI), which provided one of the most prominent places where defence and strategy were (and still are) discussed. Frequent discussants at the RUSI included members of the army and the navy, politicians, civil servants, and international lawyers.[2] These debates allow an insight into the dialogue between international lawyers and naval officers, and so enable a better understanding of the interaction between maritime strategy and international law.

Evolution of Maritime Strategic Thought

In the early 1870s, Philip H. Colomb, brother of John C. R. Colomb, and also a naval officer, began to formulate Britain's maritime strategic thought.

---

[1] Antulio J. Echevarria II, *Imagining Future War: The West's Technological Revolution and Visions of Wars to Come, 1880–1914* (Westport, CT, 2007); David G. Morgan-Owen, *The Fear of Invasion: Strategy, Politics, and British War Planning, 1880–1914* (Oxford, 2017); Andreas Rose, '"Readiness or Ruin?"—Der "Grosse Krieg" in den britischen Militärzeitschriften (1880–1914)', in Stig Förster (ed.), *Vor dem Sprung ins Dunkle. Die militärische Debatte über den Krieg der Zukunft, 1880–1914* (Paderborn, 2016), 245–390; Andreas Rose, 'Waiting for Armageddon. British Military Journals and the Images of Future Wars (1890–1914)', *Francia. Forschungen zur westeuropäischen Geschichte*, 40 (2013), 317–31.

[2] M. D. Welch, *Science and the British Officer: The Early Days of the Royal United Services Institute for Defence Studies (1829–1869)* (London, 1998); M. D. Welch, *Science in a Pickelhaube: British Military Lesson Learning at the RUSI (1870–1900)* (London, 1999).

Great Britain, International Law, and the Evolution of Maritime Strategic Thought, 1856–1914. Gabriela A. Frei, Oxford University Press (2020). © Gabriela A. Frei.
DOI: 10.1093/oso/9780198859932.001.0001

In 1872 he delivered a paper at the RUSI, in which he argued that 'it seems at first sight probable that no such thing as rule or law can be evolved except from the facts of experiment in war. It is therefore readily assumed that naval strategy is not yet in a condition to be made a subject of study.' However, so Colomb continued, 'this line of thought would be excusable after many failures to discover the hidden law or laws which may exist, but it does not excuse the neglect to seek for them.'[3] Confidence rather than hesitation drove his speech, and he made a direct appeal to naval officers and others to reflect theoretically on the scope and limitation of sea power, and to formulate principles to guide naval warfare.

Soon after, in 1874, Major-General T. B. Collinson from the Royal Engineers presented an innovative paper in which he argued that steam power 'altered maritime warfare considerably'. As long as sailing ships were dependent on wind, weather, and currents, planning naval attacks was almost impossible, which explained why in the age of sail a naval strategy was hardly possible. The introduction of steam changed this perception, because 'the power of moving in any direction at any time with nearly as much certainty as on land, has assimilated to a certain extent naval warfare to land warfare'. Collinson imagined that fleets would operate in a similar manner to armies in future wars at sea. He compared the changes from sail to steam 'as great a revolution in war as Frederick the Great did by a new system of tactics'.[4] For Collinson this 'assimilation' had been crucial for the development of maritime strategic thought, and, thus, he confidently concluded that the technological developments 'made it possible to have naval strategy as well as naval tactics, which was all that had hitherto been possible'.[5] Hence, reflections on naval and maritime warfare would lead to similar theoretical thinking as developed by Carl von Clausewitz and Antoine-Henri Jomini in the early nineteenth century for modern military strategy.[6]

---

[3] Philip H. Colomb, 'The Attack and Defence of Fleets, Part 2', *Journal of Royal United Service Institution*, 16 (1872), 1–24, here: 2; See also: Philip H. Colomb, 'The Attack and Defence of Fleets, Part 1', *Journal of Royal United Service Institution*, 15 (1871), 405–37; Barry M. Gough, 'The Influence of Sea Power Upon History Revisited: Vice-Admiral P. H. Colomb, RN', *The RUSI Journal*, 135, 2 (1990), 55–63.

[4] T. B. Collinson, 'The Strategic Importance of the Military Harbours in the British Channel as Connected with Defensive and Offensive Operations', *Journal of Royal United Service Institution*, 18 (1874), 230.

[5] Collinson, 'Strategic Importance of the Military Harbours', 230.

[6] Christopher Bassford, *Clausewitz in English: The Reception of Clausewitz in Britain and America 1815–1945* (New York, 1994); N. A. M. Rodger, 'The Idea of Naval Strategy in Britain in the Eighteenth and Nineteenth Centuries', in Geoffrey Till (ed.), *The Development of British Naval Thinking: Essays in Memory of Bryan McLaren Ranft* (London, 2006), 19–33;

In comparing sea and land warfare, Collinson concluded that 'the defeat of an army generally results at once in the occupation of territory; the defeat of a fleet is only the loss of so many ships and men, unless it opens the road to some other advantage'. In other words, 'not merely the destruction of a hostile fleet' or 'the complete annihilation of an enemy's naval resources would...necessarily terminate a war'. Rather, 'there must be some ulterior object to be gained, of which the fleets are only the means'. Collinson distinguished between three 'ultimate objects' of maritime warfare: first, 'the defence of our own [British] sea commerce, or the injury of the enemy's'; second, 'the protection of our own country [Britain] from invasion'; and third, 'the invasion of the enemy's country'. Of the three objects, the latter two were only achievable with a combined military operation. In his paper, Collinson focused on the role of the navy as part of a broader defence policy, in which the army and the navy played distinct roles.[7]

Collinson's article also highlighted the distinction between naval and land warfare. The aim in naval warfare was not victory over an enemy per se, but rather the ability to exercise control of the sea. While protection of trade and economic warfare were paramount for a sea power, Collinson went a step further in his 'ulterior objects' and stressed the importance of combined operations. These broader aims could only be achieved if the navy cooperated closely with the army. Thus, the navy's future theatre of operations would be the littoral rather than the open sea—a lesson Collinson drew from the Crimean War. Collinson concluded that Britain's future maritime strategy should focus not on decisive battles but on economic warfare and combined operations as only the latter could terminate war quickly.[8] The limitation of naval warfare was also manifested in Collinson's terminology. He used the term naval warfare to describe naval actions only, while he used the term maritime warfare to describe combined operations.

While Collinson examined strategy from the perspective of home defence, Colonel Sir Charles H. Nugent from the Royal Engineers considered it from an imperial point of view. In a two-part paper on *Imperial Defence* in 1884, Nugent identified the protection of trade as vital for the

---

Hew Strachan, 'Maritime Strategy. Historical Perspectives', *The RUSI Journal*, 152, 1 (2007), 29–33; Geoffrey Till, 'Introduction: British Naval Thinking: A Contradiction in Terms?', in Geoffrey Till (ed.), *The Development of British Naval Thinking. Essays in Memory of Bryan McLaren Ranft* (London, 2006), 1–18.

[7] Collinson, 'Strategic Importance of the Military Harbours', 230.
[8] Collinson, 'Strategic Importance of the Military Harbours', 244–5.

existence of Britain and its empire, an argument that John C. R. Colomb had already made. Nugent examined the French and Russian war threats in the 1870s and 1880s and pleaded for a British maritime strategy which focused on the protection of coaling stations and for upholding lines of communication between the centre and the periphery of the empire in war-time. For an effective imperial defence, he concluded, closer cooperation between the army and the navy was essential.[9] A few years earlier, Donald Currie, a British shipowner, provided a commercial view of imperial defence, emphasizing that 'naval supremacy' was not enough to protect Britain's economic interests at home and abroad. Rather, he argued, Britain's focus should be directed to upholding communication lines between the centre and the periphery of the empire to ensure access to graving docks and coaling stations. These issues would provide the backbone upon which a modern steam fleet could operate effectively.[10]

The discussion at the RUSI particularly addressed the lack of a combined home and imperial defence policy. Closer cooperation between the Admiralty and the War Office was essential for the formulation of a modern and effective defence policy in response to the threats from France and Russia. John C. R. Colomb had retired from service in the Royal Marine Artillery when he entered parliament as a Conservative in 1886, but as a politician he continued to argue for the integration of the two services in the context of imperial defence. He envisaged a joint general staff and a war office that not only looked at defence from the army's point of view but also from the navy's and, above all, included those of the colonies. In a speech to the House of Commons in 1888, Colomb lamented that 'the British [govern-ment] w[as] working [with] a system of national defence in two water-tight compartments without any real responsibility, and no central controlling authority for both'. Consequently, he stated that Britain's 'safety in war would have to be evolved out of dual control and divided responsibility'. For Colomb the only way forward was to create a single government position responsible for Britain's defence policy, and 'answerable for general prin-ciples, being followed both by the Army and Navy'.[11] The creation of the

---

[9] Charles H. Nugent, 'Imperial Defence, Part 1: Home Defences', *Journal of Royal United Service Institution*, 28 (1884), 427–56; Charles H. Nugent, 'Imperial Defence, Part 2: Abroad', *Journal of Royal United Service Institution*, 28 (1884), 459–513.

[10] Donald Currie, 'On Maritime Warfare; the Importance to the British Empire of a Complete System of Telegraphs, Coaling Stations, and Graving Docks', *Journal of Royal United Service Institution*, 21 (1877), 228–47.

[11] Speech of John C. R. Colomb, Hansard, 3rd series, HC Deb., 5 Mar. 1888, vol. 323, c. 238.

Committee of Imperial Defence in 1904 did not lead to service integration, as demanded by Colomb, but it provided an important platform to discuss matters of defence policy more broadly.[12]

From the debates in the RUSI we see that early concepts of naval and maritime strategy were developed by servicemen from the Royal Engineers and the Royal Marine Artillery. Their experience in combined operations gave them an insight into land as well as sea warfare, and allowed them to compare the similarities and differences between armies and navies. Another factor that influenced their thinking was the impact of new technology, which demanded much more than a quick adaptability in tactics. Contemporaries were worried about how the fundamental change in naval technology would alter the course of naval warfare, and more profoundly, British maritime strategy. In other words, technological advance had kindled the evolution of the concepts of naval and maritime strategy. Recent war experiences, such as the Crimean War, the American Civil War, and the Franco-Prussian War, provided useful reference points by illustrating the effects of technology on the changing character of war at sea and on the understanding of naval and maritime strategy.[13]

Effects of International Law on British Maritime Strategy

British maritime strategic thought was also discussed in relation to changes in international law. Prominent international lawyers appeared at the RUSI to talk about military conflicts from a legal perspective, addressing the effect of law on strategy and the conduct of warfare. Yet, no legal adviser to the British government nor an Advocate-General spoke at the RUSI.

[12] Shawn T. Grimes, *Strategy and War Planning in the British Navy, 1887–1918* (Woodbridge, 2012); Morgan-Owen, *The Fear of Invasion*, 87–126; Nicholas d'Ombrain, *War Machinery and High Policy: Defence Administration in Peacetime Britain 1902–1914* (Oxford, 1973); W. C. B. Tunstall, 'Imperial Defence 1815–1870', in *The Cambridge History of the British Empire, Vol. 2* (Cambridge, 1940), 806–41; W. C. B. Tunstall, 'Imperial Defence 1870–1897', in *The Cambridge History of the British Empire, Vol. 3: The Empire-Commonwealth 1870–1919* (Cambridge, 1959), 230–54; W. C. B. Tunstall, 'Imperial Defence, 1897–1914', in *The Cambridge History of the British Empire, Vol. 3: The Empire-Commonwealth 1870–1919* (Cambridge, 1959), 563–604.

[13] Echevarria, *Imagining Future War*; William H. McNeill, *The Pursuit of Power: Technology, Armed Force, and Society since A.D. 1000* (Chicago, IL, 1982); Donald M. Schurman, *The Education of a Navy: The Development of British Naval Strategic Thought, 1867–1914* (London, 1984), 3.

The RUSI debates focused in particular on the Declaration of Paris of 1856 and its effect on British maritime strategy as well as its impact on future war at sea. The experience of the American Civil War, which had caused so much public outcry, had received great attention from the RUSI audience. W. Vernon Harcourt, an international jurist and liberal politician, who regularly wrote commentaries for *The Times*, examined the Declaration of Paris in relation to neutral rights in 1865. Reflecting on the British experience of neutrality during the American Civil War, he argued that neutrals were treated as 'quasi-belligerents' rather than as neutrals, and that belligerents 'exercised [belligerent rights] against neutrals'. This interference from belligerents with neutrals, as Harcourt termed it, only happened because 'neutrals were suspected... [of] taking part in the war'.[14] He even went so far as to reject the American claims with regard to the *Alabama* case (see Chapter 2). In his opinion, this was not a legal issue but a question of 'international morality'. Consequently, Britain had 'to decide what measures of redress' it would pursue if a British person engaged in un-neutral service acts. Harcourt defended the rights and duties of neutrals, which had been outlined in Britain's Foreign Enlistment Act.[15]

The Declaration of Paris had also been the subject of an analysis by John Ross-of-Bladensberg, an army officer from the Coldstream Guards. He focused on Britain as a belligerent and argued that the declaration had curtailed belligerent rights and, hence, undermined the Royal Navy's ability to wage economic warfare—the most valuable weapon for a sea power. Unless a 'maritime nation... can capture the property of its enemy by sea—be that property much or little', it 'must paralyse his [the maritime nation's] military efforts, sever the sinews of his power, and bring bankruptcy upon the very resources which enable him to be aggressive'.[16] Ross-of-Bladensberg's main reference point was the Napoleonic Wars, but that all changed with the Crimean War when the two great naval powers, Britain and France, agreed to the Declaration of Paris. Comparisons between sea and land warfare can also be found in Ross-of-Bladensberg's paper. For him the main difference was that the sea was 'a barren waste' which 'cannot be occupied', and thus

---

[14] W. Vernon Harcourt, 'The Rights and Duties of Neutrals in Time of War. Part 1', *Journal of Royal United Service Institution*, 9 (1865), 322–3.

[15] Harcourt, 'Rights and Duties of Neutrals. Part 1', 322–3; W. Vernon Harcourt, 'The Rights and Duties of Neutrals in Time of War. Part 2', *Journal of Royal United Service Institution*, 9 (1865), 329–45.

[16] John Ross-of-Bladensberg, 'Maritime Rights', *Journal of Royal United Service Institution*, 20 (1876), 428.

he suggested that 'fleets do not meet each other for its possession'. Rather, the sea was 'a great highway', where 'commerce and men are transported'. Consequently, the aim of sea warfare was 'the attack and defence of foreign trade'. In conclusion, the command of the sea enabled 'a belligerent to destroy the commerce of his adversary, [and] gives him power which far exceeds, in coercive force, military strength'. Although Ross-of-Bladensberg was sceptical as to the value of the Declaration of Paris, he believed it impossible to 'tear up [the declaration] the very moment we go to war', as it would be 'neither just, wise, nor likely' that Britain would withdraw from its terms. In fact, the declaration had benefitted Britain's policy of neutrality and Britain had adhered to it in the Franco-Prussian War. Ross-of-Bladensberg concluded that peace offered 'the only moment' to withdraw from the declaration.[17] W. S. Lindsay, a British shipowner and Liberal politician, held a similar opinion, stating that the Declaration of Paris had not only 'imperilled' Britain's merchant marine but also 'the safety of the nation'.[18] Although criticism of the Declaration of Paris did not cease in the period prior to the First World War, Britain pursued a strong neutrality policy. State practice endorsed the principles of the declaration, and also defended them through the codification of international law at the beginning of the twentieth century.

Makers of Maritime Strategy

In 1890, the American naval officer Captain Alfred T. Mahan published *The Influence of Sea Power upon History, 1660–1783*, in which he considered maritime strategy in relation to politics.[19] His book, which explained the need for a strong navy to the American public, had a profound impact on US policy.[20] His work was also an inspiration for policy-makers

[17] Ross-of-Bladensberg, 'Maritime Rights', 423–46.
[18] W. S. Lindsay, 'On Belligerent Rights: The Declaration of Paris, 1856', *Journal of Royal United Service Institution*, 21 (1877), 179–204, here: 179.
[19] Alfred T. Mahan, *The Influence of Sea Power upon History, 1660–1783* (Boston, MA, 1890; reprint New York, 1987).
[20] James R. Holmes, *Theodore Roosevelt and World Order* (Washington, DC, 2006), 74–86; Scott Mobley, *Progressives in Navy Blue: Maritime Strategy, American Empire, and the Transformation of U.S. Naval Identity, 1873–1898* (Annapolis, MD, 2018); Paul E. Pedisich, *Congress Buys A Navy: Politics, Economics, and the American Naval Power, 1881–1921* (Annapolis, MD, 2016), 70–198.

worldwide.[21] Even today, the scholarly literature on maritime strategic thought highlights Mahan's contribution to the understanding of strategy. Jon Sumida has pointed out that Mahan 'transformed naval history by breaking the monopoly held by accounts of derring-do with serious analyses of naval grand strategy and the art and science of naval command'.[22]

Mahan's work was widely acclaimed in Britain, and an anonymous reviewer wrote that it was 'published at a very opportune time'.[23] Commentators such as John K. Laughton (a naval historian), Thomas Brassey (a liberal politician and editor of Brassey's Naval Annual), Cyprian A. G. Bridge (a naval officer and later director of Naval Intelligence), and James R. Thursfield (a naval historian and journalist) all praised Mahan's work and underlined his contribution to the understanding of naval and maritime strategy.[24] Thursfield described Mahan as 'one of the greatest authorities of all time on the broader issues of naval strategy'.[25] Mahan made the ideas of naval strategy and sea power popular beyond a naval audience.

Mahan was not the first to advocate a historical approach to illustrate the principles of naval and maritime strategy. John K. Laughton and Philip H. Colomb wrote their pioneering works on history and strategy in the 1870s and 1880s, using the RUSI to discuss their approach. In 1874, Laughton published 'The Scientific Study of Naval History', and Colomb

---

[21] Philip A. Crowl, 'Alfred Thayer Mahan: The Naval Historian', in Peter Paret (ed.), *Makers of Modern Strategy from Machiavelli to the Nuclear Age* (Oxford, 1986), 444–77; Roger Dingman, 'Japan and Mahan', in John B. Hattendorf (ed.) *The Influence of History on Mahan: The Proceedings of a Conference Marking the Centenary of Alfred Thayer Mahan's The Influence of Sea Power Upon History, 1660–1783* (Newport, RI, 1991), 49–66; John B. Hattendorf, 'Alfred Thayer Mahan and American Naval Theory: The Range and Limitations of Mahan's Thought', in John B. Hattendorf, *Naval History and Maritime Strategy: Collected Essays* (Malabar, FL, 2000), 59–75; Holger Herwig, 'The Influence of A. T. Mahan Upon German Sea Power', in John B. Hattendorf (ed.), *The Influence of History on Mahan: The Proceedings of a Conference Marking the Centenary of Alfred Thayer Mahan's The Influence of Sea Power Upon History, 1660–1783* (Newport, RI, 1991), 67–80; Schurman, *Education of a Navy*, 60–82; Margaret Tuttle Sprout, 'Mahan: Evangelist of Sea Power', in Edward Mead Earle (ed.), *Makers of Modern Strategy: Military Thought from Machiavelli to Hitler* (Princeton, NJ, 1943; reprint, 1971), 415–45.

[22] Jon Tetsuro Sumida, *Inventing Grand Strategy and Teaching Command: The Classic Works of Alfred Thayer Mahan Reconsidered* (Washington, DC, 1997), 99.

[23] Anonymous, 'Review: The Influence of Sea Power upon History, 1660–1783. By Captain A.T. Mahan, London 1890', *Journal of Royal United Service Institution*, 34 (1890), 1067.

[24] Thomas Brassey, 'Great Britain as Sea-Power', *Nineteenth Century. A Monthly Review*, 34, 197 (1893), 121–30; Cyprian A. G. Bridge, 'A Review on "Influence of Sea Power Upon History 1660–1783 by Captain A. T. Mahan"', *Blackwood's Edinburgh Magazine*, 148 (1890), 576–84; John K. Laughton, 'Captain Mahan on Maritime Power', *Edinburgh Review*, 172 (1890), 420–53; John K. Laughton, 'Recent Naval Literature', *Journal of Royal United Service Institution*, 37 (1893), 1161–82. See also John K. Laughton, 'The Study of Naval History', *Journal of Royal United Service Institution*, 40 (1896), 795–820.

[25] James R. Thursfield, 'The Command of the Sea', *Quarterly Review*, 177 (1893), 347.

frequently contributed to the RUSI, of which his naval prize essay of 1878 is an excellent illustration.[26] Colomb's monumental study *Naval Warfare: Its Ruling Principles and Practices Historically Treated* was published only a year after Mahan's seminal study in 1891. Colomb's work was always over-shadowed by Mahan's success, and less well known due to its lack of lucidity and persuasiveness.[27]

In 1895, Mahan published a paper on 'Blockade in Relation to Naval Strategy' in *The RUSI Journal*, summarizing the main argument of his book. Mahan examined the question of whether blockade was still central to naval warfare in the age of steam—a question which had caused much dispute among naval officers due to the changes in technology. Mahan was certain that blockade was still as relevant in the age of steam as it had been in the past, because it had 'simply widened the question, not changed its nature'.[28] For Mahan, history, not technology, was the foundation for the understanding of naval strategy. Using historical examples from the Napoleonic Wars and the American Civil War, Mahan illustrated the importance of a superior battle fleet to secure and defend command of the sea. Blockade was a central element in his understanding of naval strategy.[29]

Mahan's thinking on strategy and his methodology can be found in almost every paper presented at the RUSI. The naval prize essay, a competition run by the RUSI to stimulate discussion among aspiring young officers, offers a prime example.[30] For instance, the winner of the naval prize essay competition in 1898 was Commander George A. Ballard, who became director of Naval Intelligence in 1902 and played a crucial role in the Admiralty's war planning in 1907.[31] In his essay, Ballard was mainly con-

---

[26] Philip H. Colomb, 'Great Britain's Maritime Power: How Best Developed etc.', *Journal of Royal United Service Institution*, 22 (1878), 1–55; John K. Laughton, 'The Scientific Study of Naval History', *Journal of Royal United Service Institution*, 18 (1874), 508–27.

[27] Philip H. Colomb, *Naval Warfare: Its Ruling Principles and Practice Historically Treated* (London, 1891). For a review, see William L. Clowes [Nauticus], 'Sea Power: Its Past and its Future', *Fortnightly Review*, 54, 324 (1893), 853.

[28] Alfred T. Mahan, 'Blockade in Relation to Naval Strategy', *Journal of Royal United Service Institution*, 39 (1895), 1057–69, here: 1069.

[29] Mahan, 'Blockade in Relation to Naval Strategy', 1057–69.

[30] See, for instance, R. W. Craigie, 'Maritime Supremacy being Essential for the General Protection of the British Empire and its Commerce, to What Extent, if Any, Should our Naval Force be Supplemented by Fixed Defences at Home and Abroad, and to Whom Should They be Confided? (The Naval Prize Essay)', *Journal of Royal United Service Institution*, 36 (1892), 391–415.

[31] For a more detailed analysis of Ballard's role in the Admiralty, see Grimes, *Strategy and War Planning*; Paul Hayes, 'Britain, Germany, and the Admiralty's Plans for Attacking German Territory, 1906–1915', in Lawrence Freedman, Paul Hayes, and Robert O'Neill (eds), *War, Strategy, and International Politics: Essays in Honour of Sir Michael Howard* (Oxford, 1992),

cerned with the protection of trade. For him 'the necessary basis of any protection whatever must be a sufficient superiority in battle-ships...which in
itself would constitute the chief source of safety to our shipping, and without which it would be idle to talk of commerce existing at all'. The battle
fleet's main task was to 'destroy, capture, or blockade' the enemy.[32] However,
since blockade could not stop all enemy ships, Ballard suggested patrolling
trade routes in order to minimize attacks on the British merchant marine.
Yet, he did not think that commerce raiders were a serious threat because
coal restricted their radius of operations.[33] Ballard presented a comprehensive strategic plan, in which the protection of commerce and blockade were
the two ultimate goals of Britain's maritime strategy.[34]

The second naval prize essay that year was awarded to Captain C. F. Winter
from the Canadian Militia. He examined the value of blockade and the
necessity of the supremacy of the battle fleet for the protection of trade from
a colonial point of view. Like Colomb and others, Winter advocated closer
cooperation between the centre and the periphery of the empire. Using a
historical approach in his analysis, he concluded that '[al]though details
have altered wonderfully, the main principles of protection are the same'.[35]

Mahan had considerable impact on the RUSI debates of the 1890s, and
the emphasis shifted from technology towards historical analysis in order to
understand the principles of naval warfare and the formulation of naval and
maritime strategy. Following Mahan, the focus of the RUSI discussions also
turned towards the importance of command of the sea and blockade, rather
than the protection of trade. Here George S. Clarke, the secretary of the
Committee of Imperial Defence, who lectured on 'The Navy and the Nation'
in 1904, provides a good example. In his historical analysis, Clarke argued
that the future of Britain and the empire depended upon the 'efficiency and
sufficiency' of the Royal Navy. The empire depended on the safety of 'sea-
borne commerce' and, he suggested 'the loss of this commerce...would
bring ruin and disruption' to everyone. To prove his argument, Clarke used
examples from history to seek 'a general law', which illustrated the

---

95–116; Nicholas A. Lambert, *Planning Armageddon: British Economic Warfare and the First
World War* (Cambridge, MA, 2012), 71–84.

[32] George A. Ballard, 'The Protection of Commerce during War (Gold Medal Prize Essay)',
Journal of Royal United Service Institution, 42 (1898), 367.
[33] Ballard, 'The Protection of Commerce', 366–86.
[34] For a more detailed analysis, see Grimes, *Strategy and War Planning*, 30–2, 226–8.
[35] C. F. Winter, 'The Protection of Commerce during War (Second Prize Essay)', *Journal of
Royal United Service Institution*, 42 (1898), 507–39, here: 511.

prominent role of the navy for the prosperity of the state. For Britain the sea had been a 'constant ally' and even in the age of steam 'the old lessons of naval warfare have been strikingly reaffirmed'. Clarke concluded that the maritime strategy was therefore 'unchanged and unchangeable'.[36]

Command of the sea was also the topic of the naval prize essay in 1908. The winner, Major A. B. N. Churchill from the Royal Artillery, described command of the sea as 'a strategic condition—nothing more and nothing less. Strategically speaking, it is the aim and object of all maritime wars, because this condition must be secured in some measure before sea power can assert its influence.'[37] Using examples from British history, the author illustrated Britain's ascent as a sea power and emphasized the importance of command of the sea. Churchill, as well as the other prize winners, had closely followed Mahan's reasoning and frequently quoted other British national historians, such as Thomas B. Macaulay and John R. Seeley.[38] Naval writer James R. Thursfield focused on command of the sea as the ultimate goal in naval warfare, using the example of Trafalgar.[39] As a result, the Battle of Trafalgar was often glorified in anticipation of a future war at sea.[40]

Despite the interest in command of the sea, protection of trade remained a recurrent topic at the RUSI. At the outbreak of war, the Royal Navy would not have established command of the sea. In this short window of opportunity, attacks on British merchant ships were most likely. The naval officer Lieutenant William C. Crutchley, who later became master of a mail steamer, presented several papers, in which he focused on the merchant marine in a future maritime conflict. In his opinion the Royal Navy was not in the position to 'efficiently patrol a trade route', and hence merchant ships needed to be armed in order to defend themselves. With this proposal, Crutchley entered a legally grey area, as the conversion of merchant ships into warships was a contested issue. Nevertheless, he urged British shipowners to take their 'own initiative' to protect their ships and cargo. Mail

---

[36] George S. Clarke, 'The Navy and the Nation', *Journal of Royal United Service Institution*, 48 (1904), 30–44.

[37] A. B. N. Churchill, 'Command of the Sea: What is it? (Gold Medal Prize Essay)', *Journal of Royal United Service Institution*, 53 (1909), 435–73, here: 455–6.

[38] Churchill, 'Command of the Sea', 435–73. See also F. Fisher, 'Command of the Sea: What is it? (Third Prize Essay)', *Journal of Royal United Service Institution*, 53 (1909), 847–64; T. L. Shelford, 'Command of the Sea: What is it? (Second Prize Essay)', *Journal of Royal United Service Institution*, 53 (1909), 705–50.

[39] James R. Thursfield, *Naval Warfare* (Cambridge, 1913); James R. Thursfield, *Nelson and other Naval Studies* (London, 1909).

[40] Jan S. Breemer, 'The Burden of Trafalgar: Decisive Battle and Naval Strategic Expectations on the Eve of World War I', *Journal of Strategic Studies*, 17 (1994), 33–62.

steamers, in particular, were predestined to carry arms because many of the sailors and officers on board were in the navy reserve.[41] In another paper, Crutchley, together with H. L. Swinburne, argued that for slower merchant ships the old-fashioned convoy provided the best means of protection. In case of an outbreak of war, merchant ships had to react quickly to the new situation by changing trade routes, search bases for re-coaling and identify safe harbours in order to avoid capture.[42] John C. R. Colomb welcomed the idea of the naval reserve serving on mail steamers in order to provide adequate protection. He was more sceptical as to the feasibility of convoy as a measure of trade protection in the age of steam. First, he feared that the arrangement of convoy would interfere with trade to such a degree that it would hinder it and lead to delays. Second, British merchant ships also transported goods of other countries, for which less accurate data existed. Third, merchant steamers would be needed in wartime for the maintenance of the lines of communication between Britain and the empire, rather than for convoying slower merchant ships. Colomb reached these conclusions from his comparison with the Napoleonic Wars, and was convinced that they would hold true 'provided that we [Britain] act upon the fundamental principle', by which he meant the maintenance of a 'sufficient' fleet.[43]

When the naval thinker, Julian S. Corbett, published *Some Principles of Maritime Strategy* in 1911, he redirected British maritime strategic thought to the issues of protection of trade and economic warfare. Corbett examined maritime strategic thinking in a wider theoretical context. Influenced by Clausewitz, he focused on the control of the sea and combined army and navy operations.[44] Naval warfare could not be considered in isolation, Corbett argued. While he acknowledged the limitation of sea power, he also stressed that 'since men live upon the land and not upon the sea, great issues

---

[41] William C. Crutchley, 'Modern Warfare as affecting the Mercantile Marine of Great Britain', *Journal of Royal United Service Institution*, 37 (1893), 491–511.

[42] William C. Crutchley and H. L. Swinburne, 'Suggested Lines of Convoy in War-Time, with a Scheme of Commerce Protection', *Journal of Royal United Service Institution*, 39 (1895), 1163–88; H. L. Swinburne, 'A Scheme of Commerce Protection Protection', *Journal of Royal United Service Institution*, 39 (1895), 1170–88.

[43] John C. R. Colomb in discussion of Crutchley and Swinburne, 'Suggested Lines of Convoy', 1186–8.

[44] Julian S. Corbett, *Some Principles of Maritime Strategy* (London, 1911; reprint Mineola, NY, 2004). See also John Gooch, 'Maritime Command: Mahan and Corbett', in Colin S. Gray and Roger W. Barnett (eds), *Seapower and Strategy* (London, 1989), 27–46; Barry M. Gough, 'Maritime Strategy: The Legacies of Mahan and Corbett as Philosophers of Sea Power', *The RUSI Journal*, 133, 4 (1988), 55–62.

between nations at war have always been decided—except in the rarest cases—either by what your army can do against your enemy's territory and national life, or else by the fear of what the fleet makes it possible for your army to do'.[45] Cooperation between the navy and the army was essential and it would be a mistake to insist on the prerogative of the Royal Navy in war. In Corbett's 'notes on strategy' as part of his war course at the Royal Naval War College, he distinguished between major and minor strategy, describing major strategy as 'a branch of statesmanship which regards the Army and the Navy as parts of one force, to be handled together as the instrument of war'. In contrast, minor strategy, which he 'usually called Naval Strategy', described 'plans of operations' by distinguishing between naval, military, and combined operations. Most importantly, major and minor strategy needed to be studied together.[46]

Corbett's strategic thinking was also reflected in the naval prize essay of 1912 on the protection of trade. The winner, Commander K. G. B. Dewar from the Royal Navy, provided a paper on the relationship between war and the economy. His initial scenario assumed a European war, and he compared the economies and potential strategies of Britain and Germany. Dewar argued that, although Germany did not have to import foodstuffs and raw materials from overseas, intercepting German trade would be crucial in putting economic pressure on Germany. Britain would have to have control of the sea in order to protect its trade. He proposed a war insurance scheme to counterbalance the effects of occasional attacks from enemies on British

[45] Corbett, *Some Principles of Maritime Strategy*, 14. For a further discussion, see N. A. M. Rodger, 'The Nature of Victory at Sea', *Journal for Maritime Research*, July (2005); Schurman, *Education of a Navy*, 147–84.

[46] Strategical Terms and Definitions by Julian S. Corbett (Green Pamphlet) Royal Navy War College, No. 23, Jan. 1909, NMM [National Maritime Museum, Greenwich], CBT [Corbett Papers] 6/15. The same thought can be found in Corbett, *Some Principles of Maritime Strategy*, 8–9. See also James Goldrick and John B. Hattendorf (eds), *Mahan is not Enough: The Proceedings of a Conference on the Works of Sir Julian Corbett and Admiral Sir Herbert Richmond* (Newport, RI, 1993); Andrew D. Lambert, 'Sir Julian Corbett, Naval History and the Development of Sea Power Theory', in N. A. M. Rodger et al. (eds), *Strategy and the Sea: Essays in Honour of John B. Hattendorf* (Woodbridge, 2016), 190–200; Andrew D. Lambert, 'The Naval War Course, *Some Principles of Maritime Strategy* and the Origins of "The British Way in Warfare"', in Keith Neilson and Greg Kennedy (eds), *The British Way in Warfare: Power and the International System, 1856–1956* (Farnham, 2010), 219–53; Schurman, *Education of a Navy*, 147–84; Donald M. Schurman, *Julian S. Corbett, 1854–1922: Historian of British Maritime Policy from Drake to Jellicoe* (London, 1981); Geoffrey Till, 'Corbett and the Emergence of a British School?', in Geoffrey Till (ed.), *The Development of British Naval Thinking: Essays in Memory of Bryan Ranft* (London, 2006), 60–88; Jerker J. Widén, *Theorist of Maritime Strategy: Sir Julian Corbett and his Contribution to Military and Naval Thought* (Burlington, VT, 2012).

trade, so that food prices could be kept low, and popular panic avoided. In Dewar's scenario, command of the sea was not absolute. His vocabulary was to a large extent reminiscent of Corbett's writing. For example, he wrote that, 'if Lord Nelson had no frigates it was because these frigates were engaged on what was thought to be the equally important function of protecting the trade; and the lesson for us is to have sufficient frigates for our battle fleet and trade defence'.[47]

International Law and British Maritime Strategy

From the mid-1890s international lawyers began to lecture more frequently at the RUSI, and commented on the British experience as a neutral in the Spanish-American War of 1898 and the Russo-Japanese War of 1904–5. Their papers focused on the changes to international law and how they affected British state practice and, ultimately, the ability to protect trade and wage economic warfare. The Master of the Supreme Court, John Macdonell, delivered two lectures in 1898 that presented a general overview of recent changes in international law. The lectures received attention not least because of the outbreak of the Spanish-American War, which Macdonell had not anticipated when he accepted the invitation to speak on the issue. Addressing the rights and duties of neutrals, Macdonell rejected the view of those who thought it best to reverse the Declaration of Paris. Rather, he reminded the audience of the 'advantageous' character of the declaration for Britain as a neutral, and suggested that the country 'probably ha[d] to accept it, for better or worse, as a permanent part of maritime law'. More than that, Britain had shaped the understanding of the law of neutrality with the Foreign Enlistment Act of 1870 and the Treaty of Washington of 1871. Macdonell argued that those rules, when 'properly understood, do not go beyond what is reasonable', and yet, without reciprocity Britain's neutrality was 'as burthensome [sic] as war itself'.[48] Moreover, in situations where

---

[47] Kenneth Gilbert Balmain Dewar, 'What is the Influence of Oversea Commerce on the Operations of War? How Did it Affect Our Naval Policy in the Past, and How Does it in Present Day? (Gold Medal Naval Prize Essay)', *Journal of Royal United Service Institution*, 57 (1913), 449–500, here: 496.

[48] John Macdonell, 'Recent Changes in the Rights and Duties of Belligerents and Neutrals According to International Law, Part 1', *Journal of Royal United Service Institution*, 42 (1898), 787–811, here: 803.

'military necessity' became an acceptable means to violate existing practice, the law became fragile.[49]

The law of neutrality became again a prominent topic during the Russo-Japanese War. In 1904 the international lawyer and lecturer at the Royal Naval College, Thomas J. Lawrence, praised Britain's adherence to neutrality and addressed the challenges which Russia's behaviour posed in the recent war, particularly since it raised a more general concern about the law of neutrality. Charles H. Stockton, the drafter of the US Naval War Code, who was US naval attaché in Britain at the time, joined Lawrence in his plea for an internationally binding law of neutrality. They also received support from the chairman of the RUSI meeting, Admiral Sir R. H. Harris, who spoke from the perspective of a serving naval officer. During his long career at sea, he had often had to deal with international law but, since he did not know enough to make independent decisions, he had had to consult the Admiralty and the Law Officers of the Crown for legal advice regarding the current state practice. Having a binding law of neutrality would change that, he thought, and provide certainty for naval officers.[50]

The sinking of British merchant ships during the Russo-Japanese War had been a topic of particular interest to naval officers. Admiral Edmund R. Fremantle pleaded for a common effort by neutrals to curtail belligerent rights. Neutrals should 'insist that vessels...be taken into a port for adjudication, and not summarily sunk on the high seas'. Otherwise the captors would become 'a judge' empowered to decide whether a ship was 'really...an enemy'.[51] However, not everyone shared Fremantle's trust in the prize court system or supported his demand for the restraint of belligerent rights. At a talk delivered by the international jurist Douglas Owen at the RUSI about the value of the right to search and capture, Stewart L. Murray, a retired army officer who had previously lectured at the RUSI on food supply in time of war, dismissed the existence of international law, arguing that there was 'no such thing as International Law. The thing so-called is merely

---

[49] John Macdonell, 'Recent Changes in the Rights and Duties of Belligerents and Neutrals According to International Law, Part 2', *Journal of Royal United Service Institution*, 42 (1898), 915–40, here: 915. See also Isabel V. Hull, '"Military Necessity" and the Laws of War in Imperial Germany', in Stathis N. Kalyvas, Ian Shapiro, and Tarek Masoud (eds), *Order, Conflict, and Violence* (Cambridge, 2008), 352–77.

[50] Thomas J. Lawrence, 'Problems of Neutrality connected with the Russo-Japanese War', *Journal of Royal United Service Institution*, 48 (1904), 915–37. See also Thomas J. Lawrence, *War and Neutrality in the Far East* (London, 1904).

[51] Admiral Edmund R. Fremantle in discussion of William C. Crutchley, 'Protection of Commerce in War, with Special Reference to the Cape Route', *Journal of Royal United Service Institution*, 49 (1905), 11–12.

a collection of historical customs and precedents, and any nation powerful enough can, at any time, add fresh custom or set a fresh precedent.'[52] Owen was also critical. First, the Declaration of Paris of 1856 restricted the right of search and capture and, second, the advance of technology allowed enemy merchant ships to evade capture at sea more easily. The days of grace, granted to enemy ships at the outbreak of war, further diminished the value of capture at sea, and so Owen concluded that 'nothing will remain for us to capture but his [the enemy's] vessels caught unprepared at sea when war breaks out'.[53] Owen's lecture illustrated Britain's dilemma as to the value of the right of search and capture. In many ways, it reflected the similar discussions taking place in the Committee of Imperial Defence and the Admiralty at the same time.[54]

The Hague and London conferences brought international law and, in particular, belligerent rights to the centre of the RUSI discussions. In summarizing the results of the second Hague peace conference, Thomas J. Lawrence highlighted the achievement of an internationally binding law of neutrality. Yet, when it came to the regulation of the laws of naval warfare, he accused other participating countries of 'manipulat[ing] the rules of naval warfare in such a way as to deprive Great Britain of the advantages, springing from her vast maritime resources'.[55] Lawrence argued that 'the object of International Law is not to handicap States, so that they may all start equal in any struggle'. He pleaded for the laws of naval warfare to be 'revised on the principles of respect for justice'.[56] Navy and army officers dismissed Lawrence's moderate stance. For instance, Commander Lord Ellenborough declared that 'naval officers of all countries will continue to make law on the quarter-deck, in defiance of all Hague Regulations, and their law will remain good if their country supports them and is strong enough to do so with impunity'.[57] In reply, Lawrence reminded the audience

---

[52] Stewart L. Murray in discussion of Douglas Owen, 'Capture at Sea: Modern Conditions and the Ancient Prize Laws', *Journal of Royal United Service Institution*, 49 (1905), 1259. See also Stewart L. Murray, 'Our Food Supply in Time of War and Imperial Defence', *Journal of Royal United Service Institution*, 45 (1901), 656–729.

[53] Owen, 'Capture at Sea', 1252.

[54] Grimes, *Strategy and War Planning*; Morgan-Owen, *The Fear of Invasion*; Matthew S. Seligmann, *The Royal Navy and the German Threat 1901–1914: Admiralty Plans to Protect British Trade in a War against Germany* (Oxford, 2012).

[55] Thomas J. Lawrence, 'The Hague Conference and Naval War', *Journal of Royal United Service Institution*, 52 (1908), 486.

[56] Lawrence, 'Hague Conference and Naval War', 493.

[57] See, for instance, Commander Lord Ellenborough, RN in discussion of Lawrence, 'Hague Conference and Naval War', 495–8.

that having no binding rules would mean a return 'to absolute, complete, and utter barbarism', which he could not support. In his opinion, 'mankind' had developed the rules of war over centuries and through them had shown frequent demonstrations of restraint throughout the history of warfare.[58]

The debate on the role of international law in a future maritime war continued even after states adopted the Declaration of London in 1909. Harold F. Wyatt, an executive member of the Navy League, presented a paper at the RUSI which attacked the declaration because it undermined the Royal Navy's capability in wartime. Painting a bleak picture in which Britain faced threats from Germany, France, and Russia, Wyatt thought that Britain had already surrendered its belligerent rights with the Declaration of Paris. The British agreement at The Hague to the creation of an international prize court had deprived the Royal Navy of its 'last...freedom'. According to Wyatt, the Declaration of London was the last straw, which if ratified, would be 'a great act of national suicide'. Wyatt's argument corresponded with that of the Navy League, a proponent of a strong navy as Britain's first line of defence.[59] While the audience at the RUSI enthusiastically agreed with Wyatt, the Cambridge law professor, John Westlake, strongly opposed him. In his opinion, the Declaration of London was largely based on British practice and reflected British strategic interests and, despite its flaws, he hoped it would find approval.[60]

A similar tone to Wyatt can be found in Douglas Owen's talk at the RUSI. For him, the declaration had been a mistake because the British government had declared the 'uniformity' of the law as paramount over the protection of neutral rights to ensure food supply in time of war. Although Owen offered a more nuanced analysis than Wyatt, he called the drafters 'theorists and jurists...with no practical knowledge of commerce'.[61] Lord Ellenborough from the Royal Navy further fanned the flames when he declared that many naval officers did not think much of the declaration because 'it will be torn

---

[58] Lawrence, 'Hague Conference and Naval War', 503–5, here: 503. See also Douglas Owen, 'Our Food Supplies. Our Dependence on Overseas Food: The Emgergency Means available to us to Amplify our Supplies on Outbreak of War, and thus Prevent Food Panic, with its Danger to the State', *Journal of Royal United Service Institution*, 53 (1909), 1551–78.

[59] N. C. Fleming, 'The Imperial Maritime League: British Navalism, Conflict, and the Radical Right, c.1907–1920', *War in History*, 23 (2016), 296–322; Harold F. Wyatt, 'England's Threatened Rights at Sea', *Journal of Royal United Service Institution*, 54 (1910), 5–33. See also Matthew Johnson, 'The Liberal Party and the Navy League in Britain before the Great War', *Twentieth Century British History*, 22, 2 (2011), 137–63.

[60] John Westlake in discussion of Wyatt, 'England's Threatened Rights at Sea', 21–2.

[61] Douglas Owen, 'Declaration of London and our Food Supplies', *Journal of the Royal United Service Institution*, 55 (1911), 149–85.

to pieces and flung into the waste-paper basket when hostilities commence'.[62] Another naval officer, Admiral Sir E. R. Fremantle, also supported Owen's views, and brought the strategic thinkers, Mahan and Julian S. Corbett, into the discussion. Mahan, he remarked, had warned that the land powers 'Germany and the great central Powers of Europe' were 'so strong on land' that 'the only counterpoise' Britain had was its 'belligerents rights and the great maritime power of the British Navy'. Fremantle did not believe in an international jurisdiction as proposed by the International Prize Court as it would never 'be equally fair to an island Power and to a Continental Power'.[63]

In summary, the RUSI debate illustrated the emergence of a British school of naval and maritime strategic thought in the period 1872 to 1914. Early concepts evolved in the context of home and imperial defence in the 1870s, in response to rapid advances in naval technology, and a growing insecurity as to its effect on British maritime strategy. The study of sea power focused on both the protection of trade and economic warfare against enemies. The theoretical understanding of strategy originated from a comparison of land and sea warfare because many army and navy officers believed in its assimilation. While technology had been the point of reference in the early phase, historical analysis dominated after 1890. Following Mahan's publications, the RUSI debates changed their focus, and studies in the 1890s and 1900s examined in particular command of the sea and the strategic importance of blockade. Protection of trade and economic warfare resurfaced as important issues in 1904 during the Russo-Japanese War when British merchant ships were sunk, and Corbett's writings in the years after reflected the particular British focus of that concern.

The RUSI debates on international law urged navy and army officers to think about the relationship between law and strategy, about their visions of future maritime war, and about their preferences for what a legal framework should look like. Changes to state practice, the Declaration of Paris, and particularly the process of codification in the Hague and London conferences, prompted a broader debate at the RUSI as to the effect of international law on British maritime strategy. Two topics were of primary concern to army and navy officers, the protection of trade and belligerent rights. The two lawyers, Lawrence and Owen, who lectured most frequently at the RUSI, both taught at the Royal Naval College. While most international jurists offered a balanced analysis on the codification, some

---

[62] Commander Lord Ellenborough, RN in discussion of Owen, 'Declaration of London', 170.
[63] Admiral Sir E. R. Fremantle in discussion of Owen, 'Declaration of London', 173.

expressed a more extreme view. The RUSI debates showed that officers seemed uncertain about how international law would affect future naval warfare. Many officers doubted whether the legal framework guaranteed protection of trade, and were sceptical about the restraint of belligerent rights. Despite the criticism, the RUSI debates showed that legal questions had an impact on maritime strategic thought, and so led to a clearer formulation of British maritime strategy.

7

International Law and
the Theory of War

The sea was often described as a public highway. Thereafter, its conditions
changed in wartime, when belligerents would try to control the sea, meaning
that neutral and enemy ships were subject to search and capture. Blockade
provided another means for a sea power to deny neutral and enemy ships
access to ports or coastlines. The codification of international maritime
law restricted these belligerent rights in an attempt to restrain war at sea.
Ultimately, though, the right of search and capture made neutral and enemy
merchant ships legitimate objects in war at sea. At the Hague peace conference in 1899, the United States proposed that private property should be
made immune from capture at sea. The discussion that followed brought to
light several differences among international actors.[1]

   This chapter examines the question of the immunity of private property from capture at sea between 1856 and 1914. As it was not based on
existing state practice, its theoretical nature opened the debate on the
relationship between international law and the theory of war. This chapter
first examines the existing practice of the right of search and capture.
Second, it presents the various attempts to introduce immunity for private property at sea, in particular the Hague peace conferences of 1899
and 1907, and explains Britain's position on the issue. Third, the chapter
examines the immunity of private property at sea in relation to the theory
of war by analysing the works of international lawyers and the two
most important naval thinkers of the period, Alfred T. Mahan and
Julian S. Corbett.

---

[1] Bryan Ranft, 'Restraints on War at Sea Before 1945', in Michael Howard (ed.), *Restraints
on War: Studies in the Limitation of Armed Conflict* (Oxford, 1979), 39–52.

Great Britain, International Law, and the Evolution of Maritime Strategic Thought, 1856–1914. Gabriela A. Frei,
Oxford University Press (2020). © Gabriela A. Frei.
DOI: 10.1093/oso/9780198859932.001.0001

The Right of Search and Capture

Search and capture were a belligerent's legitimate right, which allowed it to verify the status of a merchant ship. The procedure was highly regulated. States usually issued manuals or instructions to their navies for commanding officers to follow in order to establish a rightful claim to a prize when they decided to capture a ship.[2] In times of war, warships could exercise the right of search and capture anywhere on the high seas and in the waters of belligerent parties. As a matter of principle, a belligerent warship could stop and 'visit' every neutral and enemy ship except when neutral merchant ships sailed in neutral waters or were part of a convoy (see Article 61 of Declaration of London). The capture of a merchant ship was lawful under the following conditions: if the crew resisted the right of 'visit and search', and subsequently suspicions were founded after boarding with the discovery of e.g. contraband trade; or if ship's papers, which could identify the vessel's status and that of its cargo, were incomplete. The Declaration of Paris had limited the right of capture of neutral ships but enemy merchant ships were always subject to the right of search and capture. In case of capture, a ship was brought into the nearest port of the captor for a prize court procedure, in which the lawfulness of the capture was examined.[3]

The United States and the Immunity of Private Property

Since its independence in 1776, the United States had actively advocated the adoption of the principle of immunity of private property from search and capture. These efforts resulted in a bilateral treaty between the United States and Prussia in 1785, which embodied the principle that all merchant ships would be free from capture in time of war.[4] In 1823, under US President James Monroe, the United States government approached the three major sea powers of the time, Britain, France, and Russia, to negotiate the adoption of the principle of immunity. Russia showed willingness to do so on the

---

[2] Thomas E. Holland, *A Manual of Naval Prize Law. Founded Upon the Manual Prepared in 1866 by Godfrey Lushington* (London, 1888).

[3] William E. Hall, *A Treatise on International Law*, ed. J. B. Atlay, 6th edn (Oxford, 1909), 723–39.

[4] Treaty of Amity and Commerce Between His Majesty the King of Prussia, and the United States of America, 10 Sept. 1785, http://avalon.law.yale.edu/18th_century/prus1785.asp (accessed 4 Oct. 2018).

condition that other states did the same, but Britain and France could not be persuaded. At the Paris peace conference in 1856 the US Secretary of State, William L. Marcy, declared that the United States could only agree to the abolition of privateering in return for the adoption of the principle of immunity of private property from capture at sea. However, Britain rejected the 'Marcy amendment' and the United States did not sign the Declaration of Paris in 1856 as a result.[5]

Not long after, Prussia, Austria, and Italy proclaimed the immunity of private property from capture at sea during the Austro-Prussian War of 1866. Prussia would have also adopted this position during the Franco-Prussian War of 1870–1, but France was against it. In 1871, Italy and the United States signed a bilateral treaty, obliging each other to respect the immunity of private property at sea, and allowing capture only in cases when blockade had been broken or the property at sea constituted contraband of war. In fact, Italy's Marine Code of 1865 had already declared that Italy would apply the immunity of private property at sea if the other side granted it reciprocity.[6]

The principle of the immunity of private property from capture at sea was adopted mainly in conflicts in which maritime warfare did not play a decisive factor in the outcome of the war. The principle was also pursued by states that did not have a navy strong enough to protect their trade. For them, the principle of the immunity of private property at sea offered a way to protect their trade in wartime. Major sea powers, on the other hand, were strictly against the adoption of this principle, as the British and French positions demonstrated. The only concession which they were willing to make was the adoption of the immunity of special ships, such as hospital ships, mail ships, fishing boats, ships on voyages of discovery, ships involved in the exchange of prisoners, and ships protected by days of grace or by special licence. Many of these special cases were dealt with at

---

[5] Thomas J. Lawrence, *The Principles of International Law*, 2nd and rev. edn (London, 1899), 407–8; Harold Scott Quigley, *The Immunity of Private Property from Capture at Sea* (Madison, WI, 1918); Carlton Savage, *Policy of the United States Toward Maritime Commerce in War*, 2 vols (Washington, DC, 1934), vol. 1, 9, 1–86. For a broader debate, see John B. Hattendorf, 'The US Navy and the "Freedom of the Seas", 1775–1917', in Rolf Hobson and Tom Kristiansen (eds), *Navies in Northern Waters 1721–2000* (London, 2004), 151–74; Jan M. Lemnitzer, *Power, Law and the End of Privateering* (Basingstoke, 2014), 75–95.

[6] Lawrence, *Principles of International Law*, 408–10; Charles H. Stockton, 'Would Immunity from Capture During War of Nonoffending Private Property upon the High Seas be in the Interest of Civilization?', *American Journal of International Law* 1, 4 (1907), 931–2.

the Hague peace conferences in 1899 and 1907, and resulted in the adoption of several Hague conventions.[7]

Britain and the Immunity of Private Property

Britain's opposition to the Marcy amendment at the Paris peace conference in 1856 was the first public statement by the British government on this issue, and it did not change its position throughout the period prior to 1914. Yet, the British government adopted the Declaration of Paris, which caused a public outcry as it was interpreted as leaving Britain in a vulnerable position in a future war at sea. Some did not want to accept the limitation of the right of search and capture and consequently demanded a withdrawal from the declaration as the only way to regain Britain's maritime strength. The 14th Earl of Derby argued that the declaration left Britain with its 'right arm cut off', an often-cited metaphor which was used in subsequent discussions to describe the curtailment of belligerent rights.[8] For supporters of the immunity of private property at sea, on the other hand, the declaration did not go far enough, and they feared for the protection of trade in a future maritime conflict.[9] The adoption of the immunity of private property at sea would have meant an expansion of the already disagreeable terms of the declaration. Hence, opponents argued that the immunity of private property was a further concession, which would surrender a sea power's only offensive weapon, namely the right of search and capture. Lord Derby's

---

[7] 'Convention (III) for the Adaptation to Maritime Warfare of the Principles of the Geneva Convention of 22 August 1864. The Hague, 29 July 1899', in Dietrich Schindler and Jiří Toman (eds), *The Laws of Armed Conflicts: A Collection of Conventions, Resolutions and other Documents* (Dordrecht, 2004), 373–7; 'Convention (VI) relating to the Status of Enemy Merchant Ships at the Outbreak of Hostilities. The Hague, 18 Oct. 1907', in Dietrich Schindler and Jiří Toman (eds), *The Laws of Armed Conflicts: A Collection of Conventions, Resolutions and other Documents* (Dordrecht, 2004), 1059–64; 'Convention (X) for the Adaptation to Maritime Warfare of the Principles of the Geneva Convention. The Hague, 18 Oct. 1907', in Dietrich Schindler and Jiří Toman (eds), *The Laws of Armed Conflicts: A Collection of Conventions, Resolutions and other Documents* (Dordrecht, 2004); 'Convention (XI) Relative to Certain Restrictions with Regard to the Exercise of the Right of Capture in Naval War. The Hague, 18 Oct. 1907', in Dietrich Schindler and Jiří Toman (eds), *The Laws of Armed Conflicts: A Collection of Conventions, Resolutions and other Documents* (Dordrecht, 2004), 1087–92. See also Lawrence, *Principles of International Law*, 411; Stockton, 'Immunity from Capture', 936–8.

[8] Speech of 14th Earl of Derby, Hansard, 3rd series, HL Deb., 22 May 1856, vol. 142, cc. 528–39. See also subsequent debate: Speech of Spenser Walpole, Hansard, 3rd series, HC Deb., 17 Mar. 1862, vol. 165, c. 1688.

[9] Bernard Semmel, *Liberalism and Naval Strategy: Ideology, Interest, and Sea Power During the Pax Britannica* (Boston, MA, 1986), 56–79.

speech in the House of Lords is a good example of that argument. He said: 'I look upon it as depriving her [Britain] of those natural advantages which her great maritime power has given her in war, and of the exercise of that superiority and those belligerent rights without which she is nothing.' He warned that, 'if she [Britain] remains not the mistress of the seas she falls immediately and naturally into the position of a third-rate Power'.[10] These fears were not completely unfounded, as Britain's growing dependence on the import of foodstuffs and raw materials in the second half of the nineteenth century illustrated.

Supporters of the immunity of private property from capture at sea were a minority in Britain. The Radical Liberals supported it when it was first discussed in parliament in 1856. Richard Cobden, an early spokesman for the Radical Liberals, argued that individuals should no longer be victims of maritime conflicts. A future war at sea should be a conflict only between two naval forces and leave merchants free to trade without interruption. In a private letter, Cobden wrote: 'I tell you candidly, I want to see war brought as much as possible to a duel between Governments and their professional fighters, with as little stimulus from the hope of plunder and prize-money as possible.'[11] Cobden directly attacked Britain's traditional strategy of economic warfare, a strategy primarily aimed at capturing enemy property at sea and putting economic pressure on the enemy through blockade and the right of search and capture. For Cobden, the immunity of private property from capture at sea would advance civilization. In subsequent years, several motions were proposed in parliament in favour of the immunity of private property, such as that of Thomas B. Horsfall in 1862 and of Sir John Lubbock in 1878. Yet, the motions were withdrawn before a vote took place.[12]

Merchants and shipowners were some of the most ardent supporters of the immunity of private property from capture at sea. For instance, the Manchester Chamber of Commerce made a plea in 1859 to the British government to consider its adoption. Edmund Potter, the chamber's president, argued that the British merchant marine would be put in a 'perilous position' in time of war as the Royal Navy could not provide adequate protection for

---

[10] Speech of 14th Earl of Derby, Hansard, 3rd series, HL Deb., 22 May 1856, vol. 142, cc. 528–39, here: cc. 535–6.

[11] 'Richard Cobden to William Lindsay, 29 Aug. 1856', in William S. Lindsay, *Manning the Royal Navy and Mercantile Marine. Also Belligerent and Neutral Rights in the Event of War* (London, 1877), 116.

[12] C. I. Hamilton, 'Anglo-French Seapower and the Declaration of Paris', *The International History Review*, 4, 2 (1982), 166–90; Semmel, *Liberalism and Naval Strategy*, 68–79.

the expanding British merchant marine, and that protection of trade would take away naval capacities from offensive operations. He further feared that, in case of war, merchants could choose to transport their goods by foreign ships, and that consequently people would be 'thrown out of employment'. The immediate consequence would be an increase in prices for raw materials resulting from higher war premiums or higher import costs, and 'export trade' would equally be affected.[13]

William S. Lindsay, a wealthy Lancashire shipowner and Radical Liberal MP, spoke of the legal uncertainty which shipowners faced in times of conflict, not least because the declaration had only defined broad principles rather than created clear and detailed rules. The lack of a definition of contraband, as well as uncertain rules about the right of search and capture, gave belligerents many justifications for engagement, which put shipowners at their mercy.[14] Furthermore, so Lindsay concluded from the experience of the Crimean war, blockade was no longer an effective means for Britain as a belligerent to control the sea and capture enemy ships, particularly since Britain was 'by far the largest carrier by sea' and 'any measures which stop or diminish our [British] intercourse with other countries, must inflict more injury on us than on any other neutral nation'.[15] In other words, blockade became a hindrance rather than a desirable means to protect British overseas trade.

It was obvious that, if Britain stayed neutral, the principles of the Declaration of Paris would not go far enough to provide effective protection of neutral trade. On the other hand, if Britain were a belligerent, the import of foodstuffs and raw materials would lie entirely in the hands of neutrals, and British shipowners could lose business to neutrals. Other overseas trade would be equally affected as many British merchant ships transported goods to and from foreign ports as cross-traders.[16] Rumours of war would suffice for underwriters to raise war premiums due to the risk to which shipowners would be exposed, and consequently, the British merchant marine would suffer the same fate as the American merchant marine in the American Civil War, in which it was almost annihilated. To avoid a similar catastrophe,

---

[13] Edmund Potter (President of the Manchester Chamber of Commerce) to Lord John Russell, 10 Nov. 1859, TNA, FO 881/9155X, 15–17. See also Manchester Chamber of Commerce to Lord Palmerston, 4 Jan. 1860, TNA, FO 881/9155X, 20–1; Liverpool Ship-Owners' Association to the Marquess of Salisbury, 27 Nov. 1905 (No. 11: Inclosure 1), TNA, FO 881/8672; Manchester Chamber of Commerce to the Marquess of Salisbury, 27 Nov. 1905 (No. 11: Inclosure 2), TNA, FO 881/8672.

[14] William S. Lindsay, 'On Belligerent Rights: The Declaration of Paris, 1856', *Journal of Royal United Service Institution*, 21 (1878), 189.

[15] Lindsay, 'On Belligerent Rights', 183.   [16] Lindsay, 'On Belligerent Rights', 179–87.

Lindsay demanded a concise definition of contraband, and argued a change of policy was necessary as Britain's 'vast Mercantile Marine on which we [Britain] justly pride ourselves—has become *our most vulnerable point*. For that reason alone, it is clearly to [sic] our interest to move onwards and make all private property free from capture at sea.'[17] Lindsay assumed that the navy had only limited capacity to control the sea and exercise its belligerent rights—the same argument as the Manchester Chamber of Commerce used in their plea for a policy change.[18]

Not every shipowner agreed with Lindsay. Donald Currie, for example, a Scottish shipowner and Liberal MP, trusted in the Royal Navy's ability to protect British trade and shipping routes in wartime. He even supported the idea of armed merchant ships as part of an auxiliary force. As early as 1849, a Select Committee of the House of Commons investigated ways to utilize the merchant marine as an auxiliary force for the defence of Britain. The main focus was on ocean steamships as a means to patrol trade routes. Despite enthusiasm from the owners of steamship companies, naval officers had reservations about this scheme because of technological differences between merchant ships and warships. With the improvements to steamship design in the 1880s, the Admiralty initiated subsidies for the building of ocean steamships. In return, the ships were to be commissioned into the navy in wartime to serve alongside British warships as auxiliaries. In 1885, the auxiliary forces of the Royal Navy numbered 150 steamships. Their role was limited to transporting troops, patrolling trade routes, and maintaining communications between the centre and periphery of the British Empire.[19]

Creating a naval auxiliary force from the merchant marine was controversial among shipowners. Currie, whose private interests were closely tied to those of the British government, welcomed the financial support offered by the scheme. As the owner of the Castle Line Company, he operated a steamship line between Britain and South Africa. With the help of the British government, Currie was able to expand his quasi-monopoly of the trade route, which was not consonant with free trade. Other shipowners feared that armed merchant ships were more of a target than a deterrent in wartime, and rejected the government's interference in private business.[20]

[17] Lindsay, 'On Belligerent Rights', 187.   [18] Lindsay, 'On Belligerent Rights', 187–91.

[19] Donald Currie, 'Maritime Warfare: the Adaptation of Ocean Steamers to War Purposes', *Journal of Royal United Service Institution*, 24 (1881), 81–105; Donald Currie, 'On Maritime Warfare; the Importance to the British Empire of a Complete System of Telegraphs, Coaling Stations, and Graving Docks', *Journal of Royal United Service Institution*, 21 (1877), 228–47.

[20] John Beeler, 'Ploughshares into Swords: The Royal Navy and Merchant Marine Auxiliaries in the Late Nineteenth Century', in Greg Kennedy (ed.), *The Merchant Marine in International*

The 1899 Hague Peace Conference

At the end of the nineteenth century, the question of the immunity of private property from capture at sea reappeared on the American political agenda. The reason for this renewed interest was a supposed assimilation of war at sea with the conditions of war on land. Some argued that since the codification of war on land had established the distinction between combatants and non-combatants, the same should be applied to war at sea because wars affected not only people from belligerent countries but also those from neutrals.

In 1898, Charles Henry Butler, a New York lawyer, launched a campaign lobbying for the immunity of private property from capture at sea.[21] In a memorial addressed to the US President William McKinley in 1898, Butler argued that the time was ripe for the United States to call for an international conference to discuss the immunity of private property from capture at sea. The United States had just emerged victorious from the Spanish-American War of 1898, in which it had demonstrated its maritime capabilities but had not practised the immunity of private property at sea.[22] Butler's proposal gained support from American merchants. The Chamber of Commerce of the State of New York adopted a resolution, which was presented to the US president a few days later.[23]

In his annual message to Congress on 5 December 1898, McKinley announced that the United States aspired to an international agreement on the immunity of private property at sea. McKinley explained that the experience of the Spanish-American War had 'forcibly [brought] home to us a sense of burdens and the waste of war'.[24] American businessmen widely

---

Affairs 1850–1950 (London, 2000), 5–30; Andrew N. Porter, 'Donald Currie and Southern Africa 1870 to 1912: Strategies for Survival', in Sarah Palmer and Glyndwr Williams (eds), *Charted and Uncharted Waters: Proceedings of a Conference on the Study of British Maritime History* (London, 1981), 29–53; Andrew N. Porter, *Victorian Shipping, Business and Imperial Policy: Donald Currie, The Castle Line and Southern Africa* (Woodbridge, 1986), 61–77, 85–93.

[21] Charles H. Butler, *Freedom of Private Property on the Sea from Capture During War* (Washington, DC, 1899).

[22] Charles H. Butler, 'Memorial to the President of the United States, 4 Nov. 1898', in Butler, *Freedom of Private Property*, 7–13.

[23] Report of the Committee of Foreign Commerce and the Revenue Laws, 27 Nov. 1898, in 'Proceedings of the New York Chamber of Commerce, 1 Dec. 1898', in Butler, *Freedom of Private Property*, 14–16.

[24] William McKinley, 'Second Annual Message to Congress, 5 Dec. 1898', in Gerhard Peters and John T. Woolley, *The American Presidency Project*, https://www.presidency.ucsb.edu/node/205329 (accessed 25 Oct. 2018). See also Savage, *Policy of the United States*, vol. 1, 102–3.

endorsed the president's policy announcement, as the resolutions of the Merchants Association of New York, the Chamber of Commerce of San Francisco, and the Board of Managers of the New York Produce Exchange illustrated. A few months later, the Senate approved the president's proposed policy.[25]

The British government had to respond to McKinley's announcement.[26] It still firmly opposed any change, but Arthur J. Balfour, while temporarily in power and acting on behalf of his uncle, the Prime Minister and Foreign Secretary, Lord Salisbury, noted that Britain 'would gain by the change'. He thought that Britain could better protect its trade and that, since the proposal would still exempt breach of blockade and contraband trade, ships were still liable to capture.[27] Lord Salisbury, however, rejected such a view. He questioned its practicability, particularly given the lack of definitions of contraband and blockade. Uncertainty put British trade at the mercy of foreign prize courts to decide the lawfulness of capture, which 'would be a poor reliance' according to Salisbury.[28]

Before the United States could call for an international conference in Washington, it used the opportunity to put the immunity of private property from capture at sea on the agenda at the first Hague peace conference in 1899. The issue was not part of the original conference programme, but the leader of the US delegation, Andrew D. White, wrote a memorial to the head of the Hague peace conference, in which he pleaded for widening the agenda by considering issues concerning maritime warfare.[29] The Second Commission briefly touched upon the memorial because it was concerned with the question of whether the rules for land warfare could also be adapted to maritime warfare.[30] While most of the delegates were willing to discuss the issue, the British delegate, Julian Pauncefote, was opposed to opening the agenda. As he had no instructions from his government, Pauncefote abstained from voting. On the concrete question of the

---

[25] Butler, *Freedom of Private Property*, 6.

[26] Sir J. Pauncefote (British Ambassador to the United States) to Lord Salisbury, 8 Dec. 1898, TNA, FO 881/8672.

[27] Note by Mr Balfour, 24 Dec. 1898 (No. 5: Inclosure 3), TNA, FO 881/8672.

[28] Note by the late Lord Salisbury, Dec. 1898 (No. 5: Inclosure 3), TNA, FO 881/8672.

[29] Memorial addressed by the Representatives of the Government of the United States at The Hague to His Excellency M. de Staal, President of the Peace Conference, 20 June 1899, TNA, FO 881/9155X, 60–2; Calvin DeArmond Davis, *The United States and the First Hague Peace Conference* (Ithaca, NY, 1962), 127–8.

[30] Second Commission, Plenary Meeting, 5 July 1899, in James Brown Scott (ed.), *The Proceedings of the Hague Peace Conferences. Translation of the Official Texts. The Conference of 1899* (New York, 1920), 383–411.

'inviolability of private property in naval war', which the US delegation had proposed, Feodor Martens, the president of the Second Commission, showed 'sympathy for this idea' not least because Russia had favoured it since 1823. However, Martens was also aware of its sensitivity, and cautioned that 'if inviolability is admitted, maritime nations will have to change radically their plans and projects'.[31] Hence, he thought it advisable to postpone discussions until the next conference. After a vote within the commission, from which Britain, France, and Russia abstained, the matter was put in front of the plenary conference.[32] White used the opportunity to explain the scope and limitation of the 'inviolability of private property in naval war'. He stressed that the proposal had gained support from 'several Powers', by which he meant Italy, Austria-Hungary, Germany, and Russia—all states which had signed commercial treaties containing an 'immunity' clause. White was convinced that the adoption of the proposal would 'be a crown of glory to modern diplomacy'.[33] Yet, the resistance from two major sea powers, Britain and France, could not be ignored, and White too was willing to postpone the matter until the next conference. White's speech also illustrated that the United States' proposal was less radical than it appeared. The immunity of private property did not apply in cases of contraband trade or breach of blockade. Yet, White admitted that, in order to make the immunity of private property practicable, contraband of war and blockade had to be defined more concisely. Moreover, White was convinced of the usefulness of blockade, as it was '[t]he only effective measure of terminating war by the action of a navy'.[34] Since the immunity of private property at sea did not apply in cases in which a ship headed to a blockaded port, this seemed a strong argument.[35] Although the issue was not pursued further at the conference, White had successfully prepared the ground for further discussions, so securing a major diplomatic success for the United States.[36]

White portrayed the United States' motives as 'ideal' and argued that the immunity of private property at sea was 'a question of right, of justice, [and]

---

[31] Second Commission, Plenary Meeting, 5 July 1899, in Scott (ed.), *Proceedings. The Conference of 1899*, 411.

[32] Second Commission, Plenary Meeting, 5 July 1899, in Scott (ed.), *Proceedings. The Conference of 1899*, 412.

[33] Plenary Conference, Fifth Meeting, 5 July 1899, in Scott (ed.), *Proceedings. Conference of 1899*, 47.

[34] Plenary Conference, Fifth Meeting, 5 July 1899, in Scott (ed.), *Proceedings. Conference of 1899*, 48.

[35] Plenary Conference, Fifth Meeting, 5 July 1899, in Scott (ed.), *Proceedings. Conference of 1899*, 46–50.

[36] Davis, *United States and the First Hague*, 127–8, 133–6, 175–6.

of progress for the whole world'.[37] It certainly fitted into the idea of a 'legalist empire' as Ben Coates has recently argued.[38] However, there were also dissenting opinions, most prominently that of US naval strategist Alfred T. Mahan, who had also been a member of the US delegation at The Hague. In his letters to *The New York Times*, he responded to the resolution of the New York Chamber of Commerce in 1898.[39] Mahan objected to the term private property. While he acknowledged that property was generally private, he rejected the idea that property served only a private interest. Rather, he argued that 'the exchange of goods, commerce, is the financial life of a nation, and it is now a commonplace that money is the sinews [*sic*] of war. Commerce, therefore, and especially maritime commerce, bears to the military life of a nation at large just the relation that the communications of an army in campaign bear to the efficiency of that army.'[40] The expansion of international trade would make wars less likely, not least because of the private interests at stake. The adoption of the immunity of private property at sea would therefore achieve the opposite outcome and increase the chance of war rather than diminish it. In a final point, Mahan underlined that the adoption of such a policy would constrain the strengthened US Navy's capabilities in a future war.[41] Nevertheless, Mahan was a member of the US delegation at The Hague in 1899, although he personally did not think much of the conference.[42]

Shifting Opinions

After 1900, public opinion on the issue shifted in the United States. Charles H. Stockton, serving naval officer and president of the United States

[37] Plenary Conference, Fifth Meeting, 5 July 1899, in Scott (ed.), *Proceedings. Conference of 1899*, 49.

[38] Coates, *Legalist Empire*, 86–7.

[39] Alfred T. Mahan, 'Letter to the Editor on Commerce and War I', *The New York Times*, 17 Nov. 1898, http://search.proquest.com/docview/95571033?accountid=13,042 (accessed 13 Oct. 2018); Alfred T. Mahan, 'Letter to the Editor on Commerce and War II', *The New York Times*, 23 Nov. 1898, http://search.proquest.com/docview/95565194?accountid=13,042 (accessed 13 Oct. 2018).

[40] Mahan, 'Letter to the Editor on Commerce and War I'.

[41] For a full version of the letter, see Letter addressed by Charles H. Butler to Captain Alfred T. Mahan in regard to Freedom of Private Property on the Sea from Capture during War, 24 Nov. 1898 (No. 5: Inclosure 3), TNA, FO 881/8672; Charles H. Butler, 'A Reply to Captain Mahan', *The New York Times*, 27 Nov. 1898, http://search.proquest.com/docview/9565 7494?accountid=13,042 (accessed 13 Oct. 2018), 60–7; Semmel, *Liberalism and Naval Strategy*.

[42] 'Alfred T. Mahan to James Ford Rhodes, 28 Apr. 1899', in Robert Seager II and Doris D. Maguire (eds), *Letters and Papers of Alfred Thayer Mahan*, 3 vols (Annapolis, MD, 1975), vol. 2, 633.

Naval War College, presented a different assessment of the United States' motives when he gave a speech at the American Society of International Law in 1907. The United States' position towards the immunity of private property at sea was founded upon the fact that the country did not depend on imported foodstuffs, and on the assumption that all American merchant ships would be integrated into the US Navy at the outbreak of war—a policy which had been formulated at the end of the American Civil War. However, since then the United States' economic and political situation had changed significantly. Economic growth and an expansionist foreign policy had seen the rise of the United States as a sea power by the beginning of the twentieth century. Stockton argued that the United States' 'advocacy of its [immunity's] adoption as a national policy, formerly a matter of interest', had become 'purely altruistic'. Although the right of search and capture would not always shorten a war, it was 'a weapon, which may be of some importance in time of war' against those states which relied on the import of foodstuffs and other resources.[43] Hence, Stockton insisted on retaining belligerent rights, citing Helmuth von Moltke, who argued any means that shortened a war were justified.[44] In the 'blue books' series of the United States Naval War College, one of the leading international law book series, the international jurist George Grafton Wilson also suggested that the United States should abandon the policy of the immunity of private property and instead adopt one which gradually exempted private property at sea from capture.[45]

The US Secretary of State and jurist, Elihu Root, privately shared this view because merchants would otherwise no longer be interested in keeping the peace. Rather they would put due diligence aside and become involved in risky ventures in wartime.[46] However, in the instructions for the US delegates at the Hague peace conference in 1907, Root defended the United States' official policy and underlined that the principle of the immunity of private property was 'of such permanent and universal importance that no

[43]   Stockton, 'Immunity from Capture', 942.

[44]   Stockton, 'Immunity from Capture', 943. For a broader view on US foreign policy and the role of the navy, see George W. Baer, *One Hundred Years of Sea Power: The U.S. Navy, 1890–1990* (Stanford, CA, 1994), 9–48; Walter Lafeber, *The Cambridge History of American Foreign Relations: Vol. 2: The American Search for Opportunity, 1865–1913* (Cambridge, 1993), 21–44, 129–233.

[45]   George Grafton Wilson, 'Topic V: Immunity of Private Property at Sea', in *International Law Situations* (Washington, DC, 1914), 113.

[46]   'Sir Edward Grey to Sir Mortimer Durand (British Ambassador to the United States), 6 Nov. 1906 (No. 167)', in G. P. Gooch and Harold Temperley (eds), *British Documents of the Origins of the War 1898–1914, Vol. VIII: Arbitration, Neutrality and Security* (London, 1932), 197–8.

balancing of the chances of probable loss or gain in the immediate future on the part of any nation should be permitted to outweigh the considerations of common benefit to civilization which call for the adoption of such an agreement'.[47]

Germany's growing ambitions to become a major sea power in the late nineteenth century made continued support for the immunity of private property at sea less likely. When the German Chancellor, Leo von Caprivi, responded in the German Reichstag on 4 March 1892 to a motion in favour of the immunity of private property at sea, he stressed the importance of economic warfare and expressed doubts about whether naval battles would end a war. Although Caprivi did not formally abandon Germany's position towards the immunity of private property, he implied that future war at sea would not respect the immunity of private property or the Declaration of Paris, but would rather be decided on the principle of military necessity. The British Admiralty saw Caprivi's speech as a clear sign that opinion was shifting to supporting more aggressive behaviour at sea.[48] The Foreign Office's analysis of the 'German official view' on the subject referred to a publication by Ferdinand Perels, a distinguished international jurist who taught at the Friedrich Wilhelms University of Berlin and worked as director of the civil department of the Imperial Naval Office. Perels did not think that the adoption of the immunity of private property would be possible 'in the near future'. The reason for this was plain: the British government 'maintained an attitude of persistent and determined resistance to all movements for reforming the laws of maritime warfare'.[49] Clearly Britain and Germany carefully watched each other's behaviour in the matter amid their ongoing arms race.[50]

In Britain, public opinion shifted from opposition to support of the immunity of private property. The destruction of British merchant ships during the Russo-Japanese War helped advocates, in particular merchants and shipowners, both to alert the public and to demand from the

---

[47] Elihu Root, 'Instructions to the American Delegates to the Hague Conference of 1907, 31 May 1907', in James Brown Scott (ed.), *Instructions to the American Delegates to the Hague Peace Conferences and Their Official Reports* (New York, 1916), 81–2.

[48] Leo von Caprivi, 'Reichstagsrede, 4 Mar. 1892 (187. Sitzung)', in *Stenographische Berichte über den Deutschen Reichstag*, 4553–61; Admiralty (Evan MacGregor) to Undersecretary of State to the Foreign Office (Confidential), 13 Apr. 1892, TNA, FO 97/572.

[49] The German Official View, n.d., FO 881/9155X, 59, quoted in Ferdinand Perels, *Das internationale öffentliche Seerecht der Gegenwart*, 2nd edn (Berlin, 1903), 196.

[50] Rolf Hobson, *Imperialism at Sea: Naval Strategic Thought, the Ideology of Sea Power, and the Tirpitz Plan, 1875–1914* (Boston, MA, 2001), 113–31.

government a clarification as to the protection of trade in time of war. Legal experts were split on the question. For example, William E. Hall, who was often cited in Foreign Office documents, was firmly opposed to it, not least because of the theoretical nature of the matter. In an analogy between the capture of private property at sea and the levying of requisitions on land, Hall justified the former because both aimed at interrupting trade and undermining the enemy's war efforts. Capture of private property at sea was also more humane, and less bloody and harmful than the sinking of enemy warships.[51] John Westlake, Whewell Professor of International Law at the University of Cambridge, also doubted whether the immunity of private property would stand the test of practice, and warned that a rule without reference to existing practice would more likely be breached or ignored in wartime.[52] Westlake's successor, Lassa Oppenheim, saw the right of search and capture as a state's right of 'self-preservation' and, since the rise of Germany and the United States as sea powers, 'the outcry against the capture of merchantmen has become less loud'.[53]

Advocates of the immunity of private property, such as Thomas J. Lawrence, who lectured on international law at the University of Cambridge and at the Royal Naval College in Greenwich, disputed the theoretical nature of the question. Lawrence demonstrated that in the 1860s and 1870s, treaties were enforced and immunity practised under wartime conditions, although notably in conflicts in which economic warfare was not a decisive factor. During the American Civil War, blockade rather than the capture of private property at sea brought the Confederate States of America to their knees. Only in cases in which a state depended on overseas trade could capture be a decisive factor, 'but in the vast majority of wars little advantage can be gained by driving sea-borne commerce out of hostile and into neutral ships'. Hence, Britain would gain from the adoption of the immunity of private property.[54]

Sir Robert Reid (later Lord Loreburn), who was a former Attorney-General and a future Lord Chancellor, was also among the advocates. Shortly after the Russo-Japanese War, Reid published commentaries in *The Times*, arguing that Britain, in a future maritime conflict, would fail to put decisive pressure on a continental enemy despite the Royal Navy's command of the sea. Rather, continental powers would be able to receive the necessary

---

[51]   Hall, *Treatise*, 6th edn, 437–41.
[52]   John Westlake, *Chapters on the Principles of International Law* (Cambridge, 1894), 249.
[53]   Lassa Oppenheim, *International Law. A Treatise*, 2 vols (London, 1912), vol. 2, 223.
[54]   Lawrence, *Principles of International Law*, 409, 414–16.

resources from the continent or simply import them via neutral ports. At the same time, he reckoned that a British blockade of the enemy coast could not prevent enemy cruisers from escaping and damaging British trade. The consequences for the British economy would be unpredictable as long as others could exercise the right of search and capture against British trade, which was why he argued Britain should change its policy.[55]

Another ardent supporter of the immunity of private property was Sir John Macdonell, Quain Professor of Comparative Law at the University of London. His analysis stood out because he treated the question in relation to the theory of war, and frequently referred to naval and military thinkers such as Carl von Clausewitz, Mahan, Corbett, Théophile Aube and Helmuth von Moltke. Referring to the Napoleonic Wars and the American Civil War, Macdonell highlighted that the right of search and capture of private property was less effective and decisive in modern maritime warfare than generally thought. In a future war between Britain and Germany, the capture of German merchant ships would not decisively contribute to ending a war because Germany did not rely on the import of foodstuffs and raw materials from overseas. Rather, Germany could obtain goods through neutral states, and the extensive railway system of Europe made it easy to transport those goods. Hence, neutrals rather than Germany would be the target of the exercise of the right of search and capture, meaning that it had become 'impossible' to 'injure effectively... the foreign trade of one country without injuring seriously that of others'. Therefore, it was a risky strategy, as the imports to Germany could not be stopped without greatly affecting neutrals. In essence, 'the increasing community of interests among nations, the reciprocity of services rendered by international commerce, becomes every year a greater obstacle to the free use of the right of capture'.[56] The only way forward, according to Macdonell, was to adopt the immunity of private property.

The discussion among British international jurists showed that both advocates and opponents considered the question of the immunity of private property in relation to a future war at sea. Their frequent references to the theory of war illuminated not only the close relationship between international law and maritime strategy but also demonstrated that international jurists were knowledgeable in maritime strategic thought.

---

[55] Robert T. Reid, 'The Capture of Private Property at Sea', *The Times*, 14 Oct. 1905.
[56] John Macdonell, *Some Plain Reasons for Immunity from Capture of Private Property at Sea* (London, 1910), 18.

The 1907 Hague Peace Conference

Despite the shifting opinions of key states, such as Britain, Germany, and the United States, the programme of the Hague peace conference in 1907 dealt with the question of the immunity of private property from capture at sea.[57] Feodor Martens, who, as head of the Russian delegation was chiefly involved in drafting the programme, was rather sceptical of the chances of adoption because of the notable change in the political climate since 1899, particularly in Germany and the United States.[58]

The tentative programme for the Hague peace conference of 1907 demanded an ultimate clarification on the matter from the British government. Despite public pressure, the Inter-Departmental Committee unanimously decided against the immunity of private property from capture at sea. The committee compared the impact of the immunity of private property for sea and land powers. For sea powers such as Britain, the right of capture of enemy trade was vital, while land powers would not be affected in the same way. In any case, the committee concluded that, since 'under any probable conditions of a modern maritime war our naval supremacy not only assures us unique powers of offence, but also adequate protection to our much greater commerce, the proposal involves a surrender which may be estimated at any figure up to infinity, and confers a gain which may be depreciated down to nil'.[59] The committee trusted the analysis of the Admiralty on this point, which asserted that 'British command of the sea should cause the practically complete disappearance of the enemy's mercantile flag from the high seas'.[60] The Admiralty had held this opinion since the first mention of a second Hague peace conference in 1904. It had explained to the Foreign Office the 'great benefits upon our mercantile marine', which

[57] For an analysis of the British and American position in the run-up to the second Hague peace conference, see Alan M. Anderson, 'Two Ships Passing in the Night: The United States, Great Britain, and the Immunity of Private Property at Sea in Time of War, 1904–1907', in Lori Lyn Bogle and James C. Rentfrow (eds), *New Interpretations in Naval History: Selected Papers from the Eighteenth McMullen Naval History Symposium Held at the U.S. Naval Academy 19–20 September 2013* (Newport, RI, 2018), 165–74.

[58] 'Sir Edward Grey to Sir A. Nicolson, 15 Feb. 1907 (No. 178)', in Gooch and Temperley, *British Documents on the Origins of the War 1898–1914, Vol. VIII*, 207–9.

[59] Report of the Inter-Departmental Committee Appointed to Consider the Subjects which may Arise for Discussion at the Second Peace Conference (Confidential), 21 Mar. 1907, TNA, FO 881/9041X, 1.

[60] 'Memorandum by the Admiralty on the Command of the Sea (Appendix 3), 4 Feb. 1907', in Report of the Inter-Departmental Committee Appointed to Consider the Subjects which may Arise for Discussion at the Second Peace Conference (Confidential), 21 Mar. 1907, TNA, FO 881/9041X, 62.

the 'inviolability of private property in war' would confer, but questioned whether the immunity of private property 'could be adequately guaranteed'. It was convinced that 'so long as the fleet has command of the sea the danger to our commerce will be small, as history proves'. And as such, that a change in policy would be 'detrimental' to Britain's interests.[61]

Command of the sea alone could not effectively protect British overseas trade. Consequently, the Inter-Departmental Committee recommended the introduction of a 'national insurance' scheme in order to counterbalance the risks of capture of British merchant ships at the outbreak of war.[62] This recommendation was based on the reports of the Royal Commission on Food Supply (1903–5) and of the Committee of Imperial Defence (CID). The Royal Commission suggested the introduction of a 'national indemnity' or 'national insurance' scheme.[63] The CID investigated further which of the schemes—indemnity or insurance—was preferable. A national indemnity scheme meant that the state would fully cover the extra costs, but it would also privilege shipowners. The insurance scheme, on the other hand, would require shipowners to pay a premium, and so avoid shipowners maintaining reckless businesses at state expense. The CID clearly preferred the latter.[64]

A national insurance scheme had already been discussed in 1890 when Vice-Admiral George Tryon, the Admiral Superintendent of Reserves, initiated a debate in the *United Service Magazine*, in which he suggested the adoption of an insurance scheme in wartime in order to protect British economic interests.[65] Charles Beresford, a naval officer, and George S. Clarke, secretary to the Inter-Departmental Colonial Defence Committee, immediately supported the proposal publicly.[66] Opponents feared that an insurance scheme would be seen as a replacement for a strong navy, and insisted that it should be the navy that protected trade. For Tryon and his supporters that

[61] Admiralty (C. I. Thomas) to Foreign Office (Confidential), 31 Dec. 1904, TNA, FO 881/8672, 88.

[62] Report of the Inter-Departmental Committee Appointed to Consider the Subjects which may Arise for Discussion at the Second Peace Conference (Confidential), 21 Mar. 1907, TNA, FO 881/9041X, 10.

[63] Avner Offer, *The First World War: An Agrarian Interpretation* (Oxford, 1989), 225.

[64] National Indemnity or Insurance of the War Risks of Shipping. Memorandum Prepared by Direction of the Prime Minister (Confidential), 5 Dec. 1904, TNA, CAB 38/6/118; National Indemnity of the War Risks of Shipping. Memorandum by Sir George Murray (Secret), 16 May 1905, TNA, CAB 38/9/40; National Indemnity or Insurance of the War Risks of Shipping (Confidential), 15 Nov. 1905, TNA, CAB 38/10/83.

[65] George Tryon, 'National Insurance. A Practical Proposal', *United Service Magazine*, May (1890), 184–92.

[66] Charles Beresford, 'National Insurance', *United Service Magazine*, June (1890), 279–86; George S. Clarke, 'National Insurance', *United Service Magazine*, Sept. (1890), 563–72.

was not the point. A strong navy was essential for the protection of trade but Clarke argued that 'no naval supremacy can absolutely guarantee commerce from the risks of war'.[67]

In 1905, political opinion was divided on a national insurance scheme. Charles L. Ottley, director of Naval Intelligence, was convinced that British trade did not suffer during the Russo-Japanese War as belligerents paid the increased war premiums rather than neutral shippers. In fact, he argued, they were 'a source of very handsome profits' for a neutral power, particularly since Britain profited from trading coal as contraband.[68] Figures presented to the prime minister, however, demonstrated the opposite.[69] In the end, the British government took no immediate decision, and the CID only revisited the idea of a national insurance scheme in 1913, when a sub-committee, which consisted of representatives from the railway, shipping and insurance industries, worked out a scheme bringing the two ideas together. The recommended scheme consisted of 80 per cent reinsurance from the state on all policies.[70] The Treasury had originally refused the scheme. Only when the First World War broke out did the Chancellor of the Exchequer, Lloyd George, introduce the scheme in order to reassure British trade.[71]

The state's involvement in the insurance business was a direct consequence of Britain's position on the question of the immunity of private property from capture at sea. The national insurance scheme was intended as a measure to balance Britain's conflicting strategic and economic interests.[72] To keep costs in check, the scheme was only intended as a temporary measure, particularly useful at the outbreak of a war, when the capture of merchant

[67] Clarke, 'National Insurance', 563. For further discussion, see Semmel, *Liberalism and Naval Strategy*, 102–3.

[68] Note by Charles L. Ottley on the Right of Capture, 12 Apr. 1905, TNA, ADM 1/7846; Admiralty to Committee of Imperial Defence, Draft (Confidential), 10 June 1905, TNA, ADM 1/7846.

[69] National Indemnity or Insurance of the War Risks of Shipping. Memorandum prepared by Direction of the Prime Minister (Confidential), 5 Dec. 1904, TNA, CAB 38/6/118.

[70] Maintenance of Oversea Commerce in Time of War. Report and Proceedings of the Standing Sub-Committee of the Committee of Imperial Defence (Secret), 18 Feb. 1913, TNA, CAB 16/24; Report and Proceedings of the Standing Sub-Committee of the Committee of Imperial Defence on the Insurance of British Shipping in Time of War (Secret), 12 May 1914, TNA, CAB 16/29.

[71] Speech of Lloyd George (Chancellor of Exchequer), Hansard, 5th series, HC Deb., 4 Aug. 1914, vol. 65, cc. 1941–1952. See also Franklyn A. Johnson, *Defence by Committee: The British Committee of Imperial Defence, 1885-1959* (London, 1960), 131; Matthew S. Seligmann, *The Royal Navy and the German Threat 1901-1914: Admiralty Plans to Protect British Trade in a War Against Germany* (Oxford, 2012).

[72] See also Luis Lobo-Guerrero, *Insuring War: Sovereignty, Security and Risk* (Abingdon, 2012), 57–79.

ships would be most likely. In a prolonged war, however, the CID did not rule out Britain resuming its trade with the enemy after a few months in order to secure Britain's economic position in Europe. The CID's long-term perspective on the potential effects of war on the British economy showed its appreciation for the relationship between war and economy.[73]

The British government shared the Inter-Departmental Committee's recommendation on the immunity of private property. The Foreign Secretary, Sir Edward Grey, acknowledged the humanitarian rationale for the proposal and admitted the positive effect in reducing the costs of armaments. However, Britain could never consent to the proposal, as it would have seriously impaired the navy's ability to impose a commercial blockade, which was Britain's only offensive weapon against a continental power with a large army.[74]

At the Hague peace conference, the Fourth Commission dealt with the 'inviolability of enemy private property at sea'. The wording was not accidental. It emphasized that the proposal concerned enemy property rather than neutral property. Joseph H. Choate, the United States delegate, presented the American proposal, which reflected on the United States' long-standing policy on the immunity of private property. Notably, the proposition contained two important exceptions, namely that contraband of war was not excluded from capture, and that ships destined for a block-aded port were still liable to capture.[75] Choate pleaded for the adoption of this principle 'on broad humanitarian grounds' as it would remove 'the last relic of barbarism in maritime warfare', constituting 'a great principle of justice'.[76] Future maritime warfare, so Choate was convinced, would be a collision of two enemy battle fleets, and hence 'the power to destroy [an] enemy's non-combatant ships upon the sea is no longer a very potent factor'. In fact, he said, no 'modern war' had 'been prevented or shortened by the exercise of this power [the right of search and capture], and the destruction

---

[73] Standing Sub-Committee of the Committee of Imperial Defence. Enquiry regarding Trading with the Enemy. No. 3. The Legal Position, prepared under the supervision of Professor L. Oppenheim (Secret), Oct. 1911, TNA, CAB 16/18B; Report and Proceedings of the Standing Sub-Committee of the Committee of Imperial Defence on Trading with the Enemy (Secret), 10 Sept. 1912, TNA, CAB 16/18A.

[74] Memorandum by Sir Edward Grey (Confidential), 3 June 1907, TNA, FO 881/10085X.

[75] Fourth Commission, Second Meeting, 28 June 1907, in James Brown Scott (ed.), *The Proceedings of the Hague Peace Conferences. Translation of the Original Texts. The Conference of 1907, Vol. III: Meetings of the Second, Third and Fourth Commissions* (New York, 1921), 752.

[76] Fourth Commission, Second Meeting, 28 June 1907, in Scott (ed.), *Proceedings. The Conference of 1907, Vol. III: Meetings of the Second, Third and Fourth Commissions*, 759.

of merchant shipping has been, and is likely to be, a comparatively trifling incident in the contests of nations'.[77]

Britain's delegate, Sir Ernest Satow, was categorically opposed to the American proposal. More sympathetic was the German delegate, Baron Adolf Marschall von Bieberstein, as well as his Russian colleague, N. Tcharykow, a Councillor of State, who both supported the proposal in principle but demanded the questions of blockade and contraband be resolved before the immunity of private property was dealt with.[78] The French delegate and international jurist, Louis Renault, shared the German and Russian view, assuring his colleagues that the French government was 'heartily in favour' of the immunity of private property at sea, if the questions on contraband and blockade were 'settled in the manner they [France] desire'.[79] Renault rejected the argument of an assimilation between land and sea warfare. Rather, he defended the importance of the right of search and capture, arguing that 'a belligerent must have the means of arresting the economic life of his adversary by hindering, or even supressing his commerce with the outside world'.[80] Although this measure affected individuals to a large extent, he saw it as 'less a question of individuals, whose goods are seized than of the State to which they belong and which is injured by the action against the individuals'. Hence, the right of capture constituted 'an effective means of coercion' and thus it was not 'especially cruel'. Renault's criticism was directed against prize law—a law in which the captor and the state benefited from private loss. He saw receiving prize money as being morally reprehensible and sending the wrong signal. Renault demanded the abolition of prize money so that 'the seizure of an enemy vessel or of a neutral vessel should be nothing more than an operation in the interest of the State. It is the performance of a duty, which is not to be pecuniarily remunerated any more than the performance of other duties toward the State.'[81]

The most ardent defenders of the existing practice were the British. Sir Edward Fry admitted that war was 'something of the barbarous'. Yet, the

[77] Fourth Commission, Second Meeting, 28 June 1907, in Scott (ed.), *Proceedings. The Conference of 1907, Vol. III: Meetings of the Second, Third and Fourth Commissions*, 761.
[78] Fourth Commission, Third Meeting, 5 July 1907, in Scott (ed.), *Proceedings. The Conference of 1907, Vol. III: Meetings of the Second, Third and Fourth Commissions*, 777–9.
[79] Fourth Commission, Third Meeting, 5 July 1907, in Scott (ed.), *Proceedings. The Conference of 1907, Vol. III: Meetings of the Second, Third and Fourth Commissions*, 783.
[80] Fourth Commission, Third Meeting, 5 July 1907, in Scott (ed.), *Proceedings. The Conference of 1907, Vol. III: Meetings of the Second, Third and Fourth Commissions*, 783.
[81] Fourth Commission, Third Meeting, 5 July 1907, in Scott (ed.), *Proceedings. The Conference of 1907, Vol. III: Meetings of the Second, Third and Fourth Commissions*, 784.

right of capture was of all those means 'humane' in the sense that 'no one is killed, no one is even wounded'.[82] His colleague, Satow, rejected Choate's citation of British supporters of the immunity of private property for the reason that they 'date[d] back to a rather remote period, when the conditions of commerce and of naval warfare were entirely different from what they are to-day'. He insisted that the abolition of the right of capture, together with the abolition of contraband and commercial blockade, 'would in no way diminish the inhumanity of war'.[83]

The president of the Fourth Commission, Feodor Martens, reminded the delegates before the vote that, although the immunity of private property had often been proclaimed in treaties, it was never practised in war, with the exception of the war between Prussia, Austria, and Italy in 1866, and then it had been irrelevant to the war's outcome. He also doubted whether private property at sea could be treated in the same way as private property on land. Finally, he highlighted that the adoption of such a practice would create a 'privileged situation' for businesses.[84] The vote, which ended the debate on the American proposal, showed how divided the commission was. Twenty-one states voted in favour of the immunity of private property, among them the United States and Germany, and eleven states voted against it, including Britain, France, Russia, and Japan. Only Chile abstained from voting.[85]

Other states also presented proposals but they differed from the American proposal in that they suggested changes to the existing practice rather than demanding the abolition of the right of search and capture as such. Their approach was meant to offer a solution to break the impasse.[86] The French delegation presented the most original proposal, as Louis Renault had already alluded to in his speech. His colleague, Léon Bourgeois, explained its rationale. The French desired 'to humanize and to moralize the system', based on the 'idea that war should be waged between States and should not be a source of personal profit'.[87] In practical terms this meant that states

---

[82] Fourth Commission, Third Meeting, 5 July 1907, in Scott (ed.), *Proceedings. The Conference of 1907, Vol. III: Meetings of the Second, Third and Fourth Commissions*, 790.

[83] Fourth Commission, Sixth Meeting, 17 July 1907, in Scott (ed.), *Proceedings. The Conference of 1907, Vol. III: Meetings of the Second, Third and Fourth Commissions*, 822.

[84] Fourth Commission, Sixth Meeting, 17 July 1907, in Scott (ed.), *Proceedings. The Conference of 1907, Vol. III: Meetings of the Second, Third and Fourth Commissions*, 824.

[85] Fourth Commission, Sixth Meeting, 17 July 1907, in Scott (ed.), *Proceedings. The Conference of 1907, Vol. III: Meetings of the Second, Third and Fourth Commissions*, 824–5.

[86] All proposals can be found under: Annexes, in Scott (ed.), *Proceedings. The Conference of 1907, Vol. III: Meetings of the Second, Third and Fourth Commissions*, 1121–9.

[87] Fourth Commission, Fourth Meeting, 10 July 1907, in Scott (ed.), *Proceedings. The Conference of 1907, Vol. III: Meetings of the Second, Third and Fourth Commissions*, 799.

should retain the right of capture but that 'all individual profit to the agents of the State, who exercise the right of capture, should be excluded, and that the losses suffered by individuals from captures should ultimately be borne by the State to which they belong.'[88] In other words, the French demanded the abolition of prize law and the introduction of state compensation for private loss. This was an interesting proposal because it aimed at improving existing law rather than imposing a new paradigm that did not stand a chance of acceptance. Germany and Austria-Hungary rejected the proposal because of the unforeseeable financial burdens to the state. The United States was against the proposal in principle. While Britain was undecided, it nevertheless supported the idea of a compensation scheme, which the British government had already discussed internally, but it would not consider a change in prize law. The Russian government showed a willingness to change its prize laws on the condition that all other states followed suit.[89]

The various opinions showed how split the commission was on this question. The president, Feodor Martens, concluded that this was 'the result of lack of experience and practice', and he hoped that maybe in a future war states would 'renounce the right of capture' and so 'create precedents'.[90] The nature of the question made an agreement unlikely, in particular due to the strategic impact which the immunity of private property would have on a future maritime war. Britain and France favoured the introduction of a compensation scheme for private loss as a means to mitigate the right of search and capture. Other states, such as the United States, demanded the abolition of the right of capture. No compromise seemed acceptable to either side, and so the matter was unresolved.[91]

Naval Strategists and the End of Naval Warfare

The second Hague peace conference had shown that the question of the immunity of private property from capture at sea had theoretical

---

[88] Fourth Commission, Fourth Meeting, 10 July 1907, in Scott (ed.), *Proceedings. The Conference of 1907, Vol. III: Meetings of the Second, Third and Fourth Commissions*, 799.

[89] Fourth Commission, Twelfth Meeting, 7 Aug. 1907, in Scott (ed.), *Proceedings. The Conference of 1907, Vol. III: Meetings of the Second, Third and Fourth Commissions*, 896–900. See also Sir E. Fry to Sir Edward Grey (Confidential), 10 July 1907, TNA, FO 800/929.

[90] Fourth Commission, Seventh Meeting, 19 July 1907, in Scott (ed.), *Proceedings. The Conference of 1907, Vol. III: Meetings of the Second, Third and Fourth Commissions*, 833–5.

[91] 'Report to the Committee of Examination by Henry Fromageot on the Inviolability of Enemy Private Property at Sea, n.d.', in Scott (ed.), *Proceedings. The Conference of 1907, Vol. III: Meetings of the Second, Third and Fourth Commissions*, 1024–30.

implications, which also related to the theory of war. The naval strategist, Alfred T. Mahan, was a public critic of the immunity of private property when it was first discussed at the Hague peace conference in 1899. When US President Theodore Roosevelt announced the possibility of a second Hague peace conference in 1904, Mahan urged him to reconsider the American position as the right of search and capture 'may be of immense, of decisive, importance' to the United States in the future. Mahan urged Roosevelt 'to withdraw from our old position' and instead 'fasten our grip on the sea'.[92] In reference to the *War of 1812*—Mahan's third book of the trilogy on the influence of sea power—he demonstrated the close relationship between war and trade.[93] Roosevelt could not be convinced and so Mahan approached Elihu Root, US Secretary of State, and asked him to investigate the American position on the immunity of private property at sea in light of American strategic interests in a future war. Root, who had privately favoured a policy change, forwarded Mahan's letter to the Secretary of the Navy, and consequently a General Board looked into the matter.[94] Rear Admiral Charles S. Sperry, a former president of the United States Naval War College and member of the American delegation to The Hague in 1907, had also voiced his opinion against the immunity of private property at sea. In Sperry's opinion, economic warfare was essential, and the capture of private property at sea corresponded to the interception of railways on land. Since no military commander would let trains pass with foodstuffs destined for enemy troops, he concluded that private property at sea should be subject to capture. However, despite prominent support for a policy change, the US government retained its 'traditional' position.[95]

Mahan used his 1907 publication *Some Neglected Aspects of War* to appeal for a change in American policy on the question of the immunity of private property.[96] It contained a compilation of articles from Henry S. Pritchett, astronomer, mathematician, former president of the Massachusetts Institute of Technology, and president of the Carnegie Foundation for the

[92] 'Alfred T. Mahan to Theodore Roosevelt, 27 Dec. 1904', in Seager and Maguire (eds), *Alfred Thayer Mahan*, vol. 3, 113.

[93] Alfred T. Mahan, *Sea Power in its Relations to the War of 1812*, 2 vols (London, 1905).

[94] 'Alfred T. Mahan to Elihu Root, 20 Apr. 1906', in Seager and Maguire (eds), *Alfred Thayer Mahan*, vol. 3, 157–9. See also Robert Seager II, *Alfred Thayer Mahan: The Man and His Letters* (Annapolis, MD, 1977), 506–10.

[95] Charles S. Sperry to Robert Bacon (Assistant Secretary of the State Department), 15 Dec. 1906, United States Naval War College Archives, Record Group 8, Box 87, Folder 1.

[96] 'Alfred T. Mahan to Leopold J. Maxse, 5 Mar. 1907', in Seager and Maguire (eds), *Alfred Thayer Mahan*, vol. 3, 207.

Advancement of Teaching, Julian S. Corbett, and Mahan himself.[97] The book dealt with the legal and moral aspects of war at sea, and in particular focused on the immunity of private property at sea. None of the authors had been involved in the preparatory work for the second Hague peace conference.[98] As the book's title suggested, the public had given little attention to the influence of law on the theory of war. In Mahan's analysis of the elements of sea power in his most influential book, *The Influence of Sea Power upon History*, international law was not mentioned.[99] Yet, Mahan became interested in the legal aspects of war.

In his 1907 article, Mahan argued that there was a misapprehension as to what the capture of private property at sea meant in practice. He was convinced that capture received its negative meaning because of piracy. In contrast, privateers acted in a legal framework and lawfully claimed prizes. Mahan further argued that private property was a deceptive term as the loss of private property was directed against the adversary, in particular the state. At the heart of a state's wealth was trade, and its interruption would not only affect individuals but ultimately also harm the state. Mahan used historical examples to illustrate the interaction between the state and the economy, demonstrating the effectiveness of economic warfare. In his opinion, Napoleon was defeated not as a result of the Battle of Waterloo but because of a persistent pressure from the sea, which the Royal Navy had exercised. The Royal Navy had successfully denied France essential access to resources and exchange of goods, and so had decisively contributed to ending the war. Mahan was convinced that a lesson could be learnt here and that the US government should weigh 'its policy with reference to the future... before surrendering existing powers'. A government needed to have a firm understanding of 'the geographical position of the country, its relation to maritime routes—the strategy, so to say, of the general permanent situation—and the military principles upon which maritime capture rests'.[100]

In a series of articles, which Mahan published in the *North American Review* in 1911/12, he continued to raise awareness of the need for sea

---

[97] Alfred T. Mahan, *Some Neglected Aspects of War* (London, 1907).

[98] 'Alfred T. Mahan to Julian S. Corbett, 12 Aug. 1907', in Seager and Maguire (eds), *Alfred Thayer Mahan*, vol. 3, 223. See also Seager, *Mahan: The Man and His Letters*, 505–6.

[99] Alfred T. Mahan, *The Influence of Sea Power upon History, 1660–1783* (Boston, MA, 1890; reprint New York, 1987).

[100] Alfred T. Mahan, 'The Hague Conference: The Question of Immunity for Belligerent Merchant Shipping', in Alfred T. Mahan, *Some Neglected Aspects of War* (London, 1907), 157–92, here: 183.

powers to keep the right of search and capture. Mahan was rather sceptical about the function of international law in foreign policy, because, he argued, 'law, whatever the method of its development, whether by custom or statute, cannot be so systematized beforehand as to cover all cases; partly because unforeseen conditions arising, or gradual changes of conditions evolving, existing law is by then outgrown'. As a result, he wrote, 'law often lags behind conditions, and often outlives them'.[101] Mahan focused on the inherent weakness attributable to all law, not only international law, namely that law can never capture reality in all of its facets. It would always have gaps. Mahan argued further that 'the very idea of law, its lack of elasticity, renders it too frequently inadequate to the settlement of certain classes of disputes'.[102] For Mahan, diplomacy rather than international law was more suitable for guiding relations between states, as diplomacy had shown more promise in, for example, arbitration cases.[103]

Corbett, who had studied law and lectured at the Royal Naval War College, argued similarly to Mahan in his 1907 publication in *The Nineteenth Century and After*, which was reprinted in Mahan's edited volume.[104] Despite Corbett's close relations with the Admiralty and the First Sea Lord, John Fisher, he was not a member of the British delegation. There is also no indication that he referred to Britain's state practice in his lectures on strategy at the college, and he treated the Spanish-American War of 1898 and the Russo-Japanese War of 1904–5 purely from a strategic and operational point of view.[105]

Corbett accused supporters of the immunity of private property at sea of neglecting strategic considerations in their argumentation. By using historical examples, Corbett demonstrated that the immunity of private property at sea was only 'for the benefit of weak fleets and powerful armies'.[106] Corbett dismissed the often-cited similarity between private property in land and sea warfare. Rather, Corbett argued that 'the real reason of [*sic*] the restrictions [of the capture of private property on land] was strategical and

[101] Alfred T. Mahan, 'The Place of Force in International Relations', *North American Review*, 195 (1912), 28.
[102] Alfred T. Mahan, 'Deficiencies of Law for International Adjustments', *North American Review*, 194 (1911), 674–84.
[103] See also Alfred T. Mahan, 'Diplomacy and Arbitration', *North American Review* 194 (1911), 124–35.
[104] Julian S. Corbett, 'The Capture of Private Property at Sea', in Alfred T. Mahan, *Some Neglected Aspects of War* (London, 1907; reprint of the same article in *The Nineteenth Century and After*, June 1907), 115–54.
[105] Manuscripts by Julian S. Corbett on Lectures on Naval Strategy, n.d., NMM, CBT/31.
[106] Corbett, 'Capture of Private Property at Sea', 119.

military, and not moral at all'.[107] He used the example of Gustavus Adolphus, who disciplined his troops by forbidding plunder and instead requisitioned private property to feed them. In this case, private property on land was not immune. Corbett concluded from the analysis of the treatment of private property on land that 'nations cannot be brought to their knees by the mere conflict of armies, any more than they can by the single combats of kings'. Rather, he suggested, it was 'what follows victory that counts—the choking of the national life by process of execution on property, the stagnation produced by the stoppage of civil communications, whether public or private'.[108] Comparing the conditions of private property on land with that of war at sea, Corbett rejected the idea that capturing private property at sea was more cruel than doing so on land, particularly since prize courts regulated the lawful capture of private property at sea.[109]

Corbett also examined the question of the immunity of private property at sea in regard to the theory of war. In contrast to land warfare, the sea could not be conquered in war. Rather, the sea was used for communications and trade. Denying an enemy access to the sea was essential for the success of a naval campaign as 'the value of the sea internationally is as a means of communication between States and parts of States, and the use and enjoyment of these communications is the actual life of a nation at sea'. Corbett argued that gaining 'command of the sea means nothing more nor less than control of communications. It occupies exactly the same place and discharges the same function in maritime warfare that conquest and occupation of territory does in land warfare.'[110] Corbett concluded that the capture of private property at sea had the same position as the right of requisitions on land as 'by no other means can we do what ashore is done by contributions and requisitions'.[111]

Corbett further demonstrated that economic warfare decisively contributed to shortening a war. The victories of armies and navies did not end wars, but they enabled a power to put pressure on the enemy which could eventually lead to victory. In maritime war, the control of 'the enemy's communications' enabled a power to 'paralyze his [the enemy's] seaborne commerce'. This provided the only means which 'effectively deprive him

---

[107] Corbett, 'Capture of Private Property at Sea', 124.
[108] Corbett, 'Capture of Private Property at Sea', 127.
[109] Corbett, 'Capture of Private Property at Sea', 129.
[110] Corbett, 'Capture of Private Property at Sea', 131.
[111] Corbett, 'Capture of Private Property at Sea', 132.

[the enemy] of all the sea can give him'.[112] However, if private property at sea were be exempt from capture, war would become 'impossible' because the right of capture would be abolished and blockade would not be the answer either, as a close blockade would no longer be feasible in modern warfare. This would leave a sea power in a vulnerable situation.[113]

Corbett followed up his argument in his seminal study *Some Principles of Maritime Strategy*, which he published in 1911. Here, he defended the right of search and capture as an important means to control sea communications. For Corbett, 'the object and end of naval warfare is the control of communications [and] it must carry with it the right to forbid, if we can, the passage of both public and private property upon the sea. Now the only means we have of enforcing such control of commercial communications at sea is in the last resort the capture or destruction of sea-borne property. Such capture or destruction is the penalty which we impose upon our enemy for attempting to use the communications of which he does not hold the control. In the language of jurisprudence, it is the ultimate sanction of the interdict which we are seeking to enforce.'[114] Capture put economic pressure on the enemy. Battles alone could not achieve that, and, without capture, battles would have no purpose. Consequently, he argued, 'war would become so impotent, that no one would care to engage in it'. Corbett imagined such wars as an 'affair between regular armies and fleets, with which the people had little concern' and suggested that 'international quarrels would tend to take the form of the mediaeval private disputes'. Legal battles rather than actual battles would settle disputes, which, in the words of Corbett, was 'an absurdity', and he thought 'the world is scarcely ripe for such a revolution'. For Corbett 'commerce and finance' provided 'the most powerful check on war' by which he meant that states would weigh their options before entering war because of the economic consequences of such a decision.[115] The 'fear of quick and certain loss' of private property would help prevent wars, so Corbett was convinced.[116]

The history of war played an important role in Mahan's and Corbett's writings on its theory. Historical examples demonstrated the importance of

---

[112] Corbett, 'Capture of Private Property at Sea', 132.
[113] Corbett, 'Capture of Private Property at Sea', 130–9.
[114] Julian S. Corbett, *Some Principles of Maritime Strategy* (London, 1911; reprint Mineola, NY, 2004), 91.
[115] Corbett, *Some Principles of Maritime Strategy*, 95.
[116] Corbett, *Some Principles of Maritime Strategy*, 96.

captures and highlighted their decisive impact in shortening and ending a war. However, advocates of the immunity of private property at sea used the same historical examples to make the opposite case. Although the theoretical point of view broadened the debate and understanding of the nature of maritime warfare, politicians and jurists at the Hague peace conference were concerned about the practicability of the immunity of private property. They were often accused of ignoring the strategic context, but delegates acted on behalf of their governments, and held clear instructions with little room for negotiation. Moreover, as the British preparatory work demonstrated, governments did take strategic considerations into account. What the delegates had to do was find a modus operandi to regulate capture rather than stubbornly to pursue its abolition. Here, theory clashed with practice.

More broadly, the question of the immunity of private property at sea facilitated a fundamental debate on maritime warfare, about its objectives and its objects, and whether the right of search and capture was a proportionate means for meeting them. Politicians and jurists who dealt with the matter may not have referred to military and naval thinkers, yet their terminology revealed a thorough understanding of the theory of war. For instance, in 1912 the international lawyer, Lassa Oppenheim, wrote about international law in relation to maritime strategy and the theory of war in extraordinarily sophisticated terms. In his introductory section on naval warfare he regularly referred to the US Naval War Code. He distinguished between the ends and purposes of war, the aims and means of war, and the objects of war. The purpose of war according to Oppenheim was always to 'overpower the enemy'. In contrast, the ends of war depended on politics, which could change during a war. According to Oppenheim the aims or objectives of naval warfare were the 'defeat of the enemy navy; annihilation of the enemy merchant fleet; destruction of enemy coast fortifications, and of maritime as well as military establishments on the enemy coast; cutting off intercourse with the enemy coast; prevention of carriage of contraband and of rendering unneutral service to the enemy; all kinds of support to military operations on land, such as protection of a landing of troops on the enemy coast; and lastly, defence of the home coast and the protection of the home merchant fleet'.[117] Various means could be used to achieve these aims, which included the

---

[117] Oppenheim, *International Law*, vol. 2, 216–17.

right to search and capture enemy and neutral merchant ships, seize warships, bombard the enemy coast, and blockade.[118] The gradual exemption of capture of private property at sea had limited the right of search and capture. Yet, Oppenheim did not believe that the immunity of private property at sea was likely to be adopted any time soon because 'the possibility of annihilating an enemy's commerce by annihilating his merchant fleet is a powerful weapon in the hands of a great naval Power. Moreover, if enemy merchantmen are not captured, they can be fitted out as cruisers, or at least be made use of for the transport of troops, munitions, and provisions.'[119] Oppenheim examined the immunity of private property not only in regard to the theory of war but also to politics, and concluded that the matter was for 'politicians, not for jurists' to decide. The example of Oppenheim demonstrated that international lawyers did not treat international law in isolation. Rather, they emphasized the close relationship between international law, politics, and strategy, while making a clear distinction between international law and state policy.

In summary, the debate on the immunity of private property at sea illustrated the interaction between international maritime law and the theory of war in the thinking of international lawyers, naval thinkers, and officers in the decades before the First World War. The theoretical nature of the question also revealed the limitations of politics in making law. The negotiations at the Hague peace conferences in 1899 and 1907 illustrated how difficult it was to find a practicable solution to an inherently theoretical question. Due to a lack of state practice, the question remained one of principle, which might also explain why it was hard to find common ground. At the same time, long-held positions shifted gradually in Britain, Germany, and the United States over the period between the Paris peace conference in 1856 and the second Hague peace conference in 1907, not least because of political and economic changes in those countries. Britain was willing to limit the right of search and capture in order to protect trade. On the other hand, the United States and Germany gave up their strong opposition because, as rising sea powers, they wanted greater capabilities for their naval forces in a future war. The immunity of private property at sea was foremost a political and strategic question, which divided major from minor sea powers. According to Lassa Oppenheim, minor sea powers favoured the immunity of private property for political and strategic reasons, while aspiring sea

---

[118] Oppenheim, *International Law*, vol. 2, 218.
[119] Oppenheim, *International Law*, vol. 2, 222–3.

powers had 'learnt to appreciate the value of the rule of law in war, and the outcry against the capture of merchantmen has become less loud'.[120] In all, the question of the immunity of private property from capture at sea prompted a fundamental debate on the objectives of war at sea, and yet the fears of the naval thinkers Mahan and Corbett were unfounded that it led to the end of naval warfare.

[120] Oppenheim, *International Law*, vol. 2, 223–4.

Conclusion

Sea Power, International Law, and Future Wars

In the second half of the nineteenth century, the importance of the sea as a legal and strategic space increased. With the age of steam, the sea turned from a hostile space into a commercial highway, and the foundation of modern international law enabled the creation of laws to govern this space. Britain, like no other power in that period, had a great interest in shaping this legal process, particularly since international law became an important factor in international politics. As the major sea power and the largest carrier of goods in the world, Britain's strategic as well as economic interests were at stake. Control of the sea was of great strategic importance for a sea power, and blockade and the right of search and capture were two legal instruments through which control of the sea was exercised. Britain's adoption of the Declaration of Paris in 1856 led to a fundamental debate in Britain about the role of international law in politics, and how international law would change the character of future warfare.

Parallel to the development of international law, maritime strategic thought evolved as a result of Britain's strategic vulnerability with regard to the protection of trade and economic warfare. The discussions at the Royal United Service Institution demonstrate that maritime strategic thought was shaped by the context of home and imperial defence, focusing on the concept of the control of the sea. British naval strategists and international lawyers examined how modern technological conditions affected economic warfare, and whether state practice and custom provided an adequate legal framework for the protection of trade and economic warfare. Debates highlighted the complexity of the sea as a legal and strategic space. Discussants were particularly concerned with blockade, contraband, and the right of search and capture, as well as how these would change the character of future wars, and so affect British maritime strategy. The debates demonstrated the close relationship between law and strategy in the light of the growing significance of international law in politics.

Great Britain, International Law, and the Evolution of Maritime Strategic Thought, 1856–1914. Gabriela A. Frei, Oxford University Press (2020). © Gabriela A. Frei.
DOI: 10.1093/oso/9780198859932.001.0001

Britain's state practice from 1856 to 1914 illustrates how successfully the British government used international law to protect its economic and strategic interests as a sea power. Britain's neutrality policy, formulated in 1870 with the revision of the Foreign Enlistment Act and solidified by signing the Treaty of Washington of 1871, reflected Britain's long-term state interests. As one of the leading economic powers and the world's largest carrier of goods, the law of neutrality became crucial as a safeguard for Britain's economic interests against belligerents in maritime conflict, and a strategic necessity for the protection of its trade. In fact, the reason for Britain's strict neutrality policy was its need to protect its trade in wartime, and more generally, its economic interests, both regionally and worldwide.

The revised domestic legislation enabled the British government to enforce neutrality within its jurisdiction, and hence control its citizens' behaviour. No other power had a stricter law of neutrality in place than Britain. Legal advisers played a crucial role in shaping Britain's neutrality policy and creating consistent state practice, which added to Britain's credibility as a neutral power. Responsibly for the implementation of Britain's neutrality policy lay with the Foreign Office, whose legal advisers prepared drafts and instructions, or wrote memoranda. The Law Officers of the Crown, as legal advisers to the British government, also played a crucial role in formulating and shaping Britain's state practice with regard to neutrality. They ensured that the British government reacted consistently and warned if political decisions contradicted state practice. Most importantly, their legal advice was based on Britain's long-term strategic and economic interests, and thus was also political advice.

Britain's successful neutrality policy was also the result of a smooth and effective administrative machinery which enforced the Foreign Enlistment Act. The changes to the original legislation allowed the British government to intervene swiftly and order the detention of a ship on suspicion rather than on evidence. The fact that the new legislation empowered port officials and customs authorities to observe, intervene, and execute Britain's neutrality policy made it an invaluable tool in the administrative machinery. Without these men on the spot, the implementation and enforcement of the Foreign Enlistment Act would have been impossible.

Customary international law was the result of every state's consistent behaviour and had a binding force from which a state could not easily withdraw. Only consistent state behaviour could result in the recognition of rules as customary international law. Through practice, the principles of the Declaration of Paris became binding for Britain and other states.

Britain's strict application of the law of neutrality created an obligation from which it could not retreat. For example, during the Russo-Japanese War of 1904–5 Britain applied its strict law of neutrality even though the law disadvantaged its shipbuilding industry. Consistent state practice indicated future behaviour. More generally, practice and custom were based on long-term interest, which made a state's behaviour predictable and reliable for other states. At the same time, consistent state practice also had a constraining effect on politics, as the Russo-Japanese War illustrated. Although no other sea power had similar rules in place, other states recognized Britain's state practice of neutrality. Hence, the law of neutrality in naval wars developed from a bilateral agreement between Britain and the United States into a formal international agreement with the Convention (XIII) concerning the Rights and Duties of Neutral Powers in Naval War, based on British state practice, and adopted at the second Hague peace conference.

On the other hand, inconsistent state behaviour could also have negative effects, as in the case of Britain's inconsistent position on the question of contraband. During the Revolutionary and Napoleonic Wars, Britain placed foodstuffs on its contraband list. However, with its growing dependence on the import of foodstuffs, Britain abandoned this position in the second half of the nineteenth century. When France declared rice as contraband during the Sino-French War of 1884–5, it argued that Britain had placed foodstuffs on its contraband list during the Napoleonic Wars. For the construction of its argument, the French government used Britain's inconsistency in state practice. A more delicate situation occurred during the Boer War of 1899–1902 when the British government again considered putting foodstuffs on its contraband list. Ultimately, it refrained from doing so because it feared that changing state practice could be used against it in a future conflict, and hence might harm British interests in the long term.

Changes to state practice always needed to be carefully weighed, as the example of foodstuffs as contraband during the Boer War shows. If a state disagreed with the new practice of another state, it had formally to protest against it. For example, Britain did so when France declared foodstuffs as contraband during the Sino-French War, and again when Russia put coal on its contraband list during the Russo-Japanese War. Protests were a necessary diplomatic tool to express disagreement and to avoid the creation of precedents which might have provided the basis for a new state practice. The formalization of these protest mechanisms demonstrated the importance of international law in international relations.

State practice and customary international law also provided the basis for the codification of international law at the beginning of the twentieth century. The Hague peace conferences as well as the London naval conference aimed at creating an international legal framework to govern the laws of war, and thus also to be applied to the sea. While a number of Hague conventions were the result of state practice, not all practices became law. For example, Britain's strict law of neutrality was not practicable for other states, and therefore Britain had to compromise on language and definitions in order to gain support from other states. In many ways, though, the regulation of the law of neutrality in Convention (XIII) was the result of state practice. The example of the Declaration of London of 1909 shows that the provisions were based on state practice, and that the main task of the delegates was to harmonize different practices. Codification offered an alternative to the slow process of how customary international law developed. International lawyer Lassa Oppenheim poignantly remarked that 'new interests and new inventions very often spring up with which customary law cannot deal'.[1] Yet, international lawyers and politicians were sceptical whether such a prescriptive codification would be useful in a future war.

Practice and customary international law also had a limiting effect on the process of codification. Without reference to practice, politically ambitious projects did not stand a chance of acceptance. States had also used the process of codification to push their agenda in advocating new legislation. For example, the British proposal for the abolition of contraband was rejected because customary international law distinguished between conditional and absolute contraband and the proposal would have strategically benefited Britain, a situation that was unacceptable to other states. Another example is the American proposal for the immunity of private property from capture at sea. Fears of constraining economic warfare so as to make naval warfare obsolete led to the rejection of such a far-reaching proposal at the Hague peace conferences. Hence, practice and custom, or the lack thereof, not only limited codification but also constrained political ambitions.

As a sea power, Britain remained sceptical about the process of the codification of international maritime law and the ways in which it could affect the country in future wars, as illustrated by the discussion about the Declaration of Paris. Nevertheless, the British government was a key

---

[1] Lassa Oppenheim, *International Law. A Treatise*, 2 vols (London, 1912), vol. 1, 41.

advocate for the codification of international maritime law at the beginning of the twentieth century. Britain's success at conferences at The Hague and London was based on its consistent state behaviour with respect to international law from 1856 to 1914. Britain's actions not only created precedents but also built a comprehensive state practice, which subsequently led to its recognition by other states. Britain dominated the discussions on international maritime law at the Hague and London conferences not only because it possessed the most comprehensive state practice in this area but also because of its increasing strategic and economic vulnerability as a result of its expanding trade. Consequently, strategic concerns dominated the preparatory work of the British government, and civil servants such as George S. Clarke from the Committee of Imperial Defence, and Charles L. Ottley and Edmond J. W. Slade from the Naval Intelligence Department, became important figures in analysing the legal proposals from a strategic point of view. Their involvement demonstrated the importance of international law for war-planning.

The process of the codification of international law highlighted the importance of state practice and custom. In fact, state practice and custom, as well as codification, illustrate what Martti Koskenniemi has called the dualism of international law. Law needs to be both concrete and normative in order to fulfil its function. State practice and custom emphasized the concreteness of law, describing what states actually do. On the other hand, declarations and conventions underline the normative character of law, describing what states should do. The dualism of international law cannot be resolved and is caught in what Koskenniemi describes as the apology/ utopia dilemma. State practice, such as Britain's law of neutrality, reflects the interests of a state and, therefore, tends to 'apologize' for what a state does. On the other hand, some of the Hague conventions and articles in the Declaration of London were 'utopian' as they lacked enforcement through state practice.[2]

The results of the Hague and London conferences demonstrate that the proposals took long-term strategic and economic interests into account. Britain successfully balanced its interests as a future belligerent with its interests as a future neutral power in a coming war, which meant that the British government compromised on belligerent rights while strengthening neutral rights. For example, it negotiated an internationally binding law of

---

[2] Martti Koskenniemi, *From Apology to Utopia: The Structure of International Legal Argument. Reissue with New Epilogue* (Cambridge, 1989; reprint Cambridge, 2005).

neutrality (Convention XIII) and in return accepted the limitation of the right of search and capture (Convention XI; Declaration of London, Articles 30–35 on the restriction of capture). On the other hand, Britain defended favourable terms for the law of blockade (Declaration of London, Articles 1–21) and the definition of contraband of war (Declaration of London, Articles 22–44). Britain's concessions at these international conferences were minimal as most of the 1907 Hague conventions and the Declaration of London were based on British state practice, and so safeguarded its strategic and economic interests as a potential neutral or belligerent in future wars. The legal framework, which Britain helped to create at The Hague and London, reflected Britain's interests in a future war of being able to wage economic warfare while at the same time protecting its trade. In other words, Britain used international law as an important tool to balance its own conflicting interests and to keep its options open in a future war.

While strategic considerations had a considerable influence on the practice and codification of international law, the reverse also applied. The framers of Britain's legal position at the Hague and London conferences were concerned about the strategic effect of international law on decision-making processes and the character of a future war. Britain's strict neutrality policy protected Britain's economic interests. At the same time, Britain, as the dominant sea power of the time, defended belligerent rights such as blockade and the right of search and capture as part of its maritime strategy, so aiming to exercise control of the sea in times of war. Britain used the close relationship between international law and strategy to protect its state interests.

Over the course of the nineteenth century, international law became an increasingly important political instrument, creating a new legal framework that governed relationships between states. Politicians sometimes talked hastily about their rejection of international law, and yet, the reality looked different. In contrast to the immediacies of politics, both international law and strategy were built on long-term perspectives. Britain's state practice reflected its long-term strategic and economic interests as a sea power. International law was used to balance Britain's diverging state interests as a neutral and as a belligerent, not least because it was the dominant sea power. Britain recognized the importance of consistency in state practice even if it meant applying stricter laws to itself than others. At the same time, Britain's success was also linked to its dominance as a sea power, which gave clout to its claims. Britain complied with the rules of international law because they reflected its economic and strategic interests. International law was a necessity not a luxury.

Bibliography

1. Primary Sources

(i) Unpublished Primary Sources

The National Archives [TNA], Kew

Admiralty

ADM 1   Correspondence and Papers
ADM 116   Cases
ADM 231   Foreign Intelligence Committee and Naval Intelligence Department: Naval Intelligence Reports

Cabinet

CAB 7   Colonial Defence Committee, and Committee of Imperial Defence: Minutes, Reports and Correspondence
CAB 16   Committee of Imperial Defence: Ad Hoc-Sub Committees: Minutes, Memoranda and Reports
CAB 17   Committee of Imperial Defence: Miscellaneous Correspondence and Memoranda
CAB 38   Committee of Imperial Defence: Photographic Copies of Minutes and Memoranda

Colonial Office

CO 879   Africa, Confidential Print

Foreign Office

FO 27   General Correspondence before 1906, France
FO 95   Miscellanea, Series I
FO 97   Supplements to General Correspondence before 1906
FO 800   Various Ministers' and Officials' Papers
FO 834   Confidential Print Law Officers' Opinions
FO 881   Confidential Print

Home Office

HO 45   Registered Papers

National Maritime Museum [NMM], London
Papers of Julian S. Corbett [CBT]

United States Naval War College, Newport, RI
Record Group 8 (Intelligence and Technological Archives)
Record Group 28 (President's Files)

Bundesarchiv (Federal Archives of Germany) [BA],
Berlin-Lichterfelde
R 901 Auswärtiges Amt (German Foreign Office)

Bundesarchiv–Militärarchiv (Federal Archives of Germany) [BA–MA],
Freiburg / Brsg.
RM 3 Reichsmarineamt (German Imperial Naval Office)

(ii) Published Primary Sources
Printed Government Sources
Hansard, 3rd and 5th Series
The London Gazette

Parliamentary Papers and Command Papers

Declaration respecting Egypt and Morocco, 8 Apr. 1904, in *Parliamentary Papers, France, No. 1, 1904 [Cd. 1952]*.

Foreign Enlistment. A Bill to Prevent the Enlisting or Engagement of Her Majesty's Subjects to Service in Foreign Service, and the Building, Fitting out, or Equipping, in Her Majesty's Dominions, Vessels for War-Like Purposes, without Her Majesty's License, 1870 (228), II.61.

North America. No. 13 (1863). Memorial from Certain Shipowners of Liverpool, Suggesting an Alteration in the Foreign Enlistment Act, 8 July 1863, 1863 (3200) LXXII.563.

P.P. Misc. 1 (1874): Correspondence Respecting the Proposed Conference at Brussels on the Rules of Military Warfare [C. 1010].

P.P. Misc. 1 (1875): Correspondence Respecting the Brussels Conference on the Rules of Military Warfare [Cd. 1128].

P.P. Misc. 4 (1909): Correspondence and Documents respecting the International Naval Conference, held in London, Dec. 1908–Feb. 1909 [Cd. 4554].

P.P. Misc. 5 (1909): Proceedings of the International Naval Conference, held in London, Dec. 1908–Feb. 1909 [Cd. 4555].

Report of the Neutrality Laws Commissioners Together with an Appendix Containing Reports from Foreign States and other Documents. 1867–68 (4027). Command Papers. Vol. XXXII.265.

Synopsis of the Customs Law Consolidation Bill, 1876, and the Unrepealed Sections of Existing Acts, 18 May 1876, in *Nineteenth Century House of Commons Sessional Papers, 1876, Vol. II*.

Legal Texts (International Law and British Legislation)

'Convention Respecting the Free Navigation of the Suez Maritime Canal, Signed at Constantinople on 29 Oct. 1888', in *American Society of International Law Proceedings of the Seventh Annual Meeting, 24–26 Apr. 1913*, 295–302.

'Convention (III) for the Adaptation to Maritime Warfare of the Principles of the Geneva Convention of 22 August 1864. The Hague, 29 July 1899', in Dietrich Schindler and Jiří Toman (eds), *The Laws of Armed Conflicts: A Collection of Conventions, Resolutions and other Documents* (Dordrecht, 2004), 373–7.

'Convention (V) Respecting the Rights and Duties of Neutral Powers and Persons in the Case of War on Land, The Hague, 18 Oct. 1907', in Dietrich Schindler and Jiří Toman (eds), *The Laws of Armed Conflicts: A Collection of Conventions, Resolutions and other Documents* (Dordrecht, 2004), 1399–406.

'Convention (VI) relating to the Status of Enemy Merchant Ships at the Outbreak of Hostilities. The Hague, 18 Oct. 1907', in Dietrich Schindler and Jiří Toman (eds), *The Laws of Armed Conflicts: A Collection of Conventions, Resolutions and other Documents* (Dordrecht, 2004), 1059–64.

'Convention (X) for the Adaptation to Maritime Warfare of the Principles of the Geneva Convention. The Hague, 18 Oct. 1907', in Dietrich Schindler and Jiří Toman (eds), *The Laws of Armed Conflicts: A Collection of Conventions, Resolutions and other Documents* (Dordrecht, 2004), 1082–6.

'Convention (XI) Relative to Certain Restrictions with Regard to the Exercise of the Right of Capture in Naval War. The Hague, 18 Oct. 1907', in Dietrich Schindler and Jiří Toman (eds), *The Laws of Armed Conflicts: A Collection of Conventions, Resolutions and other Documents* (Dordrecht, 2004), 1087–92.

'Convention (XII) Relative to the Creation of an International Prize Court. The Hague, 18 Oct. 1907', in Dietrich Schindler and Jiří Toman (eds), *The Laws of Armed Conflicts: A Collection of Conventions, Resolutions and other Documents* (Dordrecht, 2004), 1093–105.

'Convention (XIII) Concerning the Rights and Duties of Neutral Powers in Naval War. The Hague, 18 Oct. 1907', in Dietrich Schindler and Jiří Toman (eds), *The Laws of Armed Conflicts: A Collection of Conventions, Resolutions and other Documents* (Dordrecht, 2004), 1407–16.

Court of the Exchequer at Westminster, *Attorney-General v. Sillem and Others, Claiming the Vessel 'Alexandra' Seized under the Foreign Enlistment Act (59 George III. Chapter 69). Report of the Trial before the Lord Chief Baron and a Special Jury* (London, 1863).

Customs Laws Consolidation Act, 1853 (16 and 17 Vict., cap. 107) was later replaced; see Customs Laws Consolidation Act, 1876 (39 and 49 Vict., cap. 36), http://www.legislation.gov.uk/ukpga/1876/36/pdfs/ukpga_18760036_en.pdf (accessed 15 Oct. 2018).

Customs and Inland Revenue Act, 1879 (42 and 43 Vict., cap. 21), http://www.legislation. gov.uk/ukpga/1879/21/pdfs/ukpga_18790021_en.pdf (accessed 7 Oct. 2018).

'Declaration concerning the Laws of Naval War. London, 26 Feb. 1909', in Dietrich Schindler and Jiří Toman (eds), *The Laws of Armed Conflicts: A Collection of Conventions, Resolutions and other Documents* (Dordrecht, 2004), 1111–22.

Foreign Enlistment Act, 1870 (33 and 34 Vict., cap. 90), http://www.legislation.gov.uk/ukpga/1870/90/pdfs/ukpga_18700090_en.pdf (accessed 30 Oct. 2018).

'Instructions for the Government of Armies of the United States in the Field, 24 April 1863 (Lieber Code)', in Dietrich Schindler and Jiří Toman (eds), *The Laws of Armed Conflicts: A Collection of Conventions, Resolutions and other Documents* (Dordrecht, 2004), 3–20.

'The Laws of War on Land. Oxford, 9 Sept. 1880 (Oxford Manual)', in Dietrich Schindler and Jiří Toman (eds), *The Laws of Armed Conflicts: A Collection of Conventions, Resolutions and other Documents* (Dordrecht, 2004), 29–40.

Lloyd's Act, 1871, 34 VICT.– Ch. xxi.

'Project of an International Declaration concerning the Laws and Customs of War. Brussels, 27 August 1874', in Dietrich Schindler and Jiří Toman (eds), *The Laws of Armed Conflicts: A Collection of Conventions, Resolutions and other Documents* (Dordrecht, 2004), 25–8.

The Springbok, 72 U.S. 5. Wall. 1 1 (1866).

Treaty of Amity and Commerce Between His Majesty the King of Prussia, and the United States of America, 10 Sept. 1785, http://avalon.law.yale.edu/18th_century/prus1785.asp (accessed 4 Oct. 2018).

'The United States Naval War Code of 1900. The Laws and Usages of War at Sea', *International Law Discussions, 1903: The United States Naval War Code of 1900* (Washington, DC, 1904), 103–14.

Periodicals

Annuaire de l'Institut de droit international
Blackwood's Edinburgh Magazine
Columbia Law Review
Edinburgh Review
Fortnightly Review
International Law Discussions
Journal of Royal United Service Institution
Nineteenth Century. A Monthly Review
North American Review
Proceedings of the American Society of International Law
Reports of International Law Association
Revue de droit international et de législation comparée
Revue générale de droit international public
The American Journal of International Law
The New York Times
The Times
United Service Magazine

Books, Articles, and Pamphlets

'4th Commission-Déclaration de Bruxelles', *Revue de droit international et de législation comparée*, 7 (1875), 674–5.

Anonymous, 'Review: The Influence of Sea Power upon History, 1660–1783. By Captain A.T. Mahan, London 1890', *Journal of Royal United Service Institution*, 34 (1890), 1067.

Attlmayr, Ferdinand, *Die Elemente des Internationalen Seerechtes und Sammlung von Verträgen. Ein Handbuch für die kais. und kön. österr. See-Officiere*, 2 vols (Vienna, 1872 and 1873).

Ballard, George A., 'The Protection of Commerce during War (Gold Medal Prize Essay)', *Journal of Royal United Service Institution*, 42 (1898), 365–405.

Beresford, Charles, 'National Insurance', *United Service Magazine*, June (1890), 279–86.

Bernard, Mountague, 'Oberservations', *Annuaire de l'Institut de droit international*, 2 (1878), 128–30.

Bluntschli, Johann Caspar (Rapporteur), 'Projet de redaction nouvelle des trois règles de Washington, adopté par l'Institut', *Revue de droit international et de législation comparée*, 7 (1875), 282–3.

Bourne, Stephen, 'Increasing Dependence of this Country upon Foreign Supplies for Food: Read at Manchester Statistical Society, 11 Apr. 1877', in Stephen Bourne (ed.), *Trade, Population and Food: A Series of Papers on Economic Statistics* (London, 1880), 76–102.

Brassey, Thomas, 'Great Britain as Sea-Power', *Nineteenth Century. A Monthly Review*, 34, 197 (1893), 121–30.

Bridge, Cyprian A. G., 'A Review on "Influence of Sea Power Upon History 1660–1783 by Captain A. T. Mahan"', *Blackwood's Edinburgh Magazine*, 148 (1890), 576–84.

Bulmerincq, August von, 'Rapport', *Annuaire de l'Institut de droit international*, 7 (1885), 163–9.

Bulmerincq, August von, 'Rapport sur les délibérations et les résolutions de l'Institut relatives au projet d'organisation d'un tribunal international des prises maritimes, présenté par M. Westlake', *Annuaire de l'Institut de droit international*, 2 (1878), 113–21.

Bulmerincq, August von (Rapporteur), 'Troisième commission d'études-Droit matériel et formel en matière des prises maritimes', *Annuaire de l'Institut de droit international*, 9 (1887), 188–210.

Butler, Charles H., *Freedom of Private Property on the Sea from Capture During War* (Washington, DC, 1899).

Butler, Charles H., 'A Reply to Captain Mahan', *The New York Times*, 27 Nov. 1898, http://search.proquest.com/docview/95657494?accountid=13042 (accessed 13 Oct. 2018), 60–7.

Caprivi, Leo von, 'Reichstagsrede, 4 Mar. 1892 (187. Sitzung)', in *Stenographische Berichte über den Deutschen Reichstag*, 4553–61.

Churchill, A. B. N., 'Command of the Sea: What is it? (Gold Medal Prize Essay)', *Journal of Royal United Service Institution*, 53 (1909), 435–73.

Clarke, George S., 'National Insurance', *United Service Magazine*, Sept. (1890), 563–72.

Clarke, George S., 'The Navy and the Nation', *Journal of Royal United Service Institution*, 48 (1904), 30–44.

Clowes, William L. [Nauticus], 'Sea Power: Its Past and its Future', *Fortnightly Review*, 54, 324 (1893), 849–68.

Collinson, T. B., 'The Strategic Importance of the Military Harbours in the British Channel as Connected with Defensive and Offensive Operations', *Journal of Royal United Service Institution*, 18 (1874), 227–64.

Colomb, John C. R., *The Protection of our Commerce, and Distribution of our Naval Forces Considered* (London, 1867).

Colomb, John C. R., 'The Distribution of our War Forces. Part I', *Journal of the Royal United Service Institution*, 13 (1869), 37–56.

Colomb, John C. R., 'The Distribution of our War Forces. Part II', *Journal of the Royal United Service Institution*, 13 (1869), 57–71.

Colomb, John C. R., *Imperial Strategy with Introductory Letters Addressed to 'The Times': Forming Part 1 of 'Imperial Defence'* (London, 1871).

Colomb, John C. R., *The Reorganization of our Military Forces: Forming Part 2 of 'Imperial Defence'* (London, 1871).

Colomb, John C. R., 'The Naval and Military Resources of the Colonies', *Journal of Royal United Service Institution*, 23 (1879), 413–79.

Colomb, John C. R., 'On Colonial Defence: A Paper read before the Royal Colonial Institute, 28 June 1873', in John C. R. Colomb, *The Defence of Great and Greater Britain. Sketches of its Naval, Military, and Political Aspects* (London, 1880), 35–92.

Colomb, John C. R., *The Defence of Great and Greater Britain: Sketches of its Naval, Military and Political Aspects* (London, 1880).

Colomb, John. C. R., 'Naval Intelligence and Protection of Commerce in War', *Journal of Royal United Service Institution*, 25 (1881), 553–90.

Colomb, Philip H., 'The Attack and Defence of Fleets, Part 1', *Journal of Royal United Service Institution*, 15 (1871), 405–37.

Colomb, Philip H., 'The Attack and Defence of Fleets, Part 2', *Journal of Royal United Service Institution*, 16 (1872), 1–24.

Colomb, Philip H., *Slave Catching in the Indian Ocean. A Record of Naval Experiences* (London, 1873).

Colomb, Philip H., 'Great Britain's Maritime Power: How Best Developed etc', *Journal of Royal United Service Institution*, 22 (1878), 1–55.

Colomb, Philip H., 'Blockades: Under Existing Conditions of Warfare', *Journal of Royal United Service Institution*, 31 (1887), 733–58.

Colomb, Philip H., 'The Naval Defences of the United Kingdom', *Journal of Royal United Service Institution*, 32 (1888), 565–601.

Colomb, Philip H., *Naval Warfare: Its Ruling Principles and Practice Historically Treated* (London, 1891).

'Conclusions adoptées à Cambridge par la huitième commission, Aug. 1895', *Annuaire de l'Institut de droit international*, 14 (1895), 191–3.

'Conclusions adoptées par l'Institut', *Revue de droit international et de législation comparée*, 7 (1875), 284–7.

'Conférence de Bruxelles–Historique', *Revue de droit international et de législation comparée*, 7 (1875), 86–92.

Corbett, Julian S., 'The Capture of Private Property at Sea', in Alfred T. Mahan, *Some Neglected Aspects of War* (London, 1907), 115–54.

Corbett, Julian S., *Some Principles of Maritime Strategy* (London, 1911; reprint Mineola, NY, 2004).

Craigie, R. W., 'Maritime Supremacy being Essential for the General Protection of the British Empire and its Commerce, to What Extent, if Any, Should our Naval Force be Supplemented by Fixed Defences at Home and Abroad, and to Whom Should They be Confided? (The Naval Prize Essay)', *Journal of Royal United Service Institution*, 36 (1892), 391–415.

Crutchley, William C., 'Modern Warfare as affecting the Mercantile Marine of Great Britain', *Journal of Royal United Service Institution*, 37 (1893), 491–511.

Crutchley, William C., 'Protection of Commerce in War, with Special Reference to the Cape Route', *Journal of Royal United Service Institution*, 49 (1905), 1–21.

Currie, Donald, 'On Maritime Warfare; the Importance to the British Empire of a Complete System of Telegraphs, Coaling Stations, and Graving Docks', *Journal of Royal United Service Institution*, 21 (1877), 228–47.

Currie, Donald, 'Maritime Warfare: the Adaptation of Ocean Steamers to War Purposes', *Journal of Royal United Service Institution*, 24 (1881), 81–105.

Descamps, Edouard, *Le droit de la paix et de la guerre. Essai sur l'évolution de la neutralité et sur la constitution du pacigérat* (Paris, 1898).

Descamps, Edouard, 'Le pacigérat ou régime juridique de la paix en temps de guerre', *Revue générale de droit international public*, 7 (1900), 629–704.

Descamps, Edouard, 'Thèses sur Pacigérat', *Annuaire de l'Institut de droit international*, 20 (1904), 61–3.

Dewar, Kenneth Gilbert Balmain, 'What is the Influence of Oversea Commerce on the Operations of War? How Did it Affect Our Naval Policy in the Past, and How Does it in Present Day? (Gold Medal Naval Prize Essay)', *Journal of Royal United Service Institution*, 57 (1913), 449–500.

'Discours de M. Léon Bourgeois', *Annuaire de l'Institut de droit international*, 23 (1910), 365–73.

'Discours de M. Lyon-Caen', *Annuaire de l'Institut de droit international*, 23 (1910), 357–65.

Eardley-Wilmot, Sydney M., 'Great Britain's Maritime Power, How Best Developed etc.', *Journal of Royal United Service Institution*, 22 (1878), 435–60.

'Examen critique des traveaux de la conférence de Bruxelles', *Revue de droit international et de législation comparée*, 7 (1875), 95–111.

'Extrait du procès-verbal de la 4e séance plénière, tenue à Turin, 13 Sept. 1882, sous la présidence de M. de Pierantoni', *Annuaire de l'Institut de droit international*, 6 (1883), 177–212.

'Extrait du procès-verbal de la première séance de la Commission des prises maritimes, tenue à Wiesbaden, 5 Sept. 1881, sous la présidence de M. de Bulmerincq, *Annuaire de l'Institut de droit international*, 6 (1883), 139–52.

Field, David Dudley, *Draft Outline of an International Code* (New York, 1872).

Field, David Dudley, 'First Project of an International Code', in A. P. Sprague (ed.), *Speeches, Arguments, and Miscellaneous Papers of David Dudley Field*, 2 vols (New York, 1884), 387–96.

Field, David Dudley, *Outlines of an International Code*, 2nd edn (New York, 1876).

Fisher, F., 'Command of the Sea: What is it? (Third Prize Essay)', *Journal of Royal United Service Institution*, 53 (1909), 847–64.

Fry, Agnes, *A Memoir of the Right Honourable Sir Edward Fry, G.C.B., 1827–1918* (Oxford, 1921).

Fulton, Thomas W., *The Sovereignty of the Sea; an Historical Account of the Claims of England to the Dominion of the British Seas, and of the Evolution of the Territorial Waters, with Special Reference to the Rights of Fishing and the Naval Salute* (Edinburgh, 1911).

Gooch, G. P. and Temperley, Harold (eds), *British Documents on the Origins of the War 1898–1914, Vol. VIII: Arbitration, Neutrality and Security* (London, 1932).

Grotius, Hugo, *The Freedom of the Seas or, The Right which Belongs to the Dutch to Take Part in the East Indian Trade*, ed. James Brown Scott, trans. Ralph Van Deman Magoffin (New York, 1916).

Hall, William E., *The Rights and Duties of Neutrals* (London, 1874).

Hall, William E., *A Treatise on International Law*, 2nd edn (Oxford, 1884).

Hall, William E., *A Treatise on International Law*, ed. J. B. Atlay, 5th edn (Oxford, 1904).

Hall, William E., *A Treatise on International Law*, ed. J. B. Atlay, 6th edn (Oxford, 1909).

Hamel, Felix H., *International Law in Connexion with Municipal Statuses Relating to the Commerce, Rights, and Liabilities of the Subjects of Neutral States Pending Foreign War Considered with Reference to the Trial of the Case of the 'Alexandra', Seized under the Provisions of the Foreign Enlistment Act* (London, 1863).

[Harcourt, W. Vernon], *Letters by Historicus on Some Questions of International Law. Reprinted from the Times with Considerable Additions* (London, 1863).

[Harcourt, W. Vernon], *American Neutrality by Historicus. Reprinted from the London Times of December 22d, 1864* (New York, 1865).

Harcourt, W. Vernon, 'The Rights and Duties of Neutrals in Time of War. Part 1', *Journal of Royal United Service Institution*, 9 (1865), 313–28.

Harcourt, W. Vernon, 'The Rights and Duties of Neutrals in Time of War. Part 2', *Journal of Royal United Service Institution*, 9 (1865), 329–45.

Highmore, Joseph Nathaniel, *The Customs Laws including the Customs Consolidation Act, 1876, with the Enactments Amending and Extending that Act and the Present Customs Tariff for Great Britain and Ireland; also the Customs Laws and Tariff for the Isle of Man*, 2nd edn (London, 1907).

Holland, Thomas E., *Brussels Conference of 1874, and other Diplomatic Attempts to Mitigate the Rigour of Warfare, Delivered at All Souls College, May 10, 1876* (Oxford, 1876).

Holland, Thomas E., *A Manual of Naval Prize Law. Founded upon the Manual Prepared in 1866 by Godfrey Lushington* (London, 1888).

Holland, Thomas E., *Studies in International Law* (Oxford, 1898).

International Law Association, *Final Report of the Committee: Statement of Principles Applicable to the Formation of General Customary International Law* (London, 2000).

Kleen, Richard, *De la contrabande de guerre et des transports interdits aux neutres* (Paris, 1893).

Kleen, Richard, 'Avant-Projet de Règlement concernant les lois et coutumes de la neutralité', *Annuaire de l'Institut de droit international*, 22 (1906), 100–21.

Kleen, Richard and Brusa, Emilio (Rapporteurs), 'Contrebande de guerre et transports interdits', *Annuaire de l'Institut de droit international*, 13 (1894), 50–124.

Kleen, Richard and Brusa, Emilio (Rapporteurs), 'Avant-projet de règlement international sur la contrebande de guerre et des transports interdits aux neutres, 30 Mar. 1894', *Annuaire de l'Institut de droit international*, 14 (1895), 33–43.

Kleen, Richard and Brusa, Emilio (Rapporteurs), 'Rapport final et projet transactionnel presents au nom de la commission, 30 Apr. 1896', *Annuaire de l'Institut de droit international*, 15 (1896), 98–122.

Laughton, John K., 'Sovereignty of the Seas', *Fortnightly Review*, 5 (1866), 718–33.

Laughton, John K., 'The Scientific Study of Naval History', *Journal of Royal United Service Institution*, 18 (1874), 508–27.

Laughton, John K., 'Captain Mahan on Maritime Power', *Edinburgh Review*, 172 (1890), 420–53.

Laughton, John K., 'Recent Naval Literature', *Journal of Royal United Service Institution*, 37 (1893), 1161–82.

Laughton, John K., 'The Study of Naval History', *Journal of Royal United Service Institution*, 40 (1896), 795–820.

'Law and Customs of War on Land-Examination of the Declaration of Brussels of 1874', in James Brown Scott (ed.), *Resolutions of the Institut of International Law Dealing with the Law of Nations: With an Historical Introduction and Explanatory Notes* (New York, 1916), 7–12.

Lawrence, Thomas J., 'Recognition of Belligerency Considered in Relation to Naval Warfare', *Journal of Royal United Service Institution*, 41, 1 (1897), 1–22.

Lawrence, Thomas J., *The Principles of International Law*, 2nd and rev. edn (London, 1899).

Lawrence, Thomas J., 'Problems of Neutrality connected with the Russo-Japanese War', *Journal of Royal United Service Institution*, 48 (1904), 915–37.

Lawrence, Thomas J., *War and Neutrality in the Far East* (London, 1904).

Lawrence, Thomas J., 'The Hague Conference and Naval War', *Journal of Royal United Service Institution*, 52 (1908), 479–509.

Lindsay, William S., *Manning the Royal Navy and Mercantile Marine. Also Belligerent and Neutral Rights in the Event of War* (London, 1877).

Lindsay, William S., 'On Belligerent Rights: The Declaration of Paris, 1856', *Journal of Royal United Service Institution*, 21 (1878), 179–227.

Long, Samuel, 'Study of the Tactics of Naval Blockade as Affected by Modern Weapons', *Journal of Royal United Service Institution*, 25 (1882), 316–49.

Macdonell, John, 'Recent Changes in the Rights and Duties of Belligerents and Neutrals According to International Law, Part 1', *Journal of Royal United Service Institution*, 42, 2 (1898), 787–811.

Macdonell, John, 'Recent Changes in the Rights and Duties of Belligerents and Neutrals According to International Law, Part 2', *Journal of Royal United Service Institution*, 42 (1898), 915–40.

Macdonell, John, 'The Declaration of London', *International Law Association. Report of the Twenty-Sixth Conference held at The Guildhall London, 2–5 Aug. 1910* (1910), 89–115.

Macdonell, John, *Some Plain Reasons for Immunity from Capture of Private Property at Sea* (London, 1910).

McKinley, William, 'Second Annual Message to Congress, 5 Dec. 1898', in Gerhard Peters and John T. Woolley, *The American Presidency Project* https://www.presidency.ucsb.edu/node/205329 (accessed 25 Oct. 2018).

Mahan, Alfred T., 'Blockade in Relation to Naval Strategy', *Journal of Royal United Service Institution*, 39 (1895), 1057–69.

Mahan, Alfred T., Letter to the Editor on Commerce and War I, *The New York Times*, 17 Nov. 1898, http://search.proquest.com/docview/95571033?accountid=13042 (accessed 13 Oct. 2018).

Mahan, Alfred T., Letter to the Editor on Commerce and War II, *The New York Times*, 23 Nov. 1898, http://search.proquest.com/docview/95565194?accountid=13042 (accessed 13 Oct. 2018).

Mahan, Alfred T., *Sea Power in its Relations to the War of 1812*, 2 vols (London, 1905).

Mahan, Alfred T., 'The Hague Conference: The Question of Immunity for Belligerent Merchant Shipping', in Alfred T. Mahan, *Some Neglected Aspects of War* (London, 1907), 157–92.

Mahan, Alfred T., *Some Neglected Aspects of War* (London, 1907).

Mahan, Alfred T., 'Deficiencies of Law for International Adjustments', *North American Review*, 194 (1911), 674–84.

Mahan, Alfred T., 'The Place of Force in International Relations', *North American Review*, 195 (1912), 28–39.

Mahan, Alfred T., *The Influence of Sea Power upon History, 1660–1783* (Boston, MA, 1890; reprint New York, 1987).

Maurice, John F., *Hostilities without Declaration of War. An Historical Abstract of the Cases in which Hostilities Have Occurred between Civilized Powers Prior to Declaration or Warning. From 1700 to 1870* (London, 1883).

Noel, Gerard H. U., 'Great Britain's Maritime Power, How Best Developed etc.', *Journal of Royal United Service Institution*, 22 (1878), 461–97.

Nugent, Charles H., 'Imperial Defence, Part 1: Home Defences', *Journal of Royal United Service Institution*, 28 (1884), 427–56.

Nugent, Charles H., 'Imperial Defence, Part 2: Abroad', *Journal of Royal United Service Institution*, 28 (1884), 459–513.

'Observations of various committee members', *Annuaire de l'Institut de droit international*, 22 (1906), 121–88.

Oppenheim, Lassa, *International Law. A Treatise*, 2 vols (London, 1912).

Ortolan, Théodore, *Règles internationales et diplomatie de la mer*, 2 vols (Paris, 1845).

Owen, Douglas, 'Capture at Sea: Modern Conditions and the Ancient Prize Laws', *Royal United Service Institution, Journal*, 49 (1905), 1233–64.

Owen, Douglas, 'Our Food Supplies. Our Dependence on Overseas Food: The Emergency Means available to us to Amplify our Supplies on Outbreak of War, and thus Prevent Food Panic, with its Danger to the State', *Journal of Royal United Service Institution*, 53 (1909), 1551–78.

Owen, Douglas, 'Declaration of London and our Food Supplies', *Journal of the Royal United Service Institution*, 55 (1911), 149–85.

Perels, Ferdinand, *Das internationale öffentliche Seerecht der Gegenwart*, 2nd edn (Berlin, 1903).

Phillimore, Robert, 'Declaration of London', *International Law Association. Report of the Twenty-Sixth Conference held at The Guildhall London, 2–5 Aug. 1910* (1910), 67–88.

Quigley, Harold Scott, *The Immunity of Private Property from Capture at Sea* (Madison, WI, 1918).

'Rapport de M. Rolin-Jaequemyns', *Revue de droit international et de législation comparée*, 7 (1875), 447–552.

'Règlement international des prises maritimes, voté à Turin, 13–15 Sept. 1882', *Annuaire de l'Institut de droit international*, 6 (1883), 213–23.

'Règlement international des prises maritimes, voté à Heidelberg, 8 Sept. 1887', *Annuaire de l'Institut de droit international*, 9 (1887), 218–43.

'Règlementation internationale de la contrebande de guerre, 29 Sept. 1896', *Annuaire de l'Institut de droit international*, 15 (1896), 230–3.

'Résolutions votées dans la séances, 6–7 Sept. 1883', *Annuaire de l'Institut de droit international*, 7 (1885), 185–9.

Rolin-Jaequemyns, Gustave, 'Examen de la declaration de Bruxelles', *Revue de droit international et de législation comparée*, 7 (1875), 438–47.

Roosevelt, Theodore, 'Fourth Annual Message, 6 Dec. 1904', in Gerhard Peters and John T. Woolley, *The American Presidency Project*, https://www.presidency.ucsb.edu/documents/fourth-annual-message-15 (accessed 19 Oct. 2018).

Ross-of-Bladensberg, John, 'Maritime Rights', *Journal of Royal United Service Institution*, 20 (1876), 423–46.

Rosse, Eugène Marie Henri, *Guide international du commandant de batiment de guerre—du droit de la force* (Paris, 1891).

Scott, James Brown (ed.), *Instructions to the American Delegates to the Hague Peace Conferences and Their Official Reports* (New York, 1916).

Scott, James Brown (ed.), *Resolutions of the Institute of International Law Dealing with the Law of Nations. With an Historical Introduction and Explanatory Notes* (New York, 1916).

Scott, James Brown (ed.), *The Armed Neutralities of 1780–1800: A Collection of Official Documents Preceded by the View of Representative Publicists* (New York, 1918).

Scott, James Brown (ed.), *The Proceedings of the Hague Peace Conferences. Translation of the Official Texts. The Conference of 1899* (New York, 1920).

Scott, James Brown (ed.), *The Proceedings of the Hague Peace Conferences. Translation of the Original Texts. The Conference of 1907, Vol. I: Plenary Meetings of the Conference* (New York, 1920).

Scott, James Brown (ed.), *The Proceedings of the Hague Peace Conferences. Translation of the Original Texts. The Conference of 1907, Vol. II: Meetings of the First Commission* (New York, 1920).

Scott, James Brown (ed.), *The Proceedings of the Hague Peace Conferences. Translation of the Original Texts. The Conference of 1907, Vol. III: Meetings of the Second, Third and Fourth Commissions* (New York, 1921).

Seager, Robert II and Maguire, Doris D. (eds), *Letters and Papers of Alfred Thayer Mahan*, 3 vols (Annapolis, MD, 1975).

'Séance plénièrès—La regime de la neutralité', *Annuaire de l'Institut de droit international*, 20 (1904), 211–20.

'Séance plénièrès—La regime de la neutralité', *Annuaire de l'Institut de droit international*, 22 (1906), 345–409.

Shelford, T. L., 'Command of the Sea: What is it? (Second Prize Essay)', *Journal of Royal United Service Institution*, 53 (1909), 705–50.

Snow, Freeman, *Cases and Opinions on International Law with Notes and a Syllabus* (Boston, MA, 1893).

'Statuts votes par la Conférence Juridique international de Gand, le 10 Sept. 1873', *Annuaire de l'Institut de droit international*, 1 (1877), 1–5.

Stockton, Charles H., 'Naval War Code Memorandum, May 1900', *International Law Discussions, 1903: The United States Naval War Code of 1900* (Washington, DC, 1904), 5–7.

Stockton, Charles H., 'Would Immunity from Capture During War of Nonoffending Private Property upon the High Seas be in the Interest of Civilization?', *American Journal of International Law* 1, 4 (1907), 930–43.

Stockton, Charles H., 'The International Naval Conference of London, 1908–1909', *The American Journal of International Law*, 3, 3 (1909), 596–618.

Stockton, Charles H., 'The Codification of the Laws of Naval Warfare', in *Proceedings of the American Society of International Law at its Sixth Annual Meeting held at Washington, DC* (Washington, DC, 1912), 115–23.

Stockton, Charles H., 'The Declaration of Paris', *The American Journal of International Law*, 14, 3 (1920), 356–68.

Swinburne, H. L., 'A Scheme of Commerce Protection', *Journal of Royal United Service Institution*, 39 (1895), 1170–88.

Takahashi, Sakuyé, *Cases on International Law during the Chino-Japanese War* (Cambridge, 1899).

Takahashi, Sakuyé, *International Law Applied to the Russo-Japanese War. With the Decisions of the Japanese Prize Courts* (New York, 1908).

Thursfield, James R., *Naval Warfare* (Cambridge, 1913).

Thursfield, James R., *Nelson and other Naval Studies* (London, 1909).

Tryon, George, 'National Insurance. A Practical Proposal', *United Service Magazine*, May (1890), 184–92.

Tyron, James L., *The Inter-Parliamentary Union and its Work* (Boston, MA, 1910).

Westlake, John, *Chapters on the Principles of International Law* (Cambridge, 1894).

Wilson, George Grafton, 'General Conclusions', *International Law Discussions, 1903: The United States Naval War Code of 1900* (Washington, DC, 1904), 89–91.

Wilson, George Grafton, 'Topic V: Immunity of Private Property at Sea', *International Law Situations* (Washington, DC, 1914), 113–31.

Winter, C. F., 'The Protection of Commerce during War (Second Prize Essay)', *Journal of Royal United Service Institution*, 42 (1898), 507–39.

Woolsey, Theodore D., *Introduction to the Study of International Law, Designed as an Aid in Teaching and in Historical Studies*, 3rd edn (New York, 1872).

Woolsey, Theodore S., 'The Naval War Code', *Columbia Law Review*, 1 (1901), 298–310.

Wyatt, Harold F., 'England's Threatened Rights at Sea', *Journal of Royal United Service Institution*, 54 (1910), 5–33.

2. Secondary Sources

(i) Unpublished Theses

Ranft, Bryan, 'The Naval Defence of British Sea-Borne Trade 1860–1905' (University of Oxford, DPhil thesis, 1968).

Wilson, Bob, Fuelling the Steam Navy: Naval Coal Supplies in the Early Steam Period, 1820–1870' (University of Exeter, MA degree, 2006).

(ii) Published Secondary Sources

Abbenhuis, Maartje, *An Age of Neutrals: Great Power Politics, 1815–1914* (Cambridge, 2014).

Abbenhuis, Maartje, 'A Most Useful Tool for Diplomacy and Statecraft: Neutrality and Europe in the "Long" Nineteenth-Century, 1815–1914', *The International History Review*, 35, 1 (2013), 1–22.

Abbenhuis, Maartje, *The Hague Conferences and International Politics, 1898–1915* (London, 2018).

Abbenhuis, Maartje, Barber, Christopher Ernest, and Higgins, Annelise (eds), *War, Peace and International Order? The Legacies of the Hague Conferences of 1899 and 1907* (London, 2017).

Adams, Charles F., 'The Trent Affair', *The American Historical Review*, 17 (1912), 540–62.

Alford Jr., Neill H., *Modern Economic Warfare (Law and the Naval Participant)* (Washington, DC, 1967).

D'Amato, Anthony, *The Concept of Custom in International Law* (Ithaca, NY, 1971).

Anand, Ram P., 'Freedom of the Seas. Past, Present and Future', in Rafael Gutiérrez Girardot et al. (eds), *New Directions in International Law: Essays in Honour of Wolfgang Abendroth-Festschrift zu seinem 75. Geburtstag* (Frankfurt/Main, 1982), 215–33.

Anand, Ram P., *Origin and Development of the Law of the Sea: History of International Law Revisited* (The Hague, 1983).

Anderson, Alan M., 'Two Ships Passing in the Night: The United States, Great Britain, and the Immunity of Private Property at Sea in Time of War, 1904–1907', in Lori Lyn Bogle and James C. Rentfrow (eds), *New Interpretations in Naval History: Selected Papers from the Eighteenth McMullen Naval History Symposium Held at the U.S. Naval Academy 19–20 September 2013* (Newport, RI, 2018), 165–74.

Anderson, David H., 'Early Modern through Nineteenth-Century Law', in John B. Hattendorf (ed.), *The Oxford Encyclopedia of Maritime History*, 4 vols (Oxford, 2007), vol. 2, 330–2.

Arielli, Nir, Frei, Gabriela A., and Van Hulle, Inge, 'The Foreign Enlistment Act, International Law, and British Politics, 1819–2014', *The International History Review*, 38, 4 (2016), 642–3.

Ashton, Thomas S., *Economic and Social Investigations in Manchester, 1833–1933: A Centenary History of the Manchester Statistical Society* (Hassocks, 1977).

d'Aspremont, Jean, *Formalism and the Sources of International Law: A Theory of Ascertainment of Legal Rules* (Oxford, 2011).

d'Aspremont, Jean, 'Professionalisation of International Law', in Jean d'Aspremont, Tarcisio Gazzini, André Nollkaemper, and Wouter Werner (eds), *International Law as a Profession* (Cambridge, 2017), 19–37.

Baugh, Daniel, *The Global Seven Years War, 1754–1763: Britain and France in a Great Power Contest* (Harlow, 2011).

Baxter, James P. III, 'The British Government and Neutral Rights, 1861–1865', *The American Historical Review*, 34, 1 (1928), 9–29.

Becker Lorca, Arnulf, *Mestizo International Law: A Global Intellectual History, 1842–1933* (Cambridge, 2014).

Beeler, John, 'A One Power Standard? Great Britain and the Balance of Naval Power, 1860–1880', *Journal of Strategic Studies*, 15, 4 (1992), 548–75.

Beeler, John, 'Steam, Strategy and Schurman: Imperial Defence in the Post-Crimean Era, 1856–1905', in Greg Kennedy and Keith Neilson (eds), *Far-Flung Lines: Essays on Imperial Defence in Honour of Donald Mackenzie Schurman* (London, 1996), 27–54.

Beeler, John, *British Naval Policy in the Gladstone–Disraeli Era, 1866–1880* (Stanford, CA, 1997).

Beeler, John, 'Ploughshares into Swords: The Royal Navy and Merchant Marine Auxiliaries in the Late Nineteenth Century', in Greg Kennedy (ed.), *The Merchant Marine in International Affairs 1850–1950* (London, 2000), 5–30.

Benton, Lauren, *A Search for Sovereignty: Law and Geography in European Empires, 1400–1900* (Cambridge, 2010).

Benton, Lauren and Clulow, Adam, 'Legal Encounter and the Origins of Global Law', in Jerry Bentley, Sanjay Subrahmanyam, and Merry Wiesner-Hanks (eds), *The Cambridge World History, Vol. 6, Pt. 2* (Cambridge, 2015), 80–100.

Benton, Lauren and Ford, Lisa, *Rage for Order: The British Empire and the Origins of International Law, 1800–1850* (Cambridge, MA, 2016).

Bernath, Stuart L., *Squall Across the Atlantic: American Civil War Prize Cases and Diplomacy* (Berkeley, CA, 1970), 85–98.

Bernstorff, Jochen von, 'The Use of Force in International Law before World War I: On Imperial Ordering and the Ontology of the Nation-State', *European Journal of International Law*, 29, 1 (2018), 233–60.

Best, Geoffrey, *Humanity in Warfare: The Modern History of the International Law of Armed Conflicts* (London, 1980).

Best, Geoffrey, *War and Law since 1945* (Oxford, 1994).

Best, Geoffrey, 'Peace Conferences and the Century of Total War: The 1899 Hague Conference and What Came After', *International Affairs*, 75, 3 (1999), 619–34.

Bingham, Tom, 'The Alabama Claims Arbitration', *The International and Comparative Law Quarterly*, 54 (2005), 1–25.

Bond, Brian, 'The Effect of the Cardwell Reforms in Army Organization, 1874–1904', *Journal of the Royal United Service Institution*, 105 (1960), 515–24.

Bond, Brian, 'Prelude to the Cardwell Reforms, 1856–68', *Journal of the Royal United Service Institution*, 106 (1961), 229–36.

Breemer, Jan S., 'The Burden of Trafalgar: Decisive Battle and Naval Strategic Expectations on the Eve of World War I', *Journal of Strategic Studies*, 17 (1994), 33–62.

Bruce, Anthony, 'Edward Cardwell and the Abolition of Purchase', in Ian Beckett and John Gooch (eds), *Politicians and Defence: Studies in the Formulation of British Defence Policy 1845–1970* (Manchester, 1981), 24–46.

Butler, William E., 'Grotius and the Law of the Sea', in Hedley Bull, Benedict Kingsbury, and Adam Roberts (eds), *Hugo Grotius and International Relations* (Oxford, 1990), 209–20.

Cain, Peter J. and Hopkins, Anthony G., *British Imperialism, 1688–2000*, 2nd edn (Harlow, 2002).

Carty, Anthony, 'Doctrine versus State Practice', in Bardo Fassbender and Anne Peters (eds), *The Oxford Handbook of the History of International Law* (Oxford, 2012), 972–96.

Charlesworth, Hilary, 'Law-Making and Sources', in James Crawford and Martti Koskenniemi (eds), *The Cambridge Companion to International Law* (Cambridge, 2012), 188–202.

Chatfield, Charles, *The American Peace Movement: Ideals and Activism* (New York, 1992).

Childress, James F., 'Francis Lieber's Interpretation of the Laws of the War: General Orders No. 100 in the Context of his Life and Thought', *American Journal of Jurisprudence*, 21 (1976), 34–70.

Coates, Benjamin Allen, *Legalist Empire: International Law and American Foreign Relations in the Early Twentieth Century* (Oxford, 2016).

Cobb, Stephen, *Preparing for Blockade, 1885–1914: Naval Contingency for Economic Warfare* (London, 2013).

Coogan, John W., *The End of Neutrality: The United States, Britain, and Maritime Rights, 1899–1915* (Ithaca, NY, 1981).

Coogan, John W., 'The Short-War Illusion Resurrected: The Myth of Economic Warfare as the British Schlieffen Plan', *The Journal of Strategic Studies*, 38 (2015), 1045–64.

Cook, Adrian, *The Alabama Claims: American Politics and Anglo-American Relations, 1865–1872* (Ithaca, NY, 1975).

Crafts, Nicholas, 'Long-Run Growth', in Roderick Floud and Paul Johnson (eds), *The Cambridge Economic History of Modern Britain Vol. 2: Economic Maturity, 1860–1939* (Cambridge, 2004).

Crawford, James, *Brownlie's Principles of Public International Law*, 8th edn (Oxford, 2012).

Cross, Coy F., *Lincoln's Man in Liverpool: Consul Dudley and the Legal Battle to Stop the Confederate Warships* (DeKalb, IL, 2007).

Crouzet, François, *The Victorian Economy*, trans. Anthony Forster (London, 1982).

Crowl, Philip A., 'Alfred Thayer Mahan: The Naval Historian', in Peter Paret (ed.), *Makers of Modern Strategy from Machiavelli to the Nuclear Age* (Oxford, 1986), 444–77.

Darwin, John, *The Empire Project: The Rise and Fall of the British World-System, 1830–1970* (Cambridge, 2009).

Davis, Calvin DeArmond, *The United States and the First Hague Peace Conference* (Ithaca, NY, 1962).

Davis, Calvin DeArmond, *The United States and the Second Hague Peace Conference: American Diplomacy and International Organization 1899–1914* (Durham, NC, 1975).

Davis, Lance E. and Engerman, Stanley L., *Naval Blockades in Peace and War: An Economic History since 1750* (Cambridge, 2006).

Dhokalia, Ramaa Prasad, *The Codification of Public International Law* (Manchester, 1970).

Dhondt, Frederik, 'Recent Research in the History of International Law', *Tijdschrift voor Rechtsgeschiedenis/Revue d'Histoire du Droit/The Legal History Review*, 84 (2016), 313–34.

Dingman, Roger, 'Japan and Mahan', in John B. Hattendorf (ed.), *The Influence of History on Mahan: The Proceedings of a Conference Marking the Centenary of Alfred Thayer Mahan's 'The Influence of Sea Power Upon History, 1660–1783'* (Newport, RI, 1991), 49–66.

d'Ombrain, Nicholas, *War Machinery and High Policy: Defence Administration in Peacetime Britain 1902–1914* (Oxford, 1973).

Dowdeswell, Tracey L., 'The Brussels Peace Conference of 1874 and the Modern Laws of Belligerent Qualification', Special Issue: Law, Authority and History: A Tribute to Douglas Hay. *Osgoode Hall Law Journal*, 54, 3 (2017), 805–50.

Drew, Phillip, *The Law of Maritime Blockade: Past, Present, and Future* (Oxford, 2017).

Dudley, Wade G., 'The Flawed British Blockade, 1812–15', in Bruce A. Elleman and S. C. M. Paine (eds), *Naval Blockades and Seapower: Strategies and Counter-Strategies, 1805–2005* (London, 2006), 35–45.

Dülffer, Jost, *Regeln gegen den Krieg? Die Haager Friedenskonferenzen von 1899 und 1907 in der internationalen Politik* (Berlin, 1981).

Dülffer, Jost, 'Chances and Limits of Armament Control 1898–1914', in Holger Afflerbach and David Stevenson (eds), *An Improbable War: The Outbreak of World War I and European Political Culture before 1914* (New York, 2007), 95–112.

Dunlap, Charles J. Jr., 'Lawfare Today: A Perspective', *Yale Journal of International Affairs* 3, 1 (2008), 146–54.

Dunlap, Charles J. Jr., 'Lawfare Today…and Tomorrow', in Raul A. 'Pete' Pedroso and Daria P. Wollschlaeger (eds), *International Law and the Changing Character of War* (Newport, RI, 2011), 315–25.

Echevarria, Antulio J. II, *Imagining Future War: The West's Technological Revolution and Visions of Wars to Come, 1880–1914* (Westport, CT, 2007).

Edwards, John Ll. J., *The Law Officers of the Crown: A Study of the Offices of Attorney-General and Solicitor-General of England, with an Account of the Office of the Director of Public Prosecutions of England* (London, 1964).

Fassbender, Bardo and Peters, Anne (eds), *The Oxford Handbook of the History of International Law* (Oxford, 2012).

Ferris, John R., 'To the Hunger Blockade: The Evolution of British Economic Warfare, 1914–1915', in Michael Epkenhans and Stephan Huck (eds), *Der Erste Weltkrieg zur See* (Berlin, 2017), 83–97.

Ferris, Norman B., *The Trent Affair: A Diplomatic Crisis* (Knoxville, TN, 1977).

Fleming, N. C., 'The Imperial Maritime League: British Navalism, Conflict, and the Radical Right, *c*.1907–1920', *War in History*, 23 (2016), 296–322.

Frei, Gabriela A., 'Great Britain, Contraband and Future Maritime Conflict (1885–1916)', *Francia. Forschungen zur Westeuropäischen Geschichte*, 40 (2013), 409–18.

Frei, Gabriela A., 'Prize Laws in the War of 1812', in Tim Voelcker (ed.), *Broke of the Shannon and the War of 1812* (Barnsley, 2013), 51–6.

Frei, Gabriela A., 'Freedom and Control of the Seas, 1856–1919', in N. A. M. Rodger (ed.), *The Sea in History: The Modern World/La mer dans l'histoire. La période contemporaine* (Woodbridge, 2017), 59–69.

Frei, Gabriela A., 'The Institut de Droit International and the Making of Law for Peace (1899–1917)', in Rémi Fabre (ed.), *Les défenseurs de la paix (1899–1917)* (Rennes, 2018), 127–38.

Frei, Gabriela A., 'International Law and the First World War: Introduction', *European Journal of International Law*, 29, 1 (2018), 229–32.

Frei, Gabriela A., 'How to Wage Economic Warfare in a Globalised Economy? International Jurisdiction between State and Private Interests, 1880–1914', under peer-review.

Frei, Gabriela A., 'Legal Advisers, the Foreign Office, and Britain's Neutrality Policy, 1856–1914', in Marcus Payk and Kim Christian Priemel (eds), *Jurists in International Politics: Practice and Practitioners of International Law in the Nineteenth and Twentieth Centuries* (Oxford, forthcoming).

French, David, *British Economic and Strategic Planning 1905–1915* (London, 1982).

French, David, 'The British Army and the Empire, 1856–1956', in Greg Kennedy (ed.), *Imperial Defence: The Old World Order, 1856–1956* (Abingdon, 2008), 91–110.

Gallagher, Thomas F., 'British Military Thinking and the Coming of the Franco-Prussian War', *Military Affairs*, 39, 1 (1975), 19–22.

Gallagher, Thomas F., '"Cardwellian Mysteries": The Fate of the British Army Regulation Bill, 1871', *The Historical Journal*, 18, 2 (1975), 327–48.

García-Salmones, Mónica, *The Project of Positivism in International Law* (Oxford, 2013).

Gilje, Paul A., *Free Trade and Sailors' Rights in the War of 1812* (New York, 2013).

Goldrick, James and Hattendorf, John B. (eds), *Mahan is not Enough: The Proceedings of a Conference on the Works of Sir Julian Corbett and Admiral Sir Herbert Richmond* (Newport, RI, 1993).

Gooch, John, 'Sir George Clarke's Career at the Committee of Imperial Defence 1904–1907', *The Historical Journal* 18, 3 (1975), 555–69.

Gooch, John, 'Maritime Command: Mahan and Corbett', in Colin S. Gray and Roger W. Barnett (eds), *Seapower and Strategy* (London, 1989), 27–46.

Gooch, John, 'The Weary Titan: Strategy and Policy in Great Britain, 1890–1918', in Williamson Murray, MacGregor Knox and Alvin Bernstein (eds), *The Making of Strategy: Rulers, States, and War* (Cambridge, 1994), 278–306.

Gough, Barry M., 'The Influence of Sea Power Upon History Revisited: Vice-Admiral P. H. Colomb, RN', *The RUSI Journal*, 135, 2 (1990), 55–63.

Graditzky, Thomas, 'The Law of Military Occupation from the 1907 Hague Peace Conference to the Outbreak of the World War II: Was Further Codification Unnecessary or Impossible?', *European Journal of International Law*, 29, 4 (2018), 1305–26.

Gregory, Charles Noble, 'The Doctrine of Continuous Voyage', *Harvard Law Review*, 24, 3 (1911), 167–81.

Grewe, Wilhelm G., *The Epochs of International Law. Translated and revised by Michael Byers* (Berlin, 2000).

Grimes, Shawn T., *Strategy and War Planning in the British Navy, 1887–1918* (Woodbridge, 2012).

Grove, Eric J., 'Blockade', in John B. Hattendorf (ed.), *The Oxford Encyclopedia of Maritime History*, 4 vols (Oxford, 2007), vol. 1, 298–303.

Haines, Steven, 'The Influence of Law on Maritime Strategy', in Daniel Moran and James A. Russell (eds), *Maritime Strategy and Global Order: Markets, Resources, Security* (Washington, DC, 2016).

Hamilton, C. I., 'Anglo-French Seapower and the Declaration of Paris', *The International History Review*, 4, 2 (1982), 166–90.

Hamilton, C. I., 'The Childers Admiralty Reforms and the Nineteenth-Century "Revolution" in British Government', *War in History*, 5 (1998), 37–61.

Hamilton, C. I., *The Making of the Modern Admiralty: British Naval Policy-Making, 1805–1927* (Cambridge, 2011).

Harley, C. Knick, 'Trade, 1870–1939: From Globalisation to Fragmentation', in Roderick Floud and Paul Johnson (eds), *The Cambridge Economic History of Modern Britain. Vol. 2: Economic Maturity, 1860–1939* (Cambridge, 2004), 161–89.

Hattendorf, John B., 'Maritime Conflict', in Michael Howard, George J. Andreopoulos, and Mark R. Shulman (eds), *The Laws of War: Constraints on Warfare in the Western World* (New Haven, CT, 1994), 98–102.

Hattendorf, John B., 'Rear Admiral Charles H. Stockton, the Naval War College, and the Law of Naval Warfare', in Michael N. Schmitt and Leslie C. Green (eds), *The Law of Armed Conflict: Into the Next Millennium* (Newport, RI, 1998).

Hattendorf, John B., 'Alfred Thayer Mahan and American Naval Theory: The Range and Limitations of Mahan's Thought', in John B. Hattendorf, *Naval History and Maritime Strategy: Collected Essays* (Malabar, FL, 2000), 59–75.

Hattendorf, John B., 'The US Navy and the "Freedom of the Seas", 1775–1917', in Rolf Hobson and Tom Kristiansen (eds), *Navies in Northern Waters 1721–2000* (London, 2004), 151–74.

Hattendorf, John B., 'The War of 1812: A Perspective from the United States', in Tim Voelcker (ed.), *Broke of the Shannon and the War of 1812* (Barnsley, 2013), 1–15.

Hattendorf, John B., Simpson, B. Mitchell III, and Wadleigh, John R., *Sailors and Scholars: The Centennial History of the U.S. Naval War College* (Newport, RI, 1985).

Hayes, Paul, 'Britain, Germany, and the Admiralty's Plans for Attacking German Territory, 1906–1915', in Lawrence Freedman, Paul Hayes, and Robert O'Neill (eds), *War, Strategy, and International Politics: Essays in Honour of Sir Michael Howard* (Oxford, 1992), 95–116.

Headrick, Daniel R., *The Tentacles of Progress: Technology Transfer in the Age of Imperialism, 1850–1940* (New York, 1988).

Henshaw, Peter, 'The "Key to South Africa" in the 1890s: Delagoa Bay and the Origins of the South African War', *Journal of Southern African Studies*, 24, 3 (1998), 527–43.

Herwig, Holger, 'The Influence of A. T. Mahan Upon German Sea Power', in John B. Hattendorf (ed.), *The Influence of History on Mahan: The Proceedings of a Conference Marking the Centenary of Alfred Thayer Mahan's 'The Influence of Sea Power Upon History, 1660–1783'* (Newport, RI, 1991), 67–80.

Heydte, Friedrich August Freiherr von der, 'Die Auswirkungen der Resolutionen des Institut de Droit International im Bereich des Kriegsrechts auf die Fortentwicklung des Kriegsvölkerrechts', in Wilhelm Wengler (ed.), *Justitia et Pace: Festschrift zum 100 jährigen Bestehen des Institut de Droit International* (Berlin, 1974), 31–62.

Higgins, A. Pearce, 'The Growth of International Law: Maritime Rights and Colonial Titles, 1648–1763', in *Cambridge History of the British Empire, Vol. 1: The Old Empire from the Beginnings to 1783* (Cambridge, 1929), 538–60.

Higgins, A. Pearce, 'International Law and the Growth of the Empire', in *Cambridge History of the British Empire, Vol. 2: The Growth of the New Empire 1783–1870* (Cambridge, 1940), 842–81.

Hill, J. Richard, *The Prizes of War: The Naval Prize System in the Napoleonic Wars, 1793–1815* (Stroud, 1998).

Hinsley, F. H., 'British Foreign Policy and Colonial Questions, 1895–1904', in *The Cambridge History of the British Empire, Volume III: The Empire-Commonwealth* (Cambridge, 1959), 490–537.

Hobson, Rolf, *Imperialism at Sea: Naval Strategic Thought, the Ideology of Sea Power, and the Tirpitz Plan, 1875–1914* (Boston, MA, 2001).

Holmes, James R., *Theodore Roosevelt and World Order* (Washington, DC, 2006).

Howard, Michael, *The Franco-Prussian War: The German Invasion of France, 1870–1871* (London, 1961; reprint London, 2000).

Howard, Michael, Andreopoulos, George J., and Shulman, Mark R. (eds), *The Laws of War: Constraints on Warfare in the Western World* (New Haven, CT, 1994).

Howland, Douglas, 'The Sinking of the S.S. Kowshing: International Law, Diplomacy, and the Sino-Japanese War', *Modern Asian Studies*, 42 (2008), 673–703.

Howland, Douglas, 'Contraband and Private Property in the Age of Imperialism', *Journal of the History of International Law*, 13 (2011), 117–53.

Huber, Valeska 'Multiple Mobilities, Multiple Sovereignties, Multiple Speeds: Exploring Maritime Connections in the Age of Empire', *International Journal of Middle Eastern Studies*, 48 (2016), 763–6.

Hull, Isabel V., '"Military Necessity" and the Laws of War in Imperial Germany', in Stathis N. Kalyvas, Ian Shapiro, and Tarek Masoud (eds), *Order, Conflict, and Violence* (Cambridge, 2008), 352–77.

Hull, Isabel V., *A Scrap of Paper: Breaking and Making International Law during the Great War* (Ithaca, NY, 2014).

Imlah, Albert H., *Economic Elements in the Pax Britannica: Studies in British Foreign Trade in the Nineteenth Century* (Cambridge, MA, 1958).

Iriye, Akira, *Global Community: The Role of International Organizations in the Making of the Contemporary World* (Berkeley, CA, 2002).

Iriye, Akira and Osterhammel, Jürgen (eds), *A World Connecting: 1870–1945* (Cambridge, MA, 2012).

Jentzsch, Christian, *Vom Kadetten bis zum Admiral: Das britische und das deutsche Seeoffizierskorps 1871–1914* (Oldenburg, 2018).

Johnson, Franklyn A., *Defence by Committee: The British Committee of Imperial Defence, 1885–1959* (Oxford, 1960).

Johnson, Matthew, 'The Liberal Party and the Navy League in Britain before the Great War', *Twentieth Century British History*, 22, 2 (2011), 137–63.

Jones, Howard, *Blue and Gray Diplomacy: A History of Union and Confederate Foreign Relations* (Chapel Hill, NC, 2010).

Jones, Kate, 'Marking Foreign Policy by Justice: The Legal Advisers to the Foreign Office, 1876–1953', in Robert McCorquodale and Jean-Pierre Gauci (eds), *British Influences on International Law, 1915–2015* (Leiden, 2016), 28–55.

Jones, Ray, *The Nineteenth-Century Foreign Office: An Administrative History* (London, 1971).

Jordan, Robert S., 'The Influence of the British Secretariat Tradition on Twentieth-Century International Peace-Keeping', in John B. Hattendorf and Robert S. Jordan (eds), *Maritime Strategy and the Balance of Power: Britain and America in the Twentieth Century* (Basingstoke, 1989), 56–60.

Jouannet, Emmanuelle, *The Liberal-Welfarist Law of Nations: A History of International Law* (Cambridge, 2012).

Judd, Denis and Surridge, Keith, *The Boer War: A History* (London, 2013).

Keefer, Scott A., 'Building the Palace of Peace: The Hague Conference of 1907 and Arms Control before the World War', *Journal of the History of International Law*, 9, 1 (2007), 35–81.

Keefer, Scott A., *The Law of Nations and Britain's Quest for Naval Security: International Law and Arms Control, 1898–1914* (Cham, 2016).

Kemmerer, Alexandra and Goodwin, Morag (eds), 'From Apology to Utopia. A Symposium', *German Law Journal*, 7, 12 (2006), 977–1176.

Kennedy, David, 'International Law and the Nineteenth Century: History of an Illusion', *Nordic Journal of International Law*, 65 (1996), 385–402.

Kennedy, David, *Of War and Law* (Princeton, NJ, 2006).

Kennedy, David, 'Lawfare and Warfare', in James Crawford and Martti Koskenniemi (eds), *The Cambridge Companion to International Law* (Cambridge, 2012), 158–83.

Kennedy, Greg, 'Introduction: The Concept of Imperial Defence, 1856–1956', in Greg Kennedy (ed.), *Imperial Defence: The Old World Order, 1856–1956* (Abingdon, 2008), 1–8.

Kennedy, Paul, *The Rise and Fall of British Naval Mastery* (London, 1976; reprint with a new introduction London, 2004).

Klump, Rainer and Vec, Miloš (eds), *Völkerrecht und Weltwirtschaft im 19. Jahrhundert* (Baden-Baden, 2012).

Kolb, Robert, 'The Protection of the Individual in Times of War and Peace', in Bardo Fassbender and Anne Peters (eds), *The Oxford Handbook of the History of International Law* (Oxford, 2012), 317–58.

Koskenniemi, Martti, *The Gentle Civilizer of Nations: The Rise and Fall of International Law 1870–1960 (Hersch Lauterpacht Memorial Lectures)* (Cambridge, 2001).

Koskenniemi, Martti, *From Apology to Utopia: The Structure of International Legal Argument. Reissue with New Epilogue* (Cambridge, 1989; reprint Cambridge, 2005).

Kraska, James, 'Grasping "The Influence of Law on Sea Power"', *Naval War College Review*, 62, 3 (2009), 113–35.

Kraska, James, *Maritime Power and the Law of the Sea: Expeditionary Operations in World Politics* (Oxford, 2011).

Kubicek, Robert, 'British Expansion, Empire, and Technological Change', in Andrew Porter and Alaine Low (eds), *Oxford History of the British Empire. Vol. 3: The Nineteenth Century* (Oxford, 1999), 247–69.

Lambert, Andrew D., *The Challenge: America, Britain and the War of 1812* (London, 2012).

Lambert, Andrew D., 'The Royal Navy, 1856–1914: Deterrence and the Strategy of World Power', in Keith Neilson and Elizabeth J. Errington (eds), *Navies and Global Defence: Theories and Strategy* (Newport, CT, 1995), 69–92.

Lambert, Andrew D., 'The Naval War Course, *Some Principles of Maritime Strategy* and the Origins of "The British Way in Warfare"', in Keith Neilson and Greg Kennedy (eds), *The British Way in Warfare: Power and the International System, 1856–1956* (Farnham, 2010), 219–53.

Lambert, Andrew D., 'The Royal Navy and the Defence of Empire, 1856–1918', in Greg Kennedy (ed.), *Imperial Defence. The Old World Order, 1856–1956* (Abingdon, 2008), 111–32.

Lambert, Andrew D., 'Sir Julian Corbett, Naval History and the Development of Sea Power Theory', in N. A. M. Rodger et al. (eds), *Strategy and the Sea: Essays in Honour of John B. Hattendorf* (Woodbridge, 2016), 190–200.

Lambert, Nicholas A., *Sir John Fisher's Naval Revolution* (Columbia, SC, 1999).

Lambert, Nicholas A., *Planning Armageddon: British Economic Warfare and the First World War* (Cambridge, MA, 2012).

Lauterpacht, Hersch and Jennings, R. Y., 'International Law and Colonial Questions, 1870–1914', in *Cambridge History of the British Empire, Vol. III: The Empire-Commonwealth 1870–1919* (Cambridge, 1959), 667–710.

Leech, G., 'The Doctrine of Continuous Voyage: Its Origin and Development from the Seven Years' War (1756) to the Boer War' *Journal of the Royal United Service Institution*, 46 (1902), 1524–32.

Lemnitzer, Jan M., '"That Moral League of Nations against the United States": The Origins of the 1856 Declaration of Paris', *The International History Review*, 35 (2013), 1068–88.

Lemnitzer, Jan M., *Power, Law and the End of Privateering* (Basingstoke, 2014).

Lesaffer, Randall, 'International Law and Its History: The Story of an Unrequited Love', in Matthew Craven and Malgosia Fitzmaurice (eds), *Developments in International Law: Time, History, and International Law* (Leiden, 2006), 27–41.

Lesaffer, Randall, *European Legal History. A Cultural and Political Perspective* (Cambridge, 2009).

Lesaffer, Randall, 'Agression before Versailles', *European Journal of International Law*, 29, 3 (2018), 773–808.

Lobo-Guerrero, Luis, *Insuring War: Sovereignty, Security and Risk* (Abingdon, 2012).

Lowe, Vaughan, 'Book Review of *From Apology to Utopia*', *Journal of Law and Society*, 17 (1990), 384–9.

Lynn, Martin, 'British Policy, Trade, and Informal Empire in the Mid-Nineteenth Century', in Andrew Porter and Alaine Low (eds), *Oxford History of the British Empire. Vol. 3: The Nineteenth Century* (Oxford, 1999), 101–21.

MacDonald, Ronald St. John, *The Role of the Legal Adviser of Ministries of Foreign Affairs (Collected Courses of the Hague Academy of International Law, 156)* (Leiden, 1977), 444–9.

McKercher, B. J. C. (ed.), *Arms Limitation and Disarmament: Restraints on War, 1899–1939* (Westport, CT, 1992).

McKercher, B. J. C., 'Diplomatic Equipoise: The Lansdowne Foreign Office, the Russo-Japanese War of 1904–1905, and the Global Balance of Power', *Canadian Journal of History/Annales Canadiennes d'Histoire*, 24 (1989), 299–339.

McNeill, William H., *The Pursuit of Power: Technology, Armed Force, and Society since A.D. 1000* (Chicago, IL, 1982).

Magee, Gary B., 'Manufacturing and Technological Change', in Roderick Floud and Paul Johnson (eds), *The Cambridge Economic History of Modern Britain. Vol. 2: Economic Maturity, 1860–1939* (Cambridge, 2004), 74–98.

Makarov, Alexander N., 'Beiträge des "Institut de Droit International" zu den Problemen der internationalen Organisationen bis 1914', in Walter Schätzel (ed.), *Rechtsfragen der internationalen Organisation* (Frankfurt/Main, 1956), 257–72.

Malkin, William, 'International Law in Practice', *The Law Quarterly Review*, 49 (1933), 489–510.

Marder, Arthur J., *The Anatomy of British Sea Power: A History of British Naval Policy in the Pre-Dreadnought Era, 1880–1905*, 3rd edn (London, 1972).

Martin, Christopher, 'The 1907 Naval War Plans and the Second Hague Peace Conference: A Case of Propaganda', *Journal of Strategic Studies*, 28, 5 (2005), 833–56.

Martin, Christopher, 'The Declaration of London: A Matter of Operational Capability', *Historical Research*, 82, 218 (2009), 731–55.

Mathias, Peter, *The First Industrial Nation: An Economic History of Britain, 1700–1914*, 2nd edn (London, 1983).

Matthews, R. C. O., Feinstein, C. H., and Odling-Smee, J. C., *British Economic Growth, 1856–1973* (Oxford, 1982).

Mazower, Mark, *Governing the World: The History of an Idea* (London, 2012).

Meron, Theodor, 'Francis Lieber's Code and Principles of Humanity', *Columbia Journal of Transnational Law*, 36 (1998), 269–82.

Mitchell, Brian R., *British Historical Statistics* (Cambridge, 1988).

Mobley, Scott, *Progressives in Navy Blue: Maritime Strategy, American Empire, and the Transformation of U.S. Naval Identity, 1873–1898* (Annapolis, MD, 2018).

Morgan-Owen, David G., *The Fear of Invasion: Strategy, Politics, and British War Planning, 1880–1914* (Oxford, 2017).

Motte, Martin, *Une éducation géostratégique: La pensée navale française de la jeune école à 1914* (Paris, 2004).

Mulligan, William, *The Origins of the First World War* (Cambridge, 2010).

Neff, Stephen C., *Friends but no Allies: Economic Liberalism and the Law of Nations* (New York, 1990).

Neff, Stephen C., *The Rights and Duties of Neutrals: A General History* (Manchester, 2000).

Neff, Stephen C., *War and the Law of Nations: A General History* (Cambridge, 2005).

Neff, Stephen C., *Justice in Blue and Gray: A Legal History of the Civil War* (Cambridge, MA, 2010).

Neff, Stephen C. (ed.), *Hugo Grotius and the Law of War and Peace* (Cambridge, 2012).

Neff, Stephen C., *Justice Among Nations: A History of International Law* (Cambridge, MA, 2014).

Neff, Stephen C., 'Disrupting a Delicate Balance: The Allied Blockade Policy and the Law of Maritime Neutrality during the Great War', *European Journal of International Law*, 29, 2 (2018), 459–75.

Neilson, Keith, '"The British Empire Floats on the British Navy": British Naval Policy, Belligerent Rights, and Disarmament, 1902–1909', in B. J. C. McKercher (ed.), *Arms Limitation and Disarmament: Restraints on War, 1899–1939* (Westport, CT, 1992), 21–41.

Neilson, Keith and Otte, T. G., *The Permanent Under-Secretary for Foreign Affairs, 1854–1946* (New York, 2009).

Nichols, Barry, 'Jurisprudence 1', in Michael G. Brock and Mark C. Carthoys (eds), *The History of the University of Oxford: Volume VII: Nineteenth-Century Oxford, Part 2* (Oxford, 2011), 385–96.

Nish, Ian, 'Introduction', in Kenneth Bourne, D. Cameron Watt, and Ian Nish (eds), *British Documents on Foreign Affairs: Reports and Papers from the Foreign Office Confidential Print, Series E Asia, 1860–1914, Vol. 11: China and the Russo-Japanese War 1903–1904* (Frederick, MD, 1993), xvii–xviii.

Nuzzo, Luigi and Vec, Miloš, 'The Birth of International Law as a Legal Discipline in the 19th Century', in Luigi Nuzzo and Miloš Vec (eds), *Constructing International Law: The Birth of a Discipline* (Frankfurt/Main, 2012), ix–xvi.

Nys, Ernest, 'Codification et Consolidation', *Revue de droit international et de législation comparée*, 6 (1904), 198–212.

Nys, Ernest, 'The Codification of International Law', *American Journal of International Law*, 5, 4 (1911), 871–900.

O'Connell, Daniel P., *The Influence of Law on Sea Power* (Manchester, 1975).

O'Connell, Daniel P., *The International Law of the Sea*, 2 vols (Oxford, 1982).

O'Connell, Mary Ellen, *The Power and Purpose of International Law: Insights from the Theory and Practice of Enforcement* (Oxford, 2008).

Offer, Avner, 'Morality and Admiralty: "Jacky" Fisher, Economic Warfare and the Laws of War', *Journal of Contemporary History*, 23 (1988), 99–118.

Offer, Avner, *The First World War: An Agrarian Interpretation* (Oxford, 1989).

Osborne, Eric W., *Britain's Economic Blockade of Germany 1914–1919* (London, 2004).

Otte, T. G., 'The Foreign Office and Defence of Empire, 1856–1914', in Greg Kennedy (ed.), *Imperial Defence: The Old World Order, 1856–1956* (Abingdon, 2008), 9–29.

Owsley, Frank L., *King Cotton Diplomacy: Foreign Relations of the Confederate States of America*, 2nd edn (Chicago, IL, 1959).

Palmer, Sarah, *Politics, Shipping and the Repeal of the Navigation Laws* (Manchester, 1990).

Papastavridis, Efthymios, 'The Right of Visit on the High Seas in a Theoretical Perspective: Mare Liberum versus Mare Clausum Revisited', *Leiden Journal of International Law*, 24, 1 (2011), 45–69.

Pares, Richard, *Colonial Blockade and Neutral Rights, 1739–1763* (Oxford, 1938).

Parker, Kunal M., *Common Law, History, and Democracy in America, 1790–1900: Legal Thought before Modernism* (New York, 2011).

Parry, Clive, *Sources and Evidence in International Law* (Manchester, 1965).

Parry, Clive, 'Foreign Policy and International Law', in Francis H. Hinsley (ed.), *British Foreign Policy under Sir Edward Grey* (Cambridge, 1977), 89–110.

Patterson, David S., *Toward a Warless World: The Travail of the American Peace Movement 1887–1914* (Bloomington, IN, 1976).

Payk, Marcus M., 'Institutionalisierung und Verrechtlichung: Die Geschichte des Völkerrechts im späten 19. und frühen 20. Jahrhundert', *Archiv für Sozialgeschichte*, 52 (2012), 861–83.

Payk, Marcus M., *Frieden durch Recht? Der Aufstieg des modernen Völkerrechts und der Friedensschluss nach dem Ersten Weltkrieg* (Berlin, 2018).

Payk, Marcus M., ' "What We Seek is the Reign of Law": The Legalism of the Paris Peace Settlement after the Great War', *European Journal of International Law*, 29, 3 (2018), 809–24.

Pedisich, Paul E., *Congress Buys A Navy: Politics, Economics, and the American Naval Power, 1881–1921* (Annapolis, MD, 2016).

Pickles, John, *A History of Spaces: Cartographic Reason, Mapping and the Geo-Coded World* (London, 2004).

Piggott, Francis T., *The Declaration of Paris, 1856: A Study, Documented* (London, 1919).

Porter, Andrew, 'Lord Salisbury, Mr. Chamberlain and South Africa, 1895–9', *The Journal of Imperial and Commonwealth History*, 1 (1972), 3–26.

Porter, Andrew N., 'Donald Currie and Southern Africa 1870 to 1912: Strategies for Survival', in Sarah Palmer and Glyndwr Williams (eds), *Charted and Uncharted Waters: Proceedings of a Conference on the Study of British Maritime History* (London, 1981), 29–53.

Porter, Andrew N., *Victorian Shipping, Business and Imperial Policy: Donald Currie, the Castle Line and Southern Africa* (Woodbridge, 1986).

Preston, Richard A., *Canada and 'Imperial Defense': A Study of the Origins of the British Commonwealth's Defense Organisation, 1867–1919* (Durham, NC, 1967).

Ranft, Bryan, 'Restraints on War at Sea Before 1945', in Michael Howard (ed.), *Restraints on War: Studies in the Limitation of Armed Conflict* (Oxford, 1979), 39–52.

Reynolds, David, *Britannia Overruled: British Policy and World Power in the Twentieth Century*, 2nd edn (Harlow, 2000).

Ritter-Döring, Verena, *Zwischen Normierung und Rüstungswettlauf: Die Entwicklung des Seekriegsrechts, 1856–1914* (Baden-Baden, 2014).

Robbins, Keith, *The Eclipse of a Great Power: Modern Britain, 1870–1975* (London, 1983).

Rodger. N. A. M., 'The Dark Ages of the Admiralty, 1869–85. Part 1: "Business Methods", 1869–1874', *Mariner's Mirror*, 61, 4 (1975), 331–44.

Rodger. N. A. M., 'The Nature of Victory at Sea', *Journal for Maritime Research*, 7, 1 (2005), 110–22.

Rodger. N. A. M., 'The Idea of Naval Strategy in Britain in the Eighteenth and Nineteenth Centuries', in Geoffrey Till (ed.), *The Development of British Naval Thinking: Essays in Memory of Bryan McLaren Ranft* (London, 2006), 19–33.

Røksund, Arne, *The Jeune Ecole: The Strategy of the Weak* (Leiden, 2007).

Root, Elihu, 'The Codification of International Law', *The American Journal of International Law* 19, 4 (1925), 675–84.

Ropp, Theodore, *The Development of a Modern Navy: French Naval Policy, 1871–1904*, ed. Stephen S. Roberts (Annapolis, MD, 1987).

Rose, Andreas, 'Waiting for Armageddon: British Military Journals and the Images of Future Wars (1890–1914)', *Francia. Forschungen zur westeuropäischen Geschichte*, 40 (2013), 317–31.

Rose, Andreas, ' "Readiness or Ruin?"—Der "Grosse Krieg" in den britischen Militärzeitschriften (1880–1914)', in Stig Förster (ed.), *Vor dem Sprung ins Dunkle: Die militärische Debatte über den Krieg der Zukunft, 1880–1914* (Paderborn, 2016), 245–390.

Rose, Andreas, *Between Empire and Continent: British Foreign Policy before the First World War* (New York, 2017).

Saul, Samuel Berrick, *Studies in British Overseas Trade, 1870–1914* (Liverpool, 1960).

Savage, Carlton, *Policy of the United States Toward Maritime Commerce in War*, 2 vols (Washington, DC, 1934).

Scarfi, Juan Pablo, *The Hidden History of International Law in the Americas: Empire and Legal Networks* (Oxford, 2017).

Schlote, Werner, *British Overseas Trade from 1700 to the 1930s*, trans. W. O. Henderson and W. H. Chaloner (Oxford, 1952).

Schroeder, Paul W., *Austria, Britain, and the Crimean War: The Destruction of the European Concert* (Ithaca, NY, 1972).

Schulz, Matthias, *Normen und Praxis: Das Europäische Konzert der Grossmächte als Sicherheitsrat, 1815–1860* (Munich, 2009).

Schulz, Matthias, ' "Defenders of the Right"? Diplomatic Practice and International Law in the 19th Century: An Historian's Perspective', in Luigi Nuzzo and Miloš Vec (eds), *Constructing International Law: The Birth of a Discipline* (Frankfurt/Main, 2012), 251–75.

Schurman, Donald M., *Julian S. Corbett, 1854–1922: Historian of British Maritime Policy from Drake to Jellicoe* (London, 1981).

Schurman, Donald M., *The Education of a Navy: The Development of British Naval Strategic Thought, 1867–1914* (London, 1984).

Schurman, Donald M., *Imperial Defence*, ed. John Beeler (London, 2000).

Seager, Robert II, *Alfred Thayer Mahan: The Man and His Letters* (Annapolis, MD, 1977).

Segesser, Daniel M., *Recht statt Rache oder Rache durch Recht? Die Ahndung von Kriegsverbrechen in der internationalen wissenschaftlichen Debatte 1872–1945* (Paderborn, 2010).

Seligmann, Matthew S., *The Royal Navy and the German Threat 1901–1914: Admiralty Plans to Protect British Trade in a War Against Germany* (Oxford, 2012).

Seligmann, Matthew S., 'Failing to Prepare for the Great War? The Absence of Grand Strategy in British War Planning before 1914', *War in History*, 24, 4 (2017), 414–37.

Seligmann, Matthew S., Nägler, Frank, and Epkenhans, Michael (eds), *The Naval Route to the Abyss: The Anglo-German Naval Race 1895–1914* (Farnham, 2015).

Semmel, Bernard, *Liberalism and Naval Strategy: Ideology, Interest, and Sea Power during the Pax Britannica* (Boston, MA, 1986).

Simpson, Gerry, *Great Powers and Outlaw States: Unequal Sovereigns in the International Legal Order* (Cambridge, 2004).

Simpson, Gerry, 'International Law in Diplomatic History', in James Crawford and Martti Koskenniemi (eds), *The Cambridge Companion to International Law* (Cambridge, 2012), 25–46.

Sked, Alan, *Britain's Decline: Problems and Perspectives* (Oxford, 1987).

Spector, Ronald, *Professors of War: The Naval War College and the Development of the Naval Profession* (Newport, RI, 1977).

Spiers, Edward M., *The Army and Society 1815–1914* (London, 1980).

Sprout, Margaret Tuttle, 'Mahan: Evangelist of Sea Power', in Edward Mead Earle (ed.), *Makers of Modern Strategy: Military Thought from Machiavelli to Hitler* (Princeton, NJ, 1943; reprint 1971), 415–45.

Stagg, J. C. A., *War of 1812: Conflict for a Continent* (Cambridge, 2012).

Steinberg, Philipp E., *The Social Construction of the Ocean* (Cambridge, 2001).

Steiner, Zara S., *The Foreign Office and Foreign Policy, 1898–1914* (Cambridge, 1969).

Strachan, Hew, 'Maritime Strategy: Historical Perspectives', *The RUSI Journal*, 152, 1 (2007), 29–33.

Sumida, Jon Tetsuro, *In Defence of Naval Supremacy: Finance, Technology and British Naval Policy, 1889–1914* (London, 1989).

Sumida, Jon Tetsuro, *Inventing Grand Strategy and Teaching Command: The Classic Works of Alfred Thayer Mahan Reconsidered* (Washington, DC, 1997).

Surdam, David G., 'The Union's Navy's Blockade Reconsidered', in Bruce A. Elleman and S. C. M. Paine (eds), *Naval Blockades and Seapower: Strategies and Counter-Strategies, 1805–2005* (London, 2004), 61–9.

Sylvest, Caspar, 'International Law in Nineteenth-Century Britain', *The British Yearbook of International Law*, 75, 1 (2005), 9–70.

Sylvest, Caspar, 'The Foundations of Victorian International Law', in Duncan Bell (ed.), *Victorian Visions of Global Order: Empire and International Relations in Nineteenth-Century Political Thought* (Cambridge, 2007), 47–66.

Thirlway, Hugh, *The Sources of International Law* (Oxford, 2014).

Till, Geoffrey, 'Corbett and the Emergence of a British School?', in Geoffrey Till (ed.), *The Development of British Naval Thinking: Essays in Memory of Bryan Ranft* (London, 2006), 60–88.

Till, Geoffrey, 'Introduction: British Naval Thinking: A Contradiction in Terms?', in Geoffrey Till (ed.), *The Development of British Naval Thinking: Essays in Memory of Bryan McLaren Ranft* (London, 2006), 1–18.

Tracy, Nicholas, *Attack on Maritime Trade* (London, 1991).

Tracy, Nicholas (ed.), *Sea Power and the Control of Trade: Belligerent Rights from the Russian War to the Beira Patrol, 1854–1970* (Aldershot, 2005).

Tunstall, W. C. B., 'Imperial Defence 1815–1870', in *The Cambridge History of the British Empire, Vol. 2: The Growth of the New Empire 1783–1870* (Cambridge, 1940), 806–41.

Tunstall, W. C. B., 'Imperial Defence 1870–1897', in *The Cambridge History of the British Empire, Vol. 3: The Empire-Commonwealth 1870–1919* (Cambridge, 1959), 230–54.

Tunstall, W. C. B., 'Imperial Defence, 1897–1914', in *The Cambridge History of the British Empire, Vol. 3: The Empire-Commonwealth 1870–1919* (Cambridge, 1959), 563–604.

Turner, Barry, *Free Trade and Protection* (Harlow, 1971).

Vec, Miloš, *Recht und Normierung in der Industriellen Revolution: Neue Strukturen der Normsetzung im Völkerrecht, staatlicher Gesetzgebung und gesellschaftliche Selbstnormierung* (Frankfurt/Main, 2006).

Vieira, Mónica Brito, 'Mare Liberum vs. Mare Clausum: Grotius, Freitas, and Selden's Debate on Dominion over the Seas', *Journal of the History of Ideas*, 64, 3 (2003), 361–77.

Visscher, Charles de, 'La contribution de l'Institut de droit international au développement du droit international (Rapport spécial)', in L'Institut de Droit International (ed.), *Livre du Centenaire 1873–1973: Evolution et perspectives du droit international* (Basel, 1973), 128–61.

Warren, Gordon H., *Fountain of Discontent: The Trent Affair and Freedom of the Seas* (Boston, MA, 1981).

Welch, M. D., *Science and the British Officer: The Early Days of the Royal United Services Institute for Defence Studies (1829–1869)* (London, 1998).

Welch, M. D., *Science in a Pickelhaube: British Military Lesson Learning at the RUSI (1870–1900)* (London, 1999).

Whitney, Edson Leone, *The American Peace Society: A Centennial History* (Washington, DC, 1928).

Whittuck, Edward A., *International Canals* (London, 1920).

Widén, Jerker J., *Theorist of Maritime Strategy: Sir Julian Corbett and his Contribution to Military and Naval Thought* (Burlington, VT, 2012).

Wiley, Neville and Cameron, Lindsey, 'The Impact of World War I on the Law Governing the Treatment of Prisoners of War and the Making of a Humanitarian Subject', *European Journal of International Law*, 29, 4 (2018), 1327–50.

Wilson, Bob, 'Fuelling the Victorian Steam Navy', *Warship* (2009), https://www.researchgate.net/publication/272818419_Fuelling_the_Victorian_Steam_Navy.

Witt, John Fabian, *Lincoln's Code: The Laws of War in American History* (New York, 2013).

Wittner, Lawrence S., 'Peace Movements and Foreign Policy: The Challenge to Diplomatic Historians', *Diplomatic History*, 11 (1987), 355–70.

Wright, Charles and Fayle, C. Ernest, *A History of Lloyd's from the Founding of Lloyd's Coffee House to the Present Day* (London, 1928).

Index